After the USSR

After the USSR

Ethnicity, Nationalism, and Politics in the
Commonwealth of Independent States

Anatoly M. Khazanov

The University of Wisconsin Press

The University of Wisconsin Press
114 North Murray Street
Madison, Wisconsin 53715

3 Henrietta Street
London WC2E 8LU, England

Library of Congress Cataloging-in-Publication Data
Khazanov, Anatoly M. (Anatoly M.), 1937-
    After the USSR: ethnicity, nationalism, and politics in the Commonwealth of
Independent States / Anatoly M. Khazanov.
    334 pp.   cm.
    Includes bibliographical references and index.
    ISBN 0-299-14890-4
    1. Former Soviet republics—Ethnic relations. 2. Former Soviet republics—
Politics and government. 3. Minorities—Former Soviet republics.
    4. Ethnology—Former Soviet republics.
    5. Nationalism—Former Soviet republics.
    I. Title.
    DK33.K4527   1995
    305.8'00947—dc20   95-5696

This book has been composed in ITC Garamond

In memory of Ernest Gellner—
great scholar, great friend

We inherited from Stalinism
the imperial system,
the imperial ideology,
the imperial policy of divide and rule.
—Andrei Sakharov, 1989

The placard reads "democratization"

CONTENTS

MAPS

TABLES AND FIGURES

PREFACE

There is not one nationalism but many. There are many facets and many varieties, and the ex-Soviet Union at present may serve as their living encyclopedia. This book is an attempt at exploring the interconnections between nationalism, ethnic relations, social structure, and the ongoing political process in the Soviet and post-Soviet region. At the same time, I am trying to demonstrate the applicability of modern, Western, non-Marxist schools of thought on such crucial issues as nationalism, modernization, democracy, and civil society to the Soviet and post-Soviet materials. In my opinion these schools of thought explain the recent developments and the current situation in the former communist countries much better than the competing Marxist school of thought, not only in its original form or in its Soviet pseudodogmatic one, but also in its more sophisticated, modern, Western varieties.

The book's first chapter is devoted to the role that nationalism has played in the breakup of the Soviet Union and in undermining communist ideology in the country. In the second chapter I examine the main characteristics of a post-totalitarian society and the role of nationalism in its ideology and practice. The third chapter studies nationalism of ethnic minorities, particularly in the contemporary Russian context.

The remaining chapters are essentially case studies which substantiate further and explore in detail some theoretical points argued in the previous chapters. The fourth chapter explores the current situation in Central Asia and the impact of underdevelopment on political stability and ethnic relations in this region. The fifth chapter, based on materials from Kazakhstan, deals with nationalism in a plural society in which two numerically almost equal nationalities occupy overlapping but basically different socioeconomic niches and compete for power and economic benefits. The sixth chapter uses Yakut materials to examine nationalism of those ethnic groups in the post-Soviet Union which enjoy a certain degree of autonomy as an indigenous population but, because of internal migrations and other factors, now constitute a minority in their own homelands. The seventh chapter illustrates, mainly through the example of the

Meskhetian Turks, the situation and nationalism of those deported and dispersed ethnic groups that are not allowed to return to the territories from which they have been exiled. The last chapter is an attempt at catching up with the most recent developments in Chechnia and their implications for Russia.

In this book I make extensive use of fielddata and other materials from different parts of the Soviet Union that I was able to collect while pursuing my professional career as an anthropologist there in 1960–1980, then as a refusenik in 1980–1985, and afterwards, since 1990, during my visits to the countries of the Commonwealth of Independent States. My deep gratitude goes to my informants, friends, and colleagues there, people of different nationalities, different social strata, and different political views who during all those years provided me with information or shared with me their assessments of the ethnic and political situation in the USSR and its successor states, or assisted me in other ways. With very few exceptions, I do not mention their names because they are too numerous— literally hundreds of people. Besides, I do not wish to violate the trust of these people, which was and to a large extent still is based on the confidence that the information would be used in utmost discretion and confidentiality. I would also like to stress that the responsibility for everything that is asserted in this book is mine and mine alone.

Here, in the West, I have learned a great deal from Mark Beissinger, John Davis, Shmuel Eisenstadt, Joseph Ginat, Harvey Goldberg, Peter Golden, Herb Lewis, George Mosse, Stanley Payne, Adam Seligman, Eric Wolf, the late Abram Zloczower (with his death I lost a severe critic and a very good friend), and many other colleagues. My thanks to all of them.

I am particularly grateful to John Armstrong, Ernest Gellner, John Hall, Leonard Plotnicov, Andre Wink, and Crawford Young for reading drafts of the text and offering suggestions for its improvement. It goes without saying that only I may be blamed for the book's shortcomings.

I want to record my particular debt to Ernest Gellner for the great intellectual excitement and stimulation that I always find in his writings and in our personal contacts, and for the many years of his faithful friendship that means so much to me.

I also want to pay homage to Raymond Aron, whom, unfortunately, I never met in person. Although his works were forbidden in the Soviet Union, I became acquainted with some of them as early as the 1960s. Since then, his intellectual and personal honesty, never compromised for the sake of practical benefits, as well as his staunch position and argumentation on behalf of liberal democracy, have been exemplary to me. This book is hardly written *sine era et studio,* if the meaning of these words is conceived as the indulgence of moral equity. If the principled opposition and deep aversion to all kinds of totalitarianism mean being biased, so be it; I am biased indeed in Aron's tradition.

My warm thanks go to Dr. Levon Abramian, an Armenian anthropologist who kindly permitted me to publish some of his brilliant cartoons. I hope that readers will enjoy them as much as I and his other friends do.

I am very grateful to my doctoral student, Jeffrey C. Kaufmann, who was a great help to me in the preparation of the manuscript of this book for publication.

Thanks are also due the editors and publishers at the University of Wisconsin Press, who have been outstandingly helpful and patient. I ought to mention quite particularly Rosalie Robertson, Allen Fitchen, Raphael Kadushin, Carol Olsen, and Sheila Leary. Robin Whitaker was an admirable and very competent copy editor.

Finally, much of the recent research for this book was made possible by grants from the Wenner-Gren Foundation for Anthropological Research and the National Council for Soviet and East European Research. I also received support from the Jewish-Arab Center of the University of Haifa. It is a pleasure to express my appreciation to them.

ACKNOWLEDGMENTS

An original draft of the first chapter of this book was written by July 1992 as a paper designated for publication in the twentieth anniversary issue of *Nationalities Papers,* whose publication was delayed for two years for technical reasons. Although during my work on this book its draft was thoroughly revised and enlarged more than twice, I deliberately left intact its concluding section. The reason is that I have expressed there my views on the situation as it existed in Russia and the other CIS countries by the summer of 1992, and it would be underhanded to revise them *post factum.* Nor have they actually undergone any serious change, since, unfortunately, all the negative trends and tendencies in these countries' developments, which in my opinion made their transition to liberal democracy in 1992 far from certain, still exist and some of them have become even more conspicuous.

Chapters 4, 5, 6, and 7 incorporate some portions of several of my papers that first appeared in the following editions: "Underdevelopment and Ethnic Relations in Central Asia," in Beatrice F. Manz (ed.), *Central Asia in Historical Perspective* (Boulder, Colo.: Westview Press, 1994), 144–63; "The Ethnic Problems of Contemporary Kazakhstan," *Central Asian Survey* 14, no. 1 (1995): 243–64;"Nationalism and Neo-Shamanism in Yakutia," *MDIA* (1994): 12; and "Meskhetian Turks in a Search of Self-Identity," *Central Asian Survey,* 11, no. 4 (1992): 1–16.

I am grateful to the publishers for permission to quote from the following editions: Andrei Amal'rik, *Will the Soviet Union Survive until 1984?* (New York: Harper and Row, Perennial Library, 1971), 65; Ernest Gellner, *Spectacles and Predicaments* (Cambridge: Cambridge University Press, 1979), 339; Nancy Lubin, *Labor and Nationality in Soviet Central Asia: An Uneasy Compromise* (Princeton: Princeton University Press, 1984), 234; Timothy J. Colton, *The Dilemma of Reform in the Soviet Union* (New York: Council for Foreign Relations, 1986), 63; Karl Popper, "The Open Society and Its Enemies Revisited," *The Economist* (April 23, 1988); Manning Nash, *The Cauldron of Ethnicity in the Modern World* (Chicago and London: University of Chicago Press, 1989), 127; Milton J. Esman,

"Political and Psychological Factors in Ethnic Conflicts," in Joseph V. Montville (ed.), *Conflict and Peacemaking in Multiethnic Societies* (Lexington, Mass.: Lexington Books, 1989), 60; Czeslaw Milocz, "Some Call It Freedom," *The New York Times,* August 8, 1991; J. G. Merquior, "Thoughts on Liberalization," in John A. Hall and I. C. Jarvie (eds.), *Transition to Modernity: Essays on Power, Wealth and Belief* (Cambridge: Cambridge University Press, 1992), 337; Charles F. Furtado and Andrea Chandler (eds.), *Perestroika in the Soviet Republics: Documents on the National Question* (Boulder, Colo.: Westview Press, 1992), 44.

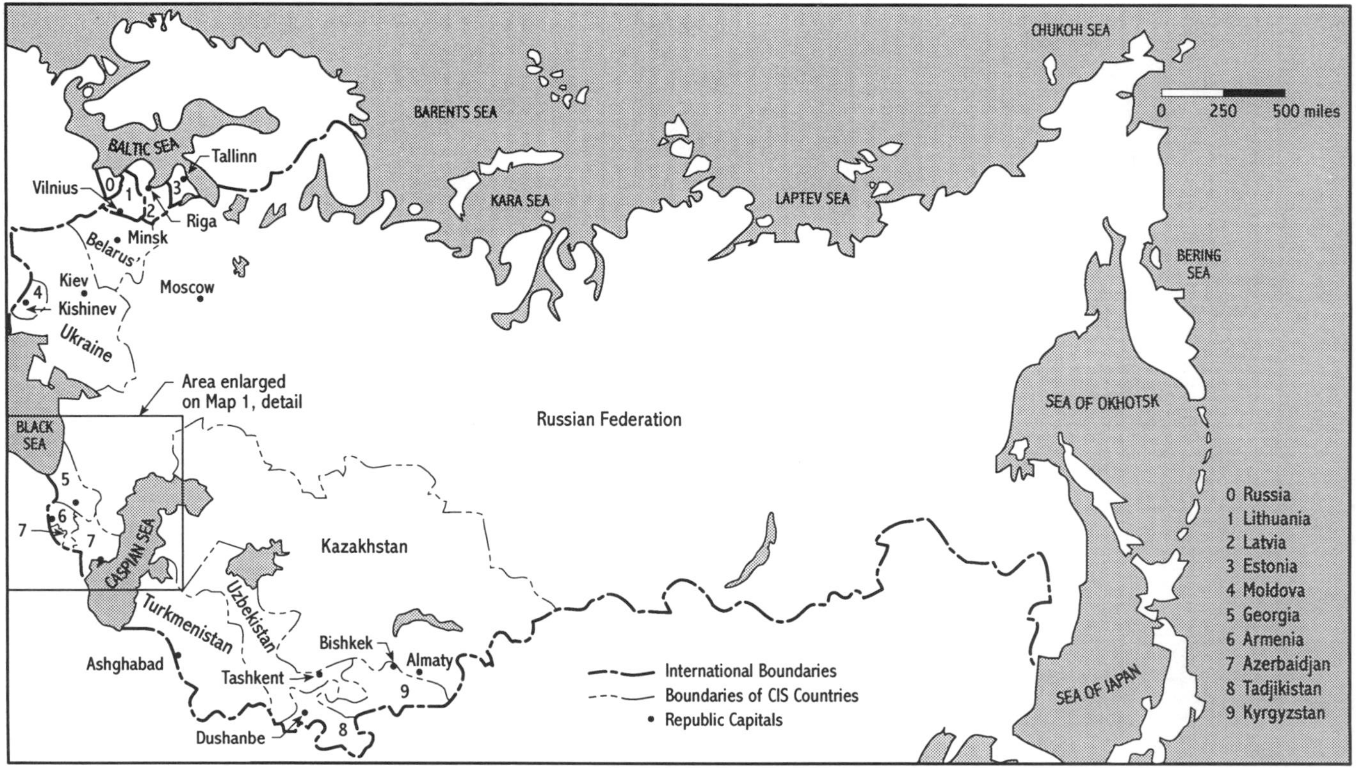

Map 1. The CIS Countries

Legend:
- 0 Russia
- 1 Lithuania
- 2 Latvia
- 3 Estonia
- 4 Moldova
- 5 Georgia
- 6 Armenia
- 7 Azerbaidjan
- 8 Tadjikistan
- 9 Kyrgyzstan

International Boundaries
Boundaries of CIS Countries
Republic Capitals

CHUKCHI SEA
BERING SEA
SEA OF OKHOTSK
SEA OF JAPAN
LAPTEV SEA
KARA SEA
BARENTS SEA
BALTIC SEA
BLACK SEA
CASPIAN SEA

Russian Federation
Kazakhstan
Uzbekistan
Turkmenistan
Ukraine
Belarus

Tallinn
Riga
Vilnius
Minsk
Moscow
Kiev
Kishinev
Almaty
Bishkek
Tashkent
Dushanbe
Ashghabad

Area enlarged on Map 1, detail

0 250 500 miles

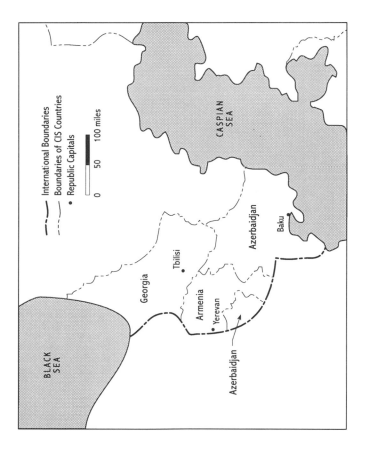

Map 1, detail

After the USSR

The acrobats *(from bottom and left)*, Marx, Lenin, Stalin, Engels, Andropov, Khrushev, Brezhnev, and Gorbachev

1

The Collapse of the Soviet Union: Nationalism during Perestroika and Afterwards (1985–Summer 1992)

> Free institutions are next to impossible
> in a country made up of different nationalities.
> —John Stuart Mill,
> "Consideration on Representative Government"

> I have no doubt that this great Eastern Slav empire . . .
> has entered the last decades of its existence . . . .
> Marxist doctrine has delayed the break-up
> of the Russian Empire—the Third Rome—
> but it does not possess the power to prevent it.
> —Andrei Amal'rik,
> *Will the Soviet Union Survive until 1984?*
> (first disseminated in Samizdat, i.e., self-published
> underground editions in the Soviet Union, in 1969)

Our times do not make much of prophets. The Soviet dissident Andrei Amal'rik went to the Gulag for his prophecy, which nevertheless turned out to be remarkably correct (of the few Western scholars who later made similar predictions, see Pipes 1975; Carrère d'Encausse 1981).

There is no reason to argue anymore that the Soviet Union was a totalitarian empire, though many on the Left have come to this conclusion too late (see, for example, Keane 1988). Although Arendt (1968: 175; first published in 1951) too optimistically hoped long ago that "the few thousand Soviet citizens who voluntarily left Soviet Russia after the Second World War and found asylum in democratic countries did more damage to the prestige of the Soviet Union than millions of refugees in the twenties who belonged to the wrong class," it has taken the curtain to fall and the empire to collapse to push some people grudgingly to admit the truth.

3

Remarkably, however, even in 1992 Motyl (1992: 312–13) considered it necessary to appeal almost apologetically to some of his colleagues, arguing that "it is not unimportant [*sic!*] that totalitarianism does, as its critics contend, have moral overtones" and that there is "nothing wrong or 'unobjective' about joining the rising chorus of Russians and non-Russians who denounce the political system inherited from Stalin, Brezhnev, and Gorbachev" because, "if anything, silence in the face of such obvious injustice may be more worthy of condemnation."

The Soviet Union was a totalitarian empire ruled by a political party, and the ruling elite of this party had the complete and uncontrolled monopoly, not only of the ideology and the legislative, executive, juridical, and punitive powers, but all kinds of economic resources as well. No wonder the majority of former Soviet people still call their society the state. The idea of civil society as something different and distinct from the state, so deeply embedded in the Western political and ideological tradition (Hall 1988; Seligman 1992), is completely alien to the Soviet one.

Before Perestroika: Soviet Nationality Policy

Although the Soviet Communist Party liked to stress its "international" ideology and composition, the Soviet ruling elite actually consisted mainly of Russians and also, immediately after the Bolshevik revolution, of "Russified members of alien nationalities *(inorodtsy)*," as Lenin called these people. It is true that in the early stages of Soviet history the latter were overrepresented at the top levels of the party—a fact that Russian right-wing nationalists stress without fail, arguing that Bolshevism was imposed upon Russians by other nationalities. But usually those people were more Catholic than the pope, and did not identify themselves with those nationalities to which they belonged by birth. As Lenin remarked regarding the Great Russian chauvinism, they tended to overdo it more intensely than ethnic Russians. In any case, as early as the late 1920s and the 1930s most of them were dismissed from the leading positions. Beginning in the early 1930s, the Soviet ruling elite increasingly relied on the support of ethnic Russians and was inclined to identify the interests of the Soviet Union with the interests of the Russian people. (It is a different matter that this identification was arbitrary and based on the primacy of the "state idea," which is characteristic not only of Soviet but also of Russian history.)

Russians have always dominated politically, economically, and culturally in the Soviet Union, far exceeding their numerical proportion in the country. They were always viewed as the stronghold of the empire. Without their support, the very existence of the Soviet Union was unthink-able. Ethnic Russians predominated absolutely in all foci of power at the all-union level. By 1986, 85 percent of the Communist Party Central Com-mittee secretaries, 83 percent of USSR ministers and state committee chairmen, and 88 percent of the top military command were Russians (Beissinger and Hajda 1990: 307). Russians controlled all other key ech-elons of power, such as the central bureaucratic apparatus, the KGB (se-cret police), the diplomatic service, and trade unions. The Russian lan-guage dominated in the Soviet Union, and on the all-union level the av-enues of social mobility were wider for Russians than for any other peoples of the USSR.

The economic policy of the center was perceived by non-Russians as a policy conducted at their expense in the interest of the Russian popula-tion. The center frequently ignored the ethnic specificity of the non-Rus-sian territories, the ecological situation in them, and the requirements for their development. In Central Asia and Moldavia (now officially called Moldova), popular opinion was that these regions were intentionally turned into appendages of the center for the provision of raw materials and agricultural products; the Baltics claimed that industrial enterprises requiring labor forces beyond local supplies were built there in order to attract a Russian population; the Armenians were convinced that ecologi-cally harmful chemical-production enterprises were being built in their republic to avert ecological danger in Russia.

The contradiction between the interests of the center and the inter-ests of the periphery affected not only non-Russian but also Russian re-gions of the country. Certain regionalist feelings became manifest in Si-beria and the Far East. However, in non-Russian regions these contradic-tions were intertwined with the nationality question. What was perceived in Russian provinces as the dictatorship of the Moscow center was per-ceived in non-Russian peripheries as a colonial policy of the Russian cen-ter. Accordingly, attempts to draw attention to local interests in Russian provinces were characterized by the center as regionalism. Analogous actions in non-Russian regions of the country were branded as national-ism that contradicts "internationalism."

Russians also played a very specific role in the Soviet government's internal migration policy. In the Soviet Union, these migrations were of-ten called interrepublic personnel exchange, and the growing polyethnic composition of many non-Russian territories of the USSR was viewed as a very positive manifestation, enabling the "internationalization" of the Soviet peoples.

The Soviet migration policy was conducted with economic as well as political considerations in mind. Industrialization in the 1930s and subsequent industrial development were completed mainly, not by the growth in labor productivity, but by drawing in masses of new workers and by developing new territories. In Central Asia and Siberia, and to a lesser degree in the middle Volga region, in Moldavia, and even in the Baltic republics, new industries were developed mainly by bringing in migrants belonging to nonindigenous ethnic groups. The participation of the native populations in this development was very limited.

The political reasons for encouraging internal migrations were obvious. In the 1920s the boundaries of the non-Russian politico-administrative units were sometimes drawn in such a way as to encompass some territories with predominantly Russian populations. This was done for two main reasons. It flattered the non-Russian nationalities (particularly since many of these territories—for example, Northern Kazakhstan—had historically belonged to them, but in the colonial period the tsarist government resettled them with Russians and other Slavs). At the same time it provided a kind of "Trojan horse" within their republics and other autonomous formations. Further migrations of the Russian population into non-Russian areas were supposed to create or increase loyal and reliable groups of the population in these areas. Control over border areas was always important for continental empires, and their governments tried to settle these regions with loyal elements. In the past, a similar practice was conducted by the governments of the Roman, Ottoman, and Chinese Empires, and by the tsarist government. Soviet "ethnic dilution policy," in Connor's (1992: 39) words, was not new, but it was implemented on a much larger scale. By 1926, there were 5.2 million Russians living outside the Russian Federation (according to its presentday boundaries). By 1939, their number had increased to 10 million; by 1979, to 23.9 million; and by 1989, to 25.3 million (Ostapenko and Subbotina 1993: 286). (See table 1.1, p. 247.)

As a result, only Armenia has preserved ethnic homogeneity. Armenians compose more than 90 percent of the country's population. By 1989, indigenous ethnic groups did not compose a majority of the population in 2 union republics (Kazakhstan and Kirgizia, the latter having changed its name to Kyrgyzstan after it became independent), in 13 out of 20 autonomous republics of the USSR, in 5 out of 8 of the autonomous regions *(oblasts),* and in 8 out of 10 of the autonomous districts *(okrugs).* The majority of other non-Russian union republics and autonomous formations in the USSR also had a complex and mixed ethnic composition, including a large Russian component. This component becomes more significant if one adds the Ukrainians into the picture. The majority of the Ukrainians, living beyond the borders of Ukraine, have become significantly Russified. The migration of not only Russian but also non-Russian populations facilitated the Soviet goal. When removed from their main ethnic territories, non-Russians often became an easier target of Russification.

An especially threatening situation for native peoples has taken place in recent decades in Estonia and Latvia. On the eve of World War II, the number of Estonians in Estonia was 92 percent; in 1959, 74.6 percent; in 1988, 61 percent (Kirch and Kirch 1988: 172–73; Rebane 1989: 87). The non-Estonian population in Estonia has tripled in the last 30 years. In the period between 1979 and 1989, when the number of Estonians in Estonia grew by 15,500 persons, the number of Russians in Estonia increased by 60,000 persons, and the number of Slavic people as a whole grew by 82,500 persons (Sheehy 1989b: 5).

From 1959 to 1969, an average of 14,300 persons per year immigrated to Latvia; from 1970 to 1978, 11,600 persons per year; and from 1979 to 1988, 9,300 persons immigrated annually (Muiznieks 1990: 19). Even in 1987–1988, 18,000 persons migrated to Latvia per year—more than during the "period of stagnation" (Peters 1989: 169). As a result, the number of Latvians in Latvia grew by 20,100 persons in the period between 1979 and 1989, and at the same time, the number of Russians and Ukrainians in this republic grew by 109,400 persons (Sheehy 1989b: 5). For this kind of situation in Latvia, a special phrase came into being—"demographic aggression of the central power." (See table 1.2, p. 248.)

By 1989, 60 million persons lived beyond the borders of their constituent republics, autonomous formations, or ethnic territories in the Soviet Union; 25 million of them were Russian. Russians had their own schools and other educational and cultural institutions all over the country, but non-Russians living beyond the boundaries of their ethnoterritorial formations were deprived of this and as a result were doomed to acculturation.

Contrary to the hopes of the Soviet leadership, internal migrations and further complications of the ethnic composition in non-Russian territories of the country did not facilitate "internationalism" and the rapprochement of the Soviet peoples; rather, ethnic friction and competition increased. Contacts between native populations and migrants were frequently limited to production and public spheres. Sensing their political supremacy in the Soviet Empire, many Russians had a dismissive attitude toward the culture and traditions of the native populations and refused to learn the local languages.

A Russian journalist (Konsratov 1989: 3) living in Moldavia and trying to explain the explosion of nationalism there stated fairly:

> Today's extraordinary events are a reaction to many years of strangling the dignity of the Moldavian people. By whom? Not by one of the union-

republic's bureaucracies, but, imagine, by those good Russian people, who, not thinking, have ignored the traditions, culture, and language of the Moldavians . . . . Why have Russians and Ukrainians living here for decades never managed to learn to say something in Moldavian? Why do even those who have just recently settled here demand privileges? Can it be because they are used to thinking of themselves as the "elder brother"?

Official Soviet ideology served to legitimize the ruling positions of the Russians. The Russians were called the elder brother of all other Soviet peoples; the latter were relegated the role of "junior brother." Only Russians were considered as deserving of the status "the great people." Beginning with the 1930s, historical chauvinism played an increasingly conspicuous role in Soviet propaganda (see, for example, the Eisenstein films glorifying Alexander Nevsky and Ivan the Terrible). Historical figures of Russian history—princes, tsars, and generals who carried out the territorial expansion of Russia—were praised as progressive, and some were declared Russian national heroes. In the city of Grozny, the capital of Chechnia, there was a monument to General Yermolov, whom the Russians consider a hero but the Chechens consider a cruel and bloody colonizer. During the perestroika period they repeatedly attempted to remove or destroy the monument, and a special police detail had to protect it 24 hours a day. Only after the collapse of the Soviet Union was the monument removed to Central Russia.

Soviet historians usually wrote about Ivan the Terrible or Peter the Great in a positive tone; analogous figures of other nationalities (such as Timur in Uzbekistan, Vytautas and Gediminas in Lithuania, or Biron in Latvia) were either portrayed negatively (as in the case of Timur) or downplayed. In the 1940s, the official doctrine took on its final form whereby the incorporation of any peoples into the Russian state was viewed as positive. Accordingly, those who resisted annexation, such as the Daghestanian Shamil', the Kazakh Kenesary Kasimov, or the Ukrainian Mazepa, became traitors and reactionaries in the eyes of the Soviet state. Non-Russian peoples of the Soviet Union could maintain their own national heroes, but only those who facilitated the annexation and incorporation of their countries and peoples into Russia (Tillett 1969; Velychenko 1994). Odintsov, the first secretary of the North Ossetian Communist Party organization in the Brezhnev period and an ethnic Russian, boldly stated that the history of the Ossetian people began only with the 1917 revolution.

In addition, the ethnic composition of the majority of non-Russian constituent republics of the USSR was very complicated. Many of them had in their territory numerous ethnic minorities living more or less compactly. Some of these minorities had autonomous formations, but most did not.

In both circumstances, their relations with the dominant nationality of the given republic and its elites were sometimes tense. Ethnic competition for economic resources and capital investments, attempts to homogenize and broaden the ethnic territory by the dominant nationalities in the republics, and sometimes even cultural-linguistic chauvinism in relations with their ethnic minorities, all made the position of the minorities rather vulnerable. Ethnic minorities often perceived this situation as discriminatory and strove to achieve or to elevate their autonomous status. This led to accusations of separatism, betrayal of republican interests, and so on, by members of ethnic majorities in corresponding republics.

The Abkhaz-Georgian conflict that has lasted for decades may serve as an example (for its detailed though very one-sided descriptions, see Miminoshvili and Pandzikidze 1990; Chervonnaia 1993). In the 1970s, the Abkhaz people, who by 1989 composed a minority (about 15 percent) in the Abkhaz autonomous republic (part of the Georgian union republic), openly protested at numerous demonstrations and rallies and conducted a letter campaign against the influx of Georgians to Abkhazia and the policy of Georgianization (teaching of the Abkhazian language and history ceased in the schools in the 1940s and resumed only in the 1980s). Some people demanded that Abkhazia be joined to the Russian Federation. In the 1970s, I asked several participants of the Abkhaz movement if they seriously thought that their situation would be better in Russia than in Georgia. They replied, "Apparently not, but we disdain Georgians even more than we dislike Russians."

In 1979, thousands of Abkhaz gathered in Lykhny, a village sacred to the Abkhaz people, and, in accordance with an ancient ritual that goes back to their pagan past, excluded the first secretary of the Abkhaz Communist Party from the Abkhaz people "for collaboration with Georgians."[1] After that, Moscow, which for several years had not interfered directly in the conflict and seemed to a certain extent pleased with the situation because it served the center's *divide et impera* policy, decided that the Abkhaz went too far. They were ordered to stop their protest immediately, and many local party leaders were removed from their positions. However, the Abkhaz were given more upper-level positions in the local administration, and the Georgian leadership was told not to carry out its policy so obviously. This could not eliminate the underlying reasons for

[1] Participants of this meeting told me that the poor man cried like a child when this happened, because he understood that his career had come to an end. The majority of Abkhaz would no longer shake his hand or even talk to him. He quickly resigned, left for Tbilisi, and was appointed to a fictitious position as a deputy minister of foreign affairs of Georgia.

the ethnic conflict, which became aggravated during the perestroika period and later turned into a full-fledged war.

At the same time, the Soviet Empire had many specific characteristics. First, from the legal point of view, its colonies enjoyed the same rights (or rather, their absence) as the metropole, that is, Russia. Second, Russia lacked many political and other institutions of her own. They dissolved into the empire's central institutions. The all-union center simultaneously fulfilled a function of the Russian center. Third, the political and cultural privileges that Russians enjoyed in the Soviet Empire were not always accompanied by the corresponding economic standing. The living standards in several republics, such as Ukraine, Belorussia (now known as Belarus'), and particularly the Baltics, were higher than in many regions of Russia (for more details see Conquest 1986; Karklins 1986; Hajda and Beissinger 1990, and many other publications).

Usually totalitarian powers fall as the result of military defeat. In Amal'rik's prophecy (1971: 64), the future Soviet-Chinese war that, in his opinion, was inevitable would cause the collapse of the Soviet Empire. On the contrary, the Soviet Empire, it would seem, has fallen apart in a long postwar development period.

However, the name "cold war" for the postwar period was no accident. Reforms were initiated in the Soviet Union only because it had lost this war in all parameters. Here Marxism became bankrupt as an ideocracy, communism as a political order, and Soviet-type state socialism as an economic system. Overextension is a common pitfall of empires. In the Soviet case economic and military overextensions accompanied an ideological one. The invasion of Afghanistan revealed this quite clearly.

The attempt to solve the problem of interethnic relations by specific Soviet methods also failed. The so-called nationality question, which the Soviet leadership so many times declared solved forever, turned out to remain a problem. Moreover, unexpectedly to this leadership and even to some shrewd sovietologists in the West,[2] during the perestroika period it became the most important internal problem of the Soviet Union.

The pretentious slogan about "the unbreakable friendship and broth-

---

[2] To provide one of many possible examples, I can refer to Colton (1986: 63), who confidently claimed: "Soviet ethnic relations are too often discussed by foreign observers in apocalyptic language, sometimes as if the Soviet multinational state were on the verge of collapsing like a house of cards. Careful reflection suggests this . . . is not a critically urgent problem. . . . Over the next ten years or so . . . , and even several decades beyond, the situation seems entirely manageable." Hough (1991) maintained virtually the same position, even in 1991. I must agree with Rywkin (1994: 8) that "Western views on Soviet ethnic reality were very much influenced by Soviet propaganda claiming that Moscow had 'solved' nationality problems" (see also Subtelny 1994).

erhood" of the Soviet peoples was always a poor cover for old and new antipathies and grievances. It would be wrong to assert that all the ethnic tensions and conflicts in the Soviet Union were exclusively the result of the Soviet nationality policy. Many of them have their roots in the history of the peoples incorporated into the Russian and then Soviet Empires. Economic, cultural, linguistic, and religious differences of the various ethnic groups influence many of these conflicts. The territorial delimitation and the borders redrawn in the Soviet period have been far from well thought-out, and sometimes (as in the case of Karabakh) they intentionally ignored the ethnic composition of the debated territories as well as the changes in this composition that were occurring for many reasons. This often gave new facets to old conflicts. Nevertheless, the Soviet nationality policy did not do much to resolve the conflicts. It has just temporarily suppressed them.

Actually this policy, the contours of which were clearly defined already in the 1930s, was quite contradictory. Its basic principles were:
1. the maintenance of an overcentralized and unitary Soviet state despite official declaration of its federative structure;
2. political domination by the Russians in the Soviet Empire;
3. suppression of all manifestations of nationalism among the non-Russian peoples including their attempts at real autonomy;
4. creation of a new social structure of all the Soviet peoples including loyal ethnic elites dependent on the Soviet state and therefore interested in its preservation;
5. enforced simplification of the ethnic composition of the USSR.

Despite several vacillations, this policy was rigorously followed from the 1930s to the 1950s, and reached its culmination in the 1960s through the early 1980s. It is true that Brezhnev's policy of "trust-in-cadres," proclaimed at the 23rd Congress of the Communist Party in 1966, entrenched non-Russian elites in local administration, which led to the development of a corrupt ethnic patronage machine. One may argue that eventually this situation contributed to their "nationalistic deviation." However, until the perestroika period, it did not affect much the goals of the nationality policy. The official Soviet concept of the ethnic situation and interethnic relations proclaimed the creation of a new historical, social, and supra-ethnic community—the Soviet people, who purportedly came about as the result of the dialectical processes of all Soviet ethnic groups simultaneously blossoming and drawing closer. Substantiating this concept, Soviet ideologists, as well as philosophers, sociologists, and anthropologists, published innumerable monotonous books and papers which were more propagandist than scientific in nature and often simply falsified the facts (about them see Khazanov 1990b). However, actually, the main goal of

Soviet policy from the 1960s to 1987 was sufficiently clear to anyone who wished to have or who did have the opportunity to conduct unbiased research. The policy attempted to force the social, cultural, and linguistic unification of all nationalities in the USSR on the basis of Russian or, more accurately, Soviet-Russian culture. The pragmatic need to control such an expansive and variegated empire dictated the policy. In other words, the Soviet nationality policy in this period was defined by a desire to homogenize the country and to turn the Soviet Union from a supranational into a quasinational state.

The ultimate goal was the complete Russification of non-Russian nationalities under the slogan "Merging the nations." This goal was openly announced by Lenin and affirmed by Khrushchev and, in the early 1980s, by Andropov (*Pravda*, December 22, 1982). Gorbachev bragged that, with difficulty, he prevented its inclusion in the new party program in 1985 (*Pravda*, January 8, 1989).

However, Lenin's goal was never pursued consistently for fear of, among other things, provoking resistance among the non-Russian peoples (Khazanov 1988: 152–54). Besides, the Soviet leaders understood that in the near future it would simply not be feasible. Instead, they set a more modest goal: acculturation and linguistic Russification of non-Russian nationalities in the USSR. The motto "Drawing the nations together" was promoted. But this, as one Russian scholar noted, "became the fig leaf for Russification" (E. S. Troitsky in a round-table discussion of the theory and practice of nationalities relations under socialism—see *Voprosy filosofii*, 9 [1988]: 72).

In order to fulfill this goal, at first higher, then secondary, elementary, and eventually preschool education began to be conducted in Russian on a growing scale in the union and especially in the autonomous republics and regions (on the Soviet linguistic policy see Kreindler 1985; Solntsev and Mikhal'chenko 1992). By the 1960s, children stopped systematically studying in their native languages in schools in the autonomous formations of the Russian Federation. The last Kalmyk-language school was closed in Kalmykia in 1963. In Ordzhonikidze, the capital of North Ossetia, there was only one Ossetian-language school left—for mentally-retarded children. In the beginning of the 1960s in Bashkiria (now Bashkortostan), the majority of national schools were converted to learning in Russian under the pretext of improving Russian-language teaching.

In Chuvashia, the Chuvash language was taught only in some elementary schools (*Sovetskaia Chuvashia*, October 8, 1992). In Mordovia, the broadcasting in Mordovian languages was only for 20 minutes a day; TV, for 5 minutes a day. In Tataria (or Tatarstan), TV in the national language operated for only 4 hours a day; in Chuvashia, for 1.8 hours; in Udmurtia, for 1.5 hours; in Mari (now known as Marii El), for 1.1 hours (Aklaev 1994: 18). In 1986, there was not one single national school or a single kindergarten in any city in Bashkiria where the teachers spoke in Bashkir (Khalim 1988: 226, 232). Matters for smaller ethnic groups were even worse. Teaching in the native languages of the native peoples of Siberia and the North was discontinued. Children were punished if they were heard to speak their native language instead of speaking Russian at school, and parents were requested not to speak their native language to their children at home (Vakhtin 1992: 18). As a result, the number of school dropouts sharply increased (*Poliarnaia zvezda*, May 27, 1976; *Pravda*, December 24, 1988). (See table 1.3, p. 249.)

Linguistic Russification had a strong effect on the union republics as well. By 1986, in the cities and district centers of Belorussia, not one Belorussian-language school was left (*Russkaia mysl'*, August 4, 1989: 7). Until recently in Ukraine, in large cities such as Zaporozh'e, Dnepropetrovsk, Kherson, Odessa, and Kharkov, there was not a single Ukrainian-language school. The same situation existed in the Crimea. In Kishinev, the capital of Moldavia, where by 1989 Moldavians made up 42 percent of the population, out of 60 high schools only 7 were Moldavian-language schools, and only 18 out of 198 kindergartens and day-care centers were conducted in Moldavian (actually Romanian). The language of higher education was predominantly Russian (Eyal 1989: 45). (See table 1.4, p. 251.)

Official Soviet statistics show the neglect of non-Russian languages, even though they were often falsified to minimize this neglect. According to these statistics, in 1972 only 55 nationalities in the USSR had some kind of education (in most cases only an elementary level) in their native language; in 1988 this number had fallen to 39. In 1940, 25.2 percent of all books and brochures in the USSR were published in languages of non-Russian peoples; in the 1960s this proportion fell to 18 percent, and in 1986, to 11 percent (Zeimal' 1988: 45).

Simultaneously, non-Russian languages were displaced from the sphere of social communication, frequently by purely administrative measures. In the middle of the 1970s, a decree was issued proclaiming that all theses for postgraduate degrees had to be presented in Russian only. All record-keeping in non-Russian parts of the USSR and all official meetings even at the lowest level were to be conducted in Russian. In Estonia, maps in Estonian disappeared (*Literaturnaia gazeta*, February 12, 1988). In Moldavia, all signs in public areas, at stations and stadiums, were exclusively in Russian. Russian was the *lingua franca* at all meetings, from Supreme Soviet sessions to collective and state farm meetings, and even conferences of the Moldavian Union of Writers (Eyal 1989: 45).

According to the 1979 census, 62.2 percent of the non-Russian population of the country was fluent in Russian. Now it is admitted in the Russian press and scientific journals that this number in several republics (for example, Uzbekistan) was overestimated, but in the 1989 census, few changes were recorded (see Appendix). According to this last census, 56.2 percent of Ukrainians were fluent in Russian, 54.7 percent of Belorussians, 60.4 percent of Kazakhs, 53.8 percent of Moldavians, 64.4 percent of Latvians, 71.8 percent of Bashkirs, 70.8 percent of Tatars (*SSSR v tsifrakh v 1989 gody* ... 1990: 38–42). In 1979, 16.3 million non-Russians considered Russian to be their first language (*Naselenie SSSR* ... 1980: 23; Guboglo 1984: 65–66). By 1989, there were 13 million such people; half of them were Ukrainians and Belorussians (Cheshko 1993: 141). This decrease may reflect the growth of nationalism more than a real situation. The number of Karelians, Komis, Komi-Permiaks, Udmurts, Mordovians, Bashkirs, and Khakas in corresponding autonomous formations of the Russian Federation who know the Russian language exceeds the number of those who know the language of their own nationalities (Yamskov 1994:68).

In multiethnic states, language is inevitably politicized (Motyl 1989: 163). The demonstrative neglect of native languages and cultures by the political elites of the non-Russian peoples was viewed favorably in Soviet official circles. The broadening use of Russian in the administration at every level was considered by Moscow as the minimal criterion of their loyalty. The Kyrgyz writer Chinghiz Aitmatov described "a special type of demagogue—a tribune-chatterer—who almost made it his prestigious profession to extol the Russian language and to depreciate his own in appropriate and inappropriate situations" (*Literaturnaia gazeta*, August 13, 1986). Ordinary Bashkirs complained that their "leadership and deputies of the Bashkir ASSR cringed and groveled before chauvinism, most of all worrying about their own privileged positions; for them it was disgraceful to give a speech even once on television or radio in the Bashkir language." Similar complaints came from Tatarstan (or Tataria): "Many leaders to this day never give speeches in their native language; some of them don't even speak it" (Koroteeva and Mosesova 1988: 8). In Moldavia, in the period when Grossul was in power, the political elite was recruited from among Russified Moldavians. Moldavians called them janizaries and *mankurts* (a synonym for *renegades*, taken from a novel by Chinghiz Aitmatov) (Ionescu 1989: 20).

Their native languages were completely unknown or known poorly not only by many officials in the party-state apparatus in non-Russian parts of the country but also even in certain circles of the intelligentsia. Many Uzbek and Kazakh ministers and other high-ranking officials needed to use the services of translators when a movement began to translate official records into Uzbek and Kazakh. Akaev, the current president of

Kyrgyzstan, admitted that he knows Russian better than his native language. The same is true with Presidents Kuchma and Lukashenko of Ukraine and Belarus'. I am personally acquainted with Ukrainian, Belorussian, Daghestanian, Tatar, Kazakh, Kalmyk, Buryat, Yakut, and Tuvinian scholars, including anthropologists, who cannot speak their native language. One of the activists of the Azerbaidjanian Popular Front, the major nationalistic organization in the country, recently confessed to me that he was hurriedly learning Azerbaidjanian.

Nevertheless, the success and the consequences of the policy of linguistic Russification were clearly overestimated by the Soviet leadership. The ever-increasing dominance of the Russian language in the Soviet Union constantly raised the required level of knowledge of this language as a sine qua non for social advancement and career promotion in almost all spheres of professional activity. As a result, members of non-Russian nationalities were placed at an additional disadvantage compared with Russians. This only intensified ethnic competition.

The policy of linguistic Russification met with strong resistance, particularly in the Baltics and in the Transcaucasian republics. In April 1978 the Supreme Soviet of Georgia adopted a new constitution for the republic. Usually, people did not pay attention to such official events, because republics' constitutions in the USSR did not have any weight. Perhaps the leadership was counting on this very apathy. If so, they were clearly mistaken. People noticed that, unlike the previous constitution, the new one did not proclaim Georgian to be the state language of Georgia. Several thousand persons, mainly students, assembled for a peaceful demonstration, demanding: "Give us back our language."

That time the authorities chose to concede. In an unprecedented move, Shevardnadze, who was at that time first secretary of the Communist Party of Georgia and should have known the mood of his fellow Georgians, met with the demonstrators and, according to my informants among them, assured them that what had happened was the result of misunderstanding. On the following day, the Georgian constitution was changed, and the Georgian language was again proclaimed to be the state language of Georgia.

A similar explosive situation existed in Yerevan, the capital of Armenia, where I happened to be in April 1978. A new Armenian constitution did not contain any mention of Armenian as the state language of the republic. Upon arriving in the city, I was told by my friends there: "Observe what will happen tomorrow morning. Our demonstrations will be more numerous and, possibly, not as peaceful." However, nothing happened the next day. The previous evening, Yerevan radio had announced without any explanation that the constitution had been changed, and Armenian again was proclaimed the state language of Armenia.

The Soviet leadership ignored the experience of many contemporary countries which has clearly demonstrated that linguistic assimilation not only does not weaken ethnic tension but often exacerbates it. The compulsory demand to know Russian at the expense of native language was considered humiliating. From the 1960s to the early 1980s, I heard the following prediction many times from members of the non-Russian intelligentsia in the USSR: If by the twenty-first century our children and grandchildren are forced to forget our own language and to speak Russian, they will, with even greater reason, state in this language, "Russians go home." Their prediction was realized significantly earlier.

However, the concept of nationality held by the Soviet state since the 1930s was completely different from that which is accepted in many Western countries. It was essentially the primordialist concept, inasmuch as it was based on the notion of descent. Moreover, in many respects it was close to conceptions that dominated in Nazi Germany. It is true that ethnic affiliation in the Soviet Union was not connected directly to race or religion. At the same time, it was not a matter of free choice for the individual. In the 1930s, when the Soviets introduced the internal passport system, they based nationality on parental identification. From then until the fall of the Soviet Empire, ethnic affiliation was inherited, and the individual, whether he or she wished it or not, inherited the parents' nationality, which was written on the birth certificate. Only the offspring of mixed marriages had the right, once in their life when they received their internal passport at the age of 16, to choose between their father's or mother's nationality.[3]

Because ethnic stratification existed in the Soviet Union, nationality was a subject of exceptional importance for the state as well as for the individual. It was noted in all identifying documents and was taken into consideration when applying to a university, for employment, for promotion, or for emigration. During the perestroika period this was admitted even by persons who were far from belonging to the liberal camp. In one of his last articles, the late Yu. Bromley (1990: 24), the leading Soviet expert on ethnicity, wrote: "The introduction of internal passports and numerous official documents in which the nationality of the individual is

[3] In the early 1980s, an acquaintance of mine who had one Russian parent and one Tatar, decided that, since he considered himself Tatar, this nationality should be written on his internal passport. Eight times he approached various offices on different bureaucratic levels, including the Ministry of Internal Affairs, arguing that his parents registered him as Russian when he was too young to make the conscious choice himself. All eight times his request was rejected. He was told unofficially that his persistence looked very suspicious and might indicate his "dissident inclinations."

written created the conditions for violating the principle of national equality and gave an unnecessary emphasis to the ethnic origins of citizens."

Thus, a very significant contradiction existed in the Soviet nationality
policy. On the one hand, the policy promoted acculturation; on the other
hand, it disparaged assimilation by placing a very serious obstacle in its
way. It denied to those individuals and groups who wanted to change
their official nationality the opportunity to do so. A significant number
of persons in the Soviet Union, particularly among dispersed nationalities
or those residing outside their ethnic formations, wanted to be registered
as Russian (or sometimes as members of titular nationalities in the non-
Russian republics) either in order to raise their ethnic status and, accordingly, improve their position in Soviet society or simply because they had
been virtually assimilated into other nationalities. But they found it impossible to do so by any legal action.

This inconsistency in the Soviet nationality policy was noticed by the
Soviet authorities themselves. Before the 1977 constitution was adopted,
some people suggested making ethnicity a matter of voluntary choice or
removing the nationality clause from identity documents. These suggestions were even published by Soviet newspapers. However, everything
remained unchanged, apparently for several reasons. On the one hand,
any changes in the existing practice of ascriptive ethnic identification
would hardly have been welcomed by many Russians, including the party
and governmental officials and even professionals and intellectuals, for
fear of competition. On the other hand, there was also the danger that
some nationalities, considering such a change as another step in the policy
of Russification, might have resisted it. The desire to have a scapegoat
that can be easily identified like the Jews might have served as an additional factor.

However, the very impossibility of crossing ethnic borders sometimes
only inspired nationalistic feelings. A Zionist movement in the late 1960s
and in the early 1970s in the Soviet Union was to a large extent revived
by some members of the very acculturated secular Jewish intelligentsia,
as a reaction against discrimination and an anti-Semitic atmosphere in the
country.

Thus, unlike modern Western nations, which emerged from a lengthy
process of nation-state formation (Kohn 1967; Smith 1986), the Soviet
Union remained underdeveloped in terms of its ethnic composition and
national structure. Events following the Bolshevik revolution artificially
interrupted and diverted the process of creating nation-states, and even
the formation of modern nations, in the territory of the former Russian
Empire. The process of modernization also remained incomplete in many

non-Russian regions of the country. The nationality policy pursued by the Soviet leadership only aggravated the situation.

Not only did Soviet legislation make ethnic affiliation ascriptive. In addition, it directly connected nationality with territory, linked ethnic status with the degree of ethnoterritorial autonomy, and made cultural autonomy dependent on the level of corresponding autonomous formation. As a result, the Soviet policy did not help to break down barriers between ethnicity and nation. Instead, by purely administrative measures it created a political hierarchy of ethnic groups, basing the hierarchy on pseudoscientific arguments and subdividing all the peoples of the USSR into *natsiia* (the most developed and consolidated peoples), *natsional'nost'* (underdeveloped nations), and *narodnost'* (ethnic groups of even lower order). Higher levels of autonomy of ethnoterritorial formations meant the provision of certain advantages to titular peoples in the spheres of education and culture, in social advancement (including various kinds of official and nonofficial affirmative action), in economic development, and simply in somehow protecting their interests. This situation resembled the Russian *matrioshka* doll, in which successively smaller figures are hidden inside the larger ones.

Accordingly, titular peoples of union republics had advantages over indigenous peoples living in autonomous republics, and those peoples in turn had advantages over peoples living in autonomous regions, not to speak of autonomous districts. Investments in culture, education, health services, and social needs were greater in the union republics than in the autonomous republics. For example, in 1988, budget appropriations for local social needs were 1,308 rubles per capita in Estonia, 800 rubles per capita in Russia, and only 212 rubles in Tatarstan. This unequal appropriation occurred despite the fact that Kama automobile production in Tatarstan alone equaled the entire production of Estonia (*Politicheskoe obrazovanie*, 8 [1989]: 99).

At the very bottom of the ethnic hierarchy were placed the dispersed nationalities and those nationalities that lived more or less compactly but did not have administrative and cultural autonomy and therefore had no institutions for defending and upholding their interests. These groups included the Germans, Poles, Jews, Hungarians, Greeks, Gagauz, Bulgarians, Crimean Tatars, Meskhetian Turks, Kurds, Uighurs, Koreans, Assyrians, Nogay, Gypsies, and several others, including many of the so-called small peoples of Siberia and the Far North. It is not by chance that some peoples of the North and Siberia are now demanding autonomy, ironically in the form of the very reservations that have always been branded by the Soviets as one of the criminal artifacts of American imperialism.

Nationalities such as the Germans, Crimean Tatars, or Meskhetian Turks were subjected to particular discrimination. Along with other "punished peoples" they were deported eastward during World War II or immediately after the war and were not permitted to return to their homeland. The Jews also faced exceptional discrimination.

Although the Soviet nationality policy resulted in some degree of Russification, it failed to eliminate, and in some ways instigated, nationalism among the non-Russian peoples of the USSR. For a long time, the very presence of this problem in the Soviet Union was denied by Soviet leaders and the scholars serving them. The concept of nationalism as a concomitant product of modernity, which is characteristic of countries with different social and economic systems, was never applied to the Soviet Union. Soviet theorists insisted that nationalism was a characteristic feature of capitalist countries only and was absolutely foreign to communist ones. In the Soviet Union, only the presence of "remnants of nationalism" was admitted and attributed to survivals from the pre-Soviet past or "the undermining activity of Western imperialism and international Zionism."

In fact, Soviet colonialism revealed the same regularities as the colonialism of capitalist countries, including the law of "colonial ingratitude." Colonialism involves the development of colonies and creates nontraditional elites; this, in turn, promotes the growth of nationalism.

More developed and modern forms of nationalism were felt the most strongly in republics such as the Baltics, which have numerous urban strata educated in the national languages and interested in promotion of these languages and the national cultures. The comparatively small numbers of these strata among the Finnic peoples of the Volga region explain the relative weakness of their national movements there.

Despite some exceptions it is impossible to speak of organized national movements in the USSR in the period being reviewed. All forms of opposition, including nationalism, were severely repressed. To be labeled a nationalist was a ticket straight to the Gulag, and the majority of political prisoners in the Soviet Union in the post-Stalin period were persons accused of nationalism (Alexeyeva 1985). In the best circumstances, organized nationalist oppositions were composed of small and usually short-lived underground groups, which, although provoking respect and sympathy, were for obvious reasons not numerous or influential enough to have much effect. Most incidents of open national unrest and disturbance that took place in the Soviet Union from the 1970s to the early 1980s (as in Tashkent in 1970, or in Tbilisi in 1978) were more or less spontaneous. Although they demonstrated a deep and powerful national antagonism, they were provoked by concrete local events. Passive resentment and protest for ethnic causes were more widespread. However, the word *dissent* means not only "open political opposition" but also "disagreement or rejection." Therefore, in the Soviet system, the declared goal of which was the creation of a single Soviet people, any activity and any behavior directed toward preserving and strengthening ethnic differences, even those that were not officially prohibited, could to a certain degree be viewed as dissent in the broad meaning of this word—first, because the fight for the preservation of various ethnic cultures and languages was incompatible with the ultimate goals of the Soviet nationality policy and, second, because an emphasis on ethnic differences was already in and of itself a hidden challenge to the Soviet leadership and its policy.

This passive and hidden opposition was present in various strata of Soviet society and took on different forms in different non-Russian regions of the USSR: an unwillingness to speak Russian in public areas; the disapproval of mixed marriages; the fight to preserve education in native languages; a demonstrative admiration of certain traditional elements of ethnic cultures and attempts to preserve them; sympathy for all political events and national movements beyond the borders of the USSR which provoked the disapproval of the Soviet leadership,[4] and so on. Such hidden dissent or simply passive non-acceptance of the Soviet nationality policy provoked anxiety in the Soviet leadership, but the leadership certainly underestimated the significance of this undercurrent.

The central leadership in Moscow in the Brezhnev period was lulled by the pseudosuccesses of its nationality policy, such as the increased knowledge of the Russian language and culture, and clearly did not realize the seriousness of the situation. The majority of the Russian population, especially the portion living in Russia itself, also was not aware of the problem. A servile press and weak feedback between the rulers and the ordinary people—a common shortcoming of all totalitarian regimes—contributed to this. The absence of civil rights and the possibility to express dissatisfaction openly on the one hand, and the almost universal use of doublespeak and doublethink on the other, also added to the distortion of the overall picture.

---

[4] A beguiling story was told to me by an Estonian journalist. One morning in May 1967, a man who was the yard-keeper of his apartment house in Tallinn, and who had formerly been a noncommissioned officer in the Estonian army during independence, then for 12 years a prisoner in the Soviet forced-labor camps in Siberia, knocked at the doors of the Estonian tenants of the house, awakening them with a cry: "Listen to what is going on. Jews are defeating Russians!" That was his interpretation of the Six-Day War in the Middle East. He certainly hoped that for this happy news he would be offered a drink, and in several cases his expectation came true.

It is true that the Soviet dissidents (see, for example, Chornovil 1968; Dzyuba 1974; Alexeyeva 1985; see also Zisserman-Brodsky 1994) and some Western experts have long warned of the growing discontent of the non-Russian peoples. However, these scholars were labeled in the USSR as professional slanderers and anti-Soviets, and dissidents were persecuted. In addition, subordinates never communicated the true situation to their superiors, saying instead what the superiors wanted to hear. Certainly the Brezhnev leadership never tried to know the truth. The impending crisis in relations with the nationalities blindsided the Soviet rulers. In this regard Gorbachev was no exception. The Soviet prime minister during the restructuring period, Nikolai Ryzhkov (1992: 208), belatedly laments the Soviet nationality policy: "We consistently hacked the bough on which we were sitting. When did we start this 'ax process'? In 1988? In 1985? In 1953? In 1937? In 1922? Or maybe already in 1917?"

In all, the frustrated nation building and ethnic competition put immense strain on the relations between different nationalities in the country. The nationality question affected the fates of the economic reforms, the political reconstruction of the country, and the recent power struggle. Among other things, the Soviet Union collapsed because of the growth in nationalism and ethnic competition as concomitant phenomena of interrelations between the core area (Russia) and its peripheral domains, and the uneven modernization of the latter.

Prelude: The Beginning of Perestroika

To have a clear understanding of Soviet developments during 1985–1992 one should not have any illusions about the initial goals of Gorbachev's reforms. Just six years after Gorbachev came to power, Dr. Stephen Cohen published a remarkable article (1991), in which he claimed that Gorbachev's real intentions were to dismantle state control and to achieve the emancipation of the Soviet Union "through privatization, democratization, and federalization of the 15 republics." (It appears that in 1992 Cohen still held this opinion; see Cohen 1992.) I do not know where he got this idea about Gorbachev's far-reaching goals. Gorbachev never claimed these goals himself, at any rate not while he remained in power. "I consider myself not only a member of the Communist Party, but a communist," reiterated Gorbachev on March 15, 1990 (*Izvestiia*, March 17, 1990), and on many other occasions (*Sovetskaia Rossiia*, May 25, 1990; *Izvestiia*, May 28, June 26, 1990, *Komsomol'skaia pravda*, March 1, 1991).

To the very end he always declared his allegiance to communism and to "socialist choice" (*Pravda*, August 23, 1991).

"We introduced perestroika not to replace the Soviet system, but to reform it. It was not in our mind to change the underlying economic and social structures of our society," asserted Egor Ligachev recently, who at one time was number two in the Communist Party hierarchy (Meeting Report 1991). A close ally of Gorbachev until 1990, Alexandr Yakovlev (1992: 128) also confirmed that the socialist order in the USSR was not questioned by those in the Communist Party's leadership who initiated the restructuring policy. Likewise, Nikolai Ryzhkov (1992: 271–72) testified that its initiator was none other than Andropov and that the underlying idea of his blueprint for reforms was the same as Gorbachev's: to speed up the economic development of the country. He asserts that glasnost and democratization, proclaimed a little later, "did not change anything in the political order of the country." These politicians are completely right. Neither Gorbachev nor his reform-minded allies in the Communist Party and state hierarchy (I would call them the liberal nomenklatura) ever wished to transform their country into a Western-type liberal democracy. In the same way, Gorbachev did not wish for or anticipate the anti-communist revolutions in Eastern Europe. He sought only to create there a group of loyal mini-Gorbachevs.

The aim of the reforms was to overcome economic stagnation and to make the Soviet Union more efficient and competitive. The reformists in the Soviet leadership also comprehended that a continuation of the arms race with the West would ruin the country, and that the Soviet foreign policy was too adventuristic and risky. The country simply could not afford it anymore.

The need for major change was felt in the Soviet Union for many years, and reforms began to be discussed with the death of Brezhnev in November 1982. However, the old guard in the ruling elite still did not have the courage to come to grips with reality. So, the most urgent problem confronting Gorbachev when he came to power was how to improve the economic situation. It is already almost forgotten that in the beginning his internal policy was far from encouraging. He merely resumed the policy of his predecessor and patron, the former KGB chief Andropov. Order, discipline, the continuation of political repression, and the demand for harder and more productive work were called *uskorenie* (acceleration) and put on the agenda. The sole innovation of his own was the hapless anti-alcohol campaign.

Of course, all these measures failed. Ordinary people lacked incentives to work better and harder, and the bureaucratic management of the economy paralyzed any initiative and innovation. A famous Soviet joke of that period was: "We pretend that we are working, and the government pretends that it is paying for our work."

Thus, Gorbachev had to come to the conclusion that limited economic liberalization was not only desirable but also necessary. However, his inconsistent attempts in this direction undertaken in 1986 and 1987 failed entirely, and one of the reasons for their failure was the resistance of the party oligarchy and bureaucracy. To overcome their resistance, beginning in 1987, Gorbachev began to look for additional support from intellectuals and those who may tentatively have been characterized as the educated urban middle strata. He initiated limited political liberalization, for which the terms *glasnost* (openness) and *perestroika* (restructuring) have been coined.

These terms were not at all new ones. The first one had come into use during the period of liberal reforms under Tsar Alexander II in the 1860s, the second during the period of Stolypin's reforms during 1906–1911. This is very significant. In both previous cases the declared goal of the reforms was to modernize the existing order, but in no way to destroy it and create a new one. Gorbachev granted reforms to the Soviet people in the same manner as some Russian tsars had done this in the past. He set his hopes on the traditional obedience of his compatriots. He was concerned only with the opposition within the ruling elite. The rest of society was supposed to approve, applaud, and obey, but in no way participate in formulating and conducting the policy of reforms.

The policy of restructuring initiated by Young Turks in the Soviet ruling elite, by Gorbachev, and by reformists such as Yeltsin, Ryzhkov, Shevardnadze, or Yakovlev was not a revolution from above but a bureaucratic attempt to vitalize the economy through a limited and controlled emancipation of Soviet society. This policy received enthusiastic support from some liberal-minded intellectuals such as Korotich, Popov, or Sobchak, who soon afterwards became known as new democrats. One should not confuse these people with the open critics of the Soviet regime, the dissidents of the 1970s and the early 1980s. Of these dissidents, including active participants of various nationalistic movements, those who had not been forced to emigrate still remained in opposition to Gorbachev. In 1986, and even in 1987, many of them still languished in the Gulag and never considered that not only would they soon be freed but also that some of them would hold parliamentary chairs. The new converts to democracy consisted mostly of those members of scientific, cultural, and other establishments who were always close to the ruling elite. (In the secret personnel lists of the Central Committee of the Communist Party such people often figured as the "nomenklatura reserve.")

In the beginning, even Gorbachev's boldest supporters did not advocate more than a mixed economy that would retain the state ownership and centrally planned production in the key sectors. Almost nobody yet dared to challenge the monopoly of political power held by the Communist Party.

However, the jinn escaped from the bottle. While it turned out that the crisis in the Soviet Union was much deeper than the Soviet leadership conceived, Gorbachev's reforms awakened the educated strata, and to a certain extent emancipated them from fear of repressions. They began to demand radical political and economic reforms and concessions that were more than what Gorbachev and his allies in the Soviet leadership were initially willing to grant them. Some of the new converts to democracy were also undergoing a process of rapid political radicalization, and the role of the oppositionists was becoming increasingly attractive to many former conformists from the stagnation period. Besides that, even the limited liberalization galvanized old tensions, grievances, and conflicts between various nationalities of the Soviet Union.

From the end of 1986 through the first half of 1987, at the onset of a period of change, representatives of the non-Russian peoples began to express in the press complaints about the Soviet nationality policy, specifically its abuses of non-Russian languages and cultures. Estonian economists and reform-minded officials began to insist on economic and financial independence for their republic. In 1987, groups sprang up in various republics to address social, cultural, and ecological problems that were often connected with the national interests of these people. Ecological movements were particularly active in Armenia, Georgia, Azerbaidjan, Estonia, Moldavia, and Uzbekistan. In September and October of 1987 in Armenia, the Greens organized unsanctioned mass demonstrations—an uncommon phenomenon in the Soviet Union at that time. There was one marked attempt at reviving nationalist opposition. In July 1986, the Helsinki-86 group was formed in Latvia, and in its very first documents it appealed to Gorbachev to hold a referendum on independence for Latvia (*Vesti iz SSSR*, 1/2 [1987]). In the beginning of 1987 anti-Russian disturbances were reported in Riga, the capital of Latvia. For several days in February 1987 Jews in Moscow staged protest demonstrations insisting on their right to emigrate from the country. In the summer of 1987, Crimean Tatars demonstrated at Red Square for the right to return to their homeland. That same year the anti-Semitic and chauvinistic Pamiat' (Memory) organization staged its first public meetings. By 1988, or even by the second half of 1987, the economic and political crisis in the Soviet Union began to be accompanied by an explosion of nationalism and tension in interethnic relations.

Perestroika in Trouble: The Resurgence of Nationalism

In a book published in 1987, Motyl came to the conclusion that non-Russians in the Soviet Union would not rebel because they could not rebel (in all fairness, one should take into account that it takes time for a book to be published). Among other factors, Motyl referred to the repressive power of the KGB, a lack of leadership and autonomous political institutions because of the seeming marginality of the dissident movements, and the conformism of non-Russian political elites, who were not likely "to bite the hand that still feeds them better than the local population" (Motyl 1987). To a large extent he was actually right, and all these factors for a long time provided the necessary means to keep the situation under control. However, by 1988 it began to change rapidly.

Theories of ethnic conflict assert that the competition for power, privilege, and scarce resources in multiethnic societies propels participants to oppose each other as members of different ethnic groups with contradicting interests (for a general survey of the literature see White 1988). Social mobilization in modernizing plural societies often relates to ethnic competition for the benefits of modernity, especially when modernization is differential and benefits are unequally spread among ethnic groups (Deutsch 1961: 493ff.; Bates 1974: 468; Glazer and Moynihan 1975: 8; Brass 1976: 231–32; Smith 1979, passim). In this respect, nationalism in many former Soviet republics has demonstrated the essential uniformity with nationalism in some developing countries.

However, the middle strata of non-Russian nationalities in the Soviet Union were unfamiliar with Western social thought. To them the policy of restructuring had a real meaning only in connection with their ethnic liberation. As soon as terror and repression in the country were significantly reduced, they started to demand more rights, or even complete independence, for their nationalities.

At the same time, Gorbachev's nationality policy, when compared with the policy of the 1960s through the early 1980s, was characterized by its halfway measures and inconsistency. It went through several stages, using various methods to which the Gorbachev leadership resorted for control over the situation in interethnic relations in the country. All of them proved to be ineffective. Gorbachev did not control events. He simply reacted to them and always with a delay. As the crisis in interethnic relations in the USSR intensified, it became increasingly obvious that Gorbachev did not want, or could not propose, a realistic way out of the crisis. Especially in the beginning, he simply did not understand the extent and particulars of the crisis, and he did not know the real mood and situation in the non-Russian regions of the country. In 1990, he himself admitted this, announcing: "Your humble servant in the first stages of perestroika sincerely assumed that here [in the nationality question] there were no serious problems" (*Izvestiia*, April 27, 1990).

For the first two years that Gorbachev held power, Soviet nationality policy, including linguistic Russification, did not undergo any substantial changes. "The nationality question inherited from the past has been successfully resolved in the Soviet Union," declared the new edition of the CPSU Program (*Programma* . . . 1986: 43), and Gorbachev affirmed this at the 27th Congress of the Communist Party of the Soviet Union in February 1987. The events in Yakutia in March-April 1986 and in Kazakhstan in December 1986 were characterized by Moscow as only nationalist riots. The January 1987 plenum of the CPSU Central Committee promised the expansion of democracy and, at the same time, admitted that negative tendencies had appeared in the USSR in the sphere of interethnic relations. Even when Gorbachev attempted to dislodge and replace the corrupted ethnic elites in order to facilitate the reforms, only one remedy was suggested: step up the fight against nationalism.

Pravda (December 28, 1986; February 13, 1987) invoked that "a decisive strike must be given against any attempts to place local interests over all-union interests" and insisted that obstacles should be removed from increasing the number of Russians in local elites and from the migration of Russians into non-Russian regions of the country. It further claimed that the populations of Transcaucasia and Central Asia lived too well at the expense of subsidies from the center.

Non-Russian republics were ordered to broaden the use of the Russian language. Ligachev stated that "the goal of creating nationalities/Russian bilingualism was and remains the key area of work in the field of interethnic relations" (*Pravda*, June 4, 1987). During his visit to Tbilisi in June 1987, Ligachev demanded a decrease in the number of Georgian students in Tbilisi University (*Zaria vostoka*, June 3, 1987). In executing this order, Georgian-language groups in several faculties were abolished and new Russian-speaking groups were formed in their place (Arkhiv Samizdata, No. 6170).

Only beginning with the second half of 1987 did the Soviet leadership gradually begin to understand that the crisis in interethnic relations in the country was significantly more profound than had been supposed, and that to overcome or at least restrain it with previous methods (i.e., repressions) was impossible. In 1988, Soviet leaders came to the realization that the Soviet nationality policy had failed. The nationality question became one of the most important and immediate internal problems of the country, on a par with political and economic reforms.

A virtual absence of civil society in the multiethnic Soviet state implied that the cooperation was most likely to be achieved by means of ethnic solidarity. In 1988–1989, national (actually ethnic) demands became the means for the political mobilization of masses in many non-Russian parts of the USSR (for a chronicle of events and their analysis see G. Smith 1990; Khazanov 1991). Thus, the "Karabakh idea" (striving for the secession of this area from Azerbaidjan) served the consolidation of Armenian society. As one Soviet publicist remarked: "Nationalities have turned into political parties" (Pomerants 1989: 26).

Rothschild (1981: 30) has pointed out that the politicization of ethnic groups is always led by elites. In the Soviet context this process was initiated by the educated middle strata, particularly by intellectuals involved in humanitarian professions.[5] Mass and organized national move-

---

[5] They are often traditionally called the intelligentsia, and in this book I occasionally, though reluctantly, follow this step. However, this term, as it was originally perceived, implied certain social and moral characterisitics (i.e., the principal opposition to the tsarist

ments, in which the former political dissidents and activists of human-rights movements sometimes played important roles, emerged and quickly radicalized the developing nontraditional forms of political opposition, including demonstrations and rallies (see, for example, Abramian 1990). Although scornfully christened by the official Soviet press as "rally democracy," these demonstrations turned out to be extremely effective in promoting the programs of these movements and in attracting wide support. Their overt or covert goals were simple: to fight against Soviet (Russian) colonialism and provide the best possible conditions to members of their own nationalities, if necessary at the expense of all others. These goals turned out to be more attractive to millions of people than the ideological glue of communism or the idea of pluralistic democracy; in any case, most of these movements and their leaders declared their allegiance to the democratic course (on various national movements in the non-Russian parts of the USSR and their programs during the restructuring period, see Bahry 1990; Chicherina 1990a, 1990b; Elabaeva 1991; Lebedev 1991; Guboglo 1992; Guboglo and Chervonnaia 1992; Furtado and Chandler 1992).

It was only later, in 1988–1989, that some political elites in the non-Russian republics also changed their policy and began to resent openly that the Moscow center never took seriously the federative character of the Soviet state, never considered sharing its power with them, and even largely deprived them of any substantial political and economic autonomy in their own republics.

In the conditions of supercentralization in the Soviet Union, all the important political and economic decisions were made by the central leadership in Moscow. The center always had complete control over all the important raw materials and industrial enterprises. More than 90 percent of industrial enterprises in a number of republics were subordinate to union ministries and departments. The income from these enterprises was at their disposal. Kazakhstan gave the center 93 percent of its income. Even Ukraine did not control more than 5 percent of its resources (*Robitnycha gazeta*, February 27, 1990). Centralization also took hold of the cultural and linguistic spheres to the extent that even the number of hours spent in union republic national schools for studying native languages and literatures had to be agreed on in Moscow.

Imperial control often requires a degree of peripheral collaboration (Doyle 1986: 38). Thus, the Soviet type of quasi consociationism, which

---

state and nonengagement in its administrative apparatus) which the Soviet functional counterparts of the prerevolutionary intelligentsia lacked.

implied accommodative behavior of non-Russian elites, was a part of the political control. However, the Moscow center always had its doubts about the non-Russian elites, if not about their loyalty to the communist regime, then about their interest in supporting and preserving the Soviet Empire and the Russians' dominance in it. The center feared that these elites would behave in opposition to the well-known Stalinist motto: National in form and socialist in content. Instead they could become socialist in form and national, even nationalistic, in content. Such a danger, in fact, was always real.

Beginning in 1988, these non-Russian elites became increasingly demanding. Many of those who unequivocally sided with Moscow and pursued a policy of open confrontation with national movements in their republics were gradually removed (in October 1988, Sandaila in Lithuania and Pugo in Latvia; in April 1989, Patiashvili in Georgia; in July 1989, Kolbin in Kazakhstan; in September 1989, Shcherbitskii in Ukraine; in November 1989, Grossul in Moldavia). Those who lost control over the situation in their republics were also removed (Demirchan in Armenia and Bagirov in Azerbaidjan in May 1988). In some of the republics (Lithuania, Latvia, Estonia), reform-minded national communists came to power for the time being and began to play along with national movements and their slogans. In other republics (Ukraine, Belorussia, Azerbaidjan, Central Asia), the "national nomenklatura," who desired to avoid implementing any substantial political and economic reforms and at the same time wished to strengthen their power at the expense of Moscow, took the lead.

In addition, in 1988–1989, interethnic relations in the Soviet Union continued to become aggravated and sometimes took a tragic turn. New antipathies and conflicts were added to old ones, and, while the means of suppression were weakening, antipathies sometimes erupted in violence. After the outbreak of the Armenian-Azerbaidjanian conflict over Nagornyi Karabakh (1988), the pogrom in Sumgait followed (February 27–29, 1989), then came disturbances in Ashghabad and Nebit-Dag (May 1 and 9, 1989), pogroms in the Fergana valley (June 1989), interethnic clashes in Novyi Uzen' and Mangyshlak (June 17–20, 1989), Abkhaz-Georgian confrontations in Abkhazia (1989), Georgian-Ossetian confrontations in South Ossetia (1989).

The emergence of national mass movements in the non-Russian union republics also strained interethnic relations. The problems and uneasiness of their ethnic minorities were clearly underestimated by the majority of these movements and were sometimes ignored or even met with open hostility. Many people in the Baltics did not hide their wish that the ethnic Russians living there would return to Russia. The same opinion regarding the Russians and other ethnic minorities became more and more vocalized in Central Asia. In Moldavia, the extremists came up with the slogan: "Russians across the Dniester; Jews in the Dniester." In Azerbaidjan and Armenia, the national movements, to put it mildly, did not hinder the Armenians' flight from Azerbaidjan or the Azerbaidjanians' flight from Armenia. Georgian nationalists carried out their threat that "the Abkhaz separatists will be taught their lesson through force."

The republican political elites and central leadership in Moscow demonstrated a complete inability, and sometimes unwillingness, not only to neutralize the interethnic conflicts but also to prevent bloodshed. Conflicts provided a convenient opportunity to distract public attention from the demands to carry out political reforms and to turn political opponents into scapegoats. The Moscow center also used the interethnic conflicts as a clear warning to its opponents regarding what could come from the weakening of its power and, even worse, from the dissolution of the Soviet Union. There is cause to believe that, both in the republics and in Moscow, there were certain forces provoking bloody confrontations.

In general, from the second half of 1988, the Soviet Union began to fall apart before our very eyes. The number of peoples, groups, and strata interested in its preservation was continually diminishing. The former superpower seemed to embody many weaknesses of the "Sick Man of Europe," as the Ottoman Empire was called at the end of the nineteenth century, or the Austro-Hungarian Empire, the other multiethnic empire that was confronted with disintegration ever since the national uprisings of 1848.

Gorbachev himself contributed much to the aggravation of ethnic tension in the country. To him national movements in the non-Russian republics of the USSR were only a "stab in the back of perestroika." Often he also demonstrated an astonishing insensitivity to the feelings of non-Russians. Thus as late as November 1987, in his speech on the 70th anniversary of the Bolshevik revolution, he stated that all peoples of the Soviet Union were filled with respect and gratitude to the Great Russian people "for its selflessness, its genuine internationalism, and invaluable contribution to the creation, development, and consolidation of the socialist union of free and equal republics" (*Pravda*, November 7, 1987). On the other hand, Gorbachev's position in the Soviet power structure, his base of support and ultimate motivation behind his reforms, left him little room for drastic changes in the sphere of interethnic relations.

In this respect, all Gorbachev's actions may be characterized as too little too late. Only at the end of 1987 did he begin to comprehend that the previous methods of carrying out the nationality policy were ineffective, and that the policy itself needed some modification. However, even in 1988, Moscow still underestimated the seriousness of the nationality question.

Moscow's underestimation is indicated by the official explanations of the exacerbation of nationality problems (on this see also Krupnik 1991). For a long time everything was blamed on foreign and internal subversion by the CIA, extremists, "enemies of perestroika," a corrupted part of the party and government apparatus in the non-Russian republics, the mafia, and so on (*Pravda*, March 21, 22, 1988, August 27, September 2, 1989; *Literaturnaia gazeta*, March 22, 1988). Curiously, the matter never went beyond obscure allusions, and the mythical organizations of instigators and extremists remained elusive. The situation continued to worsen; then, in 1988, an additional explanation was proposed.

Strained interethnic relations in the USSR began to be explained by the worsening economic situation. The new official line was that one needed only to be patient, perestroika would very soon lead to an improvement in the economy, and the ethnic conflicts would either disappear or, in any case, weaken; everyone would have full stomachs and be happy and would understand the advantages of living together in the Soviet Union. Everything sounded very Marxist, but it was not convincing to many non-Russians in the empire. It seems Gorbachev still did not understand that many of the non-Russians hoped that perestroika above all else would solve their specific ethnic problems.

Moscow began to take some indecisive steps to buy time. Beginning in late 1987, the Russification campaign was curtailed, as well as the practice of introducing ethnic Russians into the party and administrative apparatus of the non-Russian republics. At the February plenum of the CPSU Central Committee in 1988, Gorbachev, however, called only for the demonstration of more respect for the dignity, culture, language, and history of each people and promised to hold soon an important Central Committee plenum on the nationality question (*Pravda*, February 19, 1988).

At the 19th Congress of the Communist Party and the subsequent CPSU Central Committee plenum, an additional explanation for the strained ethnic situation was proposed: "deviation from Leninist principles in the nationality policy," to which Gorbachev promised to return (*Pravda*, July 5, 1988). This was certainly not enough, and the vague promises made by Gorbachev met with skepticism in the non-Russian republics, particularly since the plenum on the nationality question was put off until early 1989 (*Pravda*, July 30, 31, 1988).

The economic situation, meanwhile, continued to deteriorate, and the leaders of the more prosperous republics began to demand openly more economic independence. Remarkably, in 1988 and to some extent in 1989, even the Balts did not yet demand complete political independence. They were ready to be content with economic autonomy and the signing of a new Union Treaty aimed at the transformation of the Soviet Union into a confederation of sovereign republics. However, the Moscow center rejected their suggestions out of hand. The November 1988 plenum of the CPSU Central Committee in very vague terms promised only the perfection of a Soviet federation (*Pravda*, November 12, 1988). The Balts were clearly tired of waiting, and they went from words to deeds. On November 16, 1988, the Estonian Parliament declared the republic's sovereignty. The presidium of the USSR Supreme Soviet immediately rushed to announce the declaration unconstitutional and null and void. A high-profile conflict, often called the war of the laws, began between the center and the republics.

It was obvious that economic liberalization in the Soviet Union was impossible without a genuine political liberalization.[6] However, a political liberalization implied the dissolution of the empire. Gorbachev tried to prevent this at any cost, because it would mean that the balance of power would shift from the Moscow center to the republics. This was one of the main reasons he was so reluctant in 1989 and 1990 to carry out urgently needed economic reforms. He was simply afraid that without economic power the center would lose much of its political power.

In early 1989, Gorbachev finally recognized the gravity of the nationality question in the country and announced that the success of perestroika would depend on how the problem of interethnic relations would be solved (*Pravda*, January 6, 1989). He also admitted that it was necessary to transform the Soviet Union into a federative state, but he still strove to postpone and dilute urgent reforms. Five months later he was still making only vague promises, and warned that no borders would be redrawn and that the republics would not receive even economic independence. On several occasions Gorbachev virtually repeated Winston Churchill's analogous claim that he was not going to participate in the funeral of the Soviet Union. *Pravda* (July 12, 1989) rushed to add that the demands to redraw the Union Treaty were legally groundless. The plenum on the nationality question was again postponed. Gorbachev was clearly losing time.

Moreover, the Moscow leadership, or certain groupings in it, had still

---

[6] One may wonder whether the Chinese model was open to the Soviet Union. However, the Soviet ruling elite strongly opposed a genuine economic transformation aimed at privatization of the state-owned industrial enterprises and the dissolution of state and collective farms. In this respect Gorbachev and most of his reform-minded supporters in the elite were not very different from the diehards. The discussion of economic issues in the Soviet press at that time reveals the widespread fear that a radical reform of the central-planned and state-owned economy would contribute to separatist tendencies. The claims of the Balts only excited this apprehension.

not given up hope of dealing with the national movements by force or the threat of its application. The Tbilisi slaughter on April 9, 1989, was not an isolated event. Before this, in November 1988, a curfew had been introduced in Yerevan, the Armenian capital; the leaders of the Armenian "Karabakh" committee were arrested in December 1988; and special control over Nagornyi Karabakh was introduced in January 1989. After the events in Tbilisi, the blockade of Armenia and Nagornyi Karabakh followed, begun by Azerbaidjan in August 1989 with the clear connivance of Moscow, then came the blockade of Lithuania in April-June 1990, ordered by the Soviet government. Significantly, in his speech to the 21st Congress of the Young Communist League, Gorbachev called Lithuania "the sea frontiers to which Russia has marched for centuries" (*Pravda*, April 11, 1990). In January 1990 the troops entered Baku, the capital of Azerbaidjan. An eyewitness of the events, a journalist from Moscow, wrote that "the Soviet Army entered the Soviet city as an occupying army" (Govorukhin 1990: 10). People connected with the main Azerbaidjanian national movement, the Popular Front, told me that, according to their calculations, no fewer than 400 people died in these events. The Soviet leadership did not hide the fact that this was needed to prevent Azerbaijan's secession from the USSR (*Pravda*, January 21, 1990; *Novaia zhizn'* 5 [March 1990]).

The role of provocateur played by the center was also clearly seen in its relationship to the so-called Interfronts and Intermovements (i.e., organizations of the Russian and Russian-speaking population), which were created in the Baltics and Moldavia at the end of 1988 and the beginning of 1989. Nobody but Vadim Bakatin (1992: 49), a minister of Internal Affairs during perestroika and the last chief of the USSR KGB for a few months after the August 1991 putsch, testified that the KGB had initiated the organization of Interfronts to send a message to the recalcitrant republics: if they would not submit to the center's will they would be confronted with Interfronts, which would call for strikes, raise questions of redrawing the republics' borders, and even challenge the legitimacy of their elected powers.

The immediate organizers of the Interfronts and Intermovements were people whose interests were directly connected with the continuation of the Moscow center's hegemony. Under the guise of defending the interests of the Russian-speaking population as well as the Soviet power (i.e., in their interpretation, the preservation of the united and indivisible Soviet Union), these organizations armed themselves with chauvinistic slogans and goals. Not by chance, members of the Interfront in Estonia were nicknamed Inter nazi. Suddenly manifesting a concern about other ethnic minorities, these organizations also began to incite the Poles in Lithuania and the Gagauz in Moldavia to confront the ethnic majorities in their republics.

The Interfronts' first real actions were against new language laws adopted in several republics. Their members viewed these laws as discriminatory regarding the Russian-speaking population, that is, regarding this population's right not to know and not to want to know the languages of the indigenous population. The matter reached ludicrous proportions. In Moldavia, the Russian-speaking population protested against returning Moldavian (again, actually Romanian) to the Latin alphabet, although this should not have mattered to them because, no matter what alphabet was used, they still could not read Moldavian.

Nevertheless, in July and August 1989 in Estonia, and in September 1989 in Moldavia, strikes over the language issue occurred at enterprises where Russians constituted the majority. There were notable similarities in their organization and conduct. In both republics, the strikes were carried out under the auspices of the administrations of enterprises of all-union subordination, with the moral support of the army (in some military regiments in Estonia, meetings were held and resolutions taken to support the strikes) and with the active (including financial) support of the central ministries and departments. The strikers were paid full wages and even given scarce goods for encouragement (*Moskovskie novosti* 35 [August 27, 1989]). The strikes were a clear warning to the national movements and the republican leaderships not to go too far. In this respect, they did not fulfill their task; however, they managed to aggravate further the relations between the titular nationality and the Russian minority in each republic.

Amid this tense situation, the long-awaited plenum on the nationality question was opened in Moscow on September 19, 1989. The proposals of the Baltic delegations to turn the Soviet Union into a confederation were refuted. The approved plenum platform said that a new Union Treaty was not necessary. The only concession was a promise to convert the republics to regional economic autonomy and self-financing (*Izvestiia*, September 24, 1989). The plenum marked the end of another stage in the developing crisis in interethnic relations in the Soviet Union. The positions of the sides became clearly defined: not only the Moscow center versus the national movements but even the Moscow center versus the non-Russian republics of the USSR. It was ironic that Gorbachev began to ally himself with the most conservative elements in the non-Russian republics, against whom he had declared a decisive struggle only a few years before.

Meanwhile various strata in the non-Russian republics became entirely disappointed with the policy of the Moscow center, which they considered an imperialistic policy. They came to the conclusion that the center had deceived their hopes and expectations. Thus, in 1990, a sad joke was popular in Armenia: "Gorbachev complains: These Armenians lack any sense of humor. I have joked about openness and restructuring, and they took it seriously."

In some republics (Lithuania, Latvia, Estonia, Armenia, and Georgia) noncommunist and even anti-communist national movements came to power and stated complete independence as their goal. In others (Ukraine and Moldavia, the latter now called Moldova) the battle between national opposition groups and the old political elites continued, forcing the latter to take more radical positions on issues about the future of the USSR. Finally, in the rest (Azerbaidjan, the republics of Central Asia and Kazakhstan, and Belorussia), power remained in the hands of the conservative elites. Although they were all for preserving the Soviet Union, even they demanded that significantly more rights be given to their republics.

Only in the early 1990s did several people in the central leadership gradually begin to understand that, as the Russian saying goes, "It is not enough to bear a whip; a spice cake is also necessary." Gorbachev, for the first time, admitted the necessity of concluding a new Union Treaty (*Pravda*, March 16, 1990). However, he still strove to postpone and dilute urgent reforms. Actions by the Soviet leadership did not testify to a desire for a radical transformation of the Soviet Union. On April 3, 1990, the USSR Supreme Soviet passed a law on the procedure of republics to secede from the USSR (*Pravda*, April 6, 1990), which was formulated in such a way as to make such secession virtually impossible. In the same month, for the first time in all the Soviet Union's history, Russian was officially declared the state language.

In the summer of 1990, when the Soviet leadership at last started to negotiate the new Union Treaty with the republics, it immediately became clear that the republics and the center viewed the future of the Soviet Union differently. The majority of the republics were leaning toward the idea of a confederation with limited central power. The basis of such a confederation had to consist of horizontal ties regulated by treaties between the republics. However, a draft of the new Union Treaty published on November 24, 1990, was immediately nicknamed the union sentence (*soiuznyi prigovor*). The center wanted to retain a significant amount of authority in the political and economic spheres. Besides, obstacles worked into the text practically prevented the treaty from being amended (*Izvestiia*, November 24, 1990). It became clear that Gorbachev chose the option of what he thought was the preservation of a united Soviet Union with a strong central power at any price. In his speeches in December 1990, he did not leave any doubt that preservation of the center's power was his primary goal. In that same month, he received even more power from the Soviet Parliament, and the central leadership either got rid of reform-minded people or forced them to leave.

At the same time Gorbachev faced growing difficulties in the metropole of the Soviet Union, that is, Russia. In December 1989, Gorbachev's popularity rating in the country was 52 percent; by October 1990 it had dropped to 21 percent (*Moskovskie novosti*, November 11, 1990). While people in the street were becoming tired of growing economic hardships and angry with unfulfilled promises, the liberal supporters of Gorbachev came to the conclusion that no further reforms could be expected from him. In 1990, they began to join the opposition in growing number. The rallying point was not so much democracy as anti-communism and, indeed, the desire to oust from power the ruling elite. Far from everybody in the opposition understood the difference well.

A New Challenge to Perestroika: Russia Strives for Sovereignty

The situation became crucial to Gorbachev when he began to lose control of the Russian Federation. His archrival, Yeltsin, succeeded in temporarily creating a broad coalition of opposition forces that included populists, those communists whose interests were connected more with Russia than with the Soviet Union, some apparatchiks of the second echelons of power, liberal reformers, and even radical democrats.[7] In spite of Gorbachev's attempts to prevent Yeltsin's election, or rather because of these attempts, in May 1990, Yeltsin was elected the chairman of the Russian Parliament, and then, in April 1991, the president of the Russian Federation.

In a futile attempt to prevent Yeltsin's election as the chairman of the Supreme Soviet of the Russian Federation, Gorbachev announced that the restoration of the sovereignty of Russia would shatter the Soviet Union. He called on Russian nationalism: "We have a thousand years behind us. The Russian people have given much to unite into one family many peoples on broad expanses, so that, with the assistance of the mighty state, they could enter the [world] arena" (*Izvestiia*, May 25, 1990). Stalin himself could have subscribed to such words. These attempts on the part of Gorbachev had little effect. The predominant mood in the Russian Parlia-

---

[7] Still, some Soviet liberal observers warned at that time that Yeltsin was popular not as a democrat but as a populist and that after the democrats had helped him come to power they would be thrown off like a fur coat in the summer (*Argumenty i fakty*, March 18, 1991).

ment was expressed by the vice-president of the Russian Soviet Federative Socialist Republic (RSFSR) Supreme Soviet, Ruslan Khazbulatov, who at that time was an ally of Yeltsin. He stated that the policy of the center dissolved Russia within all-Soviet structures, to Russia's disadvantage (*Argumenty i fakty* 28 [June 14–20, 1990]).

In 1990, the situation in Russia was very complex. It was hard for Russia to free itself from the legacy of the empire, just as it was difficult for many Russians to free themselves from a certain empire-oriented psychology. For centuries the empire was part of their cultural and historical heritage, their mentality. Contrary to the non-Russian republics of the Soviet Union, in Russia the popular idea of sovereignty originally had primarily an economic and political connotation rather than a national connotation. In some republics, at first mass national movements emerged, then they achieved a victory in elections and made a declaration of sovereignty. In other republics, public pressure forced their national communists and national nomenklaturas to declare sovereignty. This phenomenon had begun on November 16, 1988, with the Estonian Parliament's declaration of that republic's sovereignty, and it continued with growing speed in 1990. Like other republics, Russia made a declaration of sovereignty on June, 12, 1990, but the proclaimed sovereignty did not concern the nation so much as the political body and territory. At that time, the so-called national patriots, pursuing far-right, chauvinistic, and pro-empire positions, were the main representatives of the national movement in Russia.

Nevertheless, by 1990, a growing number of Russians were coming to the conclusion that identifying the interests of Russia with the interests of the whole Soviet Union brought nothing but harm to Russia itself, that the Soviet Empire was too expensive and they would do better without it. One may speculate whether Yeltsin was initially committed to the independence of Russia, or simply used it to destroy his opponent, Gorbachev. What really matters, however, was that Yeltsin and the forces supporting him demonstrated tolerance, if not encouragement, of the growing separatism of the non-Russian republics of the USSR. They were ready to go as far as transforming the Soviet Union into a confederation, or even a commonwealth. Yeltsin threatened on October 16, 1990, that Russia itself might leave the Soviet Union. This attitude constituted the greatest challenge and the greatest danger to Gorbachev's power. If a majority of Russians were to come to the conclusion that their interests did not lie in the preservation of the Soviet Union, then Moscow would not be capable of putting down national movements even by force.

In August 1990, representatives of the Russian Federation proposed that the negotiations over the creation of a future union be conducted exclusively between the republics without the participation of the center

(*Moskovskie novosti* 37 [September 16, 1990]: 6). The Armenian leader Ter-Petrosian announced that he did not see the necessity for either a Union Treaty or a union constitution (*Izvestiia*, August 9, 1990). The Ukrainian leadership gave a similar opinion (*Moscow News* 34 [September 2–9, 1990]). The Baltic republics refused even to take part in work on the new Union Treaty.

In the face of such developments, Gorbachev and all those interested in the preservation of the Soviet state ran the risk of losing power. If the empire were to disintegrate, Yeltsin would become the president of Russia, the country of 148 million people, and Gorbachev would become a king without subjects.

Although some scholars consider Gorbachev's shift to the right, by the end of 1990, a "mystery" (Suny 1991: 119), there is no mystery in his actions at all. By that time, the preservation of the Soviet Union had become the main concern of Gorbachev and his allies. To prevent its disintegration he was ready to curtail openness, restructuring, and political liberalization, and to limit and postpone the economic reforms. Yeltsin summarized the existing situation in the following way: "Dividing power with the center honestly and openly did not work out .... The center will not voluntarily concede the necessary amount of power to the republics" (*Argumenty i fakty* 42 [October 1990]).

The End of Perestroika: The Dissolution of the Empire

By the end of 1990, Gorbachev became increasingly active in trying to force the will of the center on the republics, including holding a referendum which in the USSR was called the referendum under the barrel of a submachine gun. His allies in this issue were apparent: the army leadership; the KGB; those in the partocracy and bureaucracy whose interests were connected with the preservation of the empire; the military-industrial complex; and many Russian nationalists. He also tried to attract the support of some ethnic minorities in the non-Russian republics who had their own grievances against the nationalities dominating there.

During the confrontation between the union republics and the Moscow center, the phenomenon that the Soviet press called the parade of sovereignties began. One after another, various autonomous formations declared their sovereignty, including the right to all the property on their land and the natural resources in their territories. Several of them also unilaterally raised the status of their autonomies (Sheehy 1990). Many of these declarations were partly connected with the aspirations of the indigenous nationalities. At the same time, the declarations were supported by the majority of the population in each autonomous formation, of which Russians usually made up the largest part. According to reports I received from Tatar circles, even Tatarstan's proclamation to be a union republic was issued rather smoothly, and its Russian population remained calm for the most part, especially after it was reassured that the Russian language would be declared the state language on an equal basis with the Tatar language.

In this respect, the situation regarding sovereignty in the autonomous formations was just the opposite of the situation existing in the majority of the union republics, where the ethnic minorities, particularly the Russians, often opposed or were afraid of the drive for independence. As has already been noted, a lower status of autonomy meant less independence in the social and cultural spheres, less control over resources and industrial enterprises located in their territories, few tax deductions and entries from the central budget, and at the same time dual control from the union and republican powers (and in the case of autonomous regions and districts, additional control from the territories' [*krais'*] authorities). Under these conditions, Russians were as likely as non-Russians to call for elevating the political status of their formation. Local political elites in the autonomous formations were also interested in raising their status, because this meant increasing their power and the number of privileged positions. In these conditions of growing regionalism in the Soviet Union during 1990, these political elites, for the first time in many decades, saw the chance to realize their aspirations.

Interestingly, the Moscow center not only instigated separatist movements in non-Russian union republics but also did not officially interfere in the parade of sovereignties occurring in the territory of the Russian Federation. It hoped that this parade would weaken the position of its main opponent, the Yeltsin leadership. According to Galina Starovoitova, who was one of the leaders of the democratic opposition in the Soviet Parliament, Ligachev gathered the leaders of several autonomous formations of the Russian Federation in the summer of 1990 and incited them to elevate the status of their autonomies (*Sovetskaia kultura*, December 29, 1990; confirmed by personal communication). Ligachev and his supporters never denied the accusation. Gorbachev began to hint that even Russia could not avoid ethnic conflicts were it to pursue Yeltsin's course (*Pravda*, September 26, 1990).

However, Yeltsin announced that in his nationality policy he was ready to go far to meet the demands of the autonomous formations. In September 1990, he told their leaders: "Take as much autonomy as you can secure." A few years afterwards he preferred to forget about those words when he recognized that the issue of the autonomous formations of the Russian Federation might become a delayed-action bomb. In any case, in the majority of the autonomous formations, the power remained in the hands of very conservative local elites, who preferred to ally with the all-union center.

The new conservative allies of Gorbachev were not interested either in political or in economic liberalization, and the planned reforms were not implemented. In October 1990, Gorbachev rejected the plan for radical economic reforms (the so-called 500 days, or Shatalin plan) just because this plan implied the transformation of the USSR into an economic commonwealth and significantly limited the power of the all-union leadership[8] (for a good analysis of the Soviet government's economic policy in 1990 and the beginning of 1991 see S. Andreev 1991). Instead, Gorbachev gave top priority to the new Union Treaty, which by the end of 1990 was already a nonstarter.

By the end of 1990, the imperial forces in the Soviet Union had consolidated their positions and assumed the offensive. Their goals and tactics were not a secret to anyone: blackmail and threats to force the republics to be subordinate to the center; and where necessary, direct interference, using interethnic conflicts or even armed forces, to overthrow the legitimate leadership of the republics, defeat the national movements, and strengthen the positions of the local conservative circles.

By playing on the interethnic conflicts in the non-Russian republics, Gorbachev attempted to prevent them from leaving the USSR. The central Moscow leadership was manipulating the discontent of the ethnic minorities in non-Russian republics (e.g., Abkhaz and Ossetians in Georgia) by openly or silently encouraging their separatist movements. In this regard, Gorbachev's policy was apparent in Moldova, where conflicts between the Moldavian majority and the Gagauz, as well as the Russian-speaking minorities, had intensified. While not openly encouraging the separatist feelings, and even speaking out in defense of territorial integrity, Gorbachev also emphasized that peace in Moldova could be preserved only if it were to remain a part of the USSR.

Significantly, in his address to the Lithuanian Parliament on the eve of the outrages by the military in Vilnius, the Lithuanian capital, Gorbachev stressed being on guard against the restoration of "bourgeois ways" in the republic. The events in the Baltic republics soon followed. At the same time, urgently needed economic reforms were postponed again in the name of socialism. The administrative-command system, which only a year before was the object of Gorbachev's severe criticism, was again be-

---

[8] The Shatalin plan admitted: "The desire of the people for economic and political sovereignty is expressed in the adoption of declarations of state sovereignty (independence) of the republics and of legislative acts strengthening their economic independence.

"Attempts to turn the clock are hopeless; the sovereign republics believe that their common goal is the fundamental restructuring of unitary political and socioeconomic structures" (quoted in Furtado and Chandler 1992: 44).

coming his support base. In the beginning of 1991, Gorbachev openly
called upon the communists to "come out of the trenches" (*Izvestiia*,
March 1, 1991). It appeared that perestroika survived only in name.

However, the resistance was much greater than Gorbachev had anticipated. Although, by 1991, he had concentrated in his hands almost dicta-
torial power, his decrees were often not obeyed, and even in the center
his power was challenged from both sides, Left and Right. In particular
the republics challenged his power. In an atmosphere of overall political
and economic crisis in the country, their striving for sovereignty and independence was gaining momentum. Thus, in October 1990, Gorbachev's
attempts to assert the primacy of an all-union legislation over a republican one immediately met with opposition from the Russian Federation
and Ukraine.

It soon became clear that to suppress the non-Russian republics
Gorbachev would have to resort to force on a much larger scale than in
Tbilisi in April 1989, in Baku in January 1990, and in the Baltics in January
1991. Even if he had wished to resort to such force (which I doubt he
did), he could not have done so, because the Yeltsin leadership and the
general public in Russia opposed his policy. In the winter and spring of
1991, mass anti-government demonstrations and Yeltsin's ever-growing
popularity demonstrated to Gorbachev that, contrary to his expectations
at the end of 1990, the nation had not moved to the right. In Moscow
alone, on January 20 several hundred thousand people protested against
the attempted crackdown in the Baltic republics (*Moscow News* 4 [Janu-
ary 27–February 3, 1991]: 4).

Besides, the economic situation continued to deteriorate, and this worried people in the street much more than the fate of the Soviet Union. In
spring 1991, many mines and industrial enterprises in different parts of
the country went on strike. The idea of a nationwide political strike calling for the resignation of Gorbachev, the Cabinet, and the Parliament was
becoming popular in many regions of the country. The March 17 referendum on the future of the Soviet Union was won by the Soviet president,
but this did not and could not put an end to the centrifugal process in the
country. Gorbachev cautiously started to reorient his policy. On April
23, in Novo-Ogarevo, he signed with the republican leaders an agreement
which intended to turn the Soviet Union into a federation, the Union of
Sovereign States.

However, the Novo-Ogarevo accord did not strengthen Gorbachev's
position. His support base was continuing to narrow. By July 1991, about
4.2 million communists had already left the party (*Pravda*, July 26, 1991).
Particularly large defections happened in those republics where the pro-
independence movements were especially strong. Thus, when the 28th

Congress of the Communist Party of Georgia resumed its work on December 7, 1990, after an almost five-month interval, it turned out that 61 of the 666 delegates had left the party over this time, and more than 200 others chose not to attend (*Izvestiia*, December 8, 1990; January 2, 1991). As early as 1990, in the Baltics the Communist Parties, with diminishing membership, were split along ethnic lines. The new union appeared to be stillborn from the very beginning. The republican leaders considered it only a temporary compromise and remained united against the center. On August 1, 1991, in Kiev, President Bush vainly tried to persuade Ukrainians not to secede, because "freedom is not the same as independence"; however, even his unexpected support of Gorbachev on the nationality question did not help. The political struggle in Moscow was also going on, with Gorbachev still representing the center and Yeltsin the Russian Federation. Ordinary people blamed Gorbachev for the growing economic hardships. The liberal forces remained in opposition to him and continued to support Yeltsin. Meanwhile the conservatives, who had given a hostile reception to the Novo-Ogarevo agreement, accused Gorbachev of another betrayal and the destruction of communism and the Soviet Union. By August 1991, the whole Soviet society had become tired of Gorbachev.

The August 1991 putsch already has its own mythology, including the myth of mass resistance and the popular revolution. To a significant extent its real story, including the role of Gorbachev in the events, remains unclear and is yet to be written. In this chapter I will not dwell on speculations. Instead, I will concentrate on the putsch's consequences.

Curiously enough, even after the August putsch, Gorbachev still hoped to preserve the USSR, albeit in a modified form. It is often repeated that Gorbachev returned from the Crimea to a different country. However, he did not understand it, in spite of all his assurances to the contrary. While millions of people in the non-Russian republics came to the conclusion that only independence would bring them freedom and prosperity, Gorbachev considered the dissolution of the Soviet Union a catastrophe. His formula for a new, post–Soviet Union—"great Eurasian democracy"—smacked of utopia. He lost not only power but also his sense of reality, and without ceremony the republican leaders showed him the door.

After Perestroika: The Nationalities Question Remains Unsolved

I would like to return to Amal'rik's prophecy.

> The unavoidable "deimperialization" will take place in an extremely painful way. Power will pass into the hands of extremist elements and groups

and the country will begin to disintegrate into anarchy, violence and intense national [ethnic] hatred.

... The boundaries of the new states that will then begin to emerge on the territory of the former Soviet Union will be extremely hard to determine.

... But it is also possible that the "middle class" will prove strong enough to keep control in its own hands. In that case, the granting of independence to the various Soviet nationalities will come about peacefully and some sort of federation will be created, similar to the British Commonwealth or the European Economic Community (Amal'rik 1971:65).

It appears that his prediction was again very close to the truth. The disintegration of the Soviet Union and the creation of the Commonwealth of Independent States (CIS) did not and could not solve the problem of relations between the constituent states or, even more so, interethnic relations in this political region. In 1992, the Commonwealth of Independent States already had three bloody conflicts: over Nagornyi Karabakh, South Ossetia, and Pridnestrovie (Transdniestria) in Moldova,[9] and many more territorial claims and counterclaims. Ethnic minorities in practically all the former Soviet republics complained about discrimination. Some of them revealed separatist tendencies. It was uncertain for how long and in what form the CIS would survive, if at all.

I have always claimed that the breakup of the Soviet Empire was a necessary precondition to political and economic emancipation of Soviet society in general and of Russian society in particular. I still hold that opinion. However, the disintegration alone is a far cry from the emergence of democracy and civil society on the ruins of the empire.

Precisely because the Soviet Union was a totalitarian empire, its transformation involves three parallel processes: decolonization, political emancipation, and economic liberalization. However, these processes and, in particular, their simultaneous operation do not equally interest most groups and strata in the former Soviet republics. This alone makes a transition of the country to a liberal democracy much more difficult and painful than a similar development in some more homogeneous East European countries.

What happened in the country in the aftermath of the August putsch was not a democratic anti-communist revolution, as had taken place in some Eastern European countries, but rather a redistribution of power. In the Soviet Union the ruling, Communist Party–based, all-union structures collapsed before alternative democratic forces backed by specific

---

[9] By 1994, new conflicts broke out in Georgia, Abkhazia, North Ossetia (a conflict with the Ingush), Tadjikistan (the ongoing civil war), and Chechnia.

strata of society became strong enough to compete for power. Ethnic and regional elites, either old ones, who changed only their ideological garments, or newly emerged ones, defeated the center-based or center-oriented political elites. These ethnic elites considered independence the best guarantee of their positions. However, they were only paying lip service to liberal democratic principles and did not consider them their top priority. To acquire or to strengthen their prestige many leaders appealed to ethnic nationalism and populism. By 1992 such leaders were opposed by unreconstructed communists on the one hand and by even more radical nationalists on the other.

Some republics, such as Moldova, Georgia, Azerbaidjan, and even the Baltics, have adopted "nationalism by blood" (i.e., *ius sanguinis*, ethnic nationalism) as their new ideology. Other republics, such as Ukraine, Belarus', and Kazakhstan, for various reasons have declared their allegiance to "nationalism by soil" (i.e., *ius soli*, territorial nationalism) and announced their desire to achieve nation-state consolidation. However, ethnic nationalism has also begun to play a growing role in their political life, and ethnic peace in some of them has, in fact, been fragile.

The reason for the growth of ethnic nationalism in the republics of the former Soviet Union is that ideas of ethnic nationalism turned out to be more attractive to ordinary people, political elites, and even to educated middle strata in many republics of the CIS than discredited communist ideas or ideas of pluralistic democracy. As a result, in many of these republics ethnocracies replaced the partocracy, and a recognition of collective rights of certain nationalities took the upper hand over individuals' rights and freedoms. The state identified its interests with the interests of a specific nationality. The concept is not very distant from those dominating in some totalitarian countries.

Under the situation, various tensions between different republics and autonomous formations, be they political, economic, or any other, easily translated into ethnic ones. Given the demise of central power, one might predict that ethnopolitics will be a long-term phenomenon in the post-Soviet nonunion.

After Perestroika: Russia in Quest of Identity

The situation in Russia immediately after the dissolution of the Soviet Union was rather different from that in the non-Russian republics, though when one considers the hopes following the failed August putsch, the difference becomes less marked. Amal'rik had hoped that a strong middle class would be the guarantor of peace in the future commonwealth. However, this class has yet to emerge, and the current political and economic situation in Russia in no way facilitates its emergence.

The emerging political superstructure in Russia in 1992 was still very different from a democratic order based on the division of legislative, executive, and judicial powers. In some postcommunist countries of Eastern Europe, such as Poland and Hungary, first, a multiparty political system became somewhat entrenched; then the economic reforms were initiated. In Russia, on the other hand, the elected 1990 Parliament, in which unconverted communists constituted a numerous and influential faction, did not reflect a new 1992 balance of political forces in the society. Rather, the Russian leadership relied on Yeltsin's charisma more than on anything else and was not subject to any party or public control. A number of publications in the Russian press revealed that many persons in the new leadership were as prone to corruption as their predecessors, and that by 1992 the Russian bureaucracy had become the most corrupt of any in the past 70 years (see, for example, *New Times* 47 [November 26–December 2, 1991]: 15; *Literaturnaia gazeta*, January 1, 1992: 3; *Moscow News* 1 [January 5–12, 1992]: 3; and *Moscow News* 13 [March 29–April 5, 1992]: 7). A common background and mentality often united them with those members of the former party and with state apparatchiks who had retained positions in the new power structures. The new common interests of these two groups often turned out to be stronger than their recent ideological and political differences.

Already in 1992 those who strove to eliminate the imperial heritage and transform Russia into a Western-type liberal democracy began to talk about the "nomenklatura revenge" and complained that the failed coup resulted simply in the replacement of some members of the Moscow political elite by members of provincial ones. Former members of the party and the administrative-managerial bureaucracy and those intellectuals who were always close to the political establishment (in the Brezhnev period they were scornfully called professors in the party waiting rooms; see *Nezavisimaia gazeta* January 24, 1992: 2) occupied many important positions in the new government and administration.

What really mattered, however, was not the background but the policy of the new ruling elite. In 1992, in-fighting amongst its members was still going on, with different groups holding different opinions on the future of the Russian Federation and its position in the CIS. This elite did not have a firm power base in the specific strata of post-Soviet society, except for those of its members who relied upon bureaucracy and apparatchiks. The collapse of the previous order shook up the society's social structure without creating a viable new one. Democratic institutions were still in an embryonic stage and immediately came under attack from various political forces, while civil society did not emerge. The number of advocates of authoritarian rule, allegedly as a necessary and inevitable stage in the transition from totalitarianism to democracy, did not decrease.

In the economic sphere, demonopolization, denationalization, and privatization of industry, agriculture, and wholesale trade did not immediately accompany the liberalization of prices. Almost a year after the failed putsch, more than 95 percent of the economy remained in the hands of the state, or rather in the hands of the political and managerial elite (*Moscow News* 18 [May 3–10, 1992]: 10). It appeared that these people were interested in a specific kind of privatization that would permit them to divide state property among themselves or to continue to control it (Bunich 1992: 10). This meant that the middle and working classes would be deprived of any gains from forthcoming privatization. Class divisions in Russia were becoming more salient.

In addition to the economic crisis, interethnic and interrepublican tensions and conflicts remained major destructive factors. A commonwealth of such different formations will always face the problem of contradictory interests, even when things are stable politically and economically. When Russia declared herself the legal successor to the Soviet Union, and in a more tacit way to the Russian Empire, other republics conceived this as her desire to dominate in the commonwealth. The territorial claims immediately raised by many Russian politicians and enthusiastically supported by the Russian Parliament only confirmed their suspicions. In 1992, this imperial tendency was clearly taking shape both in relations with non-Russian ethnic groups of the Russian Federation (for example, in relations with Chechnia and Tatarstan) and with other republics of the former Soviet Union (for example, in relations with Ukraine, Moldova, and Georgia).

As early as 1992, consolidation of different political forces on the chauvinistic great-nation platform was quite evident in Russia. In addition to the "red- and brown-shirts," the communists and neo-fascists, these forces included the Russian nationalists, not only right-wing ones, but even many of those who only less than a year ago identified themselves with the democratic camp; in the Russian political parlance they were called demopatriots (*Literaturnaia gazeta*, February 11, 1992: 5; *Nezavisimaia gazeta*, February 13, 1992: 3). Not without reason, these forces hoped that they would be able to create a strong base of support among a growing number of disoriented people suffering from the economic and social crises. These people may have been easy prey for nationalistic slogans. Virulent anti-Semitic propaganda was rampant, and the Russian leadership did not demonstrate any sincere desire to curtail or combat it seriously. Those in the Russian government who wished to free Russian policy of its imperial past and advocate a conciliatory approach to interrepublican and interethnic relations were under strong attacks from Russian nationalists and conservatives. There were many signs that they might soon lose their influence, or even their positions. This is what actually happened soon afterwards.

The army was also very visible (Ionin 1991: 4–6). According to one opinion poll, in February 1992, 71 percent of the officers' corps was for the restoration of the USSR (*Nezavisimaia gazeta*, February 5, 1992: 30). The anticipation of a possible new putsch or of Yeltsin's own resort to authoritarian rule with nationalistic colors characterized the mood in Russia.

Conclusion I: Pragmatic

We are looking at one of the most complex and difficult transitions imaginable. It will probably be measured in years, or perhaps even in decades. The three days in August 1991 were the prologue to yet another period of political, social, and economic instability. Interethnic conflicts continue, and new independent states, many of which remain multiethnic, have been born amid violence and bloodshed. In an article submitted for publication in July 1992 (Khazanov 1994a), I claimed that the ethnic tensions and conflicts would continue to influence the political development of the Commonwealth of Independent States and its constituent republics, and singled out some specific problems in interethnic relations. I venture to make the following extensive quotation from the article with but slight stylistic changes:

1. *Ethnic competition in the economic, political, and linguistic spheres.* Economic difficulties, which are impossible to overcome quickly, will only make the situation worse and intensify the struggle for control over natural resources, industrial enterprises, and key export commodities in the territory of individual states and autonomies (such as Tatarstan, Bashkortostan, or Yakutia [see chapter 6]) and between them. Thus, in Central Asia, land and water disputes, which directly involve members of different ethnic groups, aggravate interrepublican relations in the region.

The desire to achieve higher political status and to reserve preferential treatment, privileged positions, and high-level jobs for members of one's own nationality can also intensify ethnic tension. The struggle to expand the use of languages of dominant nationalities in administrative practice, education, and culture relates, not only to the growth of ethnic awareness and the desire to prevent acculturation, but also to a more mundane goal: to place members of one's own nationality in more advantageous positions vis-à-vis competing members of other nationalities.

As a result, many nationalities, such as Tuvinians, Bashkirs, or Buryat, may follow the example of Chechens and Tatars and try to achieve more independence and/or raise the status of their political formations vis-à-vis central Russian leadership, while those who lack autonomous formations will try to create something similar. The Kumyks, Lezgin, Balkars, Ingush, Karachay, Nogay, Shapsug, and others have already expressed such a desire. In many cases this can threaten the existing political formations and offend the interests of other ethnic groups. This phenomenon has already threatened the territorial integrity of Moldova and Georgia, as well as that of Kabardino-Balkaria, Karachaevo-Cherkessia (rendered as Circassia in English), Checheno-Ingushetia,[10] and even Daghestan and Tadjikistan. This desire could threaten other republics and autonomous formations in the future.

2. Territorial disputes and conflicts. The conflict over Karabakh is the best known conflict of a territorial nature. Today, not only the Armenians and Azerbaidjanians, but also the Russians, Ukrainians, Lithuanians, Latvians, Estonians, Moldovians, Gagauz, Bashkirs, Volga Tatars, Georgians, Ossetians, Avartsy, Chechens, Ingush, Balkars, Karachay, Kabardinians, Uzbeks, Tadjiks, Kazakhs, Kyrgyz, Buryat, and other ethnic groups are already involved in territorial conflicts and disputes.

3. The problem of persons living outside their constituent state or autonomy. Today, there are about 60 million such people in the CIS; about 25 million of them are Russians. Events of the last several years have demonstrated that their situation and relations with the dominant nationality in whatever republic or country in which they reside are often the source of conflict. Attempts to lessen this problem through bilateral treaties between individual republics of the CIS, which would guarantee the rights of ethnic minorities, so far have not brought positive results.

4. The problem of dispersed and exiled nationalities includes such nationalities as the Jews, Germans, Greeks, Crimean Tatars, Meskhetian Turks, Kurds, and several others. Their situation regarding interethnic conflicts could become much worse. The first three nationalities have the option to emigrate, but others have nowhere to go. At the same time, as the examples of the Meskhetian Turks and the Volga Germans show, their return to their homeland will almost certainly meet with opposition from nationalist forces in those regions of the CIS (see chapter 7).

5. The problem of refugees from ethnic conflicts. By September 1991, there were already about 710,000 refugees, or 1 million to 1.2 million if the number of those who were forced to abandon their homes because

---

[10] In fact in the summer of 1992, the creation of a separate Ingush republic with indefinite territory within the Russian Federation was proclaimed.

of unstable circumstances, pressure from other nationalities, or a lowered ethnic status are added to the number of refugees (Vitkovskaya 1992: 11). So far only a comparatively small number of Russians have left the Baltic republics, but their out-migration from Central Asia and the Caucasus has increased significantly. The influx into Russia of a large number of refugees and involuntary migrants could complicate the political situation, because these people tend to ally with antidemocratic and chauvinistic movements.

Probably, in the near future, ethnic nationalism will remain one of the major political forces in the former Soviet Union. If the development in the country happens along the lines of political and economic pluralism and civil society emerges at least in some of its successor states, then it will be possible to avoid some of the interethnic conflicts and tensions. This may alleviate some of them, at least approximating civilized forms, but I doubt that it will completely eliminate them.

Conclusion II: Theoretic

1. Although Mill's claim that serves as one of the epigraphs to this chapter is too pessimistic, he certainly has a point (Mill 1975: 382). Social scientists used to hold that democracy reduces ethnic conflicts (Horowitz 1985: xiii). However, to function efficiently in a multiethnic environment, democracy needs a state based not on an ethnic but on a national consensus, that is, a consensus that is supported by all citizens of the given state irrespective of their ethnic affiliation.

2. It is common wisdom nowadays that neither the formal multiparty system nor more-or-less free elections constitute democracy on their own. To operate efficiently democracy needs not only individual autonomy but also voluntary though powerful and autonomous interest and corporate groups capable of developing civil society and the system of checks and balances that defend and protect the society against the state. In addition, as Seligman (1992: 182) pointed out, effective democratic society needs, not interpersonal trust based on strong ties of reciprocity and mutuality, but a specific form of generalized trust rooted in modern individualist norms.

3. Modern democracy also needs decentralized economic systems. There may be a market without democracy but never democracy without a market (Lindblom 1977: 162ff.).

4. Last but not least, modern democracy needs a strong and numerous middle class consisting of people whose incomes and livelihoods are not dependent on the state's whim or benevolence. This does not imply that

the middle class is always and everywhere a strong champion of democracy. But without a middle class that is interested in the maintenance of liberal democratic order and has a stake in it, the very existence, at any rate the stability, of the order seems precarious.

Many Russian political jokes are based on a play of similar-sounding words. At the time of the Soviet Union's collapse, a new interpretation of the famous Internationale's verse was popular in the country. Instead of "The entire world of oppression we shall destroy / To its foundation, and then / We'll build our new world," slightly different words were substituted: "The entire world of oppression we have destroyed / To its foundation, but what for?" (In Russian *zatem* means "then" and *zachem* means "what for.")

The emergence and the collapse of the communist system may be considered the two greatest social and economic experiments of our century. Let us hope that the second experiment will be more successful and less bloody than the first one.

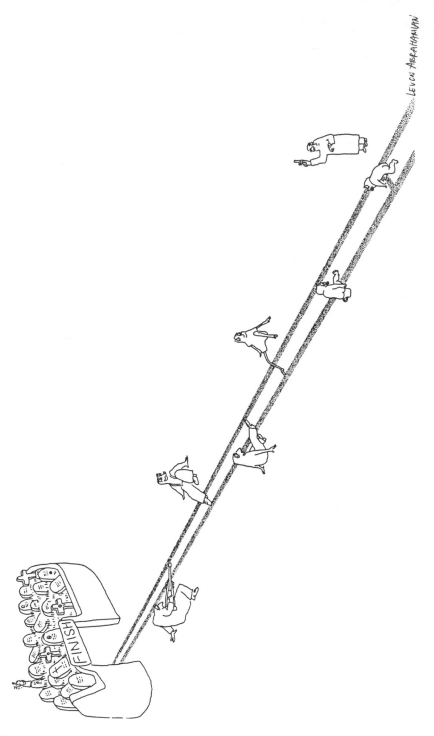

LEVON ABRAHAMIAN

The Russian signs *(left to right)*, "Damn CPSS," "Miss USSR," and "Lenin"

2

The Verse and Prose of Post-Totalitarianism (The ex–Soviet Union in 1992–1994)

> Liberty is generally established with
> difficulty in the midst of storms.
> —Alexis de Tocqueville

> Communism is the longest and the
> most difficult and painful way
> from capitalism to capitalism.
> —contemporary Russian joke

The End of History?

Recent developments in Russia and other ex–Soviet countries often contradict the prognostications of those for whom political predictions are almost a profession. Some of the failures in prognostication are connected with the essential unpredictability of the future, which always leaves open different windows of opportunity—a truth that scholars inspired by various kinds of teleologies, or by certain pragmatic considerations, are sometimes too reluctant to admit and, even more, to follow in their research. The politicians and public demand the price. Only those who claim to know what will happen by the end of the century, or beyond that in the twenty-first century, are considered experts. On the other hand, the danger of having been wrong is made insignificant. Nobody remembers or cares about the assertions of only a few years ago. Under the circumstances, the laurels of gurus, practical expertise, and interviews on TV and in the newspapers are more tempting to some attention-starved people than the honest but humble answer: "We can only analyze the current trends and discuss their possible relevance for future developments, but

54

this does not allow us to know for certain what will happen even in a year's time." Only on rare occasions may one hear the warning calls that "due deference to indeterminacy is mandatory" to careful and critical students of the Soviet Union (Young 1992: 88). Thus, I am like a hunter aiming at a very fast-moving animal. The history of the ex–Soviet Union is on the move. Whilst one is taking aim, the animal has already moved, and it is not always easy to predict where it is headed.

Another reason for many failed prognostications is connected with the confusions and even illusions surrounding the nature of change and the emerging post-totalitarian society in the ex–Soviet Union. It was often assumed that the collapse of the Soviet Empire and the communist regimes in its Eastern European vassal states would *inevitably* result in the political emancipation and economic liberalization of those societies— that sooner rather than later one would witness and cheer a Western-style order emerging on the ruins of totalitarian communism. Rejoice or beware, the end of history is coming.

However, the nation-state, civil society, liberal democracy, and welfare capitalism, the four main underpinnings of the modern Western order, have emerged and developed as a result of a prolonged historical process with its own ups and downs. To acquire them all simultaneously is a tremendous goal, the very feasibility of which for the communist countries has never had a chance to be tested in practice. So far the development in the ex–Soviet countries is so contradictory that even the movement toward liberal democracy there is far from certain, at any rate, it may still be reversed. A prosaic and sober analysis of current trends is, in this respect, more productive than the poetic but inflated expectations and incantations. The advantages of an observer who watches events living in a democratic milieu should not be neglected or, as it sometimes happens, substituted with wishful thinking. As Raymond Aron (1985: 348) has warned us: "Let us not forget: democracy is the only regime that admits—what am I saying?—that proclaims that the history of states is and must be written not in verse but in prose."

The Ex-Soviet Countries in the Aftermath of Communism

In fact, democratization is but one, and far from always the most conspicuous, of several parallel processes, interconnected but still different, which are accompanying the collapse of the Soviet Union and the breakup of the communist system.

The first of these processes is decolonization in the non-Russian countries of the Soviet Empire. As in other empires, decolonization itself in no way implies political democratization and/or drastic economic reforms; at the same time, it brings a surge in nationalism and a torrent of ethnic disputes, because a growing number of various nationalities refuse to co-exist under a single political roof.

The Soviet nationality policy eventually backfired. On the eve of the Soviet Union's collapse, nationalism became politicized ethnicity. Groups of people latched onto what were perceived to be their common ancestral experiences, often of a traumatic or, on the contrary, of a glorious nature, or both, as well as latching onto shared cultural traits, in order to unite against the political, social, and economic injustices. That was the price that Soviet colonialism had to share with Soviet totalitarianism. The absence of civil rights in the USSR and the suppression of all voluntary organizations and institutions independent of the state have made ethnicity with its ineradicable emotional appeal the focus and the rallying point of reemerging political activism.

After all, national self-determination may have little to do with civil rights and political participation (Tamir 1993: 71). The paramount goal, which by the late 1980s became so irresistibly attractive to millions of ordinary Balts, Caucasians, Ukrainians, or Moldavians, was not liberal democracy but their national liberation, sovereignty, and independence, as well as their economic prosperity, which they perceived to be directly connected with their independence (for more details see Khazanov 1991; see also Nahaylo and Swoboda 1990; G. Smith 1990; Carrère d'Encausse 1993).

Hardly anything else could be expected from people for whom liberal democracy and civil society were fairly abstract notions, while overt or covert interethnic strife and competition and the political dominance of other nationalities associated with the empire were everyday realities. The few attempts at establishing all-union democratic movements were still-born. In almost all the cases, various non-Russian national movements in the ex–Soviet Union, even those movements with a declared democratic orientation, such as the Ukrainian Rukh or the Lithuanian Sajudis, were, and still are, willing to give priority to nationalistic aspirations and goals. Ethnic solidarity became a foundation of new political identities.

No wonder national liberation in the non-Russian parts of the Soviet Union in most cases has actually turned out to be an ethnic liberation of some groups at the expense of others. The "*matrioshka* doll," the very hierarchy of nationalities occupying different positions in the ethnic pyramid, has not been destroyed in the newly emerged, independent post-Soviet countries; only the positions of different nationalities in this pyramid have been transposed. Even in Latvia and Estonia, which in several other respects have advanced on the path of the democratic political process more than other ex–Soviet countries, strict naturalization laws deny citizenship, and sometimes even permanent residency, to numerous Russians who moved to these countries after their annexation by the Soviet Union in 1940 (Kask 1994). This development was rather unexpected and disappointing to the Moscow liberals, who in the beginning of 1991, under the slogan "Hands off the Baltics," had demonstrated against Gorbachev's attempt to crush the independence-driven governments in the Baltic republics. However, liberal views of individual rights are almost always among the first victims of ethnic conflicts. Just as in other countries, "as ethnicity becomes increasingly salient, every political decision favors one community and hinders others" (Rabushka and Shepsle 1972: 85).

In all fairness, some conflicts and tension in interethnic relations in the ex–Soviet Union are inevitable and unavoidable consequences of the recent and not so recent past, as well as of the decolonization process. The emergence of new states entails the elevation in status of some languages and cultures and a lowering in status of others. Also impossible is the immediate elimination of the ethnic competition that during the last few years became even more salient in some multiethnic republics of the former Soviet Union because of the overall economic crisis and the over-population in the Caucasus, and particularly in Central Asia. Although the sine qua non of liberal states, in all their varieties, is a system of constitutional rules and practices in which individual liberty and equality are respected (Gray 1986: 75), even a liberal state is never completely neutral toward ethnicity. In the newly emerged post-Soviet states this situation is aggravated further by the redistribution of power among different nationalities and by the delay in economic reforms. As a result, positions in the government and administration remain very lucrative and highly competitive and allow those who hold political power to command the economy directly. All this leaves too much room for arbitrary and manipulative preferential policies. Ethnic affiliations outweigh an individual's merits and initiative, and they force ethnic minorities to feel their subordinate status and to defend themselves constantly in counterposition to the state's power. In practical terms, the affirmative actions in these states nowadays often tend to support not minorities but majorities.

The second process accompanying the dissolution of the Soviet Union is connected with the political transformation of its successor states. This development, which could be expected to belong to the emergence of a new, more viable, and democratic order in the CIS states, has been inadequate and, at best, very slow. The transition to post-totalitarianism has never been brokered in any of the states, and in rare cases when attempts have been made to negotiate a political change with powerful institutions of the communist regime, they have not brought satisfactory results. So far, the ideological underpinnings of the previous political order have changed much more than the order itself. In practically all these states nationalism has replaced communism as the dominating and often state-supported ideology, and all the major political forces have resorted to nationalism to legitimize their grip on power. Much less change has occurred in the composition of the ruling elites, who, with few and incomplete exceptions, still consist mainly of members of the former Communist Party and administration nomenklatura.

It is amazing, but by no means surprising, how smoothly the ideological transformation of the ruling elites has taken place: from an ostentatious devotion to communism and a declarative internationalism, which included the constant assertion of love and loyalty to the "elder brother," the Russians, to archnationalism often accompanied by overt or covert negative attitudes toward the same Russians as well as other minorities in their countries. The transformation of the former Ukrainian president Kravchuk from Saul into Paul may serve as an example. In October 1988, he was appointed the Ukrainian Communist Party's chief ideologue, a position which had always been connected with the persecution of any manifestation of Ukrainian nationalism and, in practical terms, of anybody who expressed a desire to preserve the Ukrainian language and culture. At the end of 1988 and in early 1989, Kravchuk played a very important role in the party's campaign against the major nationalistic opposition movement Rukh (Solchanyk 1991: 20). However, after his election as chairman of the Ukrainian Supreme Soviet on July 21, 1993, Kravchuk, practically without any intermediate period, established himself as an advocate of the interests of Ukraine vis-à-vis Moscow. He began to repeat almost literally those "subversive" speeches for which, only a few years before, many Ukrainian nationalists had languished in the Gulag.

Actually, for non-Russian communist political elites nationalism was more than a matter of political expedience and survival. By their very positions in the multiethnic Soviet Empire they were predisposed to nationalism, just as their Russian counterparts, as members of the dominant nationality in the empire, were predisposed to chauvinism.

From the very beginning of the Soviet regime, relations were strained between the central, Russian-dominated, elites in Moscow and the regional ethnic elites. The latter, though purged more frequently and more severely than any other ruling or privileged group in Soviet society, nevertheless repeatedly tended toward regionalism and nationalism. However, the general tendency in the changing balance of power was almost always the same: an increase in central power and a corresponding decrease of regional elites' power. It is true that in the Brezhnev period the regional elites received significant autonomy in personnel matters, particularly on the middle and lower levels; however, they were being deprived of any real political or economic autonomy, and were excluded from any real participation in serious decision making on the central level. The only task that non-Russian political elites were entrusted with was the implementation of policies dictated by Moscow. They were allowed to supervise only the daily affairs in their republics, and in addition they had to facilitate policies of cultural integration designed as mechanisms of strengthening the state's sociopolitical control, which in practical terms meant Russification. Moreover, this had to be done under the supervision of ethnic Russians introduced into their midst. Expanding the compulsory use of the Russian language in administration, education, and all channels of mass communications was considered in Brezhnev's period the minimal demonstration of loyalty (Khazanov 1988: 159ff.).

One of the classical sources of nationalism is the experience of inferiority and the response to blocked social mobility of ethnic elites (Gellner 1964; Greenfeld 1992). The non-Russian political elites realized quite well that the policy they were ordered to follow was inevitably eroding the foundation of their authority. If they were to identify their own interests completely with the interests of the ruling elite of the dominating nation and sincerely promote Russification, they would become dispensable at the same time that the avenues of upward mobility in the central foci of power open to them would remain extremely limited, even if they were to become completely assimilated. If they were to maintain the specific interests of their own nationalities, they would be suspect. Thus, their ambiguous positions in the Soviet hierarchy of power pushed them toward sovereign communism.

During my fieldwork in various parts of the Soviet Union in the 1960s and 1970s I met with some members of these elites. When demonstrating their adherence to the official line, in conversations with me, they extolled the elder brother of all the Soviet peoples—the great Russian people. When speaking more openly, they often complained, "We know the situation and the specific problems of our republic better than Moscow does. We are loyal communists. Why don't they trust us? Why don't the Moscow people understand that the policy of Russification is dangerous not only for our people but for the future of the entire Soviet Union?" In 1970, the first secretary of the Shusha regional committee of the Communist Party of Azerbaidjan said in a private conversation with me, "I am too experienced and too cynical to believe this, but sometimes it seems to me that CIA agents have forced their way into the Moscow leadership and are conducting a nationality policy in such a way as to set some Soviet peoples against others."

During the restructuring period these non-Russian elites soon discovered that the conditions of weakening central power allowed them to have it both ways under the nationalistic umbrella: they could retain privileged positions and gain more power by becoming bosses in their own home, independent Moscow. Their allegiance to communist political practices underwent very little change, but their devotion to communist ideology and to the Soviet Empire rapidly evaporated.

Besides, nationalism was a force capable of bridging the gap between the old elites and the counterelites who came to the fore during the struggle for independence (Beissinger 1992: 159–60). All the rest, to a large extent, depended, first, on the quickness of the communist-turned-nationalist conversion, on their perceptivity in borrowing the slogans of the nationalist opposition, and, second, on the readiness of the old political elites to incorporate into their midst some members of this opposition, giving them a stake in the political process. This counted more than their willingness, or rather unwillingness, to promote the democratization process. Even in those few CIS countries where the communists were ousted from the top-level leadership (significantly, in Tadjikistan, Georgia, and Azerbaidjan only for a short time), they have retained strong positions in administration, particularly on the middle and lower levels. Thus, in Azerbaidjan, during the presidency of Abulfez Elchibey, the leader of the Popular Front, of the 5,000 officials who had worked under the previous communist regime, only 120 persons were replaced with Elchibey's own people (Zinin and Malashenko 1994: 108). In Kyrgyzstan, all *akims* (heads of the local administration) without exception are former party officials (Filonyk 1994: 158). The sovereign communists' support for independence in such republics as Ukraine and Moldova allowed them to attract, or neutralize, many nationalists. In some respects, many of the educated middle strata have benefited from independence, if not economically then socially, and thus have been ready to tolerate the newly emerging regimes in the hope that they would be provided with new avenues of upward mobility. All this has been detrimental to the democratic transformation of society.

Still, it is already clear that the cementing role of nationalism for the consolidation of society has only a limited and sometimes short-term impact. As soon as independence is achieved, and exaggerated expectations of sausage nationalism do not materialize, it becomes more and more evident that different groups, and sometimes even regions, have their own vision of nationalism. Thus, in Georgia one may notice great differences in this respect between Mingrelia and Adjaria, on the one hand, and the rest of the country, on the other. Likewise, in Ukraine the differences between the western, the Transcarpathian, and the eastern and southern regions are becoming more and more conspicuous.

However, particularly dangerous are interethnic conflicts, sometimes deliberately fanned by the ruling elites. They legitimize violence as a way of reorganizing the former Soviet political space through the formation of new, postempire, ethnic hierarchies and the revision of existing political borders. This situation's additional danger to the fabric of society lies in its clear tendency to spread. It involves more and more individuals and groups who consider violence a natural state of affairs, the only way possible to defend their interests, or who become directly and indirectly interested in its maintenance to achieve their specific goals, to elevate their social standing, and so on. Moreover, in the regions affected by interethnic conflicts many new groups have emerged whose interests and positions in society, sometimes their very existence, are connected with these conflicts. In this chapter I will mention only a few of them.

The first to be singled out are refugees from the regions of ethnic conflict and tension. Many of them have lost all their possessions, houses, land, and jobs; almost all of them have become relegated to the lower levels of the social pyramid. For most of them this is not only an economic and social catastrophe but also a psychological catastrophe, aggravated by the fact that they have very little chance to improve their current standing and even less chance to return to their former homes, since their lands and houses are already occupied by other people who in most cases are their ethnic adversaries. Their only chance is revenge, a victory in the ethnic conflict. Thus, these refugees, being the victims of interethnic conflicts, have become the main protagonists in the continuation of these conflicts, a chronic source of further violence. It was the Azerbaidjanian refugees from Armenia who initiated pogroms in Baku in January 1990, and it was the Armenian refugees from Karabakh who became the backbone of the Armenian military force in the ongoing conflict with Azerbaidjan. Refugees from South Ossetia are the most active participants in the North Ossetian conflict with the Ingush, as well as in the Abkhazian war. The refugees are also playing a destabilizing role in the countries of their resettlement, easily manipulated by extremist movements and always ready to resort to violence. For example, in Georgia they became active participants in the recent civil war.

Some interethnic conflicts in the former Soviet Union have been going on for many years. In Karabakh and South Ossetia a whole generation entered its adult life with arms in hand, never experiencing peace. For members of this generation, war and violence are the only state of affairs they are used to. Only war defines their social standing, and violence provides them with glory and a livelihood; a stop to this violence would mean to them a dull and hard life for which they are completely unprepared. Besides, through these conflicts new leaders from the ranks of field commanders come to the fore and rise to prominence. In the past, some of them, such as the Georgian Dzhaba Ioseliani or the Tadjik Sangak Safarov, were ordinary criminals; most of them in normal circumstances had little chance to enter the rank of the political elites. Only violent conflict could provide them the opportunity to elevate their social status. Since their positions in the ruling elite are not secure, they are not willing to give up violence and often directly intervene by force in the political process in their countries. Remarkably, Armenia is relatively politically stable in comparison with her neighbors, Georgia and Azerbaidjan, despite her enormous economic hardships caused by the war with and the blockade by Azerbaidjan. This relative stability is somewhat connected with the fact that the first noncommunist government of the country immediately and effectively disbanded all voluntary military formations and thus politically neutralized them.

As in other parts of the world, state management of ethnic conflicts leads to an activist state with wide and discretionary power detrimental to an open political process and creates a favorable climate for the subordination of nascent civil society (Ghai 1993). As soon as the use of violence is legitimized in interethnic conflicts, the taboo against its use in the internal political process is also lifted. The paramount ethnic interests are considered to be above the law. In some Central Asian countries the old elites have imposed authoritarian rule and do not hesitate to resort to force to suppress their opponents in the worst preperestroika traditions (see chapter 4). In some other CIS countries the opposition has removed by force the legitimately elected governments. So far we have already witnessed two civil wars in the territory of the ex–Soviet Union (in Tadjikistan and Georgia), a military coup in Azerbaidjan, the authoritarian regimes of President Karimov in Uzbekistan and President Niiazov in Turkmenistan, and the military regime of General Dudaev in Chechnia. The leaderships of three Transcaucasian republics, Georgia, Armenia, and Azerbaidjan, are also rapidly acquiring many characteristics of the authoritarian regimes. In all of them the opposition press is banned or suppressed; in Armenia and Azerbaidjan the activity of several opposition parties is suspended. The irony is that in the recent past the leaders of Georgia and Armenia, Shevardnadze and Ter-Petrosian, billed themselves as democrats; nowadays they often act more like dictators. The leader of Azerbaidjan, Aliev, is an exception in this respect only because he never pretended to be a democrat.

The political development in the ex–Soviet Union proves again that the formal introduction of some democratic procedures is not enough for the liberalization of society. Stanislav Shushkevich, the former liberal chairman of the Supreme Soviet of Belarus', bitterly admitted recently that he served as a screen for the communist nomenklatura, who tolerated him for the time being only to give the impression that democracy had already come to their country (*Izvestiia*, April 8, 1994). What is really needed, after more than 70 years of totalitarian rule, is an institutional break; otherwise, democracy promulgated from above will remain largely a fiction. The sine qua non of democracy in the political sphere is a dismantling of all totalitarian institutions of the former regime. In the ex-Soviet Union they are directly connected with the continuing dominance of the old nomenklatura in governance and administration. The current political elites consist, for the most part, of the old communist ones, nowadays donning dinner jackets for the occasion and proclaiming the demise of communism. Yet they retain all the ingrained habits and mentality specific to their rank, including the lust for power not restrained by the brakes of civil society. The fact that the former party secretaries now hold governmental positions or head local administrations has not turned them into champions of democracy, since they still have almost unaccountable control of the state machinery. Likewise, all echelons of the bureaucracy, judiciary, and the repressive agencies inherited from the communist regime remain virtually the same. This is not a matter of closing the books, or of personnel continuity, or civil service employment. It is a deeper issue of power holding and officeholders' control over society. This is the tremendous and yet unresolved task of turning a Soviet-type apparatchik—almighty, arbitrary, and corrupt—into a Western-type professionally competent and impartial (at least in theory) civil servant.

Thus, one witnesses the dangerous tendency of conflating state, government, and nationality. In many CIS countries the Communist party-state is transforming not into real nation-states but rather into states with nationalistic ideologies, however, with almost the same ruling elites and little political competition—regimes in which a nationality substituted for the nation and the governance and administration apparatus dominate all spheres of public life. The road to authoritarianism is already paved, leaving too little room for the development of civil society.

It is worth noting that the Baltic republics, whose old communist structures of power were dismantled to a greater extent than those of other ex-Soviet countries, have been correspondingly more successful in their political transformation. They would be even more successful if they were to escape the excessive nationalistic fervor. Algirdas Brazauskas and his left-wing Democratic Party of Labor (the former Communist Party of Lithuania) coming to power signified the normal democratic political process, not the return of the Burokevicius-type die-hard communists. The

Lithuanian case and similar cases prove that sitting for a while on a reserve bench facilitates the transformation of some former communists into
politicians of socialist and social-democratic orientations. Luckily, the forecast with which the Lithuanian newspaper *Respublica* tried to scare voters on the eve of the elections, predicting a "Georgian scenario" for the
country (*Moscow News* 47 [1992]: 6), as might be expected, turned out
to be inaccurate. Sometimes, the politics and support base mean more
than the personalities' background, although they are often closely intertwined. It seems that at present the mainstream leftist movement in
Lithuania, just as in Poland and Hungary, is not a continuation of totalitarian communism, and this is what really matters in the democratization
process.

The third process following the breakup of the communist system could
be expected to consist of economic restructuring along the lines of a
market-oriented economy and the privatization of state-owned property.
In this respect, the development has also been unsatisfactory. In most
ex–Soviet countries profound reforms aimed at economic liberalization
have time and again been postponed or watered down, mainly because
of the ruling elites' stubborn resistance. Some Western scholars have suggested that it might be in the interest of society to allow these elites to
appropriate a significant part of the state-owned property, however un-
fair it may be, and thus, by providing them a stake in the emerging liberal
economic order, secure their peaceful participation in the democratization process (Hall 1994). In other words, it has been suggested that instead of fighting the nomenklatura it would be more expedient to buy
their interest in the reformist transformation of the society. Such wishful
thinking is divorced from the harsh post-Soviet realities, because it does
not take into account the very nature of the nomenklatura and the specificity of its functioning in what was coined, in the Soviet-Russian political
vocabulary, the command-administrative system. So far, the very limited
economic reforms are tailored to fit the nomenklatura's desire to retain
power and simultaneously to acquire wealth with few, if any, concessions
to fundamental democratic change. Gellner (1994: 124) thinks that there
are other good reasons for being soft on the nomenklatura: it is better
that they should try to save themselves by taking the funds stolen under
communism and investing them in capitalism than by turning to chauvinism. But what if they are simultaneously doing both, as in Russia today?
(In fact, with regard to chauvinism many of these people do not have to
undergo any real metamorphosis. In the recent past, they were communist chauvinists; nowadays they are becoming capitalist chauvinists. No
big difference.)

Although in Francoist Spain the major economic and social transformations substantially antedated the political ones (Pi-Sunyer 1993: 310), the opposite took place in the Soviet Union. As a result, not only political but also managerial elites, who in fact are closely associated and backed by a huge entrenched bureaucracy, remain the main obstacle for genuine economic reforms in many CIS countries. The commercialization of state management is not accompanied by genuine privatization in the main industrial, agricultural, and financial spheres; a small and dependent private sector has been allowed to emerge predominantly in trade and services. Property relations remain basically unchanged, and the key resources, enterprises, and land are still directly owned or controlled by the state apparatus.

The main reason for these circumstances consists, not in dreading the social costs of the shock or any other economic therapeutics, but in the unwillingness and inability of the ruling elites and bureaucracy to initiate those economic reforms which may be detrimental to their interests. Having been brought up in the spirit of anti-entrepreneurship and accustomed only to administrative control and distribution of economic resources and products, they are incompetent and lack the necessary managerial, marketing, and other skills and knowledge to embrace the free market successfully. Their bureaucratic experience and mentality have been shaped by the rigid communist system and are worse than useless in the new conditions; they are dysfunctional. Not without reason, the managerial elites of the industrial and agrarian sectors of the national economies fear that free-market competition would doom many enterprises and state and collective farms to bankruptcy. On the other hand, the existing monopolist positions and continuing state financial support allow these elites to survive despite their evident economic mismanagement and incapacities. In Ukraine, the state managerial elite, which consists of the members of the former economic nomenklatura, is the strongest political force; however, instead of facilitating economic reforms, it is actually hindering them.

Free prices in such conditions are a far cry from genuine economic liberalization. Retaining direct administrative control over the economy ensures that the ruling and managerial elites will retain their political power and prosperity. In the current situation, positions in the government and administration also open almost unlimited avenues of enrichment through corruption and embezzlement, which are more attractive to these elites than the risky ownership connected with private entrepreneurship not insured against the vicissitudes of open-market competition. The economic failure of countries such as Ukraine and Belarus' is the inevitable consequence of their sociopolitical situation.

What Kind of Capitalism Is Emerging in Russia?

A major player, a key player, in the ex–Soviet geopolitical arena is, of course, Russia. The Russian leadership claims (or claimed) to be anti-communist and anti-Soviet. During the last few years its existing regime was actually involved in a power struggle with its anti-democratic opponents and repeatedly declared its allegiance to a reformist course which should transform the country's administrative socialism into liberal capitalism. Movement toward the market economy has advanced further in Russia than in other CIS countries. However, by the standard of some East-Central European countries, it is too slow and uneven. It seems that the capitalism which is emerging in the country after communism has the worst characteristics of both systems. It is the state-apparatchiks-mafia oligarchic capitalism with a deteriorating welfare system in which the initial capital accumulation goes through various illegal routes and sheer criminal activities. (As the Russians are saying, the mafiocracy is replacing the partocracy in their country.) The separation of the economic, political, and public spheres meets many difficulties and strong resistance from the bureaucratic apparatus, and this apparatus has become significantly penetrated by organized crime.

Under the old regime, there was a struggle only for power. Wealth was mainly an appendage of power and had little independent existence. Nowadays their fusion assumes a new form, and there is some degree of separation of the two. Still, in Russia today, the struggle for power and wealth is, in general, one and the same thing. Not only elite officials but all levels of the bureaucracy are eager to convert their arbitrary power and connections into economic wealth. No wonder that, in spite of the proclaimed economic reforms, which supposedly should decrease the bureaucracy's influence and size, it actually continues to grow. The worst thing is that the majority of the post-Soviet bourgeoisie makes money not in the production sphere but in semilegal or illegal machinations possible only in the current political and economic climate. Many of them have nonliberal views on the economy and on politics as well. They are too dependent on and too interconnected with the still basically Soviet bureaucracy to be interested in real economic liberalization. The situation in which the state remains the principal agency of economic activities suits their interests well.

The anti-liberal economic tendency in Russia became conspicuous, not at the end of 1993, but as early as after June 1992, though at that time it was still cloaked in reformist phraseology. The new government of Chernomyrdin consists of many old-style apparatchiks. It is prone to yield to pressures from the managers of the military-industrial complex and large enterprises and the corps of agrarian directors. These managers and directors are interested in strengthening the bureaucratic control over the economy and, thus, often violate the principles of rational financial policy. Their commitment to the market economy, and particularly their ability to implement it, is doubtful.

By the summer of 1992, I claimed that the middle and working classes risked being deprived of any gains from the forthcoming privatization. At present, this is already a *fait accompli*. Privatization started not before but after the government had liberalized the prices. Together with inflation this measure almost immediately robbed the people of all their savings and, thus, prevented any possibility of their participation in the state property redistribution. The only share of state property that the ordinary Russian citizen is given is a voucher for 10,000 rubles, equal to $35 at the time of the voucher's issue. It is clear that Chubais-style voucherization is not capable of having a large-scale effect on the privatization of the economy, and is even less capable of producing a middle class of property holders. What was declared an act of social justice looks more like robbery. Managers are given various possibilities to formalize their control over enterprises. Thus, the director of Russia's largest automobile plant, employing 109,000 workers, spent 46.5 billion rubles ($28.6 million) in state-issued credits for his enterprise of buying the company's privatization vouchers for himself (*New York Times*, March 17, 1994: 5). The director of the Novosibirsk group of tin mines transformed them into a quasi–joint-stock enterprise in which he obtained the majority of stocks. He did this through various illegal machinations, including understating this enterprise's value of 1.248 billion rubles in 1992 prices (*Segodnia*, April 14, 1994: 3). Many similar cases have been revealed in the Russian press. It has also become common practice for managers of state-owned enterprises to derive incomes not from production but from subsidiary commercial activities, thereby illegally amassing enormous fortunes (*Monitor* 5, no. 18 [September 2, 1994]: 11).

In any case, in Russia today the privatization of most enterprises is either prevented or not yet started. Unprivatized enterprises make up more than 70 percent of all existing enterprises. This percentage is even higher if one takes into account that many enterprises were privatized only formally and in the worst possible way. The vast majority of joint-stock companies remain under complete control of the state apparatus (*Kommersant* 2 [January 25, 1994]: 10). In addition, handing over state enterprises to holding companies has provided their managers the right to give themselves extremely high salaries, often 100 times higher than their employers' average, with numerous additional perks, but without the obligation to make their enterprises profitable (*Izvestiia*, February 5, 1994: 1).

In agriculture the movement of private peasant farmers has not yet risen to its feet, to a large extent because of the fierce resistance of the numerous agromanagers, who strive to retain state and collective farms by administrative and economic means. So far, no more than 5 percent of those involved in agricultural production consist of individual farmers. The October 1993 presidential decree on the regulation of land relations and the development of agrarian reform in Russia has virtually programed abuses into land privatization by providing the directors of state and collective farms and the local administration the rights of land distribution.

This whole process of privatization brings into question more than the issue of social justice. Justice is almost always a train that comes to the station late, if it comes at all. After all, what kind of social justice can be expected in a country in which more than 70 years of hypocritical communist rule and its tumultuous aftermath have discredited the previously declared values and created fertile ground for cynicism and the pursuit of self-interests unrestricted by social and ethical norms? Above all, this process of privatization brings into question the issue of economic expediency. At present, the emerging class of nouveaux riches is involved mainly in speculations; its willingness and ability to stimulate genuine economic development raises many doubts.

Could It Be Otherwise?

The objective economic, cultural, and other barriers on Russia's transition to liberal democracy are enormous, and by no means should they be underestimated. The Soviet experiment is often explained, and sometimes even justified, in terms of enforced but successful industrialization and modernization of a country with a backward agrarian economy (Hobsbawm 1962: 217). As Orwell once remarked, there are mistakes that only intellectuals can make. There are still some scholars who claim that the Soviet model "up to a point worked better than anything since the breakup of the monarchies in 1918"; moreover, they claim that, not only in the Soviet Union but even in East-Central Europe, "for most of the common citizens in the region . . . it was probably the best period in their history" (Hobsbawm 1993: 62). This is a very dubious assumption, extraordinary in the current Western degree of knowledge of the repressive character of the communist regimes and incredibly insensitive to human suffering and sacrifice. It is insensitive and dubious not only because the goal does not justify the means, but also because the communist goal to become economically stronger and more efficient than the capitalist world has actually never been achieved.

The fact that at present some of the ex-Soviet countries have a fairly good chance of being relegated to Third World status indicates that the modernization policy which was pursued by the Soviet rulers with such cruelty and total disregard of human and economic cost did not achieve the creation of real and diversified industrialism. Rather, in many respects this policy was a deviation from the modernization path (Malia 1994: 509–10). The second largest economic power in the world turned out to be a fiction. Among other things this was evident in the Soviets' difficulties in conducting the second industrial revolution and their inability to pass to the third one.

Russia did not inherit from the Soviet Union a fully developed industrial society but rather an erroneously developed, or misdeveloped, economy. Some of its main characteristics are: an almost absolute priority given to the military-industrial complex, which demanded economic and material resources and scientific-technical personnel beyond all reasonable proportions; an emphasis on the extensive development of heavy industries at the expense of all other sectors of the national economy; out-of-date technologies and equipment; an agricultural sector that cannot produce enough to feed the country's population; exports similar to Third World countries' exports, consisting mainly of raw materials; an obsolete infrastructure and services; an antiquated communication system; a complete disregard for environmental problems; a negligence of the efficiency criterion, production cost, and other market mechanisms; and excessive planning and an overcentralized bureaucratic management, which during the last decades of the Soviet Union were, in addition, negatively affected by informal haggling between partly autonomous political and economic bosses. Many Russian industrial enterprises, even some branches of the economy, are so obsolete that, from the point of view of pure economic expediency without regard to the social consequences, it would be cheaper to close them down than to protect them or to try to modernize them, for which the country in any case lacks the necessary financial resources.

On the social plane a departure from totalitarianism is particularly difficult in Russia because, in fact, it involves not the re-creation but the creation, for the first time in her history, of civil society. Tocqueville often insisted that democracy signifies a state of society more than a form of government. It is very dangerous to have any illusions on this crucial issue. An important characteristic of the Russian political culture is ideological maximalism. The Russian political tradition is based, not on negotiation and compromise, but on violence—a tradition with a long history in the country. Prerevolutionary Russia, which some Russian nationalist-minded intellectuals tend now to idealize, was always an autocratic state in which the government held both legislative and executive powers and claimed the divine right to use violence against any dissident group and individual. In their turn, those who opposed the government also resorted to violence. The division of power and a notion of law, which together regulate the relations between the state and society, were almost completely alien to prerevolutionary Russian political thought.

A number of famous Russian intelligentsia of the nineteenth and early twentieth centuries, despite their high moral standards and opposition to the government, made violence the object of almost religious worship. They considered it the only way to change the existing order. Revolutionaries and terrorists were romanticized, admired as heroes; those who advocated nonrevolutionary change through a process of gradual reforms were despised as conformists and government collaborators. An incredible situation existed in Russia: some members of the upper bourgeoisie provided the financial assistance to the extreme revolutionary parties, whose very goal was the bourgeoisie's extermination. By the end of the nineteenth century, even moderate people such as Chekhov ridiculed those who hoped to achieve liberalization by developing local autonomous institutions. The famous Russian poet Valery Briusov reflected the mood of many among the intelligentsia when he wrote: "I welcome with an exultant hymn / those who will blot me out." In all fairness, the ancien régime did not inspire much optimism for a reformist course. Still, in the period of 1861–1917, the embryos of civil society were gradually emerging in the country, but they were too weak, "gelatinous," in Gramsci's terms, to change the situation, and neither the government nor the revolutionary part of the opposition was interested in their growth. The latter's contempt for civil society as the embodiment of much despised "bourgeois freedom" went back to nobody other than Karl Marx. To him the independent press, voluntary associations, right to vote, and so on, did not have an independent value; they were considered instrumental only so far as they facilitated the deliverance of power into the hands of revolutionaries (Keane 1988: 58ff.). Nevertheless, bolshevism was much more an ideology of revolutionary violence than a Western European intellectual Marxism.

Thus, when the communists seized power in Russia they argued not that violence was necessary, but rather that only they had the exclusive right to resort to violence wherever they considered it expedient, not only against their opponents but also against any group or individual whose very existence they considered detrimental to their goals.

The alleged dictatorship of the proletariat and the so-called class struggle were the only justification of such a policy. Lenin stated that revolutionary expediency was above formal law and human rights. The consequences are well known to those who wish to know them: the extermination of the aristocracy and bourgeoisie, of the active and prosperous part of the peasantry, of all "socially alien elements"; repressions of the workers; the Great Purge; mass deportations of some nationalities and discrimination of others; state-supported and -propagated anti-Semitism; and the persecution of all those who did not demonstrate their happiness with the communist regime or with any new twist in the Communist Party's policy. During the 70 years of communist rule no fewer than 30 million people, possibly even more, perished in the Soviet Union. In addition millions were imprisoned, exiled, or persecuted in other ways. This is an absolute historical record. The weak liberal tradition was not just interrupted; for all practical purposes it ceased to exist. In terms of civic continuity, in Russia today, professionals molded in the Soviet fold are even less the direct descendants of the prerevolutionary intelligentsia than the nouveaux riches are the direct descendants of the prerevolutionary bourgeoisie.

The Russian historical development suffers from excessive political and social revolutionism and insufficient reformism, from an abundance of collective identities and a lack of experience in individual political participation, from hypertrophic ethnic, religious, and social corporatism and undeveloped liberal universalism, and from a deep-rooted notion that an individual should always subjugate his interests to the public ones. These factors together prevent the development of autonomous and pluralistic structures. The prevailing identities were collective but in no way public. Communist society was collectivistic but at the same time extremely atomized. The plethora of shared public identities was absent, just like the tradition of participatory citizenship. Likewise, most Russians have grown accustomed to being guided and fed, though very poorly, by the state; many of them value the illusion of economic security above the risk of social change. Now they are left alone and in the cold, in full appreciation of the fairness of the popular Russian saying: Rescuing drowning people is their own business. A few years ago the following joke was popular in Russia: "There are two scenarios of the future development in the country—one credible, the other incredible. The credible scenario is that Americans will help us; the incredible, that we will help ourselves." At present, the joke is still popular; but aliens from other planets have been substituted for Americans.

Seligman (1995) noticed that the political discourse in contemporary East-Central Europe and the ex–Soviet Union reflects two visions of citizenship contained in two old traditions of Western political thought: the liberal (procedural) one, which views society as an assortment of autonomous individuals and voluntary associations (civil society); and the republican one, which conceives society in demos-ethnos terms, as engaged in the pursuit of a common good with subordinated individual interests. As interesting as this observation is from the point of view of political theory, it needs one clarification. This observation reflects the attitude of an outside scholar who is brought up in the Western intellectual tradition, which is alien to the Eastern European one and to those who are in practice involved there in the process of defining and redefining the relations between the state, society, and the individual. Their perception of these relations is based, not on the acquaintance with Hutcheson, Ferguson, and Smith, or with Aristotle, Machiavelli, and Rousseau, but on their own intellectual and historical experience. Thus, the century-old Russian dispute between the Westernizers and Slavophiles, which was resumed again during Brezhnev's "stagnation" period, reflects different priorities, values, and attitudes, and is based on a rather undifferentiated concept of the "other", that is, Western societies. The Slavophiles' claim that the state by its very nature is alien to the people led to their demand that the people should not interfere with state power. In practical terms this meant that the people had to reconcile themselves to authoritarianism.

Equally important in this respect is the difference between political theory and praxis. An ordinary *Homo soveticus,* whom the Russians themselves nowadays scornfully call a *sovok* (a dustpan), and his prerevolutionary predecessor were never citizens but always subjects of the totalitarian state, and, before it, the authoritarian state. They were not individuals participating in the public realm but members of certain ethnic and religious groups and of certain social classes and strata. They belonged to societies which lacked covenanted communities and instead gave saliency to ascriptive collectivities with organic ideologies and negligible universal legal protection.

In addition to economic, social, and cultural difficulties, there are many others connected with the specific historical and political circumstances of Russia's departure from totalitarianism. One problem that concerned many dissident intellectuals in the communist countries, particularly after the suppression of the Prague Spring, was whether totalitarian regimes were in principle capable of internally evolving into liberal democracies. In the West, this problem received attention from two great social thinkers, Raymond Aron and Ernest Gellner, though apparently their discussion was not directly influenced by the clandestine debate in the communist world. As far as I know, this discussion attracted less attention in the West, at any rate in the United States, than it deserved.

Aron (1968: 222ff.) was very skeptical about the Soviet Union's ability to transform into a Western-type liberal democracy, because, in his mind, communist totalitarianism represented "one of history's most lasting and most stable political forms so long as the ruling clan kept its coherence and the masses were aware of their impotence" (Aron 1977: 472). Gellner was much more optimistic. He pinned his hopes on a need for security and a regard for efficiency and integrity of the educated middle class, including technocrats and administrators. "Overt dissidents are its minuscule, heroic, probably indispensable, yet expendable advance guards, but the real battle may be won by the incomparably larger, cautious, compromising but pervasive and persistent main body, which advances like an insidious sand dune, rather than by dramatic self-immolation" (Gellner 1979: 339).

It may seem now that Gellner has won this debate, but, in fact, neither he nor Aron was completely right or wrong. Aron conceived the Soviet ruling elite as more monolithic than it actually was, or rather became, with the conditioning external and internal pressures. Gellner overestimated the rift between ideocracy, on the one hand, and technocracy and administration, on the other, in the Soviet Union. The Soviet technocrats and administrators who, by the way, more often than not belonged to the ruling and privileged strata rather than to the middle class, were molded in the fashion of a cumbersome, inefficient command and distributive system. Their consequent behavior in the period of restructuring and afterwards proved what may have been suspected earlier. A significant part of these strata, especially from their upper echelons, which were tied to the existing power structure, understood quite well that in open competition many of them would lose their perks and even positions. They might have nothing against getting rid of the official communist ideology, which set their teeth on edge, but this did not mean that they were eager to jump into a dangerous sea of economic and political liberalism. In addition, neither Aron nor Gellner apparently took into account the crucial role that external factors play in the collapse of all totalitarian regimes. Aristotle noticed long ago that internal regimes change under external forces. The Soviet Union is no exception to this.

At the risk of repeating myself I want to make one point very clear, because it is important for an understanding of the current situation in Russia. The breakup of the totalitarian order in the Soviet Union was certainly connected with the growth of nationalism, ethnic strife, economic discontent, and in-fighting within the ruling elite, especially between its central, empire-oriented and its ethnoregional groupings. However, the collapse had been initiated by the country's defeat in the Cold War. Without this defeat the regime would have continued to stagnate but would have survived for an indefinitely long period.

An anecdotal but revealing conversation that I happened to attend in 1984 may serve as an illustration of the mood of the more far-sighted members of the Soviet elite at that time. It took place in a privileged sauna club that I used to visit from time to time on the invitation of a friend. Except for him, nobody there knew that I was a refusenik and under strong pressure from the KGB; otherwise I would have been immediately thrown out of the club. The issue discussed was Reagan's Strategic Defense Initiative; the main participants in the conversation were a secretary of the Communist Party organization of one of Moscow's large research institutions and a colonel of the Soviet Air Force main staff. The secretary spoke in the tradition of official Soviet propaganda: "Colonel, let me assure you that, if necessary, the Soviet people are ready for all sacrifices—you may take our last pair of pants to match the Americans." The colonel, bored with listening to this nonsense in the relaxing atmosphere of the sauna, replied: "If necessary, we will certainly take your pants with or without your consent. If necessary, we will even take the skin off your ass. But do you think that we are capable of building anything similar to the American system with your pants and skin?" Trying to sound innocent I asked the colonel what was wrong. He explained that, in terms of scientific potential and even know-how, the country could develop a similar system, but that the technological edge was not on its side and it lacked the necessary economic resources.[1] Much later this was admitted by Gorbachev (1992: 191) himself.

This is why in the late 1980s, many intellectuals in Eastern European countries and in the Soviet Union insisted, sometimes to the dismay of liberal Western observers, that it was actually President Reagan who, by initiating a new turn in the arms race, had brought Gorbachev to power. For this reason, Reagan was much more popular than Gorbachev amongst Soviet intellectuals, contrary to their Western counterparts. However, the Cold War in many respects was a very peculiar one, and the Soviet defeat was unusual as well. The external factors had a limited impact on the consequent developments in the Soviet Union. Unlike Japan, the country lacks a General MacArthur. There is no external force there responsible for the maintenance of internal stability and in control of the democratization process (among others, this was already noted by Zaslavsky 1992: 116). The favorable circumstances which existed in other totalitarian countries, Japan and Germany, defeated in World War II, were absent

---

[1] I enjoyed this conversation so much that I immediately began to talk about it with all of my visitors from the West, as additional proof that the West should not overestimate the Soviet military might and should not be blackmailed by the Soviets. After my emigration, in 1985, I repeated this story on different occasions. Robert Conquest in the *Times Literary Supplement* (July 9, 1993) referred to the same story as having being told to him by his friend, an American "learned in all matters Russian" who allegedly also happened to be in the sauna at that moment. This puzzles me a lot. I remember quite well that there were no foreigners among the participants and witnesses of that conversation.

in the USSR. Its military-industrial complex as well as the secret police and some other totalitarian institutions were not dismantled and still continue to affect the political and economic situation in the country in a very negative way.

The Revolution That Actually Never Took Place

Recently, Gorbachev belatedly admitted (*Nezavisimaia gazeta*, April 23, 1994) that the main shortcoming of his perestroika policy was that it left the actual power and property in the hands of the nomenklatura. The ruling elites and the state apparatus in Russia have demonstrated a remarkable capability for adjustment and as a whole remain in power after they left the communist ideology out of their reckoning. One may ask, why and how did this happen at all? The answer is very simple. If a political revolution implies at least the replacement of the ruling elite, then the anti-communist revolution, so many times declared to have happened in the USSR, actually never took place. Precisely because the totalitarian structures in Russia were not completely destroyed, and decommunization along denazification lines was never carried out, the country faces additional difficulties and obstacles in her transition period.

At the time Gorbachev embraced the policies of glasnost and perestroika, his intention was to make the communist regime more efficient, even more humane, but in no way to replace it with a Western-type liberal democracy. He never accepted the line of Sakharov, whom American communists claim to be "the leader of the bourgeois opposition in the USSR" (Marcy 1990: 39). Nor did he ever wish to sell the population of the USSR and East European communist countries to international capitalism, as other Stone Age Marxists, such as Meillassoux (1993: 34), are accusing him of. The consequences of Gorbachev's policy were neither his merit nor his fault. He simply failed to comprehend that predators have a better chance of becoming vegetarians than totalitarian regimes have of acquiring a human face. Nobody but Nikolai Ryzhkov, the former Soviet prime minister and (at that time) a close ally of Gorbachev, testified that "people were still sent to jail and to psychiatric asylums for political and even economic dissidence in 1987 and even 1988" (Ryzhkov 1992: 272). Personally I do not need this reminder, because during those years several of my friends who were less lucky than I were imprisoned for their participation in the Jewish national movement in the USSR.

Gorbachev miscalculated because he did not anticipate that limited and inconsistent reforms could reveal the malady but hardly cure it. Contrary to his counterparts in Poland and Hungary (Batt 1991), Gorbachev never attempted to negotiate reforms and power sharing on the basis of compromise with the emerging democratic opposition. Thus, the problem of the popular legitimation of his leadership was never resolved. The perestroika period is now often nick-named katastroika in Russia (from the word catastrophe)—by some, because contrary to the initial blueprint of its architects, if there were any at all, it resulted in the demise of communism and the collapse of the Soviet Union; by others, because of the gap in economic expectations; by still others, because it did not immediately lead to the emergence of a liberal democratic order.

What really happened were spontaneous and haphazard, though persistent, attempts to remain in power by the more far-sighted groups among the ruling and privileged elites in the changing political situation, who sacrificed communist ideology, some institutions of the totalitarian state, and even the Soviet Union itself. The USSR ceased to exist not only because of the pressure from nationalist movements in the non-Russian parts of the country but also because, by the end of 1990, only the weakened part of the all-union nomenklatura failed to read the writing on the wall and stubbornly wished to preserve the empire, while the majority of the ruling elites came to the conclusion that they would survive better, even benefit, without this bankrupt venture. The failure of the abortive August 1991 putsch proved this beyond any doubt. An interesting, not fully comprehended, situation emerged in the Soviet Union in 1991. While Russian democratic forces vested all their hopes in Yeltsin's ascent to power, he simultaneously became the far-sighted nomenklatura's main hope for their remaining the ruling stratum in a post-totalitarian society. The ruling elite of the imperial nation, the Russians, emerged as the initiators of the empire's disintegration. Struggling for the destruction of central power, Yeltsin unambiguously disassociated Russia from the Soviet Union.

However, in at least two important respects, no clear break with the past was made. Perestroika and the ensuing events in Russia undermined the nomenklatura system as the mechanism of incorporation into the ruling elite, and particularly as the essential instrument of the Communist Party's monopolistic rule (Hill and Löwenhardt 1991). But the nomenklatura as the personnel of governance and administration survived and still remains in power. There was no real turnover of the political and administrative elite in Russia, let alone in the bureaucratic apparatus, especially on the middle and lower levels and in the provinces. The great majority of those holding high positions before 1991 are still members of the ruling elite. Research by scholars from the Institute of Sociology of the Russian Academy of Sciences (for a summary see *Izvestiia*, May 18, 1994: 2) revealed that people who in the recent past never belonged to the nomenklatura now constitute only 40 percent of the Parliament's members, 26 percent in the government, 25 percent in the president's inner circle, and 17 percent among the regional elites. Among the leadership of the parties, from right to left, they constitute no more than 42 percent. The picture is even more grim if one takes into account that many of those who did not belong to the nomenklatura are more than eager to join its ranks. There is, however, one serious difference, in terms of organization, between the political elite of the Soviet period and that of the post-Soviet period. The former was based on a principle of strict hierarchy, although this did not exclude patronage and cronyism. The latter is structured mainly on the principles of clannishness and cliquishness with, apparently, significant mafia penetration.

In all, the structure of power and privilege underwent little change, just like the inherited imperial superstructures personified by the repressive agencies and the army. There were 12,000 generals in the Soviet army, and 1,000 more generals now in the Russian army (*Literaturnaia gazeta*, October 27, 1993: 1). Only those who were unsuccessful at or incapable of, taking advantage of new opportunities want to return to the old communist system. At the same time, the majority of the former nomenklatura and apparatchiks, 20 million corrupt bureaucrats, want to retain, in one way or another, state control over the economy as the main source of their power and wealth. Their loyalty to Yeltsin's leadership is at best very dubious, their devotion to the reformist course is conditional, existing only to the extent that the emerging new order will not encroach on their lucrative positions in the government and administration but, on the contrary, will continue to provide them with political power, social advancement, and opportunities for enrichment. For all these reasons, no attempt has been made to cut the enormous Russian bureaucratic apparatus and to transform it into a civil service capable of meeting the demands of modern society and economy.

Thus, the gap between state and society did not narrow much. The state still reigns supreme. Monopartism was replaced in Russia by excessive statism. The separation of executive and legislative powers (and the judicial power as well) was never consistently maintained in post-Soviet Russia, despite a declarative struggle against the Soviet system. On the contrary, one witnesses now the actual reemergence of their combination. Ministers received the right to combine their positions in the government with the deputy's chairs (incidentally, this was made possible on the initiative of the "democrats," who hoped for quite different results at the parliamentary elections). Half of the seats in the Council of Federation, the upper chamber of the Russian Parliament, were reserved for the heads of regional administrations (on the initiative of the president or his retinue). As a result of the March 1994 elections, in the regional legislative bodies the members of executive power have a numerical majority (these very people passed the regulation which allowed them to run in this election). Thus, the nomenklatura still holds the power in the country, only this time without relying on the Communist Party's backing and in democratic disguise. The first thing that the newly elected Russian parliamentarians did was award themselves and even members of their families salaries, perks, and benefits that should make their Western counterparts from the affluent countries burst with envy.

A Missed Chance

Was this development inevitable? Exercises in alternative history never bring definite answers. Still, like a number of liberal intellectuals in Russia, I am inclined to think that at least there was a missed chance, or rather an opportunity ignored, by those who, in the late 1980s, were considered leaders of the democratic movement in the country.

By the time of perestroika, the dissident democratic movement, though enjoying the sympathies of a significant number of people, was small and disorganized because of the continuing repression and, thus, was unable to become a large-scale phenomenon in Soviet political life. The majority of its active participants were sent to the Gulag or forced to emigrate. Very few were able to return to political activity, as Andrei Sakharov, Sergei Kovalev, or Rev. Gleb Yakunin did. The vacuum was filled by the so-called democrats of the new wave. In the 1970s and the 1980s, many of them were not just sitting in the bushes, but had sufficiently rubbery spines to pursue their careers successfully, though they were unable to realize all their ambitions under the rigid nomenklatura system, whose openness became increasingly limited in the post-Stalin period. In totalitarian countries, conformism for survival should not be confused with conformism for achieving social and economic benefits. Many of the "new democrats" belonged to the privileged strata of Soviet society; actually they were bedfellows of the nomenklatura, and to achieve their high status in the recent past they had to prove their loyalty to the communist regime by paying it more than lip service. I would not evoke their past behavior if it were only a matter of moral standing. Not everyone in the Soviet Union should be expected to be a Sakharov. However, it soon became evident that their past was relevant to their political evolution. Even their hurriedly acquired anti-communism should not be overestimated, since many remained party members until 1990 or even 1991.[2] Besides,

[2] To illustrate this point it is worth mentioning beguiling facts from the biographies of some "new democrats." Sobchak and Shakhrai became members of the Communist Party

some of them either overtly or covertly favored various authoritarian models of development.

Still, the growing popularity of the struggle against the Communist Party's monopoly on power provided these people with the opportunity to become leaders of the opposition represented by the first legal democratic movements, such as Democratic Russia and some others. Although these movements united people of different political persuasions, they could have eventually evolved into organized political parties. This opportunity became very feasible in the immediate aftermath of the August 1991 putsch and the temporary ban on the Communist Party. However, it was never realized in Russia or even tested.

To call things by their proper names, the spontaneous and mass democratization movement, which received a boost from the failure of the putschists and the complete discreditation of the Communist Party and the nomenklatura, was actually abandoned by those who in August 1991 were hailed as its leaders. Instead of negotiating political change or transitional compromise, or at least exerting pressure on the ruling elite when the "democrats" were at the peak of their popularity and enjoying strong public support while the ruling elite was in deep crisis and in retreat, the democrats preferred to join the elite's ranks, to be co-opted into the basically unreconstructed power structures and the state apparatus.

The co-optation was not a negotiated process. Only Yeltsin's personal supporters were picked up, and their loyalty and personal closeness to the president served as the main criterion of their selection. However, they provided the postputsch Russian leadership with a timely democratic image and aura. Moreover, they substantially contributed to the preservation of the ruling elite. After the August putsch the "new democrats" immediately denounced the nonexistent "witch-hunt." In practical terms this was a clear signal of their unwillingness not only to prosecute the nomenklatura members but even to replace them. Moreover, this signaled that the nomenklatura members were almost unconditionally assured of retaining their power and privileges.

Among other things, those democrats who became statesmen opposed revealing the names of KGB informants and collaborators. Thus, they did not prevent these KGB associates from being manipulated by the secret police, who continued to intervene in the political process. There are

---

in 1988 and left it in 1990; Stankevich joined a year earlier, but left also in 1990. All these people were middle-aged when they joined the party: Sobchak was 51 years old, Shakhrai was 32, and Stankevich was 33 (*Argumenty i fakty* 8 [February 1995]: 2). It is difficult to believe that their joining and leaving the party was inspired by anything other than opportunistic career considerations.

serious grounds for suspicion that some of those who wished to protect the informants and provocateurs were concerned with their own, far from spotless, reputations. The Russian press revealed that some Russian politicians who first came to the fore under the democratic banner but soon became leaders of the anti-democratic forces, such as Baburin, were in fact KGB agents.

The protection of the democratization process, not revenge, was at stake when it faced strong resistance from powerful adversaries. It seems that Russia might benefit from a limited lustration, despite the many dangers of this practice. Those who oppose it on moral grounds still cannot divest themselves of illusions about the nature of the communist kingdom of curved mirrors and have forgotten about the positive effects of the analogous practice during the denazification process. It would be possible to go beyond the horizon of decommunization after it has actually taken place. In Russia it has not. In Russia carrion still lingers among the living.

The incorporation of the democrats into the ruling elite for a time created the illusion that they had come to power in Russia, and they did very little to shatter this illusion. The warnings of those who preferred to remain in constructive opposition to the government (Burtin and Molchanov 1992) were dismissed as excessive radicalism. Complaints began to be heard only long afterwards, when some democrats lost their government positions and were defeated in the parliamentary elections. Thus, Alexandr Yakovlev regretted recently that the "bureaucracy misappropriated the August victory" (*Literaturnaia gazeta*, October 27, 1993: 11). Gaidar admitted that the "Russian state cannot be considered a democratic one. . . . To a large extent the nomenklatura remains the same. They only became a little more open for a while, but only very little. They swallowed the 'best' democratic cadres and returned again to the point of departure" (*Izvestiia*, January 20, 1994: 1). The former mayor of Moscow, Popov, began to claim that after August 1991 the bloc of liberal bureaucrats and those democrats who were disposed to occupying positions in the state apparatus came to power in Russia (*Nezavisimaia gazeta*, December 10, 1993: 5). Popov asserted that this bloc was inevitable because only the state apparatus could lead the transformation process (*Russkaia mysl'*, November 26–December 1, 1993: 6). This statement, which sounds like self-justification, is dubious in its premise, since the possibility of a democratic scenario was never tested in practice. It is also analytically wrong because the alleged bloc never existed. The old bureaucratic elite did not share its power with the democrats-turned-statesmen. It simply used their temporary popularity as well as some democratic-looking procedures for the continuation of its rule over the country. When their popularity evaporated, the discredited democrats became dispensable.

And their popularity evaporated with remarkable speed, not only because the reformers came to be held responsible for the government's policy but also because of their personal misbehavior. The same people, who only a few years before had gained popularity for fighting against the privileges of the ruling elite, hurried to enjoy these privileges as soon as they joined the elite's ranks. Just when the reformers called for austerity among ordinary people, for sacrifices to make the reforms irreversible, they themselves hastily acquired various perks, luxury apartments, and *dachas* (summer houses); decorated their offices with expensive furniture imported for this occasion; appeared there with personal guards and in fancy limousines with chauffeurs, who violated traffic rules on the way; indulged in other privileges which in the Soviet Union were resented as symbols of discredited abuses of power; and proved to be prone to corruption with a greed that amazed but rather pleased the old nomenklatura, who were more experienced in these matters and who used to enjoy their privileges in a more concealed way. In 1992, one of them explained the situation to me in the following condescending words: "These people are hungry. They waited for such a long time to get their share."

Even though they were criticized in the liberal press and they understood that their behavior did not contribute to their popularity, those who became prone to corruption often could not overcome their greed. When a prominent state secretary from the reformers' camp, Burbulis, was told that his newly acquired ZIL limousine (a scornful object of bitter jokes in the Soviet Union as a symbol of undeserved privileges) did not contribute to his democratic image, he made only one concession. Arriving at democratic meetings, he ordered his chauffeur to leave his limousine around the corner to make it less conspicuous. In addition, he organized the publication of a book devoted to his alleged personal modesty and Spartan way of life (see Roiz 1993). In 1994, I discussed the matter of privileges with one Russian politician, visiting the United States, who has an impeccable democratic reputation and who currently is in opposition to the government. Even this person tried to persuade me that the problem does not deserve much attention, since the living standards of the American politicians are allegedly still higher than that of their Russian counterparts. When asked, why, in this case, not compare the living standards of ordinary Russians with that of ordinary Americans, my interlocutor admitted that the very possibility of this connection seems quite alien to the mood prevailing nowadays among the Russian democrats.

The question of privileges would not deserve special attention, since it is common knowledge that power corrupts, if it weren't a very sensitive issue in a society accustomed to egalitarian demagogy and masquerade. In the recent past, this issue greatly contributed to the discreditation of the old communist nomenklatura. Likewise, nowadays it contributes to the discreditation of those who are associated with the reform course in Russia but who began to be called the demonomenklatura. The scornful terms *shitocrats* or *democratic thieves* for the democrats (in Russian they imply the word play *dermokraty* and *demokrady* instead of *demokraty*) are inductive and alarming in this respect.

The democratic movement in Russia is still centered around personalities much more than around institutions. As soon as the democrats joined the ruling elite, loyalty to President Yeltsin was declared the main criterion of a democratic persuasion. No sincere effort has been made to organize the parties of democratic orientation under the pretext—never seriously tested in practice—that after the communist monopartism people have an aversion to all parties. The remaining organizations rapidly lost their grass-roots supporters because, among other things, their rank-and-file members were removed from participating in the formulation of their policy. They were told only to follow their leaders. The virtual absence of a stable multiparty system has meant that people have again been denied leverage for political mobilization and participation in the formulation, supervision, and correction of reform policies. Thus, another attempt was made in Russia to proceed with reforms from above, to make them top-down affairs, without popular involvement, and this soon alienated society from the reform process. The various blocs and parties of declared democratic allegiance that were hurriedly negotiated behind closed doors on the eve of the December 1993 parliamentary elections have failed to fill the political vacuum.

In just a few years the democratic leaders lost the capability of talking to ordinary people; they preferred to talk only to each other and to their followers. The number and configuration of the blocs and parties of democratic orientation that participated in the last elections reflected personal ambitions, alliances, and rivalries of their leaders more than serious political differences. Thus, Russia's Choice bloc united such different people as former political prisoners Kovalev and Yakunin, whose personal honesty and democratic persuasion were never open to doubt, the liberal economic reformer Gaidar, the careerist Kozyrev, always ready to change his views to retain his ministerial chair, and the former party-appointee Poltoranin, who already in the post-Soviet period stained his reputation with racist and anti-Semitic statements. No wonder splits have already affected the parliamentary fraction of this bloc.

It would be simplistic to ascribe everything to the egoistic careerism of the new democrats. Their blueprint for economic reforms and their political tactics have been influenced by their Balcerowicz-type sincere belief that every capitalist is good and that all good things will automatically follow the introduction of laissez faire capitalism. Hence, their implicit *enrichessez-vous* principle.

In September 1993, one reform-minded junior member of the Russian government explained his credo to me as follows: "In historical perspective it does not matter that original capital is accumulating by semilegal, or even sheer criminal, means. In the past, this happened in America and other rich capitalist countries. Eventually society will benefit from this. The children of our mafiosi and/or political capitalists will attend the best universities and become successful industrialists and financiers, their grandchildren will be famous liberal politicians, mæcenatists, and philanthropists." Maybe so. The problem is whether ordinary Russians, who during the lifespan of three generations waited for the promised advent of the communist paradise on Earth, have enough patience to wait for another three generations for the advent of enlightened capitalism.

Likewise, the reformers have contributed to the spread of what Lempert (1993:643) aptly characterized as the "cargo cult" vision of Western capitalism and its ability to sponsor reforms in Russia with billions of dollars of aid and business investment. In 1990, I witnessed an animated discussion among the editors of the Moscow liberal magazine *Znanie-Sila* concerning how to distribute $60 billion that the United States was allegedly ready to provide that very year to the country. When I asked where they got this strange idea, the editor-in-chief answered that it was common knowledge and the message that his magazine was conveying to its readers. (To be fair, some American "experts," including famous Harvard professors, contributed a great deal to these inflated expectations, saying that the figure should be closer to $100 billion, even $120 billion. The only thing they did not explain to their Russian audience was how the United States was supposed to get this money.) No wonder, when the amount of aid turned out to be much smaller, and the aid itself was largely mismanaged or appropriated by the corrupt members of the ruling elite, the general public was disappointed, and many reformers began to blame the West for their own failures.

In such conditions the relative success of reforms depends on their speed and thoroughness. However, the economic radicals in Russia were never given the freedom or enough time to realize their ideas. The reforms were initiated in liberal garments but in accordance with the bureaucratic scenario, and all the oscillations in pursuing their course reflected mainly the internal fighting between different interest groups within the ruling elite. The shock was neither accompanied nor followed by therapeutics. The reforms were soon blocked at their initial stage, at which deformed privatization is not accompanied by genuine marketization. The social danger of having free prices in the context of a state monopoly, and the emergence of a class of political capitalists dependent upon the state, is already noted in the literature (Staniszkis 1991). This is just what has happened in Russia. To many ordinary Russians the very word reforms has lost its luster, like an old coin which has lost its nominal price because its faces have been rubbed off, as did the word perestroika at the downfall of the Gorbachev era.

Russia Still at the Crossroads

In all, contrary to some East-Central European postcommunist countries, Russia still cannot work out a peaceful transition to democracy through a participatory process and consentient rules of the political game. Yeltsin's bureaucratic regime with its rapidly diminishing base of social support is too fragile to be a guarantor of the continuation of liberal economic and political reforms. The economic crisis, bouts of inflation, the danger of unemployment, together with the disillusionment of inflated expectations, substantial labor discontent, a serious drop in living standards, and a growing gap between the rich and poor, make a considerable part of the population increasingly passive (only about 35 percent of the electorate participated in the March 1994 regional elections in Russia) and incite another part toward embracing various anti-democratic movements. As one Russian liberal bitterly remarked in January 1994, the new democrats succeeded in averting people from democracy even before it got started.

After the powerful showing of the communists and ultranationalists in the first ever free parliamentary elections, one could hardly underestimate the growing danger of the country's various anti-democratic forces. No less dangerous is the tendency, under Yeltsin's leadership, to placate and compromise with them. The treaty on national accord, which leaders of most political, public, and professional organizations were persuaded by the president to sign in 1994, was hurriedly christened the Russian Moncloa pact by some observers. However, the economic and political situation in 1995 Russia is quite different from 1977 Spain. In Spain the centrists dominated in the foci of power while the extreme flanks were weakened. In Russia at present the centrist forces are weak while the opposite flanks are strong. Besides, the prestige of Juan Carlos, the head of state, and of the Suarez government in 1977 was much higher than the fading prestige of Yeltsin and of the Chernomyrdin government in 1995.

The struggle between the ethnic and national perception of the Russian state is far from over. Russia is in a period of intensifying nationalism and great-power sentiments aggravated by what is conceived by many as her national humiliation. In the growth of nationalism she lagged behind her neighbors by two or three years, but at present nationalistic sentiments have become very conspicuous in the Russian political process. Equally dangerous are attempts by some politicians from Yeltsin's camp, who themselves are nostalgic for Russia's grandeur, to use the nationalist trump card for competition with the commie-fascists and chauvinists on the populist ground. Thus, Shumeiko, the chair of the Russian Parliament's upper chamber, calls for the immediate creation of a "single Russian people" with a "single Russian ideology" (*Moscow News* 4 [January 31, 1994]: 2).

The role of the army as the political force in Russia's power struggle also raises many doubts. All indications are that neither Yeltsin nor Minister of Defense Grachev during the September-October 1993 crisis were, to the very end, sure about how the army, including the top brass, would react (Yeltsin 1994: 382–86), and Yeltsin had to pay a price for the army's eventual support. Before the fires were put out after the October 1993 showdown between the president and the Parliament, Yeltsin hurriedly convened the Russian Security Council meeting to discuss a new military doctrine. Among other things this doctrine rescinded the "no first use" nuclear weapon pledge. The vows to reduce the armed forces drastically were also abandoned. However, it appears that the military massively voted for Zhirinovsky in the last parliamentary elections. It is common knowledge that the extreme right Union of Officers, which has a goal to resist the Yeltsin "anti-people regime" and fight for the restoration of Soviet power and the Soviet Union, holds strong positions in the central apparatus of the Russian Defense Ministry and military academies, including the General Staff Academy (*Moscow News* 16 [April 12-28, 1994]: 2). A significant number of the fascist newspapers and other literature are printed by the printing house which is owned by the Russian Armed Forces General Staff (*Izvestiia*, April 8, 1995). In this situation, there is no guarantee that in case of yet another political confrontation the same military will stay in the barracks and not turn against the president or the democratic forces.

Ethnic relations within the Russian Federation (significantly, the word *federation* has been almost completely dropped from Russia's official lexicon) are far from settled. Russia is still in the process of renegotiating powers and responsibilities vis-à-vis her ethnic minorities, but there is already enough proof of a differential and sometimes discriminatory treatment of some nationalities. Thus, the Russian leadership has played a far from impartial role in the Ossetian-Ingush conflict, and Russian troops were allied with the Ossetian side in the ethnic cleansing of the disputed territory (Dement'eva 1994).

Under the pretext of fighting the mafia, even the Russian liberal press has launched a campaign against the so-called people of Caucasian nationality. Zhirinovsky's oath to drive Caucasian traders from Moscow and all other cities of Russia is, incidentally, already being accomplished by Moscow's "democratic" mayor, Luzhkov, and welcomed by the majority of Muscovites.

One can also trace many negative trends in Russia's foreign policy. Renewed pretensions about the superpower status, not backed by the country's economic and technological might, may become a destabilizing factor in world politics. I can only agree with Beissinger (1993: 110–11) that, "when imperialism dies, neo-imperialism still lives"; therefore, "the key fact about empires is the need to keep killing them." Nobody else but Yeltsin (1994: 389) admitted in his recently published memoirs that "the former Empire does not vanish easily. It prepares new and new cataclysms. It reproduces new fighters, fanatics, leaders with shoulder-straps or without them. The Empire revenges itself for its downfall." Good words, right words. If only the Russian president had always kept them in mind in his practical policy. In fact, obituaries about the demise of the Russian Empire may seem premature. Its great power ideology is now openly exposed again as a part of official ideology that wants to substitute history for Realpolitik. The famous Russian philosopher Nikolai Berdiaev's words, "Russia is doomed to be an empire," are recalled with sympathy by many intellectuals and politicians advocating a Russian version of the Monroe Doctrine.

Actually, Zhirinovsky broadcasts what many in Moscow have preferred to keep silent about but to follow in practice as far as possible. As early as the Summer of 1992, when I was in Moscow and met with some Russian politicians who at that time were responsible for formulating and conducting their country's policy toward the other ex-Soviet countries, I noticed that many of them had adopted double standards. While being champions of the democratization process in Russia, they were ready to ally with and to support anti-democratic political forces in other ex–Soviet countries if those forces were to comply with Russia's requests.

The "Zhirinovsky factor" is already serving as a catalyst for Russia's hardening policy toward these countries. Actually, some of Zhirinovsky's slogans differ little from the declarations and actions of the Russian leadership. For example, he claims that he supports Great Russia extending its territory at least to the boundaries of the former Soviet Union (Zhirinovsky 1993: 93). The military doctrine of Russia also states that the interests of the country stretch all the way to the external borders of the ex-Soviet Union. The Russian foreign minister Kozyrev, who dropped his past soft talk in order to be in line with the changing political climate in Moscow, also declared: "The countries of the CIS and the Baltics—this is a region where the vital interests of Russia are concentrated. . . . We should not withdraw from those regions which have been the sphere of Russia's interest for centuries" (*Moscow News* 3 [January 24, 1994]: 2). Finally, Yeltsin has begun to demand the placement of Russian military bases in the territory of ex-Soviet countries. The former Russian vice-premier Shokin has made an even more outspoken statement. He has admitted that Tadjikistan is already a kind of Russian protectorate and that other CIS countries, if admitted into the Russian ruble zone, will also become protectorates (*Moscow News* 47 [November 19, 1993]: 4, 6).

Russian politicians insist that keeping Russian military forces in the USSR successor countries are not attempts to restore the Soviet Union but measures for ensuring peace and security. However, Russia's policy there actually creates a zone of instability, evokes suspicion there in the reemergence of Russian hegemonism, and may result in new outbursts of anti-Russian nationalistic feelings. Azerbaidjan, Georgia, and Moldova have joined, or rejoined, the CIS under duress. Georgia had to grant Russia the right of having naval bases and deploying troops in her territory. Armenia and Belarus' have followed this example. Azerbaidjan and Moldova are pressed to do the same.

Russia interferes now in the ethnic conflicts and the internal political struggle in the CIS countries, particularly in cases where power is in the hands of forces unrelated to the old nomenklatura, and occasionally helps in overthrowing them. The ruling neo-communist regime in Tadjikistan is being propped up by Russian bayonets; as a result Russia became bogged down in the Tadjik civil war. Russia also became embroiled in ethnic conflicts in Pridnestrovie, South Ossetia, and Abkhazia, practically supporting secessionists.

Russians in the Near Abroad

The problem of Russians living in other ex-Soviet countries (the "near abroad" in the current Russian political parlance) has also become a hot political issue. In the guise of protecting ethnic kin, Russian politicians of various kinds are trying to gain the capital by fanning the nationalistic fervor. Actually, the current situation and feelings of Russians living in the near abroad[3] are very similar to those of the Europeans who lived in the former colonies of the Western powers after these colonies became independent. Their comfortable and insulated world suddenly collapsed, and without an intermediate period they had to adjust to the alien languages and cultures and find ways of integrating into local societies. (See table 2.1, p. 252.)

Being convinced in their *mission civilisatrice* and used to the protection of a powerful state, these Russians believed that knowledge of the Russian language was sufficient to live anywhere in the USSR. Sociological surveys have revealed that only a few years ago 80 percent of ethnic Russians considered their homeland not Russia but the USSR (Drobizheva 1991: 77). Having grown accustomed to the guiding principle "My address is not a house or a street, my address is the whole Soviet Union," to quote a once-popular Soviet song, they have unexpectedly found themselves in the unusual and, to them, humiliating situation of being an ethnic minority. Suddenly they are challenged by what they consider undeserved ingratitude, if not outright enmity, on the part of their former "younger brothers."

The Ukrainian ambassador to Prague was right when he claimed that even some Moscow politicians "are unable to imagine Russians in the role of a minority" (*New Times* 52 [December 1993]: 16). In addition to psychological difficulties, Russians in the near abroad are experiencing economic and social difficulties. The members of dominating nationalities are excluding the members of ethnic minorities from the power structures, managerial establishment, institutions of higher education, and some especially profitable spheres of economic activity, such as trade and service. (Incidentally, the same process is going on in Russia with respect to her ethnic minorities.) In Central Asia and the Caucasus the positions of Russians, as well as all other minorities, are particularly precarious because of overpopulation and high unemployment, which further aggravate ethnic competition.

The vast majority of Russians in the near abroad would like the Soviet Empire to be restored; Zhirinovsky is very popular amongst them. Their desire to retain Russian citizenship, or at least to acquire double citizenship, as well as their secessionist tendencies, though understandable, raise the indigenous population's suspicion that they represent Russia's fifth column in their countries.

---

[3] By 1989, their number was 25.3 million (17.4 percent of all Russians in the USSR). Since then, about 2 million Russians have already left the countries of the near abroad; of them 1 million emigrated from Central Asia.

There is no easy and equitable solution to the "Russian question," which, in fact, is only part of the broader problem of ethnic minorities and cultural pluralism in the ex-communist countries (see chapter 3). The experiences of Europeans who lived in the Western colonies demonstrate that most of them eventually chose or were forced to return to their metropolis countries. In the recent past, Yeltsin was in favor of this solution for the Russians in the near abroad. He stated several times that they would be granted not only the right but also the possibility of returning to Russia, should they so desire. A similar approach is still advocated by some liberal observers in Moscow (see, for example, Panarin 1994a: 31–35). However, it was easier for Western peoples to repatriate to their affluent countries than it is for Russians to return to a country which is in a deep economic crisis and is not welcoming her returning compatriots.

In any case the problem in general is blown out of proportion. Actually, the process of out-migration of Russians from Transcaucasia, the North Caucasus, and Central Asia began as early as the 1970s. In the period between 1959 and 1989 the number of Russians living in Georgia decreased by 66,700 persons, in Azerbaidjan (in 1970–1989) by 117,800 persons, in Armenia (in 1979–1989) by 18,000 persons (Ostapenko and Subbotina 1993: 286–87). In the period between 1979 and 1989, 850,000 Russians and other persons of European origin left Central Asia (Perevedentsev 1993: 155). The current situation only exacerbates the already existing trends. (Incidentally, in the recent past the growing out-migrations of the Russian and Slavic populations of these republics sounded an alarm to the Soviet leadership, which tried, although without result, to reverse this situation.) At present, about 80 percent of the Russians in the near abroad are living in three countries only: Ukraine, Belarus', and Kazakhstan. In the first two countries, their positions have not deteriorated in any serious way; in Kazakhstan their strength in numbers is enough to safeguard their interests somehow. Some experts predict that in the next five or six years the out-migration of Russians and other ethnic minorities from Kazakhstan will hardly exceed half a million persons (Perevedentsev 1993: 153–55). What certainly does not help the solution to the problem is Russia's current policy of using her ethnic kin's troubles to exert pressure on other ex-Soviet countries. Thus, in Latvia and Estonia she tried to link troop withdrawal to demands about the status of Russians, including demobilized military officers in these republics. The keeping of Russian troops in Tadjikistan is often explained by the desire to protect the Russian population, although of 380,000 Russians who lived there by 1989, 300,000 have already left the country. Such a policy hardly contributes to improving relations between the Russian minorities and the indigenous populations in the ex–Soviet countries.

A New Phenomenon: Post-Totalitarian Society

No poetry, anymore, please, no illusions on the Soviet move away from communism. Let us talk prose based on facts, not on hopes and expectations. So far, the main positive developments in the ex–Soviet Union are the breakup of the empire and the end of the communist order. However, this alone in no way makes the democratization process in the empire's successor states irreversible; even less does it imply their full acceptance of Western political and economic models. It may well be that these countries are facing the problem of squaring the circle. At a certain level of modernity, societies are predisposed, if not destined, to democracy. The problem is how to achieve this level and decide who has already achieved it. Most of the CIS countries, apparently, have not reached it yet.

Even with Russia the situation is far from clear. Her economy is still unreconstructed along modern lines, her society is in flux. While the nomenklatura and bureaucracy remain the most organized and powerful social strata, the new strata have not yet crystallized. Social and economic positions of the educated urban middle strata, who in the recent past were the main advocates of reforms, are deteriorating inasmuch as the livelihood of the majority of them continues to depend on the wages paid by the state. These wages are often paid with delay and are undermined by inflation. Maybe it is premature to speak about a Weimarian Russia, if one has in mind the fate of Weimarian Germany, but it is already clear that the Russian Great Leap into liberal democracy has failed to reach the safe other shore. The democratization process in the country may still be turned back.

At present, the sociopolitical space in East-Central Europe and the ex–Soviet Union is represented by a variety of postcommunist models. One of them is a post-totalitarian society, which is neither totalitarian like its communist predecessor nor liberal democratic. Still, it is already possible to speak about this society, not in purely transitory terms, but rather in structuralist terms. Its main characteristics are already evident.

1. The break from totalitarianism by the countries of East-Central Europe and the Soviet Union took place under the impact of an external situation more than through internal development (see, for example, Verdery 1991; Banac 1992). However, the internal decisions were not dictated, and external forces are unable to secure the further development of these countries toward democracy.

2. Success on the path of decommunization and democratization is to some extent connected with society's previous political experience and the degree of its resistance to totalitarianism. Not theoretical consider-

ations but purely empirical observations prove that this transition is easier when rudiments of civil society survive, or reemerge, although in more or less amorphous form beneath totalitarian structures, or at least when they are embodied by various dissident movements of democratic orientation. One should only compare the situation existing now in the Czech Republic or Poland with that in Romania, or the situation in Lithuania with that in Belarus'. The existence and the moral authority of the dissidents with their *"non possum"* challenge proved to be important, sometimes maybe even crucial, for the initial success of the breakup of totalitarian communist power, although usually it was not these people who reaped the fruits of their labor. Still, one may wonder, can Klaus escape the heritage of Havel, or can the new Polish leaders escape the heritage of Solidarity, or can even Yeltsin completely escape the heritage of Sakharov?

3. In the post-totalitarian countries of East-Central Europe and the former Soviet Union mainly the same old communist elites, inherited from the previous regime, remain in power.

In this respect again one may single out two groups of the postcommunist countries. On the one hand, we have Poland, Hungary, the Czech Republic, and maybe also Slovenia. With many serious reservations I tend also to include in this group the Baltic republics. I would rather define their society as already proto- or preliberal capitalist than as ex-communist and post-totalitarian. Some of these countries, in one way or another, have really experienced anti-communist revolutions; at any rate, the communist nomenklatura there was ousted from power. Those have-beens who remain in the power structures or have returned to power underwent a certain metamorphosis; they cannot operate anymore as representatives of their former nomenklatura class, because this class and its power base to a large extent have ceased to exist. Now these countries demonstrate better results and have more potential for further positive development.

On the other hand, in countries like Romania, Serbia, Russia, not to mention the other CIS countries, the old nomenklatura as a class, or, if one prefers, as a stratum, remains in power. It only incorporated some new members and changed the legitimation of its power. The results speak for themselves. These countries are still treading water.

4. Although some attributes and procedures of liberal democracy have been introduced into a post-totalitarian society, not only the personnel but also the previous totalitarian structures and institutions have undergone insufficient changes. The concept of the separation of powers has been used only to create a pluralism of economic and political actors in order to divide the spoils among the ruling elites, but not to develop

mechanisms of real public control and monitoring to hold the unelected bureaucracy, as well as elected officials along with their appointees, accountable (Lempert 1993).

5. In a post-totalitarian society the state continues to exercise excessive and arbitrary control over the economy.

6. Nationalism has replaced communism as the dominating and state-supported ideology in post-totalitarian societies. It is true that even countries such as Hungary and Poland have not escaped the fervor of xenophobic nationalism. However, there is still room for hope that, if their successful transition to liberal democracy continues, nationalism may recede into the background. At least there are political forces and social groupings in those countries for whom liberal democracy is more attractive than excessive nationalism. I can only hope they are strong enough to curb its detrimental impact upon emerging (or reemerging) civil society.

7. The social space for civil society in post-totalitarian countries is very narrow. The state's partial retreat from the public sphere leaves not civil society but a dangerous institutional vacuum. Stable political organizations with mass followings and specific social bases which provide institutionalized forms for political competition are still to a large extent absent; at best they are only rudimentary. Hence, there exists the real possibility of the emergence of authoritarian or semiauthoritarian regimes with nationalistic ideologies and only a few elements of a market economy.

In all postcommunist countries a lot depends on the degree of economic success (Hall 1994). Again, in this respect countries such as the Czech Republic or even Poland and Hungary provide more hope. Like it or not, although the Czech resistance to totalitarianism is symbolized by the playwright and dissident Havel, the country's consequent drive to the normality of liberal capitalism is more ensured by the pragmatic financier Klaus. Those Western intellectuals who complain that Czechs nowadays prefer sausage to any altruistic motivation forget that they themselves did not experience food and other shortages, or the suppression of their individual liberties. (I wonder if or when these people will stop their vain search for the ideal society with corresponding ideological schemes, for the Heavenly Kingdom on earth, and instead, begin to pay more attention to less exciting but more fruitful efforts for the gradual improvement the imperfect existing societies.) It is always very easy to expect others to be better and more idealistic than we are. Likewise, the real Eastern European intellectuals, despite their disappointment with many aspects of the transitional period, certainly prefer, not to whisper as they recently had to under the constant watch of Big Brother, but to speak in a loud voice, as their Western counterparts are used to doing, even if the number of their listeners and admirers has diminished. In the postcommunist context, democracy's connection with a chance for prosperity may be a better guarantee than all liberal theories together. It seems, however, that the promised and expected prosperity in post-totalitarian countries looks very dubious for the near future.

In all, the liberal democratic direction of the ongoing transformation in the ex–Soviet Union, as well as in some East-Central European countries, should by no means be taken for granted. As Merquior (1992: 337) pointed out: "It is after all possible, perhaps even probable, that the decomposition of communism ... produces a deep, dangerous social dislocation where grouping for the market and dabbling with democracy could remain very far from their 'Western,' stable institutionalization. Capitalism without its complex institutional underpinning, democracy without its constitutional anchorage could be a highly immature—and a highly volatile—post-communist situation." Post-totalitarian society, despite its inherent instability and its high level of sustained crisis, may well turn out not to be a short transitional stage but a much more lasting phenomenon. Daniel Patrick Moynihan (1993: 15) hurried too much when he stated that the "great trauma of totalitarianism ended." I hope totalitarianism has really come, or is coming, to its ignominious defeat. However, its aftereffects will be felt for generations.

Sometime in 1983 (or was it already 1984?) on a cold and windy day in Moscow, facing the likelihood of soon going to the Gulag and therefore being at that time much closer to Siberia than to the sunny Jerusalem hills or to a tranquil and green suburb in Madison, I told Ernest Gellner about my deep conviction that, paraphrasing Chairman Mao, the wind from the West would defeat the wind from the East, that is, that eventually liberal democracy would prove to be stronger and better than totalitarian communism. I must confess, however, that at that time I did not anticipate that it would happen so soon, or that the transitional period would be so painful and difficult.

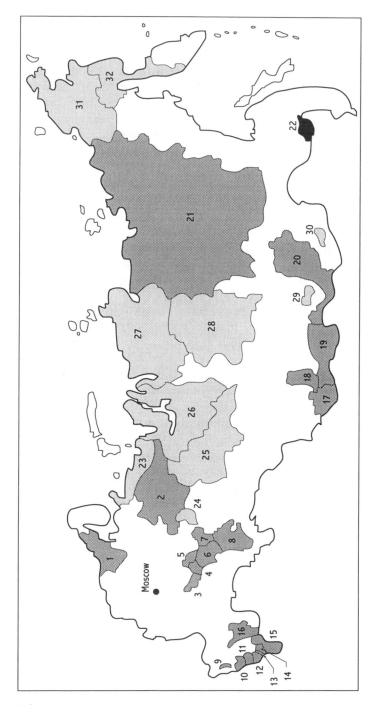

Map 2. The Russian Federation
Note: Key is on facing page.

Republics

1. Karelia
2. Komi
3. Mordovia
4. Chuvashia
5. Marii-El (Mari)
6. Tatarstan
7. Udmurtia
8. Bashkortostan
9. Adyge
10. Karachaevo-Cherkessia
11. Kabardino-Balkaria
12. North Ossetia
13. Ingushetia
14. Chechnia
15. Daghestan
16. Khal'mg Tangch (Kalmykia)
17. Altai
18. Khakasia
19. Tyva (Tuva)
20. Buryatia
21. Sakha (Yakutia)

Autonomous region

22. Jewish

Autonomous districts

23. Nenetskii
24. Komi-Permiatskii
25. Khanty-Mansiiskii
26. Yamalo-Nenetskii
27. Taimyrskii
28. Evenkskii
29. Aginskii Buryatskii
30. Ust'-Ordynskii Buryatskii
31. Chukotskii
32. Koriakskii

Key to Map 2.

95

3

Ethnic Minorities, Totalitarianism, and Democracy

> There are only two alternatives known to us:
> either a dictatorship or some form of democracy.
> And we do not base our choice on the goodness of
> democracy, which may be doubtful, but solely on
> the evilness of a dictatorship, which is certain.
> —Karl Popper, "The Open Society and Its Enemies Revisted"

The definition of an ethnic or national minority or any other minority is much less obvious than it would seem at first, especially at a time when some states are crumbling, others are being created, and ethnic conflicts acquire bloody forms. The popular, and even scientific, notion of minority is highly variable over time, space, and specific historical situations. *Minority* can be defined as a racial and/or ethnic group different from the numerically dominant one. Or it can mean a racial and/or ethnic group different from the politically dominant one. Sometimes it can even mean a cultural group, such as gays and lesbians, different from one that is currently dominant. Each of these definitions would compel us to designate different groups as minority in any particular social setting. In the United Nations even the general definition of a minority has been debated for more than 40 years, and consensus is still out of reach. To be sure, the Gypsies always constitute an ethnic minority, the *minorité par excellence*, wherever they are, while the Yakuts became such a minority only during the Soviet period of their history, and in their native or ethnic area, where only recently they had been the majority (see chapter 6). Yet there are much less clear-cut cases. The size of the Russian population in the Baltic states or Kazakhstan has shrunk only slightly in recent years. However, under Soviet rule no one viewed the Russians as an ethnic minority in these republics, while nowadays they are relegated to this status there. The Albanians in Kosovo make up about 90 percent of the population, but they can hardly be viewed as an ethnic majority even within this region, since its autonomous status has been virtually abolished, and throughout Serbia the political, cultural, and linguistic status of the Albanians is definitely lower than the status of the dominating nation. Historical examples can also be cited. In the Hapsburg Empire the Austrian Germans, despite being a minority, were the dominant nation; the Magyars also enjoyed great privileges (Barany 1971; Niederhauser 1993), while the rest, even when no fewer in number, were in fact ethnic minorities (Taylor 1948).

In the Soviet Union not only the status of ethnic minority but also sometimes even the official recognition of the very existence of one were matters of arbitrary decision by the state. The all-union and republican powers abolished and created nationalities. The number of nationalities figuring in the Soviet population census and therefore receiving official recognition was continually decreasing. There were 194 nationalities in 1929, 109 in 1939 , 106 in 1970, and 101 in 1979. However, for the 1989 census, the Institute of Ethnography of the Academy of Sciences of the USSR proposed a list of 128 existing nationalities. All these numbers clearly contradicted the number of officially recognized languages in the Soviet Union (more than 130), but such a contradiction until recently never bothered anyone. The decrease in the number of different nationalities in the USSR was officially explained by their merging.

However, for members of given ethnic groups, the question of the recognition or nonrecognition of their nationality status was not a casual one, because a negative decision eliminated whatever cultural or other institutions they may have and condemned them to assimilation. In the southeastern part of Latvia live the Latgals, an ethnic group several hundred thousand in number. Although related to the Latvians, they differ from them in religion and language. Latgals are not Protestants but Catholics, and their language corresponds to Latvian as Belorussian corresponds to Russian. This language in the Soviet period might have been heard in the churches, but it was not taught anywhere in schools for more than 40 years, and "Latvian" was written on Latgal passports.

In Georgia, the Mingrels and Svans were (and still are) refused the right to a separate nationality status; the Kryz, Budugz, and Khinalugs were refused in Azerbaidjan; in Daghestan, the Botligs, Godoberis, Kaitaks, and several others; in Tadjikistan, the Ishkashims, Rushans, Shugnans, and Yazgulems; in Ukraine, the Ruthenians and some other Carpathian groups. At the same time, various ethnic groups in the Altai were arbitrarily and administratively united into one Altai nationality.

Although individuals in the Soviet Union could not voluntarily change their nationality, whole ethnic groups were encouraged or even forced to do so by all-union powers, and especially by republic powers when they considered it expedient to their goals. Over a long period of time, Azerbaidjanian authorities forced members of all the Muslim minorities in the territory of Azerbaidjan, including the Iranian-speaking Talysh and Tats, to be registered as Azerbaidjanians. The Uzbek authorities exerted great pressure on the Uighurs and Tadjiks living in Uzbekistan territory to be registered as Uzbeks. At the same time, the Tadjik authorities registered members of the Pamir ethnic groups as Tadjiks. Since the 1950s, the Bashkir authorities began trying to increase the numbers of the Bashkir people by registering the Tatars living in the western regions of the republic as Bashkirs and even falsifying the census results (Khalim 1988: 238; Korostelev 1994: 80–81). On orders from government bodies, the Veps population of Leningrad and Vologda Oblasts was registered as Russian. A significant number of Crimean Tatars and Meskhetian Turks were forced to register themselves as Uzbeks, Tatars, or members of other nationalities. In the second half of the 1970s and the early 1980s, the mountain Jews living in Daghestan and Kabardino-Balkaria were forced to be registered as Tats; earlier the Krymchaks (the Tatar-speaking Jews) were prompted to drop their Jewish identification (Khazanov 1989).

From this it follows that, if not in every case, in many cases minority and majority statuses are more than just a matter of the arithmetic proportion of various ethnic groups within a certain state. They are also a matter of who holds the political power, and whose language and culture occupy the dominant position in the state. Ethnic minority status is an empirical reality based on the nondominant, and at times the outright subjugated, position of an ethnic group (nationality) in a state, as well as on its wish to preserve and enhance its separate status and, as a rule, on the state's recognition or nonrecognition of this status.

As soon as the intention is declared, the state's attempts to deny the ethnic status of a given minority usually exacerbate the problem instead of solving it. One illustration is the failure of the assimilationist policy conducted by the communist regimes of Bulgaria and Romania in regard to their Turkish and Hungarian minorities. The Bosnian Muslims were repeatedly told that they were only Serbs of the Islamic faith (Bracewell 1993: 148; Ramet 1994); we can presently see just how convincing and successful this claim has been. I will not be at all surprised if in the near future the Adjar also refuse to see themselves as simply Georgians who profess Islam. Initial signs of this seem to be appearing even now.

Yet the moment we encounter an ethnic minority striving to preserve or improve its separate nationality status, we face the phenomenon of nationalism. I would like to begin by pointing out three key characteristics of their nationalism. First, it has an ethnic character. The polysemy of the concept of nation is a known fact (Connor 1994: 90ff.). There are currently at least two main concepts of the nation and nationalism. In some instances the nation is identified with citizenship, and consists of collective sovereignty embodied by the state. In other instances the nation, conceived as an ethnic community, is identified with an ethnic group, nationality, or ethnos in Soviet Russian anthropological terminology, and consists of those who have a distinct ethnic self-consciousness and self-identification. In the second case the nation is but a politicized ethnicity when that ethnicity demands rights of self-determination, autonomy, sovereignty, or statehood. The status of an ethnic minority itself implies that its nationalism is always of an ethnic nature. Second, the nationalism of ethnic minorities is that of late arrivals, or losers, which are essentially one and the same; it is the nationalism of those who have missed the chance or were unable to establish or preserve their own state. Third, it is a goal-directed nationalism, aimed at achieving specific objectives of improving their ethnic position and status. In this it can differ from the nationalism of the dominant nation, which is often not an ethnic but a state or civic doctrine, or one of the ideologies, or merely a sentiment.

At the same time, the nationalism of ethnic minorities has many various aspects. Thus, their nationalism may be divided into cultural, political, and economic dimensions. Brass (1991: 48) asserts that nationalism is a political movement by definition. However, nationalism often emerges as a cultural movement, as a kind of folklorism, a yearning for the days of old, a wish to preserve the local language and culture (Hroch 1985: 22). Consider the nineteenth-century examples of Italy, the Czech lands, the Baltic countries, or Ukraine.[1] Only subsequently does it often grow into political nationalism, especially when it becomes clear that ethnic rights must be fought for (Hall 1993: 11). For this, too, there are more than enough examples. As a rule, minorities never buy tickets to enter multi-ethnic states; for instance, their free choice in joining Russia is but another myth of Soviet historiography. Tilly (1975: 3ff.) estimates that between 1500 and 1950, 475 autonomous political entities disappeared in Europe; most of them were liquidated by force. On the other hand, an exit ticket, or just a comfortable seat in the stalls, does not as a rule come free. What is totally or almost totally lacking are instances of political nationalism retracing its steps and confining itself again to the cultural

---

[1] At the same time, the role of oral tradition in the maintenance of ethnic awareness in mainly illiterate societies should not be underestimated and deserves cross-cultural study. Thus, folk songs and epics which glorified a past not hindered by foreign oppression strengthened a sense of common identity and made it possible for Serbs and Slovaks to assert their uniqueness (Okey 1982: 31–32). It is remarkable how much attention was paid to this oral tradition in Eastern European countries by such educated people as the Serb Vuk Karadˇziˇc, who were influenced by Western European ideas of nationhood.

sphere alone, once it has acquired concrete goals and become a mass movement. I am not referring to cases where minority nationalism is suppressed by force. Yet even in such cases long-range success on the part of the suppressor is far from assured. For decades battles were waged against Ukrainian, Lithuanian, Georgian, Tatar, Croatian, or Eritrean nationalism. The results speak for themselves. The Indian government is still struggling with Kashmir nationalism (i.e., nationalism of Muslims in the Vale of Kashmir), Sri Lanka with the Tamil, China with Tibetan nationalism, and so on. Whether these latter efforts are more successful than the former remains to be seen; they certainly have not been bloodless.

The causes of political nationalism among ethnic minorities are quite clear and have been researched by a number of scholars. Perhaps the best study of the subject was done by Ernest Gellner (1983). His main thesis states that modernization requires homogeneity, including cultural and linguistic unification. Maybe this thesis is stated too categorically and reflects the conviction by state managers that "national integration," which is often understood as a homogenization policy, is necessary for their accumulation and development strategies. Still the thesis is based on reality and means that bearers of the culture and language that are, legally or de facto, the dominant and especially the official ones have an advantage over those who do not belong to this culture, and who must make a special effort to embrace the dominant culture and language. In short, any given state, as a rule, has only one dominant culture; the rest can only be tolerated at best as regional cultures, or, more often, in the form of folk dances and languages spoken at home. In the developed industrial, or "postindustrial," world nothing has changed in this respect.

I need not even mention the cases when belonging to a certain nationality provides a source of direct or hidden privileges or, on the contrary, a source of discrimination; when the government, as in the Soviet Union, uses ethnic origins as a social measuring stick which makes equality of opportunities for ethnic minorities largely a fiction. This situation contains every prerequisite for the emergence of political nationalism, especially when modernization results in the emergence of educated urban strata amongst ethnic minorities who are acutely aware of their unequal status and capable of articulating their groups' demands and objectives.

Yet this is only one side of the issue. The other lies in the fact that modernization is always differential. First, it is uneven; second, its components often occur not simultaneously but sequentially. Certain strata and groups profit from it to a greater extent and more quickly than others. Where the differences are of an ethnic nature, modernization often aggravates ethnic relations. Besides, modernization presupposes mobility. A growing number of people shift locations and occupations. In contrast with traditional societies, in industrial ones children rarely continue their fathers' occupation, let alone their grandfathers'. This disrupts the ethnic division of labor. Horowitz (1985: 113) has expressed the view that the ethnic division of labor is more of a shield than a sword, smoothing rather than fueling interethnic conflicts. Indeed, as long as each ethnic group is firmly entrenched in its economic and social niche, there are fewer grounds for conflict. However, in times of rapid social, economic, and cultural changes we encounter the opposite situation: members of one ethnic group discover that the occupations which hold an increasing appeal for them have already been taken by other ethnic groups further advanced on the road to modernization. In such cases economic and social competition is inevitably transposed to the ethnic plane.

I think the increased ethnic tension in the Caucasus, Central Asia, and Kazakhstan, as well as in some other areas in the CIS, is caused in part by precisely such a situation (see chapter 5). This is not, or not much, a matter of the ill will of separate individuals and groups, of instigators, agitators, chauvinists, or ultranationalists. To be sure, there is no lack of those, but the favorable environment for their motivation and actions is created in part by the objective process of differential modernization.

It is in these situations that ethnicity becomes a political language, and political nationalism turns into a mass movement. Ethnic minorities often strive to become the majority, to grasp political power, to gain independence, to win a dominant place for their language and culture, thereby undercutting the competition of other ethnic groups by placing them in a disadvantageous position.

Much of Western social science had grown up during the first half of the twentieth century along with the belief in the supremacy of the nation-state. Despite the awareness of the historically arbitrary origin of many of them and of the great number of different ethnic groups, the common conviction among social scientists of the 1950s and 1960s was that national identities and boundaries were apt to remain constant. Pakistan's rupture producing Bangladesh was considered an anomaly as "truly stupendous that this instance stands almost alone as the breakdown of an existing post-independence state in the three decades since World War II" (Young 1976: 66). The notion of the melting pot in the United States was extrapolated internationally. It was surmised that the nation-state and modernization would eventually result in assimilation or merging of various ethnic groups and would lead to homogeneity of culture and a secular common identity for the individual citizens.

By the late 1970s and early 1980s this view was threatened. The predominance of ethnic conflict had brought the ascendancy of many existing states into question. It became clear that the only thing unusual about the Bangladesh example was its success in achieving independence. Not infrequently the presumed integrating effects of political and economic developments proved more centrifugal than conjunctive (Nagel 1986:93).

The situation that existed recently in many areas of the USSR is far from unique. It shares many features with the political nationalism of ethnic minorities in other countries, including European ones. Thus, Heiberg (1989) has shown that Basque nationalism arose as a reaction to two processes. First, it was a protest against the type of industrialization that caused the indigenous population to lose control over local resources and to feel imperiled by the influx of alien and, as a rule, better qualified migrants. Second, the Basques were upset with the take-over of real power in their provinces by remote, incompetent, and corrupt central authorities. Interestingly, this displeasure was first formulated and expressed in nationalistic terms, not in villages and not by the local political elite incorporated into the government structure, but by members of the educated urban middle strata. Were we to replace Madrid with Moscow, and the Basques with Tatars and Kazakh, or even with Tuvinians, Yakuts, or Abkhaz (the last named vis-à-vis Tbilisi), we would have a very similar picture. With some important reservations, such a state of affairs is also comparable to that in Czechoslovakia on the eve of its dissolution. True, Slovakia was not flooded by Czech migrants; yet there were widespread complaints that all the key decisions related to the country were made in Prague instead of Bratislava, and with disregard for the country's interests.

We also know about the reverse instances. An ethnic minority more advanced than others on the road of modernization also draws the conclusion that the shortcomings of being part of a multinational state outweigh the advantages. In such cases the emergence of political nationalism is also virtually unavoidable. The Catalans have opted to remain part of Spain, at least at present, because they have gained a status which gives them the upper hand in Catalonia; Slovenians, Croats, and Balts have chosen to break away. Yet in all these cases political nationalism was fueled by similar causes, though, naturally, not by those causes alone.

Finally, about economic nationalism: Economic factors are quite apt to serve as catalytic agents, exacerbators, or the chosen battlegrounds in nationalist conflicts (Connor 1984a: 356). As Nash (1989: 127) noticed: "When economic ends are sought (opportunity, wealth and income redistribution, or claims to ownership of a national patrimony) the ethnic group may approximate a political class and exhibit a form of the class struggle powered by an ethnic ideology, not a false consciousness but often a true appreciation of the existing state of economic affairs." Differential modernization always leads to a certain economic inequality among various ethnic groups within a single state, which in turn facilitates the growth of nationalism. As paradoxical as it may sound, it is the Soviet brand of state socialism that creates the most favorable environment for economic nationalism. The characteristic features of the economic system that existed in the Soviet Union were inherently unbalanced development with an emphasis on functional and branch requirements and a concentration on aggregate production totals rather than on demand served by final products, systematically distorted valuations (prices), and actual disregard for regional and ethnic factors—hence, the endless and inconclusive debate on who was subsidizing and exploiting whom (Ericson 1992: 258–59). When the so-called center, identified with the ethnic majority, is in sole control of natural resources, investments, subsidies, migration and economic policy, taxation, local budgeting, infrastructure and education, then, whether justified or not, the thought appears: "we" are exploited and discriminated against, and "we" would be better off without "them." This goes hand-in-hand with the claim: our resources belong to us, and to us alone.

National movements are always shaped by the distinctive sociopolitical and economic features of the countries where they take place. One of the factors strengthening ethnic nationalism in many ex-Soviet regions is the temporary alliance between the opportunistic political elites striving to retain power and the urban middle strata trying to ensure the dominant position of their ethnic cultures.

The hypertrophied role of the state only intensifies nationalist aspirations. At the end of perestroika it became obvious that nationalism was directly linked to statism. Every nationality, every ethnic minority, wished to gain a bigger slice of the state pie and a maximum number of decision-making positions, while believing that the ideal prerequisite for that was to gain sovereignty, statehood, and at least the highest possible autonomy. Incidentally, the very desirability of having positions in the administration, rather than, for example, in business or industry or other spheres of activity, is due to more than the nature of the Soviet totalitarian regime with its monopoly on production and distribution. It is also a testimony to the incompleteness of the modernizing process. In effect, this is a situation common to Third World countries.

Now it is time to return to the main question of why it is difficult to reduce the political nationalism of ethnic minorities, once it has arisen, to a purely cultural movement. It is true that, in modern liberal democracies, violation of individual rights on the basis of ethnic affiliation is supposed to be reduced to a minimum, although, even there, being a member of the ethnic majority bestows a number of practical advantages. For example, in none of the democratic states does an ethnic minority enjoy a real linguistic and cultural equality, which even from the practical point of view is possible in rare cases only. The democratic practice of majority rule and representational government can also weaken the political influence and encroach on the interests of ethnic minorities. The example of Switzerland—where even though the German-speaking Swiss constitute about 65 percent of the population, the entire populace is multilingual, and there is no single state language—is a rather distinctive situation which is reflective of that country's history and political setup. Swiss federalism allows citizens in minority cantons to protect their interests through such nonmajoritarian practices as the referendum procedure on federal legislation (Rogowski 1974: 127ff.; McRae 1988).

Therefore, the active part of ethnic minorities often concludes that their interests are best protected through corporate participation in the political process. This tactic does not always succeed. For example, even though political nationalism has existed for many decades in Scotland, it remains a rather weak force. However, by achieving even partial success ethnic activists are able to win many new followers, and political nationalism has a chance to grow.

All multiethnic states face the problem of choosing the policy that will convince not only the individual citizen but also every ethnic group that its treatment by the government and other ethnic groups is just and fair. Alas, achieving this in reality is extremely difficult, not to say impossible. Connor (1984b: 485) seems to have defined this dilemma the best: how to find the universal formula for achieving equality among unequals. Just like this scholar, I am afraid that such a universal formula simply does not exist, and this is borne out by the history of ethnic relations and ethnic conflicts not only in the Soviet Union but also in other contemporary states.

Nor is such a formula, one that is capable of satisfying all ethnic groups in a multiethnic state, likely to be worked out by applying the same criteria to these groups and the same principles of abstract equality and justice. No matter how noble these principles are, in reality ethnic groups are not equal, and their interests not only do not coincide but often directly contradict each other. Consider such areas as the language policy, religion, education, regional development, affirmative action, control over economic resources, environmental issues, demographic and migration policies, representation in legislative and executive branches of power, and even foreign policy.

As Gellner (1992: 250-53) noticed, nationalism invokes a number of conflicting principles: the principle of majority, the principle of territorial and historical continuity, and several others. Wherever ethnic strife exists, any argument from one side triggers two more from the opposing side, and so on *ad infinitum*, where each side has its own notion of justice. Even international law is often powerless in this respect, since it is itself ambiguous in the extreme. The right of nations and peoples to self-determination essentially contradicts the principle of inviolable state borders and the state's sovereign rights to its territory (cf. Articles 1, II, and 2, IV, of the United Nations Charter). No wonder the international normative order is very cautious with respect to the scope, limits, and application of the right of self-determination; an exception is made only for the cases of decolonization (Cassesse 1986; Mayall 1990; Buchanan 1991). The arbitrariness of such an attitude is proved by the fact that the Soviet Union was considered a colonial power only by those who had little voice in the international system of nations.

Likewise, the attempt to suppress the rebellious Chechen republic undertaken by the Russian government is considered by the West an internal Russian matter. The double standards are still valid. In fact, Chechnia is no more a part of Russia than Ireland was a part of England or Algeria was a part of France. The Chechens have a distinct culture, language, and national consciousness, and they constitute an absolute majority in their native area. Chechnia was conquered by the Russian Empire only in the 1860s, after the long and bloody Caucasian war, and the Chechens always remained the staunchest adversaries of the Russian rule in the North Caucasus. Actually, they were never completely subjugated either by the Russians or by the Soviets.

Chechnia was always kept by force, and the Russian claims that this country is an integral part of the Russian Federation are dubious not only from the historical but also from the legal point of view, because the republic refused to sign the Federal Treaty. Actually, her current ambiguous status is but another proof of the arbitrariness of the Soviet nationality policy. Had Chechnia been granted the status of a union republic rather than an autonomous republic within the Soviet Union, it would already be recognized as an independent state. The fact that at present Chechnia's clear desire to become independent is treated by the Western powers not as a national-liberation and anti-colonial movement but as a secessionist one is connected only with pragmatic political considerations, not with any objective criteria.

Still, the indigenous peoples' declaration of rights adopted by the United Nations on December 18, 1992, departs from the principle of equal rights and opportunities for all the citizens of a given state. It is interesting, though hardly accidental, that the declaration actually ignored the question of who is and is not to be considered an indigenous people. One may wonder whether or not, in the post-Soviet context, those Russians who settled in Yakutia, or in Azerbaidjan very long ago, or some Georgians who lived in Abkhazia for generations can be considered indigenous populations there.

Likewise, any suggestions aimed at overcoming the deficiencies of majoritarian democracy in plural societies by federal arrangements based on ethnic (nationality) principles (Bakvis 1987), or on consociational formulas under which ethnic groups in plural states share power as corporate communities (Lijphart 1977; van den Berghe 1981; for their criticism see Brass 1991: 332ff.; Barry 1991: 100ff.), or any other arrangement connected with territorial and/or cultural autonomy, lack a universal validity not only worldwide but also often even within one and the same state.

No wonder history and contemporary development in different parts of the world have brought some scholars to the sad conclusion that the spiral of escalating ethnic mobilization is an inevitable process in a plural society which, "constrained by the preferences of its citizens, does not provide fertile soil for democratic values or stability" (Rabushka and Shepsle 1972: 92).[2] Of course, everything would be much simpler if all the ethnic groups were of a comparable size, were to possess a compact territory and the same type of social structure, and were on a comparable level of economic and cultural development. In this case any of them, if they wish, could found an independent state with relatively little damage to others, or negotiate with other partners in creating some form of an association or federation from equal positions. Unfortunately, such a case is more a rare exception than a general rule, and for this reason alone the Czechoslovakian type of divorce is much rarer than the Yugoslavian type.

Another approach to this dilemma, already tried by Marxist doctrine, is the attempt to diminish the role of ethnic differences by inflating those of class. As we know now, this policy has proved ineffective, and not only because reality in the communist countries contradicted theory, or because, as Orwell put it, "All animals are equal, but some animals are more equal than others." Taken to its logical extreme, this principle leads to a denial of group rights based on ethnic principles. Ethnic differences are tolerated only as an inevitable yet temporary evil. After all, Marxism claims that ethnicity is only a passing phenomenon and that ultimately all nations are bound to merge into one, and before that to draw closer. However, when this policy is consistently put into practice, the tangible advantages of belonging to the ethnic majority, and the disadvantages of belonging to a minority, only increase. Assimilation can be forced or im-

---

[2] Compare this with Mill's (1975: 382) conclusion made more than 100 years ago: In multiethnic states "the influences which form opinions and decide political acts, are different in the different sections of the country. An altogether different set of leaders have the confidence of one part of the country and of another. . . . The same incidents, the same acts, the same system of government, affect them in different ways. . . . That any one of them feels aggrieved by the policy of the common ruler, is sufficient to determine another to support that policy."

posed or even made advantageous to an individual, but it is never a completely voluntary process; the strong always assimilate the weak, not the other way around. Where ethnic minorities are already self-conscious participants in the political process, the option of assimilation is generally not feasible (Weiner 1971: 182).

Ethnic differences and ethnic feelings cannot be eradicated at any given moment by either human or historical laws. Humiliation, even imaginary or overblown, never spells genuine consent; it spells only anger and hatred. In the early 1980s, in the industrial regions of Bashkiria, where Russian migrants became the majority, even saying hello to someone on a tram in the Bashkir language was perceived as a manifestation of nationalism (Khalim 1988: 243). Moldavians have often heard the following crude rebuke from the Russian population: "Come on, speak like a human being, in Russian, and don't twitter" (*Izvestiia*, August 19, 1989). On numerous occasions in different Baltic republics, I witnessed the Russians, tourists and permanent residents alike, demanding that the local population speak with them in the "Great Russian language." Now the same Russians complain about bad feelings toward them. One does not have to follow Shils (1957) or Geertz (1963) to agree that Barth (1969) and other instrumentalists have somewhat overshot the mark. Where ethnicity is concerned, culture, history, tradition, psychological factors, and emotions cannot be disregarded. In any given case one finds in ethnicity primordialist, instrumentalist, and constructivist sides. Ethnicity, though open to manipulation and exploitation, is not only a possible strategy; on the individual level it may also be a mental state (Royce 1982).

If I am right, and a universal ethnic policy in multiethnic states is impossible, then the only alternative is the possibility of a differential policy. Despite its many shortcomings, stemming from a certain departure from the principle of equal treatment of all ethnic groups, I view this approach as the most realistic in some cases.

Let me attempt to illustrate my point in the Russian context. Three distinctive features of the Russian Federation as a multiethnic state make the problem of its ethnic minorities a unique one. First, these minorities vary greatly in their population size, socioeconomic development, degree of dispersal, ratio to other ethnic groups in their homeland areas, and all the other aspects. Correspondingly, the positions and demands of these minorities also range widely: from the wish to gain maximum economic or even political independence, to the endeavor to have no more than a real cultural autonomy or simply the conditions to survive as a distinct ethnic group. (See table 3.1, p. 253.)

Second, of the 21 republics of the Russian Federation, titular nationalities constitute a majority in only 8 of them, while in 10 of them their share is about 30 percent or even less.

Third, once the federative character of the Russian state is recognized in principle, it must be admitted that this federation possesses a number of distinctive, historically formed characteristics. Unlike the United States, Germany, or Australia, Russia constitutes not a territorial but an ethnic-territorial federation. Whether this is good or bad is pointless to debate. This was decided by history, and I do not think that the practice of blaming the Bolsheviks for this arrangement, rather widespread in Russia nowadays, is justified; they simply had no choice. Be that as it may, this is the present reality, and attempts to change it trigger the resistance of non-Russian members of the federation, that is, the ethnic minorities. Political scientists have already noticed the molding effects of federal institutions. Once the federal (in the Soviet and Russian contexts, actually pseudofederal) systems are in place, they are able to ensure their own survival even while profound changes in the underlying society are going on (Bakvis and Chandler 1987: 314–17).

Nevertheless, some Russian social scientists (see, for example, V. Kozlov 1993: 62; Kukushkin 1993: 164) now call for the substitution of so-called national-cultural autonomy, of the type long ago propagated by the Austro-Marxists and for pragmatic reasons condemned by Lenin, for a national-territorial (or better, in the Russian context, an ethnic-territorial) one. The project of the Russian Constitution, suggested by the prominent Russian liberal politicians Popov and Sobchak, also implied the replacement of territorial for cultural autonomies (*Nezavisimaia gazeta*, January 26, 1993). In 1992, the policy of a gradual transition from national-territorial to national-cultural autonomies was apparently contemplated by the Russian State Committee for Nationalities. However, it was criticized at the closed meeting of the Russian government (*Nezavisimaia gazeta*, September 26, 1992), and the project was abandoned. Tishkov, the Russian anthropologist and former minister for nationality policy, is at present more realistic, admitting that in the Russian condition a national-cultural autonomy can only supplement but not replace a national-territorial one (Tishkov 1993b: 56–58). Still, the gradual transition from a national-territorial to a national-cultural principle of the state structure declared by Yeltsin in his 1994 Message to the Federal Assembly indicates that this idea is gaining support among the Russian ruling elite. Among others, it is also actively supported and propagated in numerous publications by many Russian anthropologists from the Institute of Ethnology and Anthropology of the Russian Academy of Sciences.

However, in Russia only dispersed nationalities wish to acquire cultural autonomy, which they still lack; the rest strive to retain territorial autonomy and demand an ascription of special political rights to compensate for their unequal circumstances. Once the link between an ethnic minority and a definite territory has been legally recognized and asserted through concrete measures, it is virtually impossible to change the situation in a voluntary fashion. The ethnic minority that has acquired preferential rights to or within a definite territory is unlikely to surrender these rights. Recall the outcome of the liquidation of the Hungarian autonomous region in Romania; or the factual liquidation of Albanian autonomy in Kosovo; or, what is more relevant, the Georgian-Ossetian and Georgian-Abkhazian conflicts. I believe that not only humanitarian concerns for ethnic minorities, implying some compensation for the disadvantages of belonging to a minority, but pragmatic considerations of political stability as well, often give reference to a degree of departure from the principle of universal equality for all citizens throughout a given state. While by themselves these advantages certainly cannot abolish the separatist tendencies of an ethnic minority, they can considerably weaken them. When the consequences of a divorce appear worse than the shortcomings of preserving the marriage, political nationalism may be absent or aimed at other objectives. Yet in order for this to happen, there must be the certainty or hope that the cultural, economic, and to some extent even political goals of ethnic nationalism are compatible with the multiethnic state, and that the given ethnic minority can have a real voice in the political process, at least in its own part of the country. Incidentally, even many of the liberal Western democracies are far from making an absolute out of the principle of universal equality, and grant certain preferential rights to ethnic minorities, including those related to their right to certain territories.

To come back to Russia, I see no single formula capable of taking into account and satisfying the interests of all the ethnic minorities residing there; the positioned differences are too wide between the Tatars and the Chukchi, the Tuvinians and the Cherkes, the Yakuts and the Khanty. This leaves only the possibility of a negotiating process, which should take into account the interests of each separate ethnic minority. Of course, suggesting this solution is much easier than implementing it in reality. Yet if we admit that politics is the art of the possible, then ethnic peace is a part of negotiated political culture; it can be managed and maintained only through arranged and rearranged compromises. It seems that the differential approach is the best way of meeting this objective. However, the Russian leadership, judging by the recently passed constitution and a series of other practical steps, seems to have a different opinion on the subject. The new Russian Constitution buries the Federal Treaty, under which the autonomous republics of the Russian Federation received a number of state prerogatives. No wonder that, of 21 republics, 10 opposed its adoption. In the August 12, 1993, referendum, the majority of the electorate in Bashkortostan, Tyva, Chuvashia, Mordovia, Kalmykia, Khakassia, Daghestan, and Karachaevo-Cherkessia voted against the adoption of this constitution; in Tatarstan and Chechnia the referendum did not take place at all.

At approximately the same time when Karl Marx proclaimed that in the near future ethnic differences would become irrelevant, John Stuart Mill (1975: 382) came to the conclusion that democracy is all but impossible in a country composed of different nationalities. Marx is known for being too much of an optimist; it is to be hoped that Mill was too pessimistic in his prognosis. At any rate, purely empirical observations show that liberal democracies, despite their numerous deficiencies, provide the most favorable conditions for ethnic minorities. As Winston Churchill once said, democracy is the worst form of government with the exception of all the others. The situation of ethnic minorities in many Western countries is far from ideal, even deteriorating in some of them over the past years; yet on the whole it is still better than in other regions throughout the world. Despite the Basque problem, the nationality issue is much less acute in today's Spain than it was during the Franco period. Whether Quebec remains a part of Canada or secedes, the outcome will almost certainly be free of bloodshed and civil war. So far, the tension between the Flemish and Waloon communities in Belgium is held in check through negotiated compromise.

Contemporary social science wisdom states that democracy, or rather the civil society without which liberal democracy is impossible, if it does not abolish, often weakens the threat of ethnic corporatism. Authoritarian and totalitarian regimes magnify the conflict, while liberalism is sometimes capable of diffusing it. Civil society not only guarantees but implies awareness and participation in the political process; it is based on agreement and the search for compromise. This is a necessary condition for its very existence. Based on a multitude of voluntary associations, civil society ideally provides its citizens with the opportunity to have a number of identifications and loyalties at once, and ethnic affiliation is only one of them. Besides, a multiplicity of groups which criss-cross each other reduces the centrality of any particular group (Bentley 1967). However, in order to function efficiently in a multiethnic environment, democracy needs an overall national consensus, which is impossible without a constantly negotiated and renegotiated ethnic consensus. I would very much like to think, though so far this is much more a desire than a scientific prognosis, that post-totalitarianism in the former communist countries will prove merely a transitional step toward liberal democracy, and that the emergence of civil society will in the long run relieve the tension in interethnic relations more efficiently than the totalitarian regimes which preceded it.

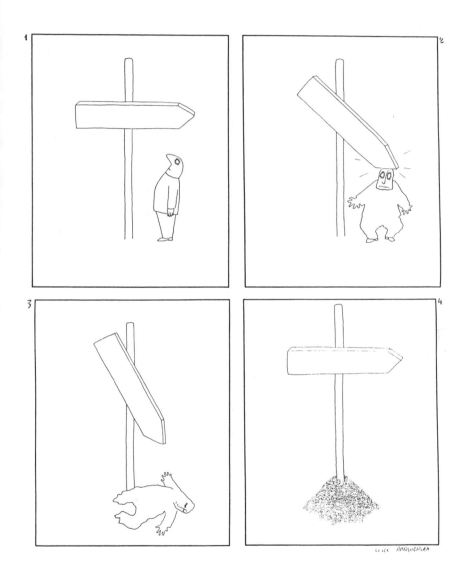

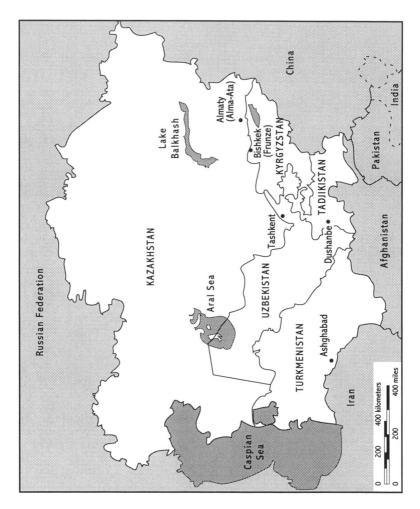

Map 3. Central Asia and Kazakhstan

4

Central Asia on a Path from the Second to the Third World

> Those who cannot remember the past
> are condemned to repeat it.
> —George Santayana, *Reason in Common Sense*

> The past is never dead, it is not even past.
> —William Faulkner

At present, Central Asia and Kazakhstan are overburdened by their past. The region's pasts are still alive and often complement one another: the precolonial past represented by what is sometimes called survivals of the traditional, or preindustrial, society; the past of the prerevolutionary colonial period; and, last but not least, the recent past of Soviet imperialism.

Of all the numerous problems that Central Asia and Kazakhstan are facing now, the most important one remains their underdevelopment (Dienes 1987: 121ff.; Rumer 1989; Allworth 1990; Critchlow 1991a; Fierman 1991; Manz 1994). Modernization was pursued in this region with a minimal participation by the native population, and none of its processes—industrialization, urbanization, the demographic revolution, the revolution in education, and occupational mobility—was fully implemented there. The so-called interregional division of labor policy carried out by the Moscow center clearly contradicted the interests of Central Asia and Kazakhstan, because it condemned the region to the role of a supplier of raw materials which left the region for other parts of the country, mainly in unprocessed form. The subsidies that the center paid Central Asian republics were only partial compensation for the profits made from unequal exchange with them. (See figure 4.1, p. 256 and figure 4.2, p. 257.)

Thus, less than 10 percent of the produced cotton remained in Central Asian republics (Ziiadullaev 1989). Varieties of Uzbek cotton were specially picked in a way that suited the textile mills in Ivanovo, in Central Russia. The local population still has to buy textiles made from its own cotton but produced in European parts of the former USSR. Nevertheless, in the period between 1970 and 1991 the center reduced its capital investments in Central Asian industry by more than a third, although Central Asia's output per capita made up only about 50 percent of the country's overall average and was continuing to drop (*Pravda vostoka,* August 30, 1989). While per capita state investments of capital in the Russian Federation were 119.5 percent of the all-union average for the years 1981–1985, and 123.1 percent for the years 1986–1988, in Uzbekistan they were correspondingly 63.9 and 48.2 percent; in Kirgizia (now Kyrgyzstan) 48.2 and 44.8 percent; and in Tadjikistan, 43.3 and 42.7 percent (*Statisticheskie materialy* . . . 1989: 317).

Underdevelopment in Central Asia

The limited industrialization of the region has been accompanied not so much by the creation of an indigenous working class as by the attraction of a work force from the European parts of the USSR. During the construction of industrial complexes, neither local needs nor local traditions were taken into account. As a result, the area contains large, heavy industry enterprises, entire industrial branches, even entire cities with the indigenous population constituting the minority, and, until recently, industrial revenues never reached the local budget (Arifkhanova 1989: 1; Rywkin 1982: 52–54). People of European origin are still the main backbone of the skilled work force and scientific-technical personnel. All the large enterprises, electric stations, oil wells, mines, railroads, aviation, and means of mass communication that were created during the Soviet period were served by engineers, technicians, and skilled workers from the industrial centers of Russia, Ukraine, and Belorussia, attracted to Central Asia by higher wages, and the possibility of receiving an apartment and good promotions (Pulatov 1990a: 7). (See figure 4.3, p. 258 and figure 4.4, p. 259.)

It is true that industrial labor is not prestigious in the eyes of the indigenous population, who prefer to be involved in trades and services. In the past, however, even those who wished to take blue-collar jobs were never given a fair chance. They were not considered sufficiently qualified, but at the same time they had limited opportunities to learn a trade (Sredniaia Aziia i Kazakhstan ... 1989: 24, 26, 41). Until recently, in the cities of Fergana Oblast it was even forbidden to employ rural people (*Pravda,* October 14, 1989).

Sixty to 65 percent of the indigenous population in Central Asia is still employed in agriculture, and complaints have often been heard that the movement of the rural population to the cities is made more difficult because of the number of Russians and other people of European origin who have settled there (see chapter 5). In Kyrgyzstan the Kyrgyz make up only 20 percent of the industrial workers and a much lower percentage in management and engineering (Soper 1988: 4). In fact, in 1991, the Kyrgyz accounted for only 8 percent of skilled workers and 3 percent of engineers and technicians in the republic (Filonyk 1994: 152; Sitnianskii 1994: 97). In Kazakhstan's industrial sector Kazakhs constitute only 21 percent, and in Tadjikistan's industrial sector Tadjiks constitute about 25 percent (Niyazi 1994: 170).

Moreover, during the Soviet period, since a good command of Russian remained a necessary requirement for social advancement and career promotion in almost all spheres of professional activity, particularly in the cities, it placed members of Central Asian nationalities in an even more unequal position in comparison with Russians, and in this way only intensified ethnic competition. In 1988, in the capital of Kirgizia, Frunze (now Bishkek), there was only one Kyrgyz-language school (*Izvestiia,* March 21, 1988). By 1990 there were three. In Tashkent, the capital of Uzbekistan, it was impossible to send a telegram or call an ambulance in the Uzbek language. Even employment applications had to be written only in Russian (*Izvestiia,* July 22, 1989).

In agriculture everything was subject to the central-imposed cotton monospecialization with the most disastrous repercussions on the economy, living conditions, and environment of Central Asia (Rumer 1987: 75–76). In the main oases the share of irrigated land sown with cotton was approximately 70 percent, and under direct orders from Moscow this continued to expand until recently. This was at the expense of the cultivation of grain, fruit, and vegetables and the production of meat and milk for local consumption, and even limited the size of family plots, from which *kolkhozniks* (collective farmers) got the lion's share of their food and income. The allotment of land for the construction of new housing in the rural regions also became a serious problem (Khazanov 1990a: 20ff.).

In Central Asia a kind of ethnic division of labor exists also in agriculture. While the native population in large part supplies the unskilled labor for cotton cultivation and pastoral production, ethnic minorities such as Russians, Ukrainians, Koreans, and Tatars, among others, prefer to be occupied in other, more mechanized branches of agriculture demanding more skilled labor (Brusina 1990: 20ff.).

A shortage of land and water in addition to ethnic competition for a limited number of jobs has resulted in growing tension in the areas with a mixed population, not only between the indigenous population and settlers and migrants of European origin, but also between the indigenous population and some Muslim ethnic minorities, such as Crimean Tatars, Meskhetian Turks, and Chechens (see chapters 7 and 8) as well as between different native nationalities. In regard to this fighting between native nationalities, one can refer to the violent conflict over land and water rights involving thousands of Tadjiks and Kyrgyz on the border between their two republics in the summer of 1989 (*Kommunist Tadjikistana,* May 31, June 28, July 15 and 21, 1989; *Pravda,* July 16, 1989), or to the brutal and bloody fighting between Kyrgyz and Uzbeks in the Osh Oblast of Kirgizia in the summer of 1990, which took at least several hundred lives (Brown 1990b: 16–18; Stepovoi and Shipit'ko 1990).

The system of education in Central Asia is also inferior to that in other parts of the former Soviet Union. One of the reasons mechanization of cotton production remains low is the former Soviet regime's ability to mobilize the almost unpaid labor of school children and students. For many years during my fieldwork in different parts of Central Asia, I met them while they worked in the fields, forced to bend their backs at the time that their counterparts in other areas of the Soviet Union enjoyed their vacations or attended classes. As a result of this practice and the neglected school system, the quality of secondary education in the rural areas is very low (Olcott 1990: 266–67).

The situation is further aggravated by the region's population explosion. Although during the last 15 years the birthrates of most Central Asian ethnic groups decreased, they still remain very high and correspond not to the Western model but to that of Third World countries (Olcott 1990: 262–63, table IA-IC). Since 1951, the population of Central Asia has more than tripled to 33 million in 1989. In 1989, more than 50 percent of the population was below age 19. There are many reasons for this situation, including low urbanization, unmechanized and labor-consuming agriculture, early marriages, a tradition in which younger members of the family support the elders, the influence of Islam, and, last but not least, pressure from tradition-oriented public opinion. From my fieldwork in different parts of Central Asia, I know that some women and men there, particularly from the urban middle strata, would like to use contraceptives and limit their number of children, but they are afraid to do it because this would expose them to condemnation by their relatives and neighbors. As a result, the region is experiencing an agrarian overpopulation. In Kyrgyzstan, arable land per one rural dweller amounts to only 0.5 hectare, in Uzbekistan it is 0.36 hectare, and in Tadjikistan 0.22 hectare (Zaionchkovskaia 1994: 3). (See table 4.1, p. 260.)

Taking all these factors into account, it should not be surprising that the area is affected by another social scourge of Third World countries—

growing underemployment and unemployment. In the 1980s, Central Asia's population grew three times faster than the number of jobs. Although Soviet statistics were not particularly precise, they revealed that in the late 1980s Central Asia and Kazakhstan had several million unemployed persons (Peterson 1987: 5, 7 n. 27). According to the most cautious estimations, by 1990, unemployment had increased to 12.5 percent, even without taking into account the unemployed mothers of many children (Zaionchkovskaia 1994: 3). In Fergana Oblast alone, one out of five youngsters entering the job market could not find employment (Bekker 1989). In 1990, in Turkmenistan unemployment was 18.8 percent (Carlson 1991: 5); in Tadjikistan, even higher. Nevertheless, the Soviet leadership acknowledged that it could not (or would not) create jobs fast enough to keep pace with the population growth. Already in the 1970s the work force in Uzbekistan grew by 250,000 persons a year, while the number of jobs outside the agricultural sector increased by only 100,000 a year (Rumer 1987: 86).

The rural population of Central Asia and Kazakhstan is usually characterized by low mobility even within their own republics. Thus, in Uzbekistan, in 1989 only 9 out of each 1,000 people moved from rural areas to cities, while in the Soviet Union in general this figure amounted to 33 (Brusina 1990: 30 n. 7). It is not only an adherence to a traditional way of life and occupations which hinders migration from villages to cities. It is easier to support big families in the village because there an individual can rely on the support of one's relatives and neighbors (communal reciprocal ties still play a very important role in Central Asia), and on the allocation of the family plot. These plots, although very small in 1987 and 1988, provided the Uzbek peasants with more than 22 percent of their income—and this according to official and therefore understated statistics (*Pravda vostoka,* November 27, 1988).

However, sometimes figures are deceptive. It is true that in the 1980s and 1990s the ratio between the rural and urban population remained almost the same. But given the particularly high birthrates in the rural regions, in practice this means that hundreds of thousands of people migrated to the cities. Thus, Bishkek, the capital of Kyrgyzstan, is at present surrounded by a ring of poor squatter districts without roads, electricity, or running water. With the emergence of these districts, since 1989 the territory of the city has increased almost twice. Sixty to 90 percent of their population does not have permanent jobs (*Vechernii Bishkek,* May 7, 1993).

In professional, educational, and linguistic respects new migrants to Central Asian cities are at a disadvantage and meet strong competition from other ethnic groups. They face the same problems that recent migrants from rural areas face in cities of some developing countries of Africa, Asia, and Latin America. It is just these people, unemployed and often homeless, who constitute a new and growing underclass in Central Asian cities (Galiev 1990: 127–28; Kostiukova 1994: 87–92; Fridman and Karazkas 1994: 15). Dissatisfied, alienated, angry, and sometimes desperate, they are often particularly hostile toward the Russians and other ethnic minorities and prove to be particularly prone to extremism, violence, and crimes. (See table 4.2, p. 261.)

It is no wonder, then, that Central Asia and Kazakhstan belong to the poorest areas of the former Soviet Union, and the standard of living there continues to deteriorate. In 1987 per capita income in Uzbekistan amounted to only 58 percent of the average Soviet income, or to 62 percent, if external revenue is taken into account (Bogdanov 1988: 27; Yu. Novikov 1990: 11). In 1988, the average per capita income of more than half of the Uzbeks and Tadjiks was below the official Soviet subsistence level, estimated at 78 rubles per month, while in Russia only 6.3 percent of the population had an income below this poverty mark (Kovalev 1989: 11; Niyazi 1994: 168). Per capita meat consumption in the rural areas of Uzbekistan was 8 kilograms per year, whereas the official Soviet average was 62 kilograms (Sheehy 1989c: 20); per capita consumption of milk, fruit, and vegetables was about a half of the Soviet average (Ziiadullaev 1989: 36; Kabilov 1989: 43). In 1990, in Turkmenistan, 40 percent of workers' families and 50 percent of *kolkhozniks'* families lived below the official poverty line (Salamatov 1990: 13). In Kyrgyzstan in 1994, the situation was even worse, since 65 percent of the whole population lived below the poverty line (*Monitor* 5 [22, October 28, 1994]: 15).

An inadequate diet, the low quality of unpurified drinking water, the lack of proper sewage systems, the excessive use of toxic agricultural chemicals that have contaminated the water, soil, and food (Uzbekistan used 54 kilograms of pesticides per hectare, while in the Baltic republics this figure was as low as 0.3 kilograms; see Rudenko 1989: 45), and primitive medical facilities result in the spread of various diseases and in a drastic increase in still-births, births of deformed children, and infant mortality (Iablokov 1988: 35–36; Velsanar 1990: 7). Infant mortality in this region is so great that in 1990 a secret instruction was issued not to register infants until they were three months old in order to "correct" the appalling statistics.[1]

In 1989, the infant mortality in Turkmenistan was 54.6 per 1,000 births, twice the USSR average; in Tashauz Oblast the figure was 64 per 1,000

---

[1] I received this information from some members of the Russian Parliament during my visit to the Soviet Union in the summer of 1990.

(Salamatov 1990: 13; Carlson 1991: 36). The situation is worse only in the Philippines, Nigeria, Angola, Chad, and in Karakalpakia, an autonomous republic in Uzbekistan, where 92 infants die out of every 1,000 born alive; of every 100 children there, 83 are born with defects. By 1989 the average life expectancy in Karakalpak villages was between 38 and 42 years, whereas in the Soviet Union as a whole it was 69 (Bohr 1989: 22). In 1990, a Karakalpak writer, T. Kaipbergenov, offered the following explanation for the absence of open protest in Karakalpakia: "All efforts of our people are focused on one thing—how to survive. We are incapable of doing anything, of being angry or looking for the culprits. We just cannot think of anything else but how to survive, how to save ourselves" (*Sovetskaia kultura*, March 31, 1990). (See figure 4.5, p. 262.)

In the last few years the public health sector throughout the region has been hit hard by the lack of funds and supplies. Long-forgotten diseases, such as malaria, tuberculosis, diphtheria, and polio, have begun to reappear.

As if all these problems were not enough, Central Asia and Kazakhstan now face an additional one: the area is literally on the brink of ecological catastrophe. Despite all the lip service paid to the need to intensify the cotton production, virtually the only way to increase it—besides a corresponding reduction in areas under all other crops or in pastures and family plots belonging to collective farmers—was to reclaim new lands, which led to the building of more irrigation systems. From 1965 to 1985, 2.5 million hectares of new land were cultivated and used mostly for cotton. As a result, cotton production increased to 75 or even 80 percent of total agricultural production, while worldwide this figure is never higher than 50 percent. However, Central Asia has limited water resources, and cotton production has already consumed outrageous amounts of water. Out of the 120–127 cubic kilometers of water that make up the overall river volume in the area, irrigation in general claims nearly 90 cubic kilometers. Of these 90 cubic kilometers approximately 60–65 are used for cotton (Wolfson 1990: 30–35; Reznichenko 1992: 40).

Such a system of reclamation inevitably results in the loss of some of the old cultivated lands (Yu. Novikov 1990: 31). Despite the absurdity of this situation, it has its own logic, though it is not based on any sound economic principle. An obsolete irrigation network (some canals, such as the Dargom in the Samarkand District and the Salar in the Tashkent region, have existed for 2,000 years) and exhausted salinized soils, on which crops are not rotated, simply cannot produce more. Irrigated lands in Central Asia have already lost 40 percent of their productivity. In Uzbekistan, 415,000–7,000,000 hectares of agricultural lands have become salinized; in Turkmenistan, 416,000–1,000,000 hectares (more than half of all irrigated land in the republic); and in Kazakhstan, 650,000 hectares (Khodzhamuradov 1984: 49; Latifi 1988).

The reclamation of this salinized land demands extensive capital investment and a reduction in the output of cotton, something Moscow was extremely unwilling to undertake and the leaders of Central Asian republics at present are unable to attempt. For the same reasons the new irrigation systems were built in total disregard of modern water-saving technology, and without appropriate drainage systems, cement facing of the canals, distilling stations, and so on. While in Israel the average efficiency of irrigation systems is 0.9, in Uzbekistan it ranges between 0.3 and 0.35. Correspondingly, in Israel the average amount of water required to produce 1 kilogram of raw cotton is 1.2–1.5 cubic meters, whereas in Central Asia 10 cubic meter are required (Wolfson 1990: 31).

The situation is particularly serious in the western parts of Central Asia and Kazakhstan. Cotton has drained the Aral Sea. It is quickly drying up because its two tributaries, the Syr Darya and Amu Darya Rivers, are completely diverted to irrigate the cotton fields. In the early 1960s there were more than 1,000 cubic kilometers of water in the Aral Sea; today, hardly more than 400–450 cubic kilometers remain there. During the last two or three decades its level diminished to 14 meters, and more and more often the sea is called Aral Kum (the Aral Desert; literally, "the Aral sand"). If urgent measures are not undertaken immediately, by the year 2005 the Aral Sea will cease to exist (Shermukhamedov 1990: 5ff.; Reznichenko 1992: 41; Micklin 1991: 42ff.). However, members of the Soviet leadership were reluctant to take any steps because they would have decreased the output of cotton. It looks as if they quietly wrote off the Aral Sea. Meanwhile, strong winds lift approximately 200,000 tons of sand intermixed with salt from the dry sea bed every day. While heavier particles are deposited on settlements 500 kilometers away from the Aral Sea, lighter particles are carried much greater distances (*Pravda vostoka,* September 3, 1989; Zuev 1991).

This is certainly a national tragedy with unpredictable consequences. The Uzbek poet Jamal Kamal (1992: 41) bemoans it in the following verses:

> Of a thousand children, a hundred die,
> Their mothers' hearts broken,
> Clear air, clean water nowhere
> in our land;
> Our soil poisoned,
> Do you care?

> Cotton grows where orchards and
> meadows were,
> I tell the truth, I do not lie,
> Fruits and meat in our villages
> nowhere,
> Tell me is this fair?
> Do you care?

Salinization of the area is accompanied by its desertification. The Kazakh steppes have been suffering from serious erosion ever since Khrushchev's virgin lands campaign. In addition, overgrazing without a seasonal rotation of pastures and a trend from multispecies to monospecies herd composition have turned vast areas of fertile pastures in Kazakhstan and Turkmenistan into sand deserts (Kotliakov, Zonn, and Chernyshev 1988: 63). Desertification in Central Asia and Kazakhstan advances on a scale comparable to those in the Sahara and the Sahel. In the past the Kara Kum and Kyzyl Kum Deserts occupied less than 24 percent of the total area of Central Asia and Kazakhstan. By now, active desertification has claimed an additional 35–40 percent of the area (Wolfson 1990: 41–42).

Ethnic Identities and Political Structure

The ethnic and sociopolitical situation in Central Asia to a certain extent also resembles the situation in many Third World countries, although the idea that Central Asia still lacks clear ethnic divisions, or that these divisions are unimportant, which was argued particularly strongly by the late Professor Bennigsen and his followers (Bennigsen and Broxup 1983; Bennigsen and Wimbush 1985; Ro'i 1991: 123ff.; cf. Atkin 1992a), seems to me groundless, just like the similar claims that the feeling of Islamic identity was stronger in Central Asia than any particular national consideration (Carrère d'Encausse 1985: 95). With due respect to their scholarship and erudition, their insistence on a common Turkestan (i.e., embracing all Central Asian indigenous peoples) and/or Muslim identity still prevailing in the area is nothing but armchair speculation. The recent development in the region speaks for itself. All those who have lived in Central Asia, or did their fieldwork there, usually do not have any doubts that Uzbeks and Tadjiks, Kazakhs and Turkmen, Karakalpaks and Kyrgyz now constitute separate nationalities with distinct self-consciousness and self-identification, and in most of the cases with clear ethnic boundaries. The number of interethnic marriages between members of indigenous Muslim groups in Central Asia is very low and is continuing to decline. Thus, those of the Tadjik intelligentsia who married Muslim but non-Tadjik women are strongly pressured by their colleagues and acquaintances who would like them to divorce (Bushkov and Mikul'sky 1992: 19).

Contrary to some assertions (Carrère d'Encausse 1992: 269), there is no undeniable sign of increasing unification of Central Asia through Islam. Muhammad Salikh, an Uzbek poet and a leader of the "Erk" Party, recently characterized the present ethnic situation in Central Asia in these sober words: "A unified Turkestan today is a 'political dream.' The peoples of Turkestan are already divided into five republics, and in each a national identity has been formed. One can't deny this process that began even during the colonial period some hundred years ago" (Bohr 1990: 20).

It is true that the Soviets contributed much to the process of ethnic differentiation in Central Asia by its political delineation, by their educational, cultural, and social policy, and by creating new political and educated elites who do not have a vested interest in a unified Turkestan but, on the contrary, are interested in a separate political existence of their ethnic groups and, correspondingly, in justifying their separateness. However, it would be an exaggeration to call this policy artificial ethnic engineering. The relative ease and success with which it was accomplished indicates that some of the preconditions had already existed before the revolution.

Central Asia has always been an ethnically and linguistically diverse region, and even its political unity in the past was achieved only in some relatively short historical periods (Khazanov 1992b: 74ff.). The circulation of ideas of pan-Turkism and pan-Islamism was limited there, and they never held sway over the soul and minds of ordinary people (Fragner 1994: 17–20). There were over 20 bloody interethnic conflicts in the nineteenth-century Kokand Khanate and even more in the Khiva Khanate (Pulatov 1990b; cf. Manz 1987: 265).

Contrary to the expectations of the Soviet leadership and the incantations of the Soviet scholars, the complicated ethnic composition in Central Asia and Kazakhstan did not evoke "internationalism" and the rapprochement of the Soviet peoples. Instead, ethnic tension has increased, and social and economic competition between members of different nationalities is growing. Actually, the Soviet differential policy toward different nationalities in individual republics facilitated not nation building but ethnic nationalism.

However, in spite of the noticeable ethnic diversity of Central Asia and the important role which it plays in political life, the process of ethnic nation building is also far from complete. Ethnic consciousness there still has a hierarchical character. An individual considers himself a member of a given ethnic group vis-à-vis other ones, but in the internal ethnic relations his parochial, regional, and/or kin-based tribal and clanal affiliations still have significant meaning and play an important role in his loyalties. Regional divisions are particularly conspicuous in Tadjikistan and Uzbekistan, while in other Central Asian republics one finds rather pure forms of tribalism.

The situation in Turkmenistan illustrates this point. Before the revolution, the Turkmen consisted of many tribes: the Yomud, Teke, Göklen, Ersari, and others. In the Soviet period, the war on tribalism was repeatedly declared victorious. But tribalism, in fact, continues to play a very important role in Turkmen politics, social consciousness, and everyday life. Tribal·affiliation is always taken into account in personal relations, marriage arrangements, career promotion, and in-fighting among the ruling elite. In the recent past, it became a common practice for the first secretary of the Communist Party of Turkmenistan to put his tribesmen in prominent and important positions in the government, administration, and even in the scientific and cultural establishment, and regional party organizations sometimes resembled tribal fiefdoms. A Turkmen who settles in the territory of an alien tribe has no prospects for social and economic advancement. In everyday life he feels the scornful attitude of his neighbors (Naumova 1991: 303). Remarkably enough, President Saparmurad Niiazov claimed that he was an orphan and, therefore, does not have a close affiliation with any particular tribe (Andreyev 1992: 21). Actually, he belongs to the most numerous Teke tribe, and the special Archive Foundation of Saparmurad Niiazov was established for the sole purpose of creating the genealogical tree of the country's first president (*Moscow News* 15 [April 15-21, 1994]: 6).

In Kazakhstan, clanal and tribal ties were very much alive until the late 1920s. At that time, members of different clan groups actively competed with each other for privileged positions in the Communist Party and local administration apparatus (Sokolovsky 1926: 24, 33). Their importance began to diminish only after the Kazakhs were forced into sedentarization and collectivization, accompanied by their mass migration during the famine of the early 1930s. Kazakhs who migrated from their lands to other parts of the country, particularly those who settled in the multiethnic districts of Northern Kazakhstan, at present understand the clan structure less well than those who continue to live in their traditional territories. However, in the purely Kazakh districts even the children are well aware of their clanal affiliation. The former first secretary of the Communist Party of Kazakhstan, Kunaev, (1992: 10-11) boasted that in accordance with Kazakh tradition he could name seven generations of his ancestors and stated that every Kazakh should be able to do the same. In some settlements the distribution of wealth depends on clan identity. This acquires a special significance with regard to commodities in short supply and gives rise to interclan rivalry for local power (Naumova 1991: 300–302). Besides, belonging to a certain *zhuz* (horde; in the past, something similar to a tribal confederation) is well known by all Kazakhs and is still important. Those who are in positions of power tend to recruit, support, and promote people of their own *zhuz*. Still, there is an unwritten rule about maintaining a certain balance between members of different *zhuz* among the republican nomenklatura (Dzanguzhin 1993: 179).

Clan and tribal membership has retained great importance in Kyrgyzstan as well, although Usubaliev, the former first secretary of the republican Communist Party, insisted that tribalism does not exist in his republic anymore and that appointments on the basis of belonging to certain tribes or clans do not have a place there (*Sovetskaia Kirgiziia,* June 26, 1988). In fact, in the 1930s through the 1950s, the majority of the leading positions were occupied by the southern Kyrgyz from the Kypchak tribe; then the balance of power began to change in favor of the northern Sary-Bagysh tribe (Filonyk 1994: 158). When Akaev, a moderate reformist, became the president of Kirgizia in October 1990, his election was connected with a struggle, not only between reformists and conservatives, but even more so between northern and southern Kyrgyz. This struggle for power was so intense that, in the opinion of some Soviet observers, it put the republic on the brink of a schism or even civil war (Ponomarev 1989: 9–10; Baialinov 1990). It is remarkable that, despite his declared negative attitudes toward tribalism, Akaev himself belongs to an old and mighty Sary-Bagysh tribe. Although some Russian newspapers like to stress that he was born into the family of a collective farmer, in Kyrgyzstan everybody knows that he is a descendant of Shabdan, a *manap* (aristocrat) from the Tynai clan (Niiazov and Baialinov 1991a: 2), who in the middle of the nineteenth century recognized and helped establish the Russian rule and was rewarded for his service by the Russian government (Dzhamgerchinov 1959: 60, 62, 73, 197, 200, 285, 343, 351, 389). Most of the positions in Akaev's entourage are occupied by those from the northern regions of Chu and Talas, especially from the Kemin District (Sitnianskii 1994: 99), while deputies from the southern regions of the republic still remain the staunchest opponents of the president (Rotar' 1993f: 3).[2] The

---

[2] In May 1994, I met with some members of the Kyrgyz delegation, which consisted of middle-level officials who visited Madison and wanted to discuss some of their specific problems with me. I asked them about the tribal affiliation of their prime minister, and in the beginning they tried to assure me that they did not know it, since tribal membership has ceased to be important in Kyrgyzstan today. After I replied that, if they were going to talk with me in the tradition of the old Soviet propaganda clichés, then we had nothing more to talk about, I immediately received information about the tribal affiliations of all Kyrgyz ministers and other high officials.

Dzhelal-Abad Oblast (administrative region) in the south became an informal center of the opposition to the political dominance of the northerners (Rotar' 1992c: 1). Akaev's decision to double the number of administrative regions (and correspondingly the number of lucrative positions in the administration) may be connected with a desire to broaden his regional support base (Dubnov 1993c: 16).

One further example: In the 1991 contest over the presidency in Tadjikistan, a candidate of the democratic and moderate Islamic forces, Davlet Khudonazarov, was defeated by a communist candidate because the latter belonged to the so-called Khudzhent (former Leninabad) faction, which has remained in power in the republic since the late 1930s. Almost all northern Tadjiks, in spite of their political differences, preferred to support their fellow countryman, Rakhmon Nabiev, while Khudonazarov was backed by the mountaineers of Match, Garm, and Badakhshan (Rotar' 1991; Vyzhutovich 1991; Niyazi 1994: 176).[3] Divisions between the northern and southern Tadjiks are often stronger than between the communists and their opposition (Niyazi 1994: 172–73). Actually, the idea of a single Tadjik nation is still in flux. Localized cultural and regional identities and differences are very strong. These differences are also conspicuous in the intraethnic division of labor. While people of Khudzhent extraction occupied many positions in the Communist Party apparatus and the government, those from Karategin controlled trade, and those from Kuliab (and later from the Pamirs) provided the bulk of the police force (Bushkov and Mikul'sky 1993: 26). Even Muslim activists are sometimes divided along regional lines (Bushkov and Mikul'sky 1992: 22ff.). The ongoing civil war in Tadjikistan, which is often explained in terms of the struggle between communists and Islamic fundamentalists, may be somewhat conceived as the struggle of regional factions that, for historical and other reasons, have chosen different political orientations and ideological garments. These factions are usually called clans, which is inaccurate because they are not based on kinship and descent. In this struggle the Khudzhent faction and its allies from Kuliab and Gissar confront the Garm, Pamir, Kurgan-Tiube, and some other factions (Rotar' 1992b: 3; Dubnov 1993b: 11; Nazrulloev 1993: 4; Niyazi 1994: 178–81). As soon as the Khudzhent-Kuliab coalition defeated the opposition, the victors began to compete for power, and at present the Kuliab "clan" holds the upper hand over the Khudzhent one (Bek 1994: 3).

The Soviet policy regarding Central Asia actually helped the preserva-

---

[3] A year and a half earlier, this candidate in a conversation with me expressed the hope, which turned out to be vain, that in Tadjikistan the political differences were becoming more important than regional ones.

tion and even the revival of tribalism and regionalism, in spite of the leadership's lip service avowing the need to fight these traditions. During the purges of the 1920s and 1930s, all the political elites of the indigenous peoples there were physically destroyed, not only the populists and enlighteners of the prerevolutionary period and the national Bolsheviks of the revolution and civil war generation, but also those who had been promoted to positions of leadership in the 1920s. The cultural elites were also destroyed. The Soviets created new political elites whose privileged positions in local structures of power were connected, not with a promotion of interests of their republics and peoples, but rather with their compliance with Moscow demands and goals and with their capabilities to implement policies dictated by the center. The positions of the top-level regional leaders depended also on their personal reputation in the center and on their allegiance to the most powerful figures in the Moscow hierarchy. No wonder, in 1959, Rashidov, the first secretary of the Communist Party of Uzbekistan, in order to please Khrushchev, suggested cutting the purchase price of raw cotton and, in 1964 in order to please Brezhnev, advocated an unlimited introduction of chemicals into cotton growing, including pesticides and defoliants, such as butifos (Levin 1989: 123–24). Instead, when the center was pleased with the performance of the regional leaders, it gave them the right to run internal affairs in their republics and to distribute preferential treatment and high-level jobs, a percentage of which were reserved for non-Russian elites in Central Asia and Kazakhstan to secure their support of the Soviet regime.

The undemocratic pyramidal structures of power which had been built with Moscow's consent and support, and the complete absence of even rudimentary elements of civil society in Central Asia, inevitably led to a situation in which the actual dispensation of power was connected with a network of personal trust, patronage, and clientage. One of the important foci of any individual's loyalty remains the groupings in which he has grown up and lived. These are the foundations of trust and thus the channels through which power is mediated and social advancement can be achieved. In these conditions it is natural that the leadership of any rank in Central Asia would try to gain the support of tribesmen or fellow countrymen.

Under these circumstances the ordinary population, which has been denied any participation in political life and has been unprotected in legal and social respects by state-imposed and state-supported institutions, also tends to rely on traditional institutions, such as kin-groups and neighborhoods (*makhalla*), and on their old traditions of mutual aid and reciprocity (Poliakov 1989). These traditional institutions also help to play down social differences in the interests of local loyalties which the Soviets failed to destroy. Local particularism, which is ruthlessly exploited by ruling elites, now inhibits the emergence of a liberal and democratic consensus. As has already been noted in other material, it is difficult to mobilize citizens on the basis of national appeals or organizations in a social structure in which most of them are involved in personal patron-client relationships, because their allegiance will be to the locality and the patron (Powell 1982: 86–87; see also Beissinger 1992: 154).

So, the Soviets failed to create a *Homo soveticus* from ordinary Central Asians. Not without reason, the structures that evolved in Central Asia are now, in the area of the former Soviet Union, sometimes called communism in its eastern feudal understanding. With equal correctness they may be called the Asian mode of production in its eastern communist understanding.

From time to time, passive nonacceptance of the Soviet nationality policy in Central Asia and Kazakhstan provoked anxiety in the Soviet leadership. However, it fought this nonacceptance with measures bordering on sheer idiocy. In Turkmenistan, people were persecuted for celebrating the festival Kurban Bairam, traditional funeral rituals were prohibited, and the wearing of the traditional women's dresses that protected them from the harsh rays of the Kara Kum sun was viewed with disapproval. In Kazakhstan, playing the *dombre*, the Kazakh national instrument, was condemned as a manifestation of national narrow-mindedness. In Uzbekistan, people were persecuted for wearing traditional clothes (the men's quilted robes, and the women's dresses decorated in national colors) and for celebrating Nauruz, the new year of the lunar calendar.

No wonder the social structure of the Central Asian nationalities in many respects can also be characterized as premodern. It consists of an upper class, which comes mainly from the former Communist Party hierarchy and people involved in government and administration, and a large lower class, the peasantry. Members of the working class and of the middle class from the indigenous population are small in number; most of the latter are white-collar workers or people involved in humanitarian professions. Blue-collar workers and a majority of the middle class were recruited from other ethnic groups—the Russians, Ukrainians, Tatars, Germans, Koreans, and several others (for additional information see Lubin 1984). (See table 4.3, p. 263.)

The Early Impact of Perestroika

At the beginning of perestroika (1986–1987) the new policy of openness and restructuring took on certain anti-Central Asian overtones. The Soviet leadership was clearly disappointed with the situation there and with the regional political elites (Khazanov 1988: 157ff.). First, the Moscow center was concerned because the regional leadership in Central Asia was blocking the "rationalizing" ambitions of perestroika. It also turned out to be incapable, or unwilling, to fight against nationalism effectively. The events in Alma-Ata (now known as Almaty) in December 1986 had significant repercussions.

Meanwhile, growing nationalism in Central Asia and Kazakhstan sometimes became an obstacle even for the foreign political goals of the Soviet Union. Thus, the invasion of Afghanistan, unpopular among all Soviet peoples, provoked particular dissatisfaction and protests from the Muslims of Central Asia, which were manifested in a series of anti-war demonstrations and evasion of military service.

Besides, the Soviet leadership began to regard the influence of Islam, especially Islamic fundamentalism, on the Muslim peoples of the USSR with serious fear. In its fight against Islam, the leadership did not consider the specifics of this religion, thus making all measures taken against it ineffective. In particular, it did not take into account the strength of the so-called parallel, or unofficial, Islam. While official Muslim spiritual authorities were under complete control of the state and were as servile as their Christian Orthodox colleagues, unregistered clergy also conducted religious rites, such as circumcision, weddings, funerals, as well as organized underground studies, and even established underground mosques. The followers of underground Islam became more active from the late 1960s, particularly under the influence of the Islamic revolution in Iran (Polonskaia 1994: 33; Kudriavtsev and Niyazi 1994: 110–11). Although most Muslims of Central Asia have not consistently been able to follow the obligations of Islam and regularly visit a mosque, they continue to consider themselves Muslims. Islam to them involves more than religion. It includes their belonging to a certain civilization, specific cultural and moral values and traditions, a specific lifestyle, and so on. Insofar as traditional institutions, attitudes, and practices in Central Asia have survived, or even revived, as undesirable but inevitable results of the Soviet policy toward the region, the role of popular Islam has remained invincible because it is inseparably linked with them (Saidbaev 1984; Wimbush 1986: 227ff.; Atkin 1989).

The Soviet leadership looked on with alarm as the observation of religious rites in Central Asia did not diminish but continued to grow (*Kommunist Tadjikistana*, September 3, 1988). The local leadership demonstrated its inability, and often its lack of desire, to oppose Islam seriously. Many officials, especially from the ranks of the lower leadership, were rather successful in combining an outward devotion to communist dogma with the observation of many Islamic practices in their private lives (*Pravda,* November 16, 1985; *Pravda vostoka,* August 13, 1987). Thus, I have heard many stories from the communists in Central Asia about how they bypassed the prohibition against circumcising children, the violation of which could have meant their exclusion from the party or being fired from work. Usually, they sent their children to older relatives, or went away on business trips, and then explained that their irresponsible kinsmen performed this rite without their knowledge and consent. At the 27th Congress of the Communist Party of Uzbekistan, news circulated that Sherkulov, the former first secretary of the Samarkand regional party organization, personally participated in building improvements on a *mazar,* a holy man's tomb (*Pravda,* February 5, 1988).

In the secret CPSU Politburo resolution of 1986, Islam was declared an obstacle to socioeconomic development (Saidbaev 1991: 3). The following year, the previously hidden anxieties of the Soviet leadership were made public. Beliaev, a commentator close to the ruling circles, announced that the export of the Islamic revolution was more than propaganda, and that an Islamic infrastructure existed in Central Asia that created a very favorable atmosphere for foreign interference (*Literaturnaia gazeta,* May 13, 1987). The appearance of a movement toward pure Islam, especially in Tadjikistan since 1977, was also noted (*Kommunist Tadjikistana,* January 31, February 12, 1987). Its adherents borrowed (or were given) the name Wahhabites from the followers of the strict form of Sunni Islam practiced in Saudi Arabia, although they were not directly connected with this form. Actually, only a very small number of the adherents of pure Islam in Central Asia called themselves the Wahhabites. Usually they began to do this after they had made the hajj to Mecca (Kudriavtsev and Niyazi 1994: 125, n. 14). They criticized the existing moral order, the official clergy, and the corrupt sociopolitical system in Soviet Central Asia (Chicherina 1990b: 79–82; Bushkov and Mikul'sky 1992: 25ff.; Polonskaia 1994: 65).

In November 1986, Gorbachev, while stopping in Tashkent on his way to India, ordered the local leadership to conduct an "uncompromising fight against religion" (*Pravda vostoka,* November 25, 1986). After his critical observations, many communists were excluded from the party for observing religious rites (*Pravda vostoka,* August 13, 1987). In Turkmenistan alone more than 200 communists were expelled from the party for circumcising their children (*Kultura,* September 21, 1991). In Tadjikistan in 1985–1987, 24 activists of the underground Islamic movement were imprisoned (Kudriavtsev and Niyazi 1994: 112).

The threat of Islamic fundamentalism, potential or real, as it existed in the first half of the 1980s, was overestimated by the Soviet leadership, maybe because, as one Russian scholar noted, nowhere was "Islamophobia more prevalent than in the country's political leadership" (Goble 1990: 23). However, the events in Iran and Afghanistan actually influenced the Muslims in Central Asia, in whose minds and hearts Islam became identified with anti-colonial liberation movements. From the end of the 1970s a growing number of people in Central Asia began to listen to broadcasts of the Teheran radio, and audio cassettes of Khomeini's speeches were widely circulated there (Spillover Effects . . . 1980; Iranian Religious Propaganda . . . 1987; Malashenko and Moskalenko 1992: 5).

Third, the political elites in Central Asia and Kazakhstan began to be considered by the center as too conservative to put reforms into practice. The anti-corruption campaign and the so-called Uzbek affair—which had been secretly initiated during the Andropov reign, made public under Chernenko (Pechenev 1991), and revived with Gorbachev's coming to power—exposed their complete corruption, incompetence, and ineffectiveness. However, to a significant extent this sad state of affairs was a result of Moscow's own policy toward Central Asia. While corruption there is endemic—the population is used to it and considers it a normal state of things—members of the central leadership for a long time closed their eyes to it, particularly because some of them received their share of bribes (Gdlian and Ivanov 1994).

Cotton production in Uzbekistan has been in decline since the early 1980s (averaging 4.9 million tons a year) (Ziiadullaev 1989: 31). However, Moscow's demand remained the same: Cotton at any cost. This resulted in a popular, but bitter, joke in Uzbekistan: "If you don't plant cotton, you will be planted in jail; if you don't bring it in, you will be put out" (in colloquial Russian the verb *posadit'* means both "to plant" and "to imprison," and the verb *ubrat'* means "to harvest" and "to sack") (Minkin 1988: 26). The local leadership, unable to meet Moscow's constantly increasing demands, resorted to different types of deception, including falsification of cotton production figures and bribes.

In 1986, the "Uzbek affair" reverberated across the entire Soviet Union. At the 27th Congress of the Communist Party, Gorbachev and Ligachev chose Uzbekistan as the object of especially harsh criticism. Ligachev proposed shaking up the Uzbek elite. Ninety percent of the personnel of the Central Committee of the Communist Party of Uzbekistan was changed. Serious personnel changes were also made in Uzbekistan's Council of Ministers, the presidium of the Supreme Soviet, the militia, the regional party apparatus and government, and ministries. A massive wave of arrests and dismissals affected different strata of Uzbek society. Thousands of foremen, agronomists, *kolkhoz* (collective farm) and *sovkhoz* (state farm) directors, and other lower-level specialists and administrators upon whose work the organization of cotton growing depended, were subjected to various punitive measures (Gdlian 1989: 88-89). To a lesser, but still significant, degree repression was carried out in other Central Asian republics as well.

The decisions made at the January 1987 plenum of the Soviet Communist Party Central Committee and some consequent practical measures definitely put the republics of Central Asia and Kazakhstan at a disadvantage. They were told that, although the center was short of capital to contribute much to the development of the region, they should give the center an even larger part of their financial and material resources.

Another demand was to get rid of obstacles to the migration of Russians into the area and their introduction into the local elites. A growing out-migration of the Slavic population from Central Asia and Kazakhstan sounded an alarm to the Soviet leadership, which tried, although without positive results, to change the situation. *Pravda* expressed discontent, claiming that, "in several republics, the most prestigious professions were turned into the unique privilege for persons of that or another nationality" (*Pravda,* September 27, 1987). The entire campaign involved a number of concrete measures. Thus, hundreds of officials in the party and administrative apparatus were taken from the center, moved to Uzbekistan, and given substantial promotions. They were locally nicknamed the landing force of the limited contingent (Rizaev 1990: 32)—a clear allusion to the occupation troops in Afghanistan, which the Soviet press always called the limited contingent. According to Igitaliev, the former chairman of the Supreme Court of Uzbekistan, a "triumvirate" of Russians was sent to Uzbekistan from Moscow to serve as the de facto governors of the republic: Anishchev, the second secretary of the Communist Party of Uzbekistan; Ogarok, the first deputy chairman of the Council of Ministers; and Romanovsky, the deputy chairman of the presidium of the republic's Supreme Soviet (Critchlow 1990: 20). Moscow also expressed dissatisfaction with the fact that in Central Asia members of the national intelligentsia and student population were becoming too numerous and exceeded the ratios for the native ethnic groups (*Pravda,* February 13, 1987). Some practical measures followed. For example, the number of Kazakh students in higher learning institutions of Kazakhstan was limited (Alimdzanov 1989: 217). (See table 4.4, p. 263.)

For a long time a large part of the Central Asian population had high hopes for improving the situation in agriculture with a plan to divert Siberian rivers to Central Asia, no matter how ludicrous the plan was ecologically and economically. When in 1986, the center, under the influence of Russian public opinion, finally shelved the plan without any appropriate reconsideration of Central Asian ecological policy (Micklin 1987:

67–68), this was perceived there as one more manifestation of a colonial policy that strangled the interests of the periphery for the interests of the Russian metropole (Atchabarov and Sharmanov 1990: 117ff.).

It became clear that Gorbachev's leadership was incapable of helping the Central Asian republics overcome their economic hardships. Instead, it recommended the same solutions to the problem that had been advocated in vain during the Brezhnev period: reducing the birthrate and transferring a part of the Central Asian population to unpopulated or underpopulated parts of Russia—to the non-black earth zone, the Urals, or even Siberia.

One may suspect that these suggestions had strong political connotations. Because of differences in the birthrates and the out-migration of Slavs from Central Asia, the ratio of natives to Russians there was changing to the advantage of the natives. Moscow was afraid that this tendency would result in a growth of nationalism. Thus, Victor Kozlov, a Soviet ethnographer and demographer who was one of the champions of the policy of Russification, frankly admitted his alarm concerning the danger presented by the ethnic homogeneity of Central Asian republics (i.e., the growth of the indigenous population there) to the position of Russians in the Soviet Union (V. Kozlov 1988, 1990).

However, both of the suggestions failed. Ordinary people in Central Asia simply ignored the family planning campaign, and many intellectuals there publicly denounced it (Sheehy 1988b: 1–7). All attempts to persuade or lure the Central Asians to migrate to Russia also failed to make headway (Rywkin 1982: 76ff.).

The Emergence of National Movements

Public opinion in Central Asia was set acutely against what it considered the colonialist policy of the center. Because vertical social structures with widespread patronage and clientage are still characteristic of Central Asian society, economic and other benefits there are distributed in accordance with, not only an individual's general standing in the society, but also his position in these social structures. When the power of a patron diminishes, his clients are at a disadvantage. By 1988, a growing discontent with the existing conditions affected all strata in Central Asia and Kazakhstan. In the different republics, national groups and organizations began to emerge in which the intelligentsia, and the educated urban middle strata in general, played the most active and organizing role and tried to articulate consistent programs of political goals and actions (for more details see Khazanov 1991: 82ff.; see also Chicherina 1990b; Ponomarev 1991).

Of all these movements, the one with the largest membership was Birlik (the Movement for Preserving the Natural, Material, and Spiritual Wealth) in Uzbekistan, formed in November 1988 by 18 intellectuals. Among its original demands were the end of "cultural imperialism" and colonial exploitation of Uzbekistan, democratization of the political life, and finally, sovereignty of the republic. Its popularity quickly grew, and in 1989, despite the active opposition of the Uzbek leadership, it was able to organize a series of rallies and demonstrations. Similar, though less successful, attempts have been made in other Central Asian republics.

However, the formation of the national movements in Central Asia and Kazakhstan took place in significantly more difficult conditions than in many other regions of the Soviet Union. National intelligentsias there are a rather new phenomenon. Although they now demonstrate the same "colonial ingratitude" that other colonial powers have faced in the recent past, they are a creation of the Soviet regime (Allworth 1989: 380ff.). They lack a tradition of democratic political process and do not have a clear vision of the political future for their republics, in the form of either Western-type liberal democracies or any other system. Instead, they tend to incline toward ethnic nationalism because to them the dominance of their own nationality in their respective republic is the best safeguard and an improvement of their own position in society. Thus, the rights and identity issues have become closely intertwined. A liberal democratic system, based on an individual's merit and competence, guaranteeing equal rights to all citizens regardless of ethnic membership, began to be considered detrimental to the interests of politically strong but economically disadvantaged nationalities.

Besides, members of the national intelligentsias in Central Asia are still not numerous, are often quite corrupt, and are tied to the old political elite and the official power structure more closely than in other parts of the former Soviet Union. Most of them are involved in culture, education, and humanitarian professions, which were always under the strictest control of the Communist Party. Until recently, most of them have been obedient servants of the communist leadership, particularly because a significant part of the system of higher education was turned into a marketplace where admission to a university and even a university diploma, as well as professional positions, could be acquired for money or through patronage. Contrary to the European parts of the USSR, Central Asia in the Brezhnev period lacked a dissident movement. It is notable that during perestroika many leaders of informal national organizations in Central Asian republics preferred to escape anti-communist slogans, were rather moderate in their political demands, and were ready for collaboration with local political elites. Often their criticism of these elites was leveled more at personalities than at institutions.

No wonder that on January 17, 1992, when Muhammad Salikh, the leader of the Erk Party, tried to ease the atmosphere at the university campus in the Uzbekistan capital of Tashkent after the student demonstration had been dispersed by police the previous day, participants of a protest rally booed him because of his previous moderate stand toward the government (Usmanov 1992: 3). It is also remarkable enough that even such influential and internationally known figures in the Central Asian cultural elite as the Kyrgyz writer Chinghiz Aitmatov or the Kazakh poet Olzhas Suleimenov never openly sided with the opposition and preferred to maintain good relations with the political elite.

During the restructuring period the opposition in Central Asia and Kazakhstan turned out to be not influential enough to lead broad and stable national movements with clear social and political goals. From time to time they were temporarily able to inspire an urban underclass and part of the rural population with nationalistic slogans, but they often failed to suggest to them an attractive alternative or to control them. Besides, they began to face competition from groups of Islamic orientation. In the late 1980s, attempts were made to organize various Islamic parties within the borders of separate republics or even within the whole area (Brown 1991d: 12ff.; Atkin 1992a: 63–66), although most of these groups had primarily a local following. However, they definitely had an influence on certain strata of Central Asian societies.

One should give credit to the perspicacity of Lubin (1984: 234), who already in the early 1980s noticed that, in Uzbekistan

> for the indigenous nationalities, a perceived worsening quality of life has already become linked with the presence of "outsiders" in their republic. The possibility of a more extreme economic slowdown in Uzbekistan . . . would hold immense ethnic implications which go beyond purely economic considerations alone. It could spark deep-seated nationalist hostilities and resentments which would be difficult to contain.

An underclass and rural population have turned out to be particularly prone to extreme forms of ethnic nationalism and to slogans like "Down with the cotton," "Uzbekistan for Uzbeks," "Russians out of Tadjikistan," or "Priority to the indigenous people in Kazakhstan." They are looking for a scapegoat to avenge all miseries in their life, and they find it, or are encouraged to try to find it, in others: infidels, Russians and other people of European origin, neighboring ethnic groups, and particularly ethnic minorities in their midst.

Interethnic relations in Central Asia and Kazakhstan deteriorated during perestroika. After unrest in Ashghabad and Nebit-Dag (May 1 and 9, 1989), pogroms of the Meskhetian Turks in the Fergana valley followed (June 1989), then riots in Novyi Uzen' and Mangyshlak (June 17–20, 1989), clashes in Buka and Parkend (March 3, 1989), unrest in Dushanbe (February 11–14, 1990), a pogrom in Andijan (May 2, 1990), fighting between Kyrgyz and Uzbeks in the Osh Oblast (spring-summer 1990), and clashes in Namangan (December 2, 1990).

For a long time everything has been blamed on various subversive forces. The Moscow center liked to point to the extremists, the Islamic fundamentalists, the "enemies of perestroika," the corrupted faction of local political elites, the mafia, and so on. The regional leadership preferred to blame informal organizations, such as Birlik in Uzbekistan or "Kyrgyzstan" in Kirgizia. The opposition in Central Asia also claimed that the violence was the result of instigation, but it pointed blame in the opposite direction—at local and central authorities and the KGB. Be that as it may, the whole matter of ethnic violence never went behind more or less obscure allusions. So far only one thing is clear: there are different forces in Central Asia which, in spite of their contradictory interests, are ready to play with the fire of ethnic conflicts, and in an atmosphere of overall crisis they can always find a receptive and explosive social environment.

The Last Years of Perestroika

Because the political culture of the masses in Central Asia and Kazakhstan is very low, conservative political elites retained their power there during the whole restructuring period. In spite of all their grievances against the center and their desire to strengthen their power at the expense of the center, beginning in 1988, most of them clearly preferred to side with Moscow against the democratic movement in the Soviet Union in general, and against the opposition movements in their own republics. Thus, all of them were for preserving the Soviet Union and for a new Union Treaty. It was not by chance that the Central Asian deputies at the sessions of the USSR Congress of People's Deputies and Supreme Soviet were the most docile and always voted the way the central leadership wished.

In its turn, beginning in 1988, the Gorbachev leadership clearly changed its policy and expressed its support of the conservative political elites in Central Asia. It also demonstrated an increasing readiness to close its eyes to their old and new sins, as long as they controlled the situation in their republics and did not insist on a fundamental transformation of the Soviet Union. As early as late 1987 attempts to introduce ethnic Russians into the political elites and administrative apparatus of the Central Asian republics were curtailed and then practically abandoned. Thus, in July 1989, the first secretary of the Communist Party of Kazakhstan, Kolbin, whose name had been indelibly connected with the events in December 1986 (see chapter 5), was recalled from the republic. In 1989, Moscow recalled from Central Asia the "landing force," those Russians that it had sent into leadership positions there during the anti-corruption campaign. Scathing attacks on the corrupt command-control apparatus in Central Asia turned into a growing reliance on that apparatus.

It is not surprising then that, between 1988 and 1991, all attempts to organize national movements and parties in Turkmenistan immediately met with opposition from the Turkmen leadership, which more than once announced that the creation of unofficial organizations in the republic would be a "blind, absurd mimicry" (*Turkmenskaia iskra*, April 29, 1989). The leadership's opposition to the Popular Front in Turkmenistan was based on the conception that all issues concerning the republic's population could be solved by official political organizations. On January 15, 1990, the minister of justice of Turkmenistan proudly announced on Soviet television that there were no unofficial groups in his republic.

In keeping with the spirit of the times, Turkmenistan passed a law on sovereignty on August 22, 1990, but, both before and after this decision, the national opposition continued to be severely suppressed. Niiazov, the first secretary of the Communist Party of Turkmenistan, was elected president in an election in which he had no opponents and received about 99 percent of the votes. This "unanimous support of the people," the expression used by the servile Turkmen press, even provoked comments about the irony from the liberal Moscow press (*Moskovskie novosti* 4 [November 4, 1990]: 5).

In Uzbekistan in 1989 and 1990, the opposition remained popular among the masses, but the political elite, using all of its organizational capabilities and administrative pressure, such as a ban on some opposition activities, ensured its victory in the elections to the republic's Parliament in February and March 1990 (*Izvestiia*, February 16, 1990). Among its 500 members, the opposition held no more than 50–60 seats. Besides, the Uzbek leadership provoked or encouraged a split in Birlik, from which a moderate branch broke away to form the Erk Party. The declaration of sovereignty made on June 20, 1990, remained a symbolic act. The demands made by the republic's leadership to Moscow were moderate, primarily dealing with economic issues.

A similar policy was practiced by the Tadjik and Kyrgyz leaderships. To remain in power, the political elites in these republics did not hesitate to instigate or resort to violence. In 1988, Makhkamov, the first secretary of the Communist Party of Tadjikistan, spoke out against the creation of the Popular Front in his republic. Under pressure from the Tadjik leadership, unofficial organizations, which had begun to appear in late 1988, either fell apart or remained with few participants (Chicherina 1990b). Within a year, political life in Tadjikistan was primarily defined by the consequences of the unrest in its capital, Dushanbe, on February 11–14, 1990. There is reason to assume that this unrest was provoked by the local elite, who knew that dissatisfaction with them was strong and feared losing power in the upcoming elections to the Supreme Soviet of the republic (*Kommunist Tadjikistana*, February 1, 1990; Mirrakhimov 1990: 2).

The unrest was of a nationalistic kind and was directed against the European or Europeanized population. However, simultaneously, a demand was put forth for the resignation of the local leadership (Shoismatulloev 1994). The leadership promised to do this, but the promise seemed no more than a tactical maneuver. Control over the situation was restored with the help of the army. An emergency plenum of the Central Committee of the Communist Party of Tadjikistan with the participation of representatives from Moscow was quickly held, and as could have been expected, the Tadjik leader Makhkamov did not resign (*Pravda*, February 17, 1990). Elections to the Parliament took place during the ensuing state of emergency, and the local elite was victorious (*Pravda*, February 25, 1990). On November 30, Makhkamov, refusing to hold national elections, was elected president of the republic by the Tadjik Parliament (*Moscow News* 51 [December 30, 1990—January 6, 1991]: 60). The state of emergency in Dushanbe was not lifted until 1991; however, the opposition was soon revived in Tadjikistan (*Izvestiia*, December 3, 1990, and July 10, 1991).

In Kirgizia, the political elite also refused to enter into constructive dialogue with the national opposition, represented by the movement "Kyrgyzstan," which appeared in early 1990. At the same time, the political elite tried to play along with nationalism by placing the ethnic Kyrgyz in privileged positions. The explosive situation that developed in the Osh Oblast, where tension between the Kyrgyz and Uzbeks was growing, was not a secret to anyone (*Izvestiia*, July 25, 1990), but there were no measures taken to alleviate the situation (*Sobesednik* [4 January 1990]; *Izvestiia*, June 25, 1990). The Congress of the Kyrgyz Communist Party, which took place during the Uzbek-Kyrgyz confrontations and during a state of emergency in the capital of the republic, tried to place the blame for the bloody events in the Osh Oblast (Brown 1990b) on the "Kyrgyzstan" movement and reelected almost all the old leaders, headed by First Secretary Masaliev (*Pravda*, June 19, 1990). In July 1990, at the time when "Kyrgyzstan" was being persecuted, news began coming from Kirgizia that the ruling powers, including the KGB, were secretly supporting extremist organizations: the Kyrgyz Osh Aimagy (which is Kyrgyz for "land of Osh," or the People of the Osh Region movement) and the Uzbek Adolat (which is Uzbek for "justice," or the Justice movement) (*Novoe russkoe slovo,* August 6, 1990; for the KGB explanation of these events, see Razakov 1993).

As a result, many representatives of the party apparatus were elected in the summer of 1990 to the Supreme Soviet of the republic (*Ekspress-khronika* 26 [June 26, 1990]). Nevertheless, the Osh events upset the situation in Kirgizia, and put Masaliev's position in jeopardy. His desire to preserve the compromised leaders and to incite tribal passions turned out to be extreme even for less conservative members of the local elite. Under pressure from the movement "Kyrgyzstan," Akaev, the candidate from the reformist circles, was elected president of the republic on October 27, 1990 (Baialinov 1990).

The situation was somewhat different in Kazakhstan, where the most acute problem was power sharing among different ethnic groups, mainly between Kazakhs and Russians (see chapter 5). (According to the Soviet census of 1989, of Kazakhstan's 16,463,000 people, Kazakhs constituted 39.7 percent, while Russians made up 37.8 percent.) In the late 1980s and in the early 1990s, their relations continued to grow tense. By 1990, several emerging Kazakh parties and movements (Azat, Alash, Zheltoksan) were openly demanding the republic's complete independence and secession from the Soviet Union. In October 1990, when the republic's Parliament made a declaration of sovereignty, many Kazakhs picketed it, carrying the slogan "Don't sign the Union Treaty" (*Izvestiia,* December 9, 1990). In such conditions, Kazakhstan's president, Nazarbaev, expressed his readiness to sign the Union Treaty, but at the same time he tried to introduce some changes in the treaty and categorically took a stand against changing the borders of the republic.

The Current Situation and Its Prospects

Some Western scholars predicted that the Central Asians would be the first to revolt against the Soviet Empire (Carrère d'Encausse 1981). Actually, the opposite took place. Before the March 17, 1991, referendum on the future of the USSR, all Central Asian leaders stated that their republics were overwhelmingly in favor of the preservation of the Soviet Union. Even President Akaev stressed that Kirgizia had no other realistic choice but to remain part of the USSR. Docile electorates complied with their president's desires. Of those who participated in the referendum, Uzbekistan voted 93.7 percent in favor of preserving the union; Kazakhstan, 94 percent; Kirgizia, 94.5 percent; Tadjikistan, 96 percent; and only 2 percent opposed the measure in Turkmenistan (Brown 1991c: 1–3). With the exception of President Akaev, who faced an attempted minicoup in his own republic (Niiazov and Baialinov 1991b: 30), all other Central Asian leaders either gave conditional approval to the August 1991 coup in Moscow or preferred to take a wait-and-see position (Brown 1991g: 43ff.). Because of the economic weakness and political instability of the region, members of the Central Asian leadership to the very end were the most persistent champions of keeping the Soviet Union intact. Its dissolution has created many new problems for them.

The main problem of the local political elites is how to remain in power in the new conditions of independence. For this they spare no efforts, and it seems that for now they are doing this quite successfully. In Uzbekistan, Turkmenistan, Tadjikistan, and to a large extent in Kazakhstan and Kyrgyzstan, the power is still in the hands of the old nomenklatura and the Communist Party's apparatus existing under different names.

It is obvious that Central Asia is a long way from a liberal, Western-type, democracy, and many political scientists in Russia and in the West foresee only two possible developments there: a dictatorship by former communist leaders, or a dictatorship by Muslim fundamentalists (Eickelman and Pasha 1991: 634ff.). The first development has already taken place in Turkmenistan, Uzbekistan, and Tadjikistan.

Turkmenistan's president, Niiazov, expressed his attitude toward democracy in his country by bluntly stating that "formal democracy is a burden for the people" (Andreyev 1992: 20), and that "Western-style democracy does not suit us" (Zhukov 1991: 6). He frankly claims that "one should be a complete idiot if he were to allow the formation of the opposition only because, in the opinion of some people, this corresponds to the idea of democracy" (*Russkaia mysl'*, November 6, 1992: 4). His own vision of democracy has a very peculiar character. He is promoting a multiparty system on the basis of the former Communist Party only. Veteran communists are to rally into a new Communist Party, secretaries of rural districts and other communists formerly responsible for agriculture are to launch the Dekhan (Peasants') Party. Other communists can join the Democratic Party headed by Niiazov (Zhukov 1992a: 4; Sakhatov 1993: 3).

Khudaiberdy Khalliev, a Turkmen writer, says that "in the degree of openness Turkmenistan can be compared with Russia in the same way as the USSR of yesterday could be compared with the West" (Ukhlin 1993: 14). The opposition organization Agzybirlik now has to operate underground, and individual dissidents are severely persecuted. The best-known case is the trial of Shiraly Nurmuradov, a poet and playwright, who in his epigrams dared to ridicule the president. He was sentenced to three years in a labor camp on a false accusation of swindling (Rumshiskaya and Cherkasov 1991: 34–35). Shortly before U.S. secretary of state James Baker visited Turkmenistan in early 1992, police, in the Soviet tradition of the 1970s and the early 1980s, which I still remember too well, detained or put under house arrest those whom they called destructive elements, that is, everyone who was publicly critical of the government (Sakhatov 1993: 3). The authorities resorted to the same practice on other occasions as well (*Russkaia mysl'*, November 27, 1992: 5; *New Times* 18 [April 1993]: 1). The Niiazov cult of personality also bears features that are characteristic of the Soviet tradition. For instance, he was the only presidential candidate in the election. Today he is officially called Turkmenbashi (the leader of Turkmen people).[4] In 1994, the editor-in-chief of *Yashlyk* magazine was dismissed after the government newspaper, *Turkmenistan*, claimed that the magazine's editorial staff ignored the "outstanding merits of the great leader of Turkmen people, teacher of independence and builder of independent Turkmenistan Saparmurad Niiazov–Turkmenbashi" (*Monitor* 5, no. 18 [September 2, 1994]: 3). The same year Niiazov himself decreed that those who spread gossip about the leadership of Turkmenistan should be arrested and prosecuted.

The record of Uzbekistan's president, Karimov is no better. His country's independence allowed him to throw away even those mild restraints that perestroika imposed upon his actions. The Communist Party was renamed the People's Democratic Party, and the former regional (*oblast'*) party secretaries became the *khakims*—the governors of administrative regions. But six months after the August 1991 coup in Moscow, the legal opposition in Uzbekistan was crushed. Karimov even refused to sign those of the CIS agreements that were concerned with the observance of human rights (*Nezavisimaia gazeta,* May 7, 1993: 3; Kalinkin 1993: 13–15).

Karimov does not tolerate any criticism of or objection to his policies. Vice-President Mirsaidov was removed from his post a month after he was elected in December 1991, as soon as he showed an inkling of independent thinking (Rotar' 1992a: 2; Portnikov 1992a: 4; Azamova 1992a). The students' protests against soaring prices in Tashkent, in January 1992, were suppressed with the utmost cruelty. At least two students were killed,

---

[4] In 1994, Turkmenistan's Meli-Mejlis (Parliament) worked out a new decree concerning the use of the president's title in the mass media, while translating from Turkmenian into any other language. The decree reads: "Many mass media, including Russian, are too frivolous in using the term 'Turkmenbashi,' the title of the Turkmen people's leader." The decree envisages imposing a fine for systematic distortions in the president's title (*Monitor* 5, no. 17 [August 19, 1994]: 16).

dozens were wounded and beaten, and thousands were sent away from the Uzbek capital (*Ekspress-khronika* 3/233 [January 1992]; *Komsomol'-skaia pravda*, January 25, 1992: 2; Mursaliev 1992: 2; Usmanov 1992: 4; Fyodorov 1992: 5). Opposition papers were shut down, and other papers, including mass media publications, have come under strict censorship (Gafarly 1994: 5). Even the dissemination of liberal Russian newspapers have been practically banned in Uzbekistan (Orlik 1992: 1, 2). Uzbek readers are barred and banned from familiarizing themselves with any views on particular problems other than the official views. Since February 1990, Uzbekistan has had a decree banning open-air rallies and demonstrations.

Opposition parties, even those who, like the Erk Party, have wished to play a constructive role in the changing political scene and who in the recent past sought a dialogue with the government, are virtually forced to work underground. Their leaders are terrorized, beaten, jailed, or forced into political exile; their activists are fired from their jobs or denied employment by the government. Some of the opposition leaders have even been kidnapped by the Uzbek secret police (the National Security Service is the new name for the KGB in Uzbekistan) from the territory of other CIS republics (Olgun 1992: 36; *Russkaia mysl'*, December 12, 1992: 4, and February 12, 1993: 1, 20; Azamova 1992b: 50).

Karimov has a personal reason to maintain good relations with the United States. His daughter is married to a banker from New Jersey, and his son-in-law's brother has been appointed Uzbekistan's representative to the UN (Andreyev 1992: 21). However, he certainly prefers to sacrifice his international reputation for more power at home.

The Uzbek leadership was clearly scared by the events in Tadjikistan, where the former communists were temporarily ousted from power. They use the fighting in the neighboring republic and the rapid revival of Islam in some regions of Uzbekistan as justification for the crackdown on the opposition. They used to avow that Uzbekistan is not yet ready for democracy and that stability in the country should be maintained at any cost. Uzbekistan's foreign minister, Abdurazakov, explains his government's iron-handed policy in the following words: "If you are the head of a family and someone begins to act up, you must assert your authority to keep everyone in line" (Burke 1992: 10). During his visit to Germany in 1993, President Karimov stated: "It is not necessary for us to adopt Western democracy spiritually alien to us. We shall have our own, national democracy which will help Uzbekistan become one of the leading countries of the world." The kind of national democracy that Karimov has in mind is clear from the same interview quoted above, in which he mentioned that he found answers to all serious questions of our time in the Code of the medieval despot Timur (*New Times* 45 [November 1993]: 29). In its turn, the opposition claims that it could respond to the suppression with mass disobedience or armed resistance, but is not doing this because it does not want a civil war, preferring instead, peaceful, constitutional methods of the political process (personal communication with Abdumannob and Abdurahim Pulatov, leaders of the Birlik movement; see also *Moscow News* 36 [1992]: 5).

In Tadjikistan, the communists smashed the government of national accord formed after the events of April 1992 and have returned to power in a bloody civil war, in which, according to still very loose estimates, no fewer than 50,000 persons were killed and about 300,000 became refugees (Brown 1993: 35; *Nezavisimaia gazeta,* February 6, 1993: 1; *Russkaia mysl',* February 12, 1993: 1, Rotar' 1993e: 3; Rotar' 1993g: 3; Aiubzod 1993: 6; Bushkov and Mikul'sky 1993; Rubin 1994). During this war they had no aversion to using criminals with a number of convictions, such as Sangak Safarov, who at the November 25, 1992, session of the Tadjik Supreme Council boasted, "We [i.e., the pro-Communist Popular Front] have broken the back of democracy in Tadjikistan and soon we'll drive this scum to a place whence it will never reappear neither in Central Asia nor in Russia" (Dubnov 1993b: 12). The communists declared Safarov a "people's hero" and a "father of the nation"; however, as some observers had predicted (*Russkaia mysl',* March 26–April 1, 1993: 7; Yemelyanenko 1993: 4), they got rid of him as soon as there was no need of him anymore. Safarov and his lieutenant Faizali Saidov were murdered on March 30, 1993, under unclear circumstances (*Russkaia mysl',* April 9–15, 1993: 5). However, it seems that the "red terror" still remains the main weapon of the Tadjik government in its struggle against the opposition (Panfilov 1993c: 3; Rotar' 1993b: 3; Lebedeva and Panfilov 1994: 2). Among other measures imposed on all opposition parties and movements, the Tadjik Supreme Council in June 1993 officially banned the Democratic Party, the Islamic Renaissance Party, the Rastokhez movement, and the regional movement Lali Badakhshon. Some observers assert that, without the assistance of the Russian 201st Division, the current regime would not be able to stay in power even for two days (Bek 1994: 3).

The second prognosticated development in the region, a dictatorship by Muslim fundamentalists—an idea used by many Russian politicians and observers as well as by the Russian press to scare their readers and to justify Russia's policy in the region—seems at present less plausible. It is true that Central Asian society is turning to Islamic values and traditions, though they are conceived quite differently by different groups and strata of the population. Scripturalist Islam is trying to bring popular Islam closer to itself through religious enlightenment (Panarin 1994b: 23). The number of mosques, religious enlightenment centers, and religious schools for men and women is growing. In 1989, there were only several hundred mosques in Central Asia and Kazakhstan; by 1991, their number had increased to 5,000 (Landa 1993: 39). By 1993, their number exceeded 5,000 in Uzbekistan alone (Usmanov 1994: 3). In the Fergana valley mosques have been or are being built in every *makhalla*, and their general number already approaches that which existed in the times of the Kokand Khanate (Satvaldyev 1991: 1, 14). In Turkmenistan the number of clergy has recently risen several times. The number of mosques has jumped from 16 to 181, and more are planned to be built in the near future (*Novaia Nezavisimaia gazeta*, July 15, 1994). In Kazakhstan the number of mosques increased from 125 in 1978 to more than 300 in 1992 (Sultangalieva 1994: 76).

Such Central Asian leaders as Presidents Niiazov and Karimov hurried to demonstrate their devotion to Islam and, in 1992, made a hadj to Mecca. (Remarkably, one of Karimov's entourage during this pilgrimage complained: "The greatest difficulty with the visit to Saudi Arabia was abstaining from drinking alcohol and smoking" [Andreyev 1992: 19]). Karimov also swore his presidential oath on the Koran in January 1992. In Turkmenistan the history of Islam has been included into the high school curricula by presidential decree. Their flirting with the religion in an ideological vacuum is characteristic of all CIS countries, and may be better understood considering Yeltsin's frequent attendance at Russian Orthodox churches, or the Georgian leader Shevardnadze's sudden baptism. However, the expanding role of Islam in Central Asian politics is an undeniable fact.

The state-supported (in the recent past, the state-appointed) "official" clergy still prefers to ally with its governments and is against the politicization of the religion. (The only exception was the Tadjik religious leader Kazikolon Khodziakbar Turadzonzoda's unsuccessful involvement with the opposition in the political struggle in his country.) Thus, in Turkmenistan the text of the daily prayer sanctioned by the official clergy reads: "Oh, powerful Allah, protect independent Turkmenistan and bring luck to our beloved Motherland and honorable President Saparmurad Turkmenbashi in all his intentions" (*Novaia Nezavisimaia gazeta*, July 15, 1994). However, this clergy is challenged by more radical clerics from the middle and lower levels who accuse them of conformism and corruption (Malashenko 1992: 3). In nearly all Central Asian countries social protest of the impoverished and pauperized strata is connected with new developments in the religious life, which sometimes take a fundamentalist turn, including demands to clericalize the social life and even to create an Islamic state (Nurullayev 1992: 9).

In some regions, especially in the Fergana valley, alcohol is practically forbidden, and women are forced to cover their faces. Even in Kyrgyzstan, where the observance of Islamic law by the former nomads before the Bolshevik revolution was the weakest in Central Asia, it has been decided that a mosque will be built in every Kyrgyz settlement. When the pope's nuncio visited Bishkek in April 1992, the Commission of Volunteer Muslims gathered 150,000 signatures appealing for "a ban on the activity of foreign missionaries on Kyrgyz territory." (To put this request in its proper perspective, I must add that in 1993 the Russian Orthodox church approached President Yeltsin and Khazbulatov, the speaker of the Russian Parliament, with a similar request.) When the poet Ernis Turchenov published his translation of the Koran into Kyrgyz, young Muslims accused him of corrupting the Holy Writ. The zealots held a meeting in the central square of Bishkek demanding "Death to Turchenov!" and forcing the poet into hiding (*Izvestiia,* April 28, 1992; Andreyev 1992: 19).[5]

Still, the danger of Islamic fundamentalism should not be overestimated, at any rate in the short run, because it meets with resistance from the ruling political elites, their more liberal-minded opponents, and even the officially sanctioned clergy. All Central Asian leaders insist that their states will remain secular ones. In all of them the activities of Islamic parties are banned.

In 1991, at a rally in Namangan, in the Fergana valley, President Karimov promised that Uzbekistan would become an Islamic republic and that he personally would strengthen the Islamic faith in his country. However, he soon forgot his promise. One of his appointees recently stated that Islam in Uzbekistan will be just what Karimov wants it to be. The Islamic spring that flourished in the country since 1990 until the beginning of 1992 was superseded by a short autumn, and then by winter. Religious institutions were again put under strict state control. Officials who demonstrated too much sympathy toward Islam were dismissed. Some mullahs were arrested (Usmanov 1994: 3; Polonskaia 1994: 36–37).

Besides, it seems that at present a majority of Muslims in Central Asia and Kazakhstan do not support the idea of clerical totalitarianism. In part, the movement to disseminate knowledge about Islamic dogmas and normative practice can be seen as an attempt to re-create and reintegrate this religion as a component of national culture and self-awareness. Thus, one opinion poll has demonstrated that 65 percent of the Kazakh students consider Islam an integral part of the Kazakh culture (personal com-

---

[5] In this respect, the atmosphere in Kazakhstan is more liberal. The publication of the Koran's Kazakh translation was welcomed by a large number of people and did not meet any serious resistance. I received several copies of it as gifts during my visit to the country in January 1995.

munication with Dr. Alma Sultangalieva). A poll conducted in 1991–1992 in Uzbekistan revealed that many town women do not accept a number of Islamic canons and are critical of the basic tenets and commandments of Islam, although they regard them as part of an educated person's cultural heritage. Most girls and young women, in both the town and the countryside, accept the teachings of Islam only theoretically (Konstantinova 1993: 12). The current upsurge in Islamic activism is to a large extent the search for self-identity and sometimes a desire to return to the idealized and imaginary past as a reaction against modernization in its Soviet-type colonial variety. Even many of those who call themselves fundamentalists, such as the members of the Islamic Renaissance Party, claim that they consider the spread of religious education as their main objective and do not support the creation of an Islamic state based on the shariah. Thus, Abdulla Utaev, a leader of the Islamic Renaissance Party in Uzbekistan, stated that "Uzbekistan's government should be secular, and all forms of belief or non-belief should be respected; but Islam should occupy a central place in public life" (Cavanaugh 1992: 20).

Besides, it is difficult to imagine that fundamentalist Islam will be, in the nearest future, a threat in Central Asia, given the absence of scripturalist Islamic knowledge for over more than seven decades. Kazikolon Turadzonzoda has described the current situation in these sober words: "What Islamic republic can possibly exist, if a mere three percent of the population can read the namaz the real way?" (*Moscow News* 36 [1992]: 14).

Nevertheless, the peril remains that the liberal and nationalist opposition, who exploited Islam in the struggle for virtually secular goals, may have the tables turned on them. This can happen, considering that those who are concerned with the promotion of their vision of religious values may use politics as the vehicle by which they impose their views upon the majority of the population. Still, at present the main danger lies at the opposite extreme.

Some Central Asian leaders like to present themselves as a bulwark against fundamentalism, thus justifying their dictatorship—an argument that is often tacitly bought in Russia and in the West. Fearing a loss of power, leaders of Tadjikistan and Uzbekistan label all their political opponents an Islamic threat. Actually, the opposite may become true. When secular opposition is weak and suppressed, disillusioned and dissatisfied ordinary people may turn to fundamentalism as a political force against their oppressive, corrupted, and inefficient rulers. This is just what happened in Tadjikistan, where since 1993 the repressions have radicalized the Islamic movement. Sociological studies in Andijan and Namangan, in Uzbekistan's part of the Fergana valley, demonstrate that the majority of those who call themselves fundamentalists there consist of young people who are unfamiliar with Islamic teaching but are certain that it means social justice and moral purity (Landa 1993: 39).

I would also not completely rule out the third and, realistically speaking, apparently the most desirable development that is feasible in at least some Central Asian countries: an autocratic or semiautocratic regime of moderate reformists. Actually, they already exist and are represented by Nazarbaev in Kazakhstan and to a lesser degree by Akaev in Kyrgyzstan. In the current situation, they are certainly the lesser evil; however, one should have no illusion about them. Both of these leaders are often praised by the press and politicians as the champions of democracy in Central Asia, but, in fact, they are quite authoritarian. Nazarbaev's sympathy toward authoritarian rule, allegedly as a transitional stage from totalitarianism to democracy, is well known; he does not pretend to hide it or his high opinion about the South Korean or even Chinese models of development (Brown 1991e: 10; Bogert 1991: 39; *Komsomol'skaia pravda* 1991: 2; *Izvestiia,* December 3, 1991: 1–2; Kiyanitsa 1992: 4; S. Kozlov 1993a: 4). Recently he tried to impose a moratorium on activities of all political parties and movements, except his own newly created Union of People's Unity (S. Kozlov 1993b: 3; S. Kozlov 1993g: 3). The independent press and other mass media in Kazakhstan are operating in difficult conditions under constant pressure from the government (S. Kozlov 1993d: 3). International observers claim that the 1994 parliamentary elections in the country cannot be considered free because state authorities directly intervened in them and thus influenced their results (S. Kozlov 1994: 3). Soon afterwards Nazarbaev dissolved the Parliament and, following the example of his counterparts in Turkmenistan and Uzbekistan, extended his presidency until the year 2000 through the referendum, which in Central Asian countries can hardly be characterized as a democratic measure. In Kyrgyzstan, there are discussions about a "quiet transition to Akaev's dictatorship," which is expressed in a popular joke: "Communism has gone—Keminism has come" (Kemin is the birth-place of Akaev). Some of those who call themselves democrats accuse Akaev of betraying democratic principles (*Moscow News* [November 15–22, 1992]: 10). At present he is also maneuvering to extend his presidency without holding a new election.

The main problems that these leaders are facing now consist, not in their uneasy relations with democratically oriented organizations, but rather in their connections with the former communists. They still prefer this group or have to rely upon it because, among other things, the communists occupy the dominant positions in the government and administration and constitute the most serious political force in the Parliaments. Thus, the communists are able to sabotage any serious attempts at reform.

In 1993, President Nazarbaev complained that the government of Kazakhstan had proved its complete insolvency. He caustically remarked that an anti-crisis program is a manual for Kazakhstan's bureaucrats in the same way that the *Decameron* is a handbook for a bishop (Samoilenko 1993: 1). Even in Kyrgyzstan, the only Central Asian country where the Communist Party and state ceased to be one (the Communist Party there was suspended after it had expressed support for the putsch leaders in August 1991 and is functioning now under the name the Party of Communists of Kyrgyzstan [Azamova 1991; Andreyev 1992: 20]), President Akaev is still very susceptible to pressure from the former party functionaries (Ivanov 1992a: 8). The conflict between the executive and legislative powers, with the majority of the latter made up of members of the former party nomenklatura, was recently at its apex in Bishkek, as it recently had been in Moscow in 1993.

Even though some observers call nationalism in Central Asia an *a posteriori* phenomenon, since it gained strength only after the dissolution of the Soviet Union (Zubov 1993: 168), so far the ideology of ethnic nationalism has turned out to be the strongest of all competing ideologies in Central Asia. This is the case primarily because ethnic nationalism proved its compatibility both with the mainstream Islamic revival and with national communism of the post-Soviet period. In Tadjikistan the "democrats" from the Rastokhez movement and from the Democratic Party, who demanded liberal and market oriented reforms but at the same time demonstrated strong nationalistic inclinations, forged an alliance with the members of the Islamic Renaissance Party against the communists. In other Central Asian countries, as in some former Western colonies, nationalism propagated by the ruling and cultural elites is considered instrumental in societal consolidation and independent statehood building.

It is true that the political leaders of Kazakhstan and Kyrgyzstan, the most multiethnic republics in the region with a very significant Russian population (the Russians constitute about 37 percent of the whole population of Kazakhstan and more than 20 percent in Kyrgyzstan), have declared their desire to achieve nation-state consolidation in their republics. However, at present the issues of sharing power and the economic benefits of modernization in both of these republics remain unsolved.

Interethnic tension and competition in Kazakhstan drove President Nazarbaev to argue for civil accord and interethnic accommodation in the country. So far he has proved to be a very skillful politician who is capable of keeping interethnic tension under control, albeit he is not able to defuse it. However, one may wonder whether and for how long he will be capable of maneuvering in the future.

The situation in Kyrgyzstan is similar to that in Kazakhstan and also does not favor an adjustment to an interethnic social environment. The situation is further aggravated by the competition for scarce land resources. Increasing numbers of Kyrgyz are migrating from the mountainous regions to the more fertile areas of Kyrgyzstan, but the arable lands there are already occupied by Russians and some other ethnic minorities. In addition, the growth in unemployment affects the Kyrgyz more than any other ethnic group in the republic. Just as in Kazakhstan, most of the noncommunist political organizations in Kyrgyzstan, even those that declare their allegiance to democratic principles, have split along ethnic lines. While the Kyrgyz support Asaba (Revival), Erkin Kyrgyzstan (Free Kyrgyzstan), and some other parties with a certain nationalistic appeal, the Russian population gives its sympathy to the Slavic Fund (Verkhovsky 1991: 6; Ivanov 1992a: 2; Ivanov 1992b: 2; S. Bekmakhanov 1992: 6; Dubnov 1993d: 16).

The prevailing conditions in Central Asia and Kazakhstan do not favor the possibility of a political, or even an economic, unification of the region. Central Asian leaders have met several times to discuss their countries' bilateral or regional economic cooperation, including the establishment of a common market, a bank for reconstruction and development, custom-free borders, and other measures. However, some attempts made in this direction were not particularly successful. The Central Asian Regional Union, which was founded on January 24, 1993, at the Central Asian leaders' meeting in Tashkent, has so far turned out to be stillborn (*Russkaia mysl'*, January 15, 1993: 3). It remains to be seen whether the 1994 agreement between Uzbekistan, Kazakhstan, and Kyrgyzstan on the creation of a single economic space (Zainutdinov 1994b: 2) will be fulfilled; as yet it has not been put into practice.

There are several reasons for these failures. The economies of Central Asian countries are to a large extent not complementary, and each leader is concerned mainly with his own country's problems. When, in the beginning of 1992, Turkmenistan increased 50-fold the price of its gas, without any consideration of its neighbors' financial situation, Tadjikistan and Kyrgyzstan were put on the brink of energy starvation (Narzikulov 1992: 4). The introduction of a national currency in Kyrgyzstan was strongly disfavored in Uzbekistan and Kazakhstan (Denisenko 1993a: 3; Denisenko 1993b: 3; Denisenko 1993c: 3). Political competition and discord should also be taken into account (Novoprudsky 1993: 8; Usmanov 1993b: 11). Ideas of Turkestan unity are still alive, or rather resuscitating, in circles of the Uzbek ruling elite and among some members of the Uzbek intelligentsia, who hope that, as the most numerous ethnic group, the Uzbeks will dominate in a united Turkestan. A semiofficial Uzbek newspaper has the audacious title *Turkestan*. However, sober observers understand that "a single state is utopia in today's conditions" (interview with Abdurahim Pulatov in *Umid/Hope* [Fall 1992]: 41).

Uzbekistan's intervention on the side of the communists in the civil war in Tadjikistan is a clear indication of its intentions. One of the Tadjik leaders, Rakhmonov, flatters President Karimov by calling him the father of all Tadjiks (Dubnov 1993b: 11, 12; *Russkaia mysl'*, March 26–April 1, 1993: 7; Nazrulloev 1993: 4; Panfilov 1993a: 3). Kyrgyzstan has already indicated its dread of its stronger neighbor (Dubnov 1993c: 1; Sitnianskii 1994: 98). At one time, disagreements between Kazakhstan and Uzbekistan also became public knowledge (Usmanov 1992: 11).

In addition, territorial claims and counterclaims between Tadjiks and Uzbeks (on Bukhara, Samarkand, the Zerafshan Oasis, parts of the Fergana valley, and some other territories), Uzbeks and Kyrgyz (on the Kyrgyz part of the Fergana valley), Uzbeks and Kazakhs (on some territories along the Syr Darya and Arys' Rivers), Kyrgyz and Tadjiks (on the northern Pamirs, the alpine pastures in the Alay and Transalay Ranges, and some other territories), Turkmen and Kazakhs (on the Mangyshlak Peninsula), and so on; water disputes between Uzbekistan and Turkmenistan; and other disputes and tensions between different Central Asian ethnic groups do not facilitate their unity (Helgesen 1994: 145–46, 151).

The internal situation in Central Asia is also connected with its international standing. Russia still remains the main political and economic partner for all Central Asian countries, although there are serious difficulties in their relations with Russia. Kyrgyzstan and Kazakhstan would prefer closer cooperation between CIS countries and are clearly disappointed with Russia's position on the issue. Their numerous attempts to provide the Commonwealth of Independent States with real economic power remain unsuccessful (Portnikov 1992b: 1; Ardaev 1992b: 2; S. Kozlov 1993c: 2; S. Kozlov 1993e: 3; Konovalov 1993: 5). Akaev complained that Kyrgyzstan was nearly forced out of the ruble zone (Dubnov 1993d: 15). Similar complaints were made by Uzbekistan's and Kazakhstan's leaders. Niiazov, Turkmenistan's president, has repeatedly said that the very existence of the CIS is senseless (Andreyev 1992: 22). In its turn, Russia above all other things prefers stability, apparently, as the best guarantee against the threat of Islamic fundamentalism. For this illusive goal Russia is ready to sacrifice its declared democratic principles. Turkmen, Tadjik, and Uzbek secret services operate against their political opponents even in Moscow with the connivance of the Russian authorities (Petrov 1993: 3). Russian troops helped the communists in Tadjikistan return to power and are still assisting them in the continuing civil war. The liberal Russian press has already sounded the alarm that this policy is fraught with consequences similar to the invasion of Afghanistan (Dubnov 1993b: 12–13; *Russkaia mysl'*, March 26–April 1, 1993: 7; Panfilov 1993a: 3; Rotar' 1993c: 1). More and more frequently Russia has been accused of pursuing a neoimperialist policy in Central Asia based on the *divide et impera* principle. In particular, Russia strives to prevent both a political alliance of Central Asian states and their attempts at economic cooperation (Kasenov 1994: 1, 3).

Meanwhile, different Muslim countries, such as Turkey, Iran, Pakistan, and Saudi Arabia, have already begun to compete for influence in the Central Asian region. For a time its countries considered Turkey their most desirable and attractive partner and, among other things, a link to America. Central Asian leaders hoped that the United States would back Turkey in its economic assistance to their countries. President Karimov declared Turkey an elder brother of Uzbekistan, just as Russia was called in the country until recent times. President Akaev praised Turkey as "a morning star for the Turkic[-speaking] republics of Central Asia" and claimed that relations with this country would have the most important meaning in Kyrgyzstan's foreign policy. Even Nabiev, the former president of Tadjikistan, the only Iranian-speaking country in Central Asia, which has traditionally looked with suspicion on the neighboring Turkic-speaking countries, presented to Mr. Demirel a golden heart symbolizing Central Asia's bond with Turkey (Davlet-uulu 1992: 12; Andreyev 1992: 21). The cultural and economic presence of Turkey is increasing in Central Asia, but claims that it has an important role to play in stabilizing the Central Asian region (Winrow 1992: 101) seem premature to me. Turkey does not possess the capital and know-how so desperately needed for the modernization of this region. It seems that the Turks, ethnically close to the majority of Central Asian peoples, have enough strength merely to confirm this affinity but not to promote Central Asia's economic growth.

In spite of several attempts to promote Iran's presence in Central Asia, it is still far from being influential. However, Iran has concluded some important economic deals with Turkmenistan. Among other things, Teheran proposes to build a railway and road from Ashghabad to northern Iran with an outlet to the Persian Gulf. In fact, this idea was put forward in the time of the shah, but it was not developed for political reasons. Pakistan's presence in the region is even less visible, although Pakistani leaders, since the time of Zia ul-Haq, have been cherishing the dream of creating a "strategic deep front" in view of its confrontation with India. In comparison with Turkey and Iran, Pakistan has relatively weak historical and ethnic ties with Central Asian countries. Even more important is the fact that the economies of the two regions are oriented toward different markets and are likely to compete rather than implement one another in the future (Borisov and Vladimirov 1992: 2). Surprisingly, Arab countries have expressed limited interest in the Central Asian region. Saudi Arabia is concerned mainly with the promotion of Islamic learning; other Arab countries are even less involved. No wonder that, without hesitation, all Central Asian countries, have established diplomatic relations with Israel and are demonstrating their interest in the Israeli expertise in industry, trade, and especially agriculture.

Meanwhile, there is no improvement in the ecological situation, and the economy of the region is in a serious crisis. The breakup of the Soviet Union has taken a heavy toll on the Central Asian countries. The rapid fall in the exchange rate of local currencies, introduced after their failures in the ruble zone, put them in a very difficult situation. Their industry and agriculture, in the past almost totally oriented toward the Russian metropole's needs, are overcentralized, with obsolete machinery and equipment, poor technologies, low productivity, and an undeveloped infrastructure. Most of the region's industry was dependent on supplies from Moscow, and at present the production in many enterprises has ground to a halt, and increasing numbers of factory workers have been laid off. The Kyrgyz economy, devoid of reliable raw materials and energy sources and forced to import them, has found itself on the brink of collapse. Russia has cut quotas for supplies of metals by one-third; of oil, by two-thirds. In 1992, total economic production in Kyrgyzstan fell by 27 percent, and it continues to plummet. The living standard, especially of the provincial indigenous population, continues to decrease; in many places people live on home-baked bread and tea. They also face growing unemployment (Dubnov 1993d: 15). In Uzbekistan, President Karimov's August 1992 promise of a better life proved to be a big price hike. Prices on food stuffs and manufactured goods are almost as high as in Russia, while wages are much lower (Usmanov 1993a: 11). The civil war has brought Tadjikistan to the verge of complete economic disaster; more than 80 percent of its industrial enterprises are destroyed or damaged. Hunger is widespread, particularly in the southern regions of the republic and in the Pamirs (*Russkaia mysl'*, February 12, 1993: 1). Even Turkmenistan, with its gas deposits and dreams of becoming a "gas Kuwait," has had to introduce food rationing. The living standards have begun to decline rapidly in Kazakhstan, another country rich in mineral resources. In addition, Russians who have lost their elder brother status and turned into an ethnic minority in Central Asia, along with other nonindigenous peoples, are leaving the region in growing numbers. This is creating a shortage in the professional and skilled labor force. (See table 4.5, p. 264.)

Actually, the out-migration of Russians and other ethnic minorities already exceeded their in-migration to Central Asia during the last 15 or 20 years. This process accelerated in the 1980s and particularly during the last few years. (See table 4.6, p. 264.)

In 1989–1992, 10 percent of the Russian and Russophone population left Turkmenistan, 16.5 percent left Kyrgyzstan, and 25 percent left Uzbekistan. As a consequence of the civil war in Tadjikistan, 300,000 of the 387,000 Russians who lived in the republic have already left this country. Altogether, by 1994, 1 million Russians and Russophones had left Central Asia (excluding Kazakhstan) for other countries. According to some estimates, at least 1–1.5 million more ethnic Russians will migrate to Russia before the year 2000. In fact, the only factor preventing more people from immediate emigration is the enormous difficulties involved with re-settling in Russia now (Panarin 1993: 14; Rotar' 1993a: 3; Rotar' 1993d: 3; Rotar' 1994: 5; Perevedentsev 1993: 155).

With the possible exception of oil-and-gas-rich Turkmenistan and Kaza-khstan, the economic crisis in Central Asia will undoubtedly not be over-come in the near future. Serious economic reforms in the Central Asian republics and Kazakhstan have so far not begun. The scale of structural changes is not even worth mentioning. In Kyrgyzstan even the smallest enterprises have not yet been privatized (Dubnov 1993d: 15). President Karimov likes to talk about the "Turkish model of development" as the best match for Uzbekistan, but, in actuality, he simply strengthens the state monopoly. The presidential office instructs the republic's Ministry for Foreign Economic Relations in matters concerning which foreign firms it may sign agreements with (Portnikov 1992c: 3; Azamova 1992a). In the beginning of 1994, the Uzbek government announced, with great pomp, the new economic reforms (Zainutdinov 1994a: 2), but so far they have not materialized. Turkmenistan's government favors a state-regulated economy and the preservation of the collective farm system. State-run enterprises in the country still account for 99 percent of production, and severe restrictions are imposed on entrepreneurship (Zhukov 1992b: 3; Andreyev 1992: 21).

Even the transition to the market economy and the reduction in cot-ton production or its intensification will hardly bring immediate results or help the region out of poverty. Thus, considering that one-fifth of all labor in cotton production is connected to water, a reduction in water consumption can reduce the labor force by 6–12 percent (Wolfson 1990: 32–33). This and similar developments will inevitably lead to an increase in unemployment and to the further pauperization of that significant part of the population which is fraught with ethnic and social unrest. When the Uzbek government removed control over prices on January 16, 1992, an immediate result was the students' spontaneous protest in Tashkent (*Ekspress-khronika* 3/233 [January 1992]).

With few exceptions, such as Kazakhstan's billion-dollar oil contract with the American corporation Chevron (S. Kozlov 1993a: 3; S. Kozlov 1993f: 9), attempts to attract foreign capital have not yet been lucrative. Many of them, like Akaev's dream of turning Kyrgyzstan into an Asian Swit-zerland, are not based on sound economic estimates. No wonder he strives for Western investments in Kyrgyzstan without great success. One of his aides complained, "We were patted on our back with approval by our American and German friends, but no money was given" (Andreyev 1992: 20). Two years of the "special path" of Turkmenistan, which hoped for a quick transformation into the "Central Asian Kuwait," failed to material-ize. A country devoid of a developed gas-processing industry and capable of only selling raw fuel became helpless when the CIS customers put for-ward their own harsh demands. Nevertheless, in the worst Third World countries' tradition, the Turkmen leader carries out grandiose projects such as the building of a luxurious international airport and five-star hotels in Ashghabad, a city where the water-supply and sewage systems remain hazardous to the health of its residents. This occurred at the time when the government had to introduce food rationing.

Given the geographic location of Central Asia, its shortage of infrastruc-ture and skilled labor, its political instability and completely corrupted and inefficient administration (the former prime minister of Kyrgyzstan, who was dismissed for corruption, remarked that in his country only fools and lazy persons are not involved in embezzlement [Baialinov 1994: 6], but the new government has already been criticized by President Akaev for the same practice), the prospect of large-scale foreign investments into the region seems rather dubious. At first, the Japanese took an interest in this Asian region, a region that was new to them, but their enthusiasm soon waned.

All in all, in the few years of the post-Soviet period, Central Asia and Kazakhstan have come to be what, in truth, they were during the whole Soviet period: another Third World region with unsolved structural prob-lems and minimal potential for rapid economic and sociopolitical devel-opment. The future does not look particularly bright for the region. So-cial disorder, and even violent riots in spontaneous and sometimes very unpleasant forms, may soon be a social reality.

For several decades the Soviet Union liked to refer to the Central Asian example as the model for successful development along socialist lines, which the Third World countries were encouraged to emulate. In fact, very little was achieved in more than 70 years of ruthless communist rule, which cost the peoples of this region millions of lives, but failed to get them out of poverty or to change drastically the foundation of their tradi-tional organization. Those people in Third World countries, and in the West as well, who, in their search for the best solution to the problem of underdevelopment and modernization, have been inspired by the Cen-tral Asian example (or, to put it bluntly, were sometimes intentionally or unintentionally brainwashed and cheated by Soviet propaganda) should seek other solutions.

5

Ethnic Stratification and Ethnic Competition in Kazakhstan

> When camels are fighting, flies are dying.
> —Kazakh proverb

> A great principle, commonly little employed,
> is that nothing happens without sufficient reason.
> —Gottfried Wilhelm von Leibnitz

It is already asserted in the literature that ethnic specialization may motivate ethnic groups in the direction of complementary rather than competitive occupations and reduce ethnic tensions (Horowitz 1985: 113; see also Enloe 1973: 29). It is also assumed that, in times of rapid political and social changes and instability, accompanied by drastic economic fluctuations, the opposite is often true, and ethnic divisions of labor may only strain interethnic relations, especially if one ethnic group is identified with an alien outside power. Actually this issue deserves further examination. It may well be that in some cases of rapid change one kind of ethnic division of labor simply substitutes for another. Still, there is sufficient proof that in conditions of modernization and industrialization increased spatial and occupational mobility may increase social distance between ethnic groups (Chazan 1986: 138), while differential economic growth in ethnically divided societies may further exacerbate ethnic tensions (Esman 1989a: 482–83, 489). In this respect, nationalism in Kazakhstan, as in many other former Soviet republics, demonstrates the essential uniformity with nationalism in other developing countries. When ethnic groups become conscious communities (Brass 1976: 226) in response to a supranational state and/or competition with other ethnic groups, they strive to maintain separate identities within the larger heterogeneous society as the best guarantee of political and economic advancement.

While some Soviet scholars (Mukomel' 1989; Poliakov 1992; cf. Chesko

1990) still explain nationalism in Central Asia and Kazakhstan by the fact that their societies remain somewhat traditional, in my opinion, the opposite is true, and nationalism there is much more connected with still insufficient but ongoing modernization and with the emergence of new urban social strata (Khazanov 1994c).

I have already noted that the nationality policy which the Soviet leadership pursued during the last decades was fraught with potential conflicts. The ethnic structure of the state remained extremely rigid. At the same time, this policy facilitated the emergence of new educated strata among the titular nationalities in the non-Russian parts of the country whose competitive advantage depends on their members' privileged positions there vis-à-vis other nationalities (Khazanov 1988, 1991; cf. Zaslavsky 1992). As in many Third World countries (Emerson 1960: 44; Shibutani and Kwan 1965: 445ff.), it is these people who are now the main promoters of ethnic nationalism in different countries of the Commonwealth of Independent States.

Historical Background

Kazakhstan with its 2,717,300 square kilometers of territory was the second largest republic of the USSR. According to the Soviet census of 1989, of Kazakhstan's 16,463,000 population, Kazakhs constituted 39.67 percent; Russians, 37.82 percent; Germans, 5.82 percent; and Ukrainians, 5.44 percent. Smaller ethnic groups compose the rest. (See tables 5.1 and 5.2, p. 265.)

The highly diverse ethnic composition of Kazakhstan is the result of a long and sometimes tragic history. In the past the country was the exclusive domain of pastoral nomads. In the second half of the eighteenth century and in the first half of the nineteenth century, Russia subdued and annexed Kazakhstan. Soon afterwards, the Russian government ousted the Kazakhs from their summer pastures and sometimes even from their winter quarters and replaced them first with Cossack and then with Russian peasant settlers (Demko 1969). About 1.5 million new colonists from European Russia came to Kazakhstan at the end of the nineteenth century and in the beginning of the twentieth century (Dakhshleger 1965: 51). Kazakh pastoral nomads were gradually removed to the arid areas of Central and Southern Kazakhstan.

The Russian colonization of Kazakhstan and corresponding crisis in the traditional pastoral nomadic economy, unsuccessful uprisings, and the turmoil years of the revolution and civil war resulted in a sharp decrease in the country's percentage of Kazakh population. The proportion of Kazakhs fell from 91.4 percent in 1850 to 58.5 percent in 1926. Then, in the early 1930s came the traumatic events of forced collectivization and bloody settlement of Kazakh nomads on fixed lands, followed by the famine that decimated their herds and altogether cost them around 1.5–2 million souls. Another half million people had to flee from the country (Abylgozhin, Kozybaev, and Tatimov 1989; Kozybaev and Kozybaev 1994: 182ff.). In just a few years, about 550,000 nomadic and seminomadic households were forced to settle in waterless regions where not only agriculture but even pastoralism was impossible; others moved to towns and cities, where they found little work, not even unskilled jobs (Nurmukhamedov, Savosko, and Suleimenov 1966: 195–96; Olcott 1987: 179–87).

Meanwhile, the Russian and Slavic migrations to Kazakhstan continued, and by 1939 the number of Russians there began to exceed the number of Kazakhs. In the 1930s and 1940s the industrialization of the republic stimulated these movements, and in the 1950s so did the so-called virgin lands campaign, aimed at sowing wheat on huge tracts of land in the Northern Kazakhstan steppes. The last campaign generated, in less than 15 years, 3 million hectares of sand and made about 12 million hectares of land liable to wind erosion (Uteshev and Semenov 1967: 5; Gerasimov 1969: 442ff.; McCauley 1970; Komarov 1978: 53). However, it brought to Kazakhstan another 1.5–2 million new settlers from the European part of the USSR (Rybakovskii 1987: 185).[1] By 1939, the number of Russians in Kazakhstan had doubled the number there in 1926; by 1979 this number had more than doubled again. In addition, in the 1930s and particularly in the 1940s, Kazakhstan became one of the main territories for resettlement of various deported groups and peoples, such as the Poles, Koreans, Germans, Chechens, Ingush, Meskhetian Turks, Kurds, and Greeks, among many others.

In all, by 1962, the proportion of Kazakhs in Kazakhstan had dropped to 29 percent. However, during the last 30 years their overall proportion in the republic began to increase again because of their high birthrate and a decline in the influx of nonindigenous groups, above all of Russians. By 1991, the share of Kazakhs in the total population of Kazakhstan had already reached 42 percent (Orazbekov 1991: 51); by 1993, 43.2 percent; while the Russians' share had decreased to 36.4 percent (Suzhikov et al. 1993: 53, 55). It appears that Kazakhs have a good chance of becoming a majority in their country again by the beginning of the next century. (See table 5.3, p. 266.)

---

[1] Nazarbaev (1991a: 35) claims that their number amounted to even 2.5 million people.

This confidence in the ethnic future of the Kazakhs after the period when their very survival as a people was in jeopardy contributed to a growth in their nationalism, which in the first postwar decades was at a rather low level. Nationalism became more conspicuous during the later years of the Kunaev's rule, who until his dismissal in December 1986 held for 24 years the position of the first secretary of the Communist Party of Kazakhstan. Although Kunaev was no less corrupt than other Soviet politicians of the Brezhnev period, he was, and still remains, rather popular among the Kazakhs.[2] He tried to advocate for the interests of Kazakhstan in the central government, to give preference to Kazakhs over Russians in the republic, and to move them into many key positions in the administration (Olcott 1987: 240ff.; Kunaev 1992). Thus, he managed to protect the famous Kazakh poet Olzhas Suleimenov when the latter was accused of nationalist deviation.

At the end of the 1970s, when the Moscow leadership became worried about the immigration of Soviet Germans to West Germany, it tried to solve this problem at Kazakh expense. Moscow toyed with plans to create a German autonomous formation in Kazakhstan, in the territory of Tselinograd Oblast. However, the Kazakh leadership prevented this formation by leaking this information to the public. Anti-German rallies followed in Tselinograd, and the plans for German autonomy had to be revoked (Cheshko 1988: 14).

The ethnic composition in Kazakhstan was further complicated by the growing linguistic Russification of its population. No fewer than 700 Kazakh-language schools were closed (*Nezavisimaia gazeta*, May 5, 1992: 5), many Kazakh children began to study in the Russian-language schools, and a part of urban Kazakhs, particularly the youth, have at present very limited knowledge of the Kazakh language (Asylbekov 1991:45). By 1989, 2,021,596 school children in Kazakhstan attended the Russian-language schools, while 923,990 attended the Kazakh-language schools (Naumova 1992: 35). However, this did not result in the rapprochement of different nationalities in its territory. On the contrary, ethnic tension increased, and social and economic competition between members of different ethnic groups grew. The number of intermarriages between Kazakhs and Slavs was far below the Soviet average of mixed marriages (Kalyshev 1991: 49).

---

[2] In 1989, one of the Moscow newspapers complained that the bronze bust of Kunaev had not been removed from the central square of Alma-Ata, despite his dismissal and the following criticism of his policy (*Izvestiia*, September 2, 1989).

Social Structure and Ethnic Division of Labor

As in other Central Asian countries, Kazakh social structure remains in many respects premodern. It consists of the upper class, which includes people involved in government and administration (most of them in the recent past belonged to the former Communist Party hierarchy), and the large lower class, the peasantry. Members of the working class and of the middle class from the indigenous population are few in number. Blue collars and a majority of the middle class come from other ethnic groups— Russians, Ukrainians, Tatars, Germans, Koreans, and several others. Kazakhs provide 51 percent of the administrative personnel but only 3.0 percent of the skilled labor and 11.3 percent of the unskilled labor (Aitov 1990: 53).

With respect to European Russia, Kazakhstan always was a peripheral region. As in similar cases in the capitalist world system (Wallerstein 1974), its economy became specialized in extractive and primary products to supply the core area (Asylbekov 1991: 43). Of Kazakhstan's export trade to other Soviet republics, 70 percent consisted of raw materials and 12 percent of half-finished products (Suzhikov et al. 1993: 90). The limited industrialization of Kazakhstan conducted by the Moscow center involved the attraction of a work force from the European part of the USSR, not the creation of an indigenous working class. The participation of Kazakhs in this development was insignificant. However, unlike capitalist countries, which usually recruit immigrants from other regions to perform unskilled labor (Hechter 1976: 216ff.), Kazakhstan attracted immigrants from European Russia to occupy those positions in industry that demanded skilled labor and, thus, they became a labor aristocracy.

The construction of industrial complexes did not take into account local needs or local traditions. While the production of consumer goods in Kazakhstan is underdeveloped and more than 60 percent of consumer goods have to be imported into the republic (Asylbekov 1991: 43), it contains large mining and heavy industry enterprises (including a defense industry), which are operated mainly by the people of Slavic and German origin or by migrants from the Caucasus. In 1979 the Kazakhs constituted only 20.8 percent of the urban population of the republic; 69.1 percent of them continued to live in the rural areas (Naumova 1991: 295). In 1977, they constituted only 13 percent and, in 1987, 21 percent of industrial workers (Sacks 1990: 91). In the ferrous metal industry the Kazakh workers constitute only 8.6 percent; in coal mining, 9.2 percent; in engineering and metalworking industries, 12.6 percent; and in woodworking, 15.6 percent (Suzhikov et al. 1993: 66).

Until recently, 93 percent of Kazakhstan's industry was directly subordinate to the all-union ministries in Moscow. The republic's tax revenue from these enterprises constituted only 0.03 percent of its budget. Their employees were not Kazakhstan workers but rather Soviet Union workers. They virtually embodied the union center, its defense and heavy industries, space research, and military power. They were far from integrated into the local society, and often considered themselves more as representatives of the center vis-à-vis Kazakhs (Kuanyshev 1991: 40; Suzhikov et al. 1993: 80). Kazakhstan no longer needs many of them in their former capacity, and many Kazakh nationalists regard the "union people" as a potential "fifth column."

Of Kazakhstan's 71 districts, those with a predominantly Kazakh population are economically the most backward and have the highest percentage of unemployed (*Kazakhstanskaia pravda*, April 21, 1989). The developmental lag and the ethnic division of labor that hinder Kazakh participation in modern sectors of the economy have contributed to a growth in ethnic competition. The violent disturbances and interethnic conflicts of the summer of 1989 in Novyi Uzen', Munaishi, Dzetybai, and other centers of oil industry in the Mangyshlak Peninsula in Western Kazakhstan (*Izvestiia*, June 20, 21, 23, 1989; *Kazakhstanskaia pravda*, June 22, 1989; *Pravda*, June 22, 23, 1989; *Leninshil zhas*, July 14, 1989; Sheehy 1989a; Rorlich 1989) demonstrate where this situation is going. The central, Moscow-based organizations pumped oil from there for decades. In order not to build schools, hospitals, and day care centers, they brought in temporary workers from the North Caucasus and other parts of the Soviet Union. These people received better pay and living conditions. In addition, migrants from the Caucasus managed to seize many lucrative positions in trade and services (Samoilenko 1989). The central organizations viewed the local Kazakh population as a burden despite the fact that they constitute the majority in Novyi Uzen' and neighboring towns and settlements. Every three months airplanes brought a new shift of 12,000 people to Mangyshlak. These shifts included not only skilled oil-industry workers, but also secretaries, cooks, and even office cleaners, while 18,000 Kazakh youths remained unemployed with nowhere to go (Zhambulov 1991: 98). As a result, the Kazakhs began to demand the expulsion of migrants of Caucasian origin and the provision of jobs for their own unemployed population. Mobs went on a rampage which lasted for several days and resulted in several deaths, numerous injuries, and great damage to various consumer enterprises and services. Only after these disturbances did Moscow give the order to provide some Kazakhs with jobs (Asylbekov 1991: 44).

An ethnic division of labor exists also in agriculture. Kazakhs supply most of the unskilled labor for pastoral production and, to a lesser degree, for cotton cultivation. Ethnic minorities such as Russians, Ukrainians, Germans, and Koreans, among others, prefer to be occupied in other, more mechanized, and better paid branches of agriculture (Brusina 1990: 20). This situation also has a long history. Thus, the virgin land campaign in Kazakhstan was at Kazakh expense. In Northern Kazakhstan their livestock-raising state and collective farms were closed, and Kazakh employees were prevented from becoming involved in grain production.

The amalgamation of collective farms (*kolkhozes*) into larger units during the Brezhnev period again affected Kazakh peasants and pastoralists in a negative way. It abandoned many Kazakh small settlements (*auls*). Furthermore, directors of newly created state farms (*sovkhozes*) offered jobs only to young male Kazakhs; old herdsmen (*chabans*) remained in their *auls* (Alimdzanov 1988).

Moreover, the Soviet state confiscated about 20 million of the 270 million hectares of Kazakhstan's grazing and arable lands for numerous military grounds and ranges, the nuclear test site at Semipalatinsk, and the satellite and missile test center at Baikonur (*Nezavisimaia gazeta*, May 26, 1993: 6). There were virtually no Kazakhs among their employees, and the state ousted the indigenous population from these lands (Nazarbaev 1990: 3; Kunaev 1992: 234). Although the anti-nuclear movement in Kazakhstan has united people from different ethnic groups, some Kazakh intellectuals claim that ethnic Kazakhs have suffered more than other groups as a result of the nuclear-weapons tests. They refer to Kazakh villagers who were used as human guinea pigs during above-ground nuclear tests in the 1950s, and to those who for three decades suffered and died from the consequences of radiation leaks. The Soviet military and public health service always denied this fact (Brown 1991a: 29; Brown 1991b; Eremeev 1991; Lushin 1992).

The overpopulated Kazakh rural regions of the republic also suffer from erosion, salinization, and desertification, the results of erroneous agro-technology, overgrazing, and a trend from multispecies to monospecies herd composition. In 1989, salt marshes occupied about 650,000 hectares in Kazakhstan (Wolfson 1990: 40–42). During the last few years, an increasing number of Kazakhs have migrated from overpopulated Southern Kazakhstan to the northern, grain-producing parts of the country, thus, pressing the Russian population, which is in the majority there. A growing competition in the economic and social spheres has resulted in deteriorating ethnic relations in Northern Kazakhstan (Alexandrov 1994: 24).

Besides this, during the last 20 or 30 years many Kazakhs began to move from overpopulated and underemployed rural areas to the cities. Thus, in 1970, Kazakhs made up only 12.4 percent of the population in

Alma-Ata (now Almaty), the capital of Kazakhstan; in 1979, they constituted 16.7 percent; and in 1989, already 22.5 percent (Brown 1990a: 19). In the 1970s Kazakhs became one of the most mobile ethnic groups in the Soviet Union (*Naselenie SSSR* . . . 1983: 39–40, table 12). (See table 5.4, p. 266.)

Educationally and professionally, the new migrants from the rural areas are at a disadvantage and encounter strong competition from other ethnic groups. Moreover, social advancement and career promotion for the urban population require a good command of Russian. This puts the Kazakhs in an underprivileged position in comparison with Russian-speaking urbanites and intensifies ethnic competition. Furthermore, if the new migrants fail in the cities, they usually cannot return to their villages and small towns, because their jobs, if they had any, are already occupied by other people.

At best, these people can find only unskilled jobs in the cities. They have little sympathy for the Russians, whom they tend to associate with foremen, team leaders, and superiors of different rank, in other words, with the urban population's alien, competing, and privileged group. Both groups have different incomes, values, life-styles, and maintain few contacts with each other (Galiev 1990). At worst, the new Kazakh migrants constitute a new and growing underclass in the cities of Kazakhstan. In the summer of 1990, when some of these desperate people lost any hope for government assistance, they illegally seized plots of land near Alma-Ata, which created an explosive situation in the capital (Ponomarev 1991: 21, 31, 33). In this respect, the situation in Kazakhstan is very similar to conditions in some other developing countries. The movement of rural groups into urban sectors dominated by ethnic groups with distinctive linguistic and cultural traits precipitates ethnic conflict and ultimately nationalism (Brass 1976: 234).

Interethnic and Intraethnic Competition

At the same time, opportunities for social advancement in the political sphere, and some other prestigious or profitable spheres, are better for the Kazakhs than for other ethnic groups in the republic. Through various kinds of official and unofficial affirmative actions undertaken during the communist period and continuing afterwards, they are overrepresented in virtually all republican foci of power. Also, in the ratio of Kazakhs to other ethnic groups, there is a greater number of both Kazakh intelligentsia trained in the humanities and students in general. In the 1979–1989 period, the proportion of Russians occupied in the administration decreased by 8.2 percent; in science, by 12.3 percent; in trade and ser-vices, by 8.7 percent (Ostapenko and Subbotina 1993: 296). The reasons for this situation are quite obvious and connected not only with ethnic favoritism.

The successful implementation of colonial rule often depended on the participation of some of the indigenous population (see, for example, Mutiso 1975 for an analogous situation in Kenya in the colonial period), and the Soviet policy toward Kazakhstan was no exception. During the purges of the 1920s and 1930s the state physically destroyed the political elite in Kazakhstan. It also destroyed the cultural elite (Kommunistiches-kaia partiia Kazakhstana 1990: 61; Kozyrbaev 1990; Kuderina 1994). Ac-cording to recently published but very incomplete data, from 1930 to 1953 the state sentenced 35,000 of these people to various punishments, and shot more than 5,000 of them (*Kazakhstanskaia pravda*, February 16, 1990).

The Soviets created in Kazakhstan a completely new political elite. In this elite, ethnic Kazakhs outnumbered members of all other ethnic groups because the recruitment to this elite was based, to a significant extent, on ethnic affiliation. An exception was made only for the most important position, the first secretary of the Communist Party of Kazakhstan. Dur-ing the whole Soviet period only 4 of 22 of these secretaries were ethnic Kazakhs (*Literaturnaia gazeta*, November 28, 1990: 11).[3]

The Kazakh political elite's privileged positions in the local power struc-tures depended on their compliance with all of Moscow's demands and goals, and with their capabilities to implement policies dictated by the center. In addition, they had to embrace the Russian language and, at least in public, some of the Russian culture and life-style. In return Mos-cow gave them the right to run internal affairs in Kazakhstan and to dis-tribute preferential treatment and high-level jobs. In order to secure their support the Soviet regime reserved a significant percentage of these jobs for Kazakhs.

It is true that in the beginning of the restructuring period a growing number of Russians were introduced into this elite and administrative apparatus by the Moscow center. However, they were sent to Kazakh-stan from other republics.[4] The local Russian population continued to complain about discrimination in political and educational spheres.

---

[3] Remarkably, one of the slogans of the Kazakh demonstrators in Alma-Ata, in Decem-ber 1986, was: "To each people its own leader" (Asylbekov 1991: 43).

[4] In this respect the appointment of Kolbin, a Russian who had no connection with Kazakhstan whatsoever, to the position of first secretary of the Republican Party organiza-tion, which was made by the Moscow center without any consultation with the local lead-ership and resulted in the serious disturbances in Alma-Ata in December 1986, may serve

Although the educational level of Kazakhs in Kazakhstan is still lower than that of Russians there (in 1979, 69 out of 1,000 Russians compared with 56 out of 1,000 Kazakhs had a higher education), the number of educated Kazakhs is growing. The Kazakh political elite encouraged this process, sometimes at the expense of other ethnic groups. At the same time an ethnic division of labor still exists in Kazakhstan among those in the educated strata. While the educated Kazakhs are mainly involved in the humanities, the Russians dominate in engineering, the natural sciences, medicine, and so forth.

In almost all social levels in Kazakhstan, different nationalities occupy specific niches in which other groups are underrepresented. Thus, all of them feel victimized. Each group hinders the social and professional advancements of the other. Each group perceives this sectional unevenness in ethnic divisions of labor as oppressive and discriminatory. As a result, the tense situation has emerged in which some social differences take on ethnic colors, and social mobility struggles with ethnic boundaries. This contributes to a general deterioration of interethnic relations in the republic.

Intraethnic competition among the Kazakhs further complicates the interethnic competition in Kazakhstan. Belonging to a certain *zhuz* (in the past, something similar to a tribal confederation) is still important to the Kazakhs. In particular, this factor is used in the struggle for power between regional political elites (Kuandykov 1994: 22). There are many members of the Middle (Srednii) Zhuz among the Kazakh intelligentsia, and in the 1920s–1930s their predominance was even more significant. At the same time, Kunaev, the long-serving first secretary of the Communist Party of Kazakhstan in the Brezhnev period, tried to put his fellow tribesmen from the southern *oblasts* of Kazakhstan, that is, those from the Great (Starshii) Zhuz, into positions of power. Moscow officially condemned this policy after Kunaev lost power. However, his successor, Kolbin, in just the first 18 months of his incumbency, tried to eliminate favoritism toward Kazakhs from the Great Zhuz but then abandoned this attempt. Some members of the Kazakh intelligentsia complained to me that Nazarbaev, today's leader of Kazakhstan, owes his career to Kunaev, and continues the policy of encouraging members of the Great Zhuz. This is hardly true; some articles in the Russian press claim that Nazarbaev

as an example. (Much has already been published about the Alma-Ata unrest, and the number of publications is growing. See, for example, *Alma-Ata: 1986* [1991]; *Izvestiia*, November 15, 1989, and September 27, 1990; *Kazakhstanskaia pravda*, November 18, 1989; Arkhiv Samizdata, Nos. 6434, 6435, 6436; Focus on Kazakhstan 1990; Brown 1990d: 20–21; Nazarbaev 1991a: 177ff.; Kunaev 1992: 267ff.).

belongs to the Junior (Mladshii) Zhuz (Kiyanitsa 1992), although others (*Moscow News* 15 [April 15–21, 1994]: 6; see also Helgesen 1994: 148) confirm that he is indeed a member of the Great Zhuz. Be that as it may, the persistent attention paid to the *zhuz* affiliations is indicative by itself.

Nazarbaev's desire to move the capital of Kazakhstan from the southern city of Almaty (formerly Alma-Ata) to the northern Akmola (named Tselinograd from 1961 to 1992) may be partly explained by his desire to weaken the influence of the southern clans on the state apparatus (Ardaev 1993). Incidentally, Nazarbaev claims that the Central Committee of the Soviet Communist Party was well informed of the situation and was deliberately playing with tribal differences among the Kazakh leadership in order to set these people against each other and make them even more docile (Nazarbaev 1991b: 4).

Today, one should not overestimate the intraethnic competition among the Kazakhs. It is certainly only of secondary importance and is much less salient than, for example, among the Kazakhs' southern neighbors, the Turkmen (Naumova 1991: 302–3). It is possible that the importance of ethnic subdivisions within the Kazakh community will diminish in the future because of intensive internal migrations and a growing number of marriages between members of different *zhuz* (Dzanguzhin 1993: 179). On the other hand, I would not completely exclude the future possibility of a revival in tribalism in Kazakhstan if the proper conditions emerge. There is already some evidence that the growing competition for pastures among the Kazakh pastoralists results in increasing salience of clanal divisions (personal communication, Dr. Alma Kunanbaeva).

The Political Development

When ethnicity is salient in the social structure of modernizing society, different ethnic groups contest political participation, power sharing, economic opportunities, and cultural status, and tend to incline, in Connor's terms (Connor 1973), toward ethnic nationalism. Kolbin's aforementioned appointment provoked the indignation of Kazakh youths, and on December 17 and 18, 1986, at least 5,000 students and young workers protested in Alma-Ata. Amongst their slogans one was particularly remarkable: "Perestroika is going on, but where is democracy?" (Nazarbaev 1991a: 179).

Spetsnaz (special purpose) troops, military cadets, and internal troops from various cities were called against the demonstrators. In addition, the Russian civil population (especially from the "people's patrols"—the auxiliary of the police), armed with clubs, metal picks, and other weapons made for this occasion at the industrial enterprises of the city, were used to put them down. In several parts of Alma-Ata, particularly in the working-class neighborhoods, the Russian blue-collar workers organized hunts for all Kazakhs appearing in the streets (Kubekov 1990).

According to official reports, six people died; however, Kazakh sources suspect that the state covered up the deaths of at least 58 people or even more (*Zheltoksan* 2 [1993]: 2). (The exact number will never be known, since a few years afterwards most of the archives on these events were deliberately destroyed to hide the truth.) More than 1,700 people were wounded. About 8,500 people were held or arrested, and many of them were beaten. In the following repressions, hundreds of Kazakhs were sentenced to prison internment, fined, or fired from work. Many Kazakhs were obliged to leave the city either to avoid troubles or because they were ordered to do so. About 3,000 students were expelled from the universities and other educational institutions. Nevertheless, despite all attempts, the prosecutor and the KGB failed to present proof that the disturbances had been organized.

The events in Alma-Ata were characterized by Moscow as nationalistic riots. Kazakhstan's leadership was ordered to take immediate measures "for improving the education of the workers in the spirit of internationalism" (*Pravda*, December 26, 1986). The Soviet press began a staged campaign to fight against Kazakh nationalism. Some of the Kazakh newspapers were accused of publishing more material about the Kazakh people than about the Russians living in Kazakhstan. The literary magazine in the Kazakh language was criticized for publishing Kazakh authors instead of translating the writings of authors working in other languages. Another magazine was censured for publishing articles about the Kazakh clans and tribes, and particularly for articles about the growth of the Kazakh population in the republic. Solomentsev, the chairman of the Committee for Party Control in the CPSU Central Committee, pronounced the first and only kindergarten opened in Alma-Ata in the Kazakh language to be a "breeding ground of nationalism" (*Ogoniok* 26 [June 1989]).

The further development in the Soviet Union soon forced Moscow to reconsider its policy toward Kazakhstan and to agree reluctantly on the opposite interpretation of the events in its capital. However, the damage has been done. Kazakhs consider these events not only the first mass action against Soviet colonialism during the perestroika period; the events also had a traumatic impact on interethnic relations in the republic.

Kazakhstan's stability is fragile. In October 1990, when President Nazarbaev persuaded, or rather forced, some leaders of the Kazakh major opposition groups in Alma-Ata to declare a two-year moratorium on demonstrations in the capital, others promptly staged a demonstration against the moratorium (*Izvestiia*, March 13, 14, 1990). In June 1992, the opposition resumed demonstrations, which this time took on an open anti-government character (*Izvestiia*, June 17, 22, 23, 1992).

The ethnic peace in Kazakhstan is very fragile and exists mainly because of the quantitative parity of the two major ethnic groups. However, the worsening economic situation and growing unemployment[5] have clearly strengthened Kazakh malevolence toward the ethnic minorities in the republic, including the Muslim ones. Thus, in July and August 1990, Kazakhs clashed with Chechens in the Dzhambul Raion (District). In the beginning of 1992, activists of the Kazakh organizations Azat and Kazaktili forced Chechens and Ingush living in the Novyi Mir settlement in the Taldy-Kyrgan Oblast to sell their houses for a mere trifle and immediately leave Kazakhstan (*Nezavisimaia gazeta*, February 4, 1992: 3). In the summer of 1991, Meskhetian Turks living in the Enbekshikazakhskii Raion were warned by their Kazakh neighbors there that they would either have to leave or face the music (Khovratovich 1991). In 1992, a total of 370,000 people, including about 250,000 Russians, left Kazakhstan. In the near future the situation may become even worse, because it is expected that by the year 2000 at least 1 million more Kazakh youths will move from the rural areas to the cities (Tatimov 1990: 104; Suzhikov et al. 1993: 141).

With the exception of the former Communist Party, which was renamed the Socialist Party at the end of 1991, all other political organizations, parties, and movements in Kazakhstan in 1988-1992 were organized or split along ethnic lines (Bychkova 1990). The paramount motivation behind the Kazakh organizations is to preserve the territorial integrity of the republic. Solzhenitsyn's proposal to annex Northern Kazakhstan, published in "How We Should Build Russia" (*Literaturnaia gazeta*, September 18, 1990), led to protests from a wide spectrum of Kazakh intelligentsia and youths and to the demonstrations in Alma-Ata on September 21-23, 1990. These Kazakhs reminded the Russians that the Omsk Oblast in the Russian Federation was once Kazakh territory (*Literary Gazette International*, November 1990: 5).

As early as 1990, several emerging parties and movements (Azat, Alash, and Zheltoksan) were openly demanding the republic's complete independence and secession from the Soviet Union (Brown 1990c: 10-11; Ponomarev 1991: 27ff.). In October 1990, when the republic's Parlia-

---

[5] In 1993, Kazakhstan's gross domestic product decreased by 12.9 percent from what it had been in 1992, and the volume of industrial production fell by 16.1 percent; agricultural production, by 9.8 percent; and construction and assembly work, by 25 percent. The production of main foodstuffs fell drastically: meat, by 12.6 percent; sugar, by 36.1 percent; margarine, by 48 percent; and butter, by 25.4 percent. Kazakhstan's cabinet of ministers has admitted that the country was on the verge of hyperinflation and that price increases are out of control (*Moscow News* 8 [February 25-March 3, 1994]: 7).

ment made a declaration of sovereignty, many Kazakhs picketed it carrying the slogan "Don't sign the Union Treaty" (*Izvestiia*, December 9, 1990). Significantly, one clause of this declaration states that in the future the right to regulate migration to Kazakhstan will belong to the republic itself (*Kazakhstanskaia pravda*, October 28, 1990). Beginning in 1988, the most outspoken champions of Kazakh nationalism started to call for a complete halt to in-migration of Russians to Kazakhstan (*Kazakhstanskaia pravda*, February 4, 1988; see also Sheehy 1988a). Significant numbers of Kazakhs do not hide their desire for Russians, Ukrainians, Germans, and other non-Kazakhs to leave Kazakhstan (*Nezavisimaia gazeta*, April 20, 1993: 5). The saying "We bid farewell to Germans [freely immigrating to Germany] and shake hands with them; we turn Russians out by kicking their backs" is rather popular nowadays in nationalistic circles.

All political arguments ultimately boil down to whether the republic should evolve into a Kazakh ethnic state or a multiethnic national state. Just as in Assam, Malaysia, Sri Lanka, Fiji, not to mention the former Soviet republics, nationalists in Kazakhstan use the "indigenous" issue (and in addition, the consequences of Russian and Soviet colonialism) as an argument for providing Kazakhs priority and special political status. In the political arena, Russians are already at a disadvantage. After the May 1990 election, the percentage of Kazakh deputies in Kazakhstan's Parliament (Supreme Soviet) increased from 46.7 to 54.72, while the percentage of Russian deputies decreased from 41.0 to 28.8. One of the reasons for this change was that Kazakhstan remained the only Soviet republic where a peculiar electoral system was (deliberately?) retained. Its elected deputies came not only from electoral districts but also from public organizations, such as trade unions, the Academy of Sciences, and the Union of Writers. The leadership of these organizations traditionally consisted mainly of Kazakhs. As a result, of 88 deputies elected by them, 61 (69.3 percent) were Kazakhs (cf. with 133 Kazakh deputies, 49.3 percent of all the deputies elected from territorial districts) (Tishkov 1991). In the parliamentary elections of March 1994, which in the opinion of international observers were not free of the government's pressure and manipulation, the Kazakhs won 103 of 177 seats (58 percent of the total number); Russians, 49 seats; Ukrainians, 10 seats; the rest of the seats were won by members of other ethnic minorities that will be represented by 1–3 deputies (S. Kozlov 1994).

Many Kazakhs also worry that radical economic privatization and the transition to a market economy will hurt the descendants of pastoral nomads, who do not have any tradition of commerce and free enterprise and will inhibit, rather than facilitate, the emergence of a strong Kazakh middle class (Ardaev 1992a). Thus, the nationalistic Republican Party expressed the concern that privatization of land and industrial enterprises would be detrimental to the interests of Kazakhs, "whose psychology is not yet ready for market economic principles" (*Nezavisimaia gazeta*, April 11, 1992). Remarkably enough, President Nazarbaev explained his antipathy to outright ownership of land by pointing out that to permit such ownership would be alien to the heritage and mentality of the former nomads (Brown 1991f: 25). The last decree on the state farms' sale implies only short-term and long-term lease but still not the private ownership of land (*Segodnia*, January 27, 1994: 1; *Izvestiia*, April 1, 1994: 2).

The fight for a wider use of the Kazakh language in education, culture, and administrative practice relates, not only to the growth of ethnic consciousness and the desire to prevent acculturation, but also to the mundane motivation to place the Kazakhs in more advantageous positions with respect to other ethnic groups. Not without reason, the Slavs in the republic are afraid of the policy of "Kazakhization," which they consider an "infringement on other people's rights" (Svoik and Lan'ko 1994: 43–44). While 60.4 percent of the Kazakhs know the Russian language, only 0.9 percent of the Russians and 0.6 percent of the Ukrainians in Kazakhstan can communicate in Kazakh (*SSSR v tsifrakh v 1989 gody ...* 1990: 38). The language law of September 1989, which declared Kazakh to be the state language of Kazakhstan and required its eventual widespread use in public life, led to protests from the Russian-speaking population.[6]

The fact that the Kazakhs are today a minority in Northern Kazakhstan further aggravates the interethnic relations in the country. In 1989, their percentage in the Kokchetav Oblast was 28.9; in the Pavlodar Oblast, 28.5; in the Kustanai Oblast, 22.9; in the Tselinograd Oblast, 22.4; and in the Karaganda Oblast, only 17.2 (Brown 1990a: 19). Remarkably, the Kazakh nationalistic parties are receiving the strongest support in these very regions (personal communication with S. Aktaev, one of the leaders of the Azat movement and the Republican Party). Also significant is the fact that the Kazakh immigrants from Mongolia are settled in Northern Kazakhstan. Its Russian population considers this a deliberate attempt to change the ethnodemographic situation (*Nezavisimaia gazeta*, January 18, 1994: 4).

---

[6] The language issue is becoming important also to those educated Kazakhs who in the recent past were caught up in the forces of linguistic acculturation. Nowadays a good command of the Kazakh language is an asset in administrative, educational, and cultural spheres, and the acculturated part of the Kazakh intelligentsia faces growing competition from those to whom the Kazakh language remained the mother tongue. However, so far this situation has not brought a majority of this faction of the intelligentsia to ally with the Russian-speaking non-Kazakh groups.

Despite the agreement on the inviolability of interrepublican borders made by the leaders of the Commonwealth of Independent States, some Russians living in northeastern and northwestern Kazakhstan, encouraged by sympathetic nationalists in Russia, want these territories transferred to Russia as the best guarantee against lowering their positions and status (Carlson 1990). The Ural and Semirek Cossacks are particularly persistent in this respect; no wonder their relations with Kazakhs are deteriorating (*Kazakhstanskaia pravda*, September 2, 1990; *Izvestiia*, September 18, 1991; *Nezavisimaia gazeta*, October 3, 1991; Kiselev 1991; Desiatov, 1991b). In January 1995 an *ataman* (chief) of the Semirek Cossacks told me that their ultimate goal is to make all of Kazakhstan a part of Russia and that to achieve this goal the Cossacks are ready to take up arms. However, the Cossacks are not alone. Before the adoption of the declaration of Kazakhstan's sovereignty in October 25, 1990, the Ust'-Kamenogorsk City Soviet of the *oblast* of the same name, where Russians make up a majority of the population, threatened to secede from Kazakhstan if discussion of the declaration was not stopped and the law on language not suspended.

Demands to create Russian territorial autonomy or autonomies in Kazakhstan met with strong opposition from Kazakhstan's government and Kazakh public opinion (*Nezavisimaia gazeta*, April 20, 1993: 5). In 1994, the Russian mass media reported cases of persecution of the leaders of the Russian community in Northern Kazakhstan (*Segodnia*, April 15, 1994). Likewise, Kazakhstan's constitution excludes double citizenship—another demand by the Russians in the country—and President Nazarbaev resists Russia's persuasion to grant it to her compatriots because this would mean that almost half of Kazakhstan's population could become Russian citizens (*Nezavisimaia gazeta*, February 5, 1993: 2; March 19, 1994: 1). He also made quite clear that any territorial claims to Kazakhstan by Russia would imply unavoidable bloodshed (*Nezavisimaia gazeta*, May 6, 1992: 5). He is certainly alarmed that Zhirinovsky's claims have a sympathetic ear among some, more moderate, Russian politicians (*Nezavisimaia gazeta*, December 23, 1993: 3). Once, he even stated that Russia's policy toward the Russian population of Kazakhstan resembles the policy of Nazi Germany toward the Sudeten Germans (*Radio Liberty*, November 24, 1993).

Remarkably, the promotion of nationalism concerns the intelligentsia more than it concerns some groups in the political elite in Kazakhstan, although interethnic tension and competition are felt even within the Socialist Party. Apparently, the multiethnic composition of Kazakhstan was one of the reasons President Nazarbaev argued for civil accord and interethnic accommodation in the republic and for the preservation of the Soviet Union. On many occasions he declared his allegiance, not to "nationalism by blood," but to "nationalism by soil," which means that his official goal is to make Kazakhstan a nation-state based on citizenship and habitation. He constantly emphasizes that no one ethnic group should have privileges in the republic. During the 1991 presidential electoral campaign he stated, "I will never call a single person in Kazakhstan a migrant" (Kiyanitsa 1991). So far Nazarbaev has proved to be a very skillful politician who is capable, if not of defusing interethnic tension, then of keeping it under control. However, one may wonder whether and for how long he will be capable of maneuvering in the future. The Kazakh intelligentsia appeals to him "to help his own people" and reproaches him for "neglecting interests of the Kazakh people." On the other hand, the Russian-speaking population reproach him for being led by Kazakh nationalists; they claim that although Nazarbaev avoids publicly favoring Kazakhs, this is just what he is doing in his practical measures (Desiatov 1991a).

Nevertheless non-Kazakhs in Kazakhstan certainly consider Nazarbaev the least evil of the possible alternatives. Of the whole electorate, 98.8 percent voted for him in the December 1, 1991, elections (*Izvestiia*, December 2, 1991); of the 150,000 people who voted nay, the majority were supporters of Kazakh nationalist movements (mainly the supporters of Alash and Zheltoksan). They criticize Nazarbaev for being a "poor defender of the indigenous population."[7]

It is clear that today the issue of power sharing between different nationalities in Kazakhstan remains unsolved. Although Nazarbaev vigorously denies that different nationalities in his country are put in unequal conditions and insists that there is no discrimination against anyone who does not know Kazakh (*Nezavisimaia gazeta*, January 6, 1994: 3), the Russians in Kazakhstan hold the opposite opinion. Not without reason they complain that they already are denied some prominent and lucrative positions under the pretext that they do not know the Kazakh language, which was elevated to the status of the state language of the country, while the Russian language was granted the ambiguous status of being the language of interethnic intercourse (*Nezavisimaia gazeta*, April 20, 1993: 5; January 6, 1994: 3). Some Russian deputies of the new Parliament have already stated that they are going to demand that both languages be declared the state languages of Kazakhstan. The virtual absence of consociational or federate structures makes developing a bargaining political culture a particularly difficult task. The communists have failed to secure ethnic accord. It remains to be seen whether the recently emerged new parties, which consist mainly of the former communists and are not based on an implied ethnic principle, be it the presidential

---

[7] One should also take into account that there were no alternative presidential aspirants.

Union of People's Unity or the centrist National Congress of Kazakhstan, are capable of doing better by commanding the "ethnic center," like, for example, the Alliance Party (now the National Front) in Malaysia (Stubbs 1989), and thus fostering an interethnic accommodation.

Conclusions

As in other plural modernizing countries with a growing mobility in the population, in Kazakhstan objective demands of cultural homogeneity required by the economic base of social life conflict with ethnically connected social differences, which hinder the flow of personnel across the lines of social stratification (Gellner 1983: 94–96). It is just these differences that have become a source of explosive polarization and social disunity, while ethnically unmarked differences remain tolerable.

In this respect the situation in Kazakhstan and in some other republics of the former Soviet Union resembles the situations in other multiethnic countries. The competition for political participation, economic opportunities, and cultural status virtually ensures that "ethnicity will remain an important criterion for political organization and that ethnically based claims will maintain a prominent place on the addenda of the state" (Esman 1989b: 60).

"The working men have no country. We cannot take from them what they have not got," claimed the Founding Fathers in the *Communist Manifesto* (Marx 1973: 84) in a belief that class membership and rational economic interest will erase ethnic solidarity and, eventually, ethnic differences (Connor 1984b). Many ethnic communities in the former Soviet Union came to a different conclusion. Now, as then, they consider blood much thicker than the ink that was spilt to convince them of the opposite. Ethnic differences became and continue to be more salient and more important than class ones; ethnic membership began to be considered the best leverage for social mobility and economic advancement. In an atmosphere of overall economic and political crisis, ethnicity has become the common political language for the Kazakhs and millions of members of other nationalities. Nationalistic demands have turned out to be the effective means for political mobilization of the masses in the country, which until recently declared internationalism a component of its official ideology. The ethnic corporatism, implicitly or explicitly, makes equality of opportunities for members of competing ethnic groups fictitious to a large extent (Gordon 1975: 106). This may explain why nationalism in the newly emerged Commonwealth of Independent States has usually taken not state-associated or civic but ethnic form.

Map 4. Yakutia

6

Yakutian Nationalism
in a Search for Identities

> When side by side for a long time
> An old and strong people lives with a small one,
> The younger people is treated unfairly
> In secret and patently, but always in everything.
> —Kulakovsky, *Snovidenie shamana*

The opening epigraph presents lines taken from the poem "The Dream of the Shaman" by the classic author of Yakut literature, Alexei Kulakovsky (1877–1926), called Eksekiuliakh Alexei (Aquiline Alexei). This poem is known virtually by all educated Yakuts; it was practically forbidden for many decades, but that only increased its popularity.

One variety of nationalism existing now in the ex-Soviet Union is represented among others by such peoples as the Abkhaz, Mari, Buryat, and Bashkirs, who enjoy a certain degree of autonomy as indigenous populations but, because of internal migrations and other developments, constitute a minority in their own homelands. One of their main concerns and priorities is to assert a privileged position in their respective autonomous formations. Yakutia illustrates this situation well.

Located in East Siberia, Yakutia (Sakha)[1] is crucial to the future of the Russian Federation. Although its population density is very low, only one person per 0.9 square kilometer, Yakutia occupies 3,103,200 square kilometers, an area roughly six times larger than France. The country is enormously rich in diamonds, gold, coal, oil, gas, tin, silver, antimony, tungsten, timber, and other natural resources.

Russian experts in interethnic relations in Moscow currently consider Yakutia relatively quiet and tend to underestimate the troubles the Russian

---

[1] Sakha is the self-appellation of the people. They resent the name Yakuts, which the Russians call them. Since April 1992 the official name of the country is the Sakha Republic (Yakutia).

government may face there in the future (Yamskov 1992: 47–48). Actually, at present the situation in the republic is fraught with tension and conflicts.

Background

The Yakuts are the northernmost Turkic-speaking people. In the thirteenth and fourteenth centuries, or even earlier, their ancestors migrated from the Lake Baikal area to the middle Lena River and the lower Viliui and Aldan Rivers, and then gradually spread to the Arctic Ocean shores, assimilating some indigenous ethnic groups along their way (Okladnikov 1949: 299ff.; Levin and Potapov 1956: 269–70; Forsyth 1992: 55–57, 165, 176; Seroshevsky 1993: 174ff.). Even in East Siberia the Yakuts retained strong pastoralist traditions in economy and culture because of the meadowlands along the Lena and some of its tributaries. These provided pastures and hay for their unique breeds of horses and cattle, which are well adjusted to the harsh environment. The Yakut horse has the ability to uncover grass that is under as much as 50 centimeters of snow (and the snow cover lasts in the country for seven to eight months a year).[2]

Since the seventeenth century, Yakutia has come under Russia's sway; however, despite the colonial exploitation and contrary to other indigenous Siberian ethnic groups, the Yakuts have demonstrated a remarkable capability of accommodation and enterprising skills. The Yakuts spread far and wide beyond the Lena area, particularly in the northeastern and western directions. The Yakut language became a lingua franca all over East Siberia. The number of Russians who settled in Yakutia was very limited; as late as 1917, the Yakuts and other indigenous groups constituted about 90 percent of the country's population.

In prerevolutionary times a significant part of the Russian minority in Yakutia consisted either of political exiles or of those who had lived there for many generations, were involved in agriculture, and were well acquainted with the Yakut culture and language. In the past, the Yakut language was more widespread among the Russians living in the country than it is today (Argunov 1985: 65–66). In the nineteenth century, it was said that, even at the governor's evening parties in Yakutsk, it was heard

---

[2] Unfortunately, in the 1940s and the 1950s, to a large extent these breeds were spoiled by incorrect cross-breeding imposed by the followers of the notorious Lysenko. Horses and cattle of the breeds ill-suited to the northern environment were brought to Yakutia from European Russia despite the difficulties connected with the distance and the absence of railroads and highways in the republic. Those who were reluctant to obey the order and to cross-breed were threatened with imputation of sabotage.

among the Russian guests (Argunova 1992: 13–14; Forsyth 1992: 165). However, there are still 1,311 Russians in Yakutia who consider the Yakut language their mother tongue; 7,460 Russians are fluent in Yakut (Natsional'nyi sostav ... 1990: 20). Until recently intermarriages were rather frequent. Many members of the Yakut political elite, such as President Mikhail Nikolaev, have Russian mothers or spouses. All these factors have helped to reduce ethnic tension to some extent.

However, during the last 25 years the development of mining has resulted in an influx of new migrants from European Russia and other eastern Slavic republics. As a result, the proportion of Yakuts in the overall population of the republic has dropped from 90 percent in 1920, to 43 percent in 1970, to 36.6 percent in 1979, and to 33.4 percent in 1989. (See table 6.1, p. 267.)

The development of the mining regions in Yakutia has greatly altered the ethnographic, demographic, and social structure of the country (Fedorova 1993: 44ff.). Powerful state trusts were subordinated directly to the central ministries in Moscow. They were excluded from the competence of the government of Yakutia, which has never shared in the revenues from their enterprises. They became a "state within a state" in Yakutia. In 1989, the Yakut diamonds alone brought the Soviet Union $1.7 billion (Marchintsev, Krivochapkine, and Kopylov 1992: 25); however, the government of Yakutia controlled only 4 percent of the republic's industries and received only 1 percent of their revenues. Industries other than mining, the infrastructure, and services remain undeveloped, and agriculture is in decay. The republic still has to import 90 percent of foodstuffs and manufactured goods. By 1989, of 73 autonomous republics, *krais,* and *oblasts* of the Russian Federation, Yakutia was 70th in terms of provision with dwellings and last in public services and amenities (Maksimov 1990: 8).

The intensive development of mining has resulted in the deterioration of the environment (Maksimov 1990: 13; Marchintsev, Krivochapkine, and Kopylov 1992: 25ff.), which is particularly pronouced in the conditions of the Far North, where the environment is extremely fragile and susceptible to degradation. In Viliui, a region in the historical heartland of Yakutia, the rivers are polluted, the taiga forest is destroyed, and the indigenous peoples' life span is an unacceptable 40–45 years (Savvinov 1992: 29ff.; Krivochapkine 1992: 35ff.).

While the indigenous population was virtually prevented from participation in the mining industries and their traditional economic activities were deteriorating, the new migrants enjoyed higher wages, bonuses, better living conditions and provisions, and some other privileges, such as "northern wage-increments," which were denied to the local population (Maksimov 1990: 9). As a result, the living standards of Yakuts are twice as low as the republic's average and much lower than the general average in Russia. In spite of the severely cold climate, only 63.2 percent of apartments and houses in the rural districts of Yakutia have central heating; 22.1 percent of them have running water; and 17 percent of them are supplied with a sewerage system (Diakonov 1992).[3] The death rate of the rural population of Yakutia is twice as high as the urban one (Maksimov 1990: 12).

In spite of incentives, many new migrants cannot adapt to the harsh northern environment. Often they turn back after they have made some money, serving only one or two terms of their contracts (three or six years). In 1959–1989, the migration turnover in Yakutia reached 4.1 million persons (*Sotsialisticheskaia Yakutia*, June 30, 1990). These temporary migrants, a portion of whom consists of criminals (*Sotsialisticheskaia Yakutia*, July 21, 1989), do not have any respect for, or interest in, the indigenous peoples and their cultures. Furthermore, they are not concerned with the preservation of the environment, and tend to look down on the Yakuts. The policy of Russification also affected Yakuts in a negative way. In the 1960s, the Yakut schools were ordered to teach only in Russian beginning in the seventh grade. Simultaneously, a number of Yakut-language schools and preschool educational institutions were drastically curtailed. In 1989–1990, the education of 22 percent of Yakut school children was conducted only in Russian. In 1986, in Yakutsk, the capital of the republic, only 16 percent of the Yakut school children were fluent in their native language (Argunova 1992: 75).

It is not surprising that interethnic relations in Yakutia have deteriorated during the last decades. Opinion polls revealed that 68–75 percent of Yakuts complain that Russians did not demonstrate a respect for Yakut traditions, culture, and language (Maksimov 1990: 15). In 1986, the tension resulted in open clashes between the Yakut and the Russian students in Yakutsk. Actually, this was the first open outbreak of interethnic strife during the restructuring period, and many Yakuts are proud to note that they were the first non-Russian group at that time who publicly protested against what they considered the colonialist attitude. However, my informants in Yakutia insist that these clashes were actually provoked by the KGB, who wished to use them as a pretext to step up preventive measures against a growing Yakut nationalism.

To a large extent, the division of labor in Yakutia coincides with ethnic divisions. In seven industrial and mining districts of Yakutia, the Yakuts

---

[3] I am most grateful to N. Diakonov for his kind permission to quote from his manuscript in this chapter.

divisions. In seven industrial and mining districts of Yakutia, the Yakuts constitute less than 20 percent of the whole population. In the Mirninskii District, where the diamond mining is concentrated, the Yakuts constitute only 3.8 percent of the population. The majority of the agricultural population consists of Yakuts (271,219 persons out of 362,102), whereas in the mining sector Russians dominate and occupy all privileged positions. Until recently all directors and other managerial personnel of mining enterprises were appointed by Moscow and were not accountable to the government of Yakutia. However, while economic power in Yakutia belongs to Russians, it is not accompanied by their political power. (See table 6.2, p. 267.)

In the republican political elite the Yakuts are overrepresented. This is due, first, to the Soviet nationality policy's provision of some members of indigenous ethnic groups with privileged positions in the local party apparatus and administrations in order to secure their support (Khazanov 1991: 57ff.) and, second, to the association of many Russians in Yakutia, particularly the most influential managerial-administrative personnel in the mining industry, with Moscow rather than Yakutia, and to their lack of interest in the local political process. The political passivity of the Russians in Yakutia and the system of electoral districts, which favors the rural population, have created a situation in which 46.3 percent of the deputies of the Supreme Soviet of Yakutia elected in 1990 were ethnic Yakuts. In Il Tumin, as the new Parliament elected in December 1993 is called, ethnic Yakuts held 31 of 51 seats, while Russians held only 14 seats (Zykov 1994: 8). Ethnic Yakuts constitute 67.6 percent of the ministers and 80 percent of the heads of local administration (Ivanov 1994: 93).

The Yakuts had a developed national consciousness even before the October Revolution. The first Yakut nationalist organization, the Yakut Union, was founded as early as 1906. In the 1920s, a cultural organization, Sakha Omuk (the Yakut People), a nationalist literary journal *Cholbon* (The Morning Star), and influential intellectuals continued to resist the Sovietization and Russification of their country. In their turn, the Soviets launched several campaigns against the so-called Yakut nationalist movement, during which many members of the Yakut intelligentsia perished (Kolarz 1969: 103; Chichlo 1987: 372; Nikolaev and Ushnitskii 1990). However, a new intelligentsia has emerged. In spite of only 94,011 Yakuts living in the cities in 1989, the members of this intelligentsia are relatively numerous, well-educated, sensitive to any deterioration of the Yakuts' positions in their republic, and capable of articulating nationalistic goals.

Political Nationalism

In daily life interethnic relations in Yakutia are deteriorating. Mixed marriages, which are particularly resented by Yakut nationalists (Utkin 1991: 10) are much rarer now than in the recent past, and small-scale fights provoked by Russian youths dating their Yakut peers, or similar events, are at present rather common. Because of the ratio of Yakuts to Russians in the republic, complete independence from Russia is not considered an immediately feasible goal by the majority of Yakuts. However, they certainly wish to occupy a privileged status as the indigenous and titular nationality in the republic. During the perestroika period they wished to elevate Yakutia's status to that of an all-union republic. At present they also desire that Yakutia gain more sovereignty within the Russian Federation. In the latter respect, aspirations of the political elite, which consists mainly of the former communists, and the nationalistic Yakut intelligentsia coincide. Moreover, these aspirations enjoy the support of some Russians, particularly those who are living outside the mining regions and/ or do not consider their residence in the republic a temporary one. Though these Russians are afraid of the growing Yakut nationalism, they tend to support the leadership of Yakutia in its struggle with the Moscow leadership over control of the republic's economic resources. A prevailing opinion in Yakutia is that, given its richness in diamonds, gold, oil, and minerals, and its small population (1,094,065 persons in 1989 and 1,061,700 in 1994), the living standards in the republic would easily reach that of Kuwait if they were not exploited by Moscow.

The Soviet government of Gorbachev was, and now the Russian governments are, clearly unwilling to comply with Yakutia's requests, and would like to consider diamonds mined in the republic as federal property. For some time, the president of Yakutia, Mikhail Nikolaev, who is apparently on good personal terms with Yeltsin, hoped to win concessions from Moscow by demonstrating the republic's loyalty in actively supporting the Federal Treaty. In the spring of 1992, his efforts were apparently being rewarded. On March 31, just three hours before signing the Federal Treaty, Nikolaev and Yeltsin signed an economic agreement that should provide Yakutia with 25 percent of the diamonds mined in its territory, a revenue share from the diamonds sold on the foreign markets, and a right of ownership on newly discovered deposits. In addition, the Yakut government received the right to appoint the top managerial personnel in the mining industry. To the dissatisfaction of the Russian managerial elite in Yakutia, President Nikolaev began to appoint ethnic Yakuts to key positions in the mining industry. Thus, for the first time in history an ethnic Yakut became the head of the Yakut Gold Corporation (Yakut-zoloto). This put the Parliament of Yakutia in a jubilant mood, and in April 1992 it ratified the Federal Treaty practically without any discussion. Shortly, their mood sobered when it became apparent that the Russian government was not going to fulfill the agreement. In August 1992, President M. Nikolaev complained that Yakutia was still not receiving the promised revenues and that shareholding in the joint-stock company Diamonds of Russia-Sakha, established in July 1992, was controlled by the Russian government.

By summer's end in 1992, Yakutia began to ally with Tatarstan and Bashkortostan against the Russian government and suspended the payment of federal taxes. In the summer of 1993, the vice-president of Yakutia complained in very sharp words that the Chernomyrdin government had not fulfilled its economic obligations to Yakutia and that Yakutia was in a kind of economic blockade (*Nezavisimaia gazeta,* July 8, 1993: 3). At present, a sometimes overt and sometimes covert struggle for Yakut diamonds continues. By the end of 1993, the Yakut government had secured for the republic a share of profits from the diamond sales, and for the first time could draw up a budget without subsidies; however, it remains to be seen whether this agreement with the central government in Moscow will last long.

In the political sphere President Nikolaev certainly wishes to win more independence from Moscow; however, he clearly understands that politics is an art of the possible, and he is demonstrating a remarkable pragmatism and flexibility. Thus, in the summer of 1993, he was strongly against the proposed project of the Russian Constitution, which he called a unitary one that ignored the right of non-Russian peoples to self-determination and sovereignty on their indigenous territories (*Nezavisimaia gazeta,* June 30, 1993: 2). However, by the end of 1993, he apparently had accepted the inevitable and ceased to oppose the new constitution (*Literaturnaia gazeta,* December 1, 1993: 11). In the December 12, 1993, referendum the majority of the Russian population voted for the adoption of the new constitution, while the majority of the Yakuts voted against it (Drobizheva 1994: 149).

Just like many other leaders in the CIS and in the Russian Federation, Mikhail Nikolaev clearly wishes to concentrate in his hands as much power in the republic as possible. He is already accused of authoritarian tendencies (Drobizheva 1994: 149). Even directors of libraries are appointed now by the president. However, to a large extent, his internal positions depend on his ability to uphold the republic's interests and on his success in maneuvering between the two major ethnic communities in Yakutia. He repeatedly stresses that all nationalities in the republic have common goals: to regain ownership of economic resources and to become rich.

So far Nikolaev has apparently enjoyed the support of the majority of Yakuts, while many Russians consider him a lesser evil. However, he also faces growing criticism from both sides. In the last few years, the Yakut nationalistic movement has made remarkable progress in the republic's political arena. In the summer of 1992, during my visit to Yakutia, I met and had long conversations with many leaders and activists of this movement. At present, it is represented mainly by Sakha Omuk (the Union of Yakut People), the organization that concentrates its activities in the political and cultural spheres. Significantly enough, it keeps the name of its predecessor, the Yakut organization that was condemned by the Soviets as secessionist and destroyed in 1928.

By 1991, Sakha Omuk numbered 5,000 members, a significant figure if one takes into account the relatively small number of Yakuts. In our conversations its leaders stated quite frankly that the ultimate goal of Sakha Omuk is an independent state in which Yakuts would become the most powerful and numerically strongest nationality. They were less specific about how the latter goal could be reached; however, it appears that their hopes are connected with a restriction of migration to Yakutia and with a voluntary out-migration of non-Yakuts from the republic. A demand to limit the in-migration is widespread in Yakutia. In 1985–1989, 304,938 persons migrated to Yakutia while 262,112 persons left it (Diakonov 1992). However, in 1993–1994, the deteriorating living conditions motivated about 50,000 Russians to leave Yakutia (personal communication, Vladimir Nikolaev; see also Zykov 1994: 5). As a kind of compromise, the Yakut nationalists are ready to consider as part of the indigenous population those Russians and other non-Yakuts who have lived in Yakutia for several generations (Nikolaev 1990). However, they insist that temporary residents should be denied the republic's citizenship and suggest at least a six-year residence qualification as a precondition for the citizenship application.

In spite of their radical views, the Sakha Omuk activists, particularly their actual leader, Vladimir Nikolaev (unrelated to Yakutia's president), are influential political figures in Yakutia. They are not devoid of pragmatism and have demonstrated their capability to make temporal alliances with various political groups, including the Russian organizations of democratic orientation.

President Mikhail Nikolaev was elected in December 1991 with the strong support of Sakha Omuk. Since then his relations with this organization sometimes became more strained. However, there is some evidence that he was rather pleased with its activities and demands because they allowed him to demonstrate the moderation of his own positions. In his negotiations with Moscow he liked to point out that he acted under heavy pressure from Sakha Omuk and that some decisions of Yakutia's Parliament were made against his will. Thus, in April 1992, despite extremely cold weather (-35° C), about 2,000 people responded to the call from Sakha Omuk and the Yakut student organization Eder Saas and picketed the session of the republican Supreme Soviet, demanding an adoption of the new constitution. This constitution proclaimed the sovereignty of the republic, including its right to self-determination, although at President M. Nikolaev's insistence the clause which declared a right to secession from the Russian Federation was rejected. By 1994, the leaders of Sakha Omuk were practically incorporated into the Yakut political elite. This development is resented by the leaders of the more radical nationalist organization Sakha Keskile (Sakha Perspective) (Ivanov 1994: 95).

However, the greatest challenge to the internal stability and peace in Yakutia consists now of separatist tendencies already revealed in the Russian-dominated mining regions of the republic. As in other parts of the former Soviet Union, such as Pridneprovie and Northern Estonia, in Yakutia the secessionist movement was originally instigated by the managerial elite, who consider themselves representatives of the central administrative apparatus and are influenced by the chauvinist forces in Moscow. Already in June 1991, the Supreme Council of Yakutia was warned that Aldanskii, Lenskii, Mirninskii, and Neriungrinskii Raions (Districts) would secede from Yakutia and join Russia if Yakutia were to secede from Russia (*Molodezh Yakutii*, June 11, 1991). At present, the secessionist forces in Yakutia are playing with the idea of creating the Lena Slavic Republic, which would include not only the aforementioned districts but even the capital, Yakutsk, in which Russians constitute the majority (*Molodezh Yakutii*, April 30, 1992). Separatist tendencies are particularly strong in the Mirnenskii District (Ivanov 1994: 93–94), but they exist also in the Kolyma and the middle Indigirka regions (Tishkov 1993a: 32). Such developments would certainly provoke a civil war in Yakutia.

The Yakuts also watch with great alarm the emergence of the Cossack movement in the republic, although before the revolution the Cossacks there never constituted a separate administrative and economic body. Surprisingly enough, President M. Nikolaev does not oppose this movement and even supports it financially, apparently in an attempt to please the Russian community and to have a trump card in dealing with the Yakut nationalists (Drobizheva 1994: 143). However, considering the destructive role that the Cossack movement now plays in other parts of the CIS, it may also turn out to be detrimental to the interethnic relations in Yakutia.

Cultural Nationalism and the Reemergence of Shamanism

As in many other parts of the Soviet Union and the Russian Federation, the perestroika period and the subsequent disintegration of the empire were accompanied in Yakutia by a growth not only in political but also in cultural nationalism. In the cultural sphere the Yakuts have insisted on a revival of their traditional culture and on reinstituting the Yakut language in their schools. However, the most remarkable development is their recent complete rejection of Orthodox Christianity, to which they were forced to convert 300 years ago, and their enthusiastic return to shamanism.

The traditional religion of the Yakuts, like that of most of the indigenous peoples of Siberia, is often called shamanism. A discussion of this religious phenomenon is certainly beyond the scope of this chapter; therefore, I must limit myself to a few remarks on the problem.[4] As Lewis (1984: 3) aptly remarked, "The term shaman belongs to that limited category of ethnographically specific concepts which are used cross-culturally outside their own native contexts." It becomes even less precise if every witch doctor and medicine man, every person who is a medium or possessed by a spirit, every divinator or fortune teller is considered to be a shaman. Shamanism conceived in this way was found, and correspondingly described as such, in almost all parts of the world. However, the situation seems quite different if one agrees that shamanism is more than certain acts aimed at controlling spirits, acts which are based on a belief in some individual's ability to serve as an intermediary between this world and other ones. Then it becomes clear that shamanism, connected with a specific cosmology (the three zones of the universe—the upper world; the middle, earthly world; and the lower world) and the sacred world tree, with journeys of the soul (mystical flights to other worlds), and with other out-of-body experiences, as well as with specific religious practices (ecstatic techniques), is a culturally restricted phenomenon located in North Asia and, possibly, some adjacent areas.

As soon as an attempt is made not to confine shamanism simply to its own practice but to connect it to specific cosmological ideas and systems, and to an artistically expressive cognition of the world, it is easy to demonstrate that these particular cosmological ideas and systems, and this cognition, cannot be reduced to and characterized through practice

---

[4] An extensive discussion of the problem of shamanism and arguments for my own position on the issue will be provided in my forthcoming book *Nomads, Sedentaries, and Missionaries: World Religions in the Eurasian Steppes.*

only, because taken separately this practice can be found in different religious systems in various degrees (Eliade 1951).

Apparently, in the past the indigenous Yakut religion, with its developed pantheon *(aiyy)*, its belief in a supreme deity (Yuriung Aiyy Toion), and its veneration of Heaven, Earth, and natural forces, shared some common characteristics with the religions of other Turkic-speaking pastoralist peoples. In all probability, the so-called white shamans *(aiyy oiuuna)* were more priests of the heavenly deities than real shamans. They did not use drums, did not fall into trances, and did not have assisting spirits. In fact the "white shamans" played a key role and offered *kumys* (fermented mare's milk) to the fire during Ysyakh, the most important religious festival, usually celebrated in June and connected with the coming of summer (Levin and Potapov 1956: 302; Alexeev 1975: 77ff.; Diakonova 1990: 48ff.; for additional information on Yakut shamanism see Balzer 1990; Ksenofontov 1992; Seroshevsky 1993: 593ff.).

The Yakuts' forced conversion to Orthodox Christianity began in the second half of the eighteenth century, and by the nineteenth century all Yakuts were officially considered Christians (Shishigin 1991). By 1917, Orthodox churches were built in all districts of Yakutia. A few Yakuts even became Christian priests. The conversion led to a gradual disappearance of the old Yakut religion and its priests, the white shamans. Contrary to expectation, however, shamanistic beliefs and shamans who protected Yakuts from evil spirits (the so-called black shamans), although persecuted by the Russian church and administration, survived and continued to enjoy a great deal of support, prestige, and respect. They even began to perform some functions that in the past had belonged to the priests, the white shamans.

Communism, as a secular religion, was much more jealous than any sacred one. The Soviet communists in their struggle against shamanism and shamans in Siberia turned out to be more persistent, cruel, and merciless than the prerevolutionary Russian missionaries and priests. In the 1920s, the shamans were made "enemy number one" of the Soviet regime in all regions inhabited by the indigenous populations of Siberia and the Far East (Kolarz 1969: 74ff.). Yakutia was no exception (Alexeev 1975: 179–81; Vasilieva 1992: 98; Gorokhov 1992: 101). I was told many stories about the shamans who were interrogated, coerced into pledging that they would renounce their activities, trialed, expelled, imprisoned, and even executed. Many hereditary lines of the shamans were destroyed because, in accordance with Yakut beliefs, shamanic abilities were transmitted, although not necessarily directly, only within certain families and lineages (Alexeev 1975: 130).

Nevertheless, some shamans managed to survive, although they had to lie low, and shamanistic beliefs have proved to be more persistent than might have been expected. A lack of organized and hierarchical structure turned out to be an advantage to shamanism. During perestroika and afterwards, it became clear that, after 300 years of the Yakuts' formal conversion to Russian Orthodox Christianity and after 70 years of severe suppression of shamanism by the Soviets, shamanism is still alive.

For a society which only recently has stepped onto a path of modernization, and in the social and economic conditions of instability that have often resulted in psychological stress, the resurgence of shamanism should not be particularly surprising. At present, most Yakuts, including Russified educated people, believe, or pretend to believe, or wish to believe, in the existence of mediums between the natural and supernatural forces. Russian Christianity has been completely abandoned. Even in funerals the Yakuts are returning to their old burial practice.

However, shamanism in Yakutia has also acquired a new characteristic. While traditional shamans still living in remote villages, jealous of each other's success, wish only to be able to continue their practices and are not interested in modern ways of self-advertising, the number of self-proclaimed shamans, who in the recent past were historians, physicians, and professionals, is growing. The new shamans use the mass media, give press conferences, and participate in other modern activities. By 1992, there were at least two professional organizations of shamans in Yakutia that were at odds with each other. They were competing for influence and material support, and were accusing each other of being quacks and false shamans. This is a unique development in the long history of shamanism in the country, which is, to a large extent, connected with changing attitudes of the Yakut educated strata.

It is certainly not enough to explain the growing popularity of shamanism in Yakutia only in terms of a persistence of "cultural survivals." Religion became ethnicized and politicized in many regions of the ex–Soviet Union. To the nationalistic Yakut intelligentsia, shamanism not only acquired an aura of political rehabilitation as an institution persecuted by the Soviet regime, it also became one of the symbols of their struggle for sovereignty and independence. The collapse of the official atheistic communist ideology and its social myths resulted in religious revivals everywhere in the ex–Soviet Union, be it Christianity, Islam, or Buddhism. In many cases, this revival is directly connected with a growth in ethnic nationalism and a desire to rediscover the lost ethnic values and to return to ethnic roots. In this respect, there is nothing extraordinary in the Yakuts' desire to return to shamanism, which they perceive now as their national religion, except that this means a rejection of not only communism as the Soviet ideology but also Orthodox Christianity as the alien religion of

Russian colonizers. Similar revivals of shamanism exist at present among other northern peoples of the Russian Federation (Simchenko 1993: 5ff.; cf. Hoppál 1992), while attempts to substitute an old pagan religion for Orthodox Christianity are conspicuous among the Mari and to a lesser degree among the Chuvash.

What one is witnessing now in this respect is not so much a revival of an old religion as a response to pressures of the Russian culture, an attempt to create a new cultural identity disguised in the old garments which are connected with ethnic nationalism and the desire to separate from and to resist Russian cultural supremacy. One self-proclaimed shaman, a university-educated man with many admirers, told me that, although there are shamans among all the indigenous peoples of Siberia, there has never been even one ethnic Russian among them, and that, apparently, the Russians are genetically or spiritually unable to become shamans. It was obvious that he enjoyed this situation.

One Yakut philosopher, recently a professor of Marxism-Leninism and, therefore, a dedicated atheist *ex officio,* now pathetically declares: "Shamanism will exist, as long as the Yakut people exists" (Novikov 1992: 39). Even many former communists, including the president of Yakutia, who believe neither in God nor in the devil, claim now that shamanism should be cherished at least as a part of the Yakut ethnic culture and as a treasury of still-useful folk medicine.

Actually, the Yakut intelligentsia is contributing much to the revival of shamanism (Balzer 1993). But what is propagated in practice is something new and quite different from traditional shamanism, something that may be called neo-shamanism. In fact, this is but another example of what Hobsbawm (Hobsbawm and Ranger 1992) calls "invented tradition." In this respect, the ongoing debate in Yakutia over what exactly should be conceived as shamanism is quite remarkable. The Yakut intelligentsia is striving to present shamanism as a phenomenon transcending religious practice, as a custodian of high moral standards, and as a protector of the environment. They wish to demonstrate a compatibility of shamanism with modern science, aesthetics, ethics, and philosophy. New pseudo-scientific myths are created. Thus, the president of the Association of Alternative Medicine, V. Kondakov, insists that shamans are capable of "teleportation of their electric power doubles in order that their images attend several places simultaneously" (Okoneshnikov 1992: 112).

The Yakut intelligentsia is propagating shamanism in several ways. A growing interest in shamans as medicine men may be partly explained by the dissatisfaction in modern medicine, which in Yakutia, as everywhere in Russia, is in crisis. The low quality of medical service and the shortage of doctors and medicine in many cases encourage the people to turn to

traditional medicine, which in Yakutia was always connected with shamans. The intelligentsia provides a rationale for this trend by accentuat-
ing positive effects of curing seances in terms of psychotherapy, folk
medicine, or individuals' extrasensual abilities (Grigorieva 1991). A special department for studying shamans' medical practices has already opened in Yakutsk.

The intelligentsia also advertises the folklore tradition regarding shamanistic prowess, shamanic graves, toponymy, and accoutrements (Balzer
1992b: 18; Simchenko 1993: 30) and disseminates stories about great shamans of the past and present across the country. Actually, this tradition is
far from genuine folklore; it is rather a pseudofolklore tradition, because
a significant role in its restoration and propagation is played by the modern mass media (TV, videos, professional journalists), as well as writers,
artists, and scholars. Numerous publications on shamanism and its complex cosmology, exhibitions in local museums, theatrical performances,
the so-called shamanistic rituals currently accompanying many public
events, or even political life, contribute much to the popularity of shamanism, albeit already in very modified form. This trend is expressed in
the formation of the rock group Ay-Tal, in Yakutsk, which has set old shamanistic tunes to modern music.

I have attended several other performances aimed at illustrating various scenes of the shamans' life and prowess, as well as shamanistic rituals, costumes, and accoutrements. All these performances attracted full
houses. The performers were professional actors. Some of them have
recently discovered that participation in such performances is more profitable and popular than in any other play. The Yakut intellectuals who
accompanied me were ambiguous in their feelings toward these performances. On the one hand, they pointed out that these performances
were nothing more than kitsch and had little resemblance to traditional
shamanistic rituals. On the other hand, it was apparent that they enjoyed
them very much, and they mentioned the positive role of these portray-
als in propagating the traditional Yakut culture and folklore.

To provide another example, I can refer to Ysyakh, a traditional Yakut
festival which for many years was considered to be suspicious in the eyes
of the Soviet authorities. Nowadays Ysyakh is opening again with pray-
ing to the heavenly divinities and with other traditional rituals. However,
this restored festival has more symbolic than religious meaning. Not genuine white shamans but professional actors are performing the rituals. Nevertheless, the audience enjoys it and conceives it in terms of returning to
one's roots and of restoring a national culture, in which shamanism should
play an important role.

I would rather characterize neo-shamanism as a pseudoreligious movement which has certain political overtones and which is based on some sort of invented and/or reconstructed tradition. This invention of modern cultural symbols in the name of old tradition is motivated by political and social feelings and has a strong sense of nationalism.

This becomes even clearer if one turns to Tengrianism, which some members of the Yakut intelligentsia, particularly the traditionalists united in the organization Kut-Sür, are striving to restore, either in the framework of an alleged old Yakut religion (Aiism) or as an indigenous religion of all Turkic-speaking peoples (Utkin 1991). With respect to Aiism and Tengrianism one cannot apply the prefix "neo." What is being propagated nowadays as Tengrianism is a completely artificial conception that has nothing in common with religions of those Turkic- and Mongol-speaking peoples who revered Tengri as the supreme sky-deity. Thus, there are those who wish to erect a temple of Tengri in Yakutsk despite the fact that the pagan Turks, like any nomads, never worshiped their deities in temples.

However, it would be wrong to dismiss this interest in Tengrianism as an intellectual exercise confined to an overzealous minority. It also reveals the growing Pan-Turkic feelings. Some Yakut cultural and political organizations already maintain various contacts with similar Tatar, Bashkir, Azerbaidjanian, Uzbek, and other organizations in the CIS and wish to establish closer ties with the foreign Turkic-speaking countries. Since at present almost all Turkic-speaking peoples profess Islam, the Yakuts' relation to them is asserted through the linguistic affinity and alleged common indigenous religion. No wonder old hypotheses about the Turkic origin of Sumerians, Scythians, Sakas, and many other ancient peoples, widespread in Turkey in the 1920s and 1930s but at present considered utterly wrong and obsolete, are nowadays popular in Yakutia (Nikolaev 1990).

Ethnic Awareness of the Smallest Minorities

Just as in some other Soviet and then post-Soviet formations, the ethnic hierarchy and ethnic relations are not confined to relations between Russians and non-Russians only. There are also several other ethnic groups living in the territory of Yakutia who belong to the so-called small peoples of Siberia and the Far North. Altogether they number 22,274, constituting 2.14 percent of the whole population of Yakutia. The most numerous of them are the Evens (8,668 persons, 0.79 percent of the whole population). The growth in ethnic awareness, common to all ethnic groups in the former Soviet Union, has affected the Evens as well. While Yakuts complain that Russians discriminate against them, Evens complain, not without reason, that they are discriminated against by Yakuts, who they say have a scornful attitude toward them as a "wild, forest" people. In the past, there was no Even-language education whatsoever, and Even children attended only Yakut schools. So far very few changes are noticeable in the educational sphere even now. More than half of Evens consider the Yakut language their mother tongue (Ivanov 1994: 106), and many Evens still communicate, even with each other, in the Yakut language. Actually, very few of them, mainly persons of the older generation, are sufficiently fluent in their own language. Some Evens prefer to hide their ethnic affiliation, and when meeting with strangers call themselves Yakut.

In order to change this situation and "to facilitate the survival of peoples of the North," on April 21, 1989, the Eveno-Bytantaiskii District (Raion) was created in Yakutia. Among the population of this district Evens number 916 (33.2 percent of the whole population); Yakuts number 1,738 (62.9 percent); Russians, 47 (1.7 percent); and others, 62 (2.2 percent). However, Evens received some material and other privileges with respect to Yakuts in this district, in particular, a disproportionately high number of administrative positions. As a result, many offspring of mixed Yakut-Even marriages, who in the recent past chose a Yakut nationality on their internal passports and other identification documents, now prefer to be considered Evens.

Conclusions

Just as in many other countries of the Commonwealth of Independent States, in Yakutia, reinvented cultural symbols which stress ethnically marked differences serve the goals of ethnic mobilization. Culture, language, ethnicity, and politics are entwined in the nationalistic movement in which an ethnic group pursuing the goal of its social and economic advancement becomes a conscious community that strives to maintain a separate identity within the larger heterogeneous society. In this situation, the recommendation made by a British scholar (Vitebsky 1990: 316) to devise "an acceptable way of distinguishing 'national development' and 'self-determination' from 'nationalism'" is hardly plausible (who will devise this distinction anyway?).

At present, the internal peace in Yakutia is fragile. To a large extent, future developments depend on the general situation in the Russian Federation and on the policies of the Russian government. If Yakutia wins a higher stake in the exploration of and benefits from its mineral riches, the living standards of all its nationalities may be improved and, though ethnic tension and competition will not be eliminated, they may be reduced. Otherwise the situation may soon become aggravated. In this case, the situation in Yakutia will affect the situation in the whole Siberian region.

7

People with Nowhere To Go: The Plight of the Meskhetian Turks

You are a scholar, you should know the truth.
Tell me who is responsible for our continuing sufferings.
Stalin? Brezhnev? Gorbachev? Who?
—question directed to me by
a Meskhetian Turk in Moscow, August 1990

A truth, banal today, deserves to be repeated:
The Soviet Union was created by a totalitarian party
responsible for unspeakable crimes against humanity.
—Czeslaw Milocz, "Some Call It Freedom"

Among many ethnic problems of the Soviet Union, and now of the Commonwealth of Independent States, one of the most poignant is the problem of those deported and dispersed nationalities that for decades have not been allowed to return to the territories from which they were exiled: the Crimean Tatars, Germans, Kurds, Meskhetian Turks, and several others. They were placed at the very bottom of the Soviet ethnic hierarchy and often were subject to particular discrimination that was sanctioned by the central authorities (Alieva 1993). Not only the policies of the central and regional elites, but also real cultural and religious differences, as well as ethnic competition in the worsening economic situation, often fuel prejudices, ill will, and discrimination by the ethnic majorities toward deported minorities in their midst.

General contours of the policy toward Meskhetian Turks, Germans, and Crimean Tatars were formed by Moscow. Crimea has been a favorite resort area for many Russians, including party officials and the KGB, who for fear of "anti-Soviet and alien elements" were reluctant to support the return of the Crimean Tatars to the peninsula. Uneven relations with West Germany and the overall position of the USSR on the German question had an effect on the Soviet attitude toward ethnic Germans within the

192

USSR. Also, Soviet leaders clearly did not want to lose the hard-working and qualified work force that was needed in Kazakhstan and West Siberia.

At the same time, the demands of these peoples often affect other ethnic groups. The local authorities and a majority of the population of those territories from which they were banished are against their return to their homelands. The ideological self-justification has been the alleged negative past of these exiled peoples. In the mass consciousness, the image of Russian Germans has been associated, if not with fascists, then with their kin; the image of Crimean Tatars, with that of collaborators and participants in execution squads; the image of Meskhetian Turks, with Turkish Muslims, aggressors, the historical enemies of Christian Georgia and its culture.

Official Soviet propaganda has contributed to these negative associations. In the exhibits in the Crimean museum of local lore in the territory of the former khans' palace in Bakhchisarai, Crimean Tatars were presented as barbarians, primordial enemies of the Russian and Ukrainian peoples.[1] On the pages of numerous Crimean publications about World War II, Tatars were presented as traitors and accomplices of the fascists. Even a TASS (Telegraph Agency of the Soviet Union) announcement from June 24, 1987, contained a series of slanderous statements.

For many years, the Soviet leadership tried to suppress the Crimean Tatars' movement to return to their homeland by using repressive measures, including imprisoning Tatar activists. Then it began to claim that the Crimea was already populated so densely that there was simply no room for the Crimean Tatars. This argument was circulated at the time when active measures were being carried out to attract thousands of new settlers from Russia and Ukraine to the Crimea.

Beginning in 1989, the Crimean Tatars began returning independently to the Crimea in growing numbers and without the permission of the Soviet authorities. In the changing political climate, it became more and more difficult to inhibit their return, as before, by administrative and police methods. However, the Moscow center, tending toward the opinion that it had no other option than to allow the Crimean Tatars to return to their homeland, met with opposition from the local population and au-

---

[1] It is worth noting that, in talking to local Russian and Ukrainian inhabitants during my trips to the Crimea from the 1950s to the 1970s, I noticed differences in relation to the Crimean Tatars between the old-timers and migrants from the postwar period. Those who were personally acquainted with the Tatars and had lived with them side by side until the war had much more patient and objective attitudes toward them than those who had never actually laid eyes on a Tatar. All of this, of course, is not by chance. Personal experience made the older population of the Crimea less receptive to the anti-Tatar propaganda, while in the eyes of these old residents, their long habitation of the Crimea made their own right to this territory unquestionable.

thorities of the Crimea. Despite this opposition, by summer 1993, about 230,000 persons, almost a half of the Crimean Tatars, had returned to the Crimea (Vozgrin 1994: 25); however, to date, their continuing return aggravates interethnic tension on the peninsula.

The movement of the Russian Germans for their return to the Volga region (Povolzh'e), where before World War II they had an autonomous republic, did not become as broad as the Crimean issue. Many Germans before deportation lived not in the Volga region but in other parts of the Soviet Union. In addition, many Germans migrated or wished to migrate to Germany. Nevertheless, some part of the German population of the USSR and its unofficial leaders began actively propagating the "Povolzh'e option," indicating that only this could prevent the disappearance of the German language and culture in the USSR and present to the Soviet Germans an alternative to emigrating. In 1989, the Soviet government seemed worried about the growing emigration and was leaning toward the Povolzh'e option. The USSR Supreme Soviet made the decision to restore German autonomy in principle. Those among the Russian Germans who sided with this option proposed a carefully formulated, although hardly realistic, plan for their return to the area, in which it was emphasized that the Russian population would not suffer from this and would even gain from the supposed economic boom and possible aid from Germany (Vormsbekher 1989). However, the Russian population there, often overtly instigated by local party and Soviet leaders, met the proposal concerning the restoration of the German autonomy with opposition. In connection with this, USSR people's deputy Vorob'ev (1990: 23) wrote about the negligence and tolerance of the USSR leadership "toward the maneuvers of the local party apparatus, seemingly organizing mass protests of the Russian population of the Saratov Oblast who supposedly will have nowhere to go if the German autonomy is restored."

Gorbachev's leadership retreated and the plan was shelved. Instead, the creation of an association on the rights of extraterritorial autonomy was proposed to the Germans, which they decisively rejected (Pain 1990a).

Yeltsin's record is no better. For some time, Yeltsin tried to keep silent about Volga autonomy, so as not to inflame passions. However, in September 1991 he declared that the best way to solve the German problem would be to create tolerable conditions for them in the places to which they had been exiled under Stalin. A little later, he suggested that Germans be given autonomy in such far-off locations as the Amur River area or the northern part of the Sverdlovsk Oblast. Still later, he suggested setting up German autonomy in the territory of the Kapustin Yar missile-testing range in the Volgograd Oblast, next to the salt lakes of Elton and Baskunchak. This barren territory is one-tenth as large as the prewar German autonomous republic in the Volga area. In addition, Yeltsin promised the local Russians that Germans would receive autonomy only in the districts where their number would exceed 90 percent of the whole population, which is practically an impossibility (Isakov 1991). To the Germans this "generosity" was but another proof that they could hardly expect a sympathetic and fair attitude about their plight in Russia. In 1989, 120,000 Soviet Germans immigrated to Germany; in 1990, 120,000; in 1991, 150,000 (*Izvestiia*, February 4, 1994). It is very likely that their immigration to Germany will continue.

I will illustrate the situation further by using the example of another so-called punished people of the Soviet Union: the Meskhetian Turks. Before the tragic events in the Fergana valley of Uzbekistan in the summer of 1989, very few people in the Soviet Union, much less in the West, knew about even so much as the existence of this people (for some general information, see Bennigsen and Wimbush 1985:216–18; Akiner 1986:261; Wixman 1988:134; Panesh and Ermolov 1990:16–24). Even in the books by Conquest (1970b) and Nekrich (1978) the Meskhetian Turks occupy much less space than other deported peoples. Sheehy's (1973) report is an exception.

No wonder their ethnic history is rather obscure. This is an issue deserving attention because, just as in the case of many other ethnic groups in the Soviet Union and its successor states, their history affects their present situation.

According to an opinion that at one time was rather popular in the Georgian historiography, the Meskhetian Turks who speak the Kars dialect of the Turkish language and belong to the Hanafi school of Sunni Islam are simply Turkicized Georgians converted to Islam in the period between the sixteenth century and 1829, when the region of Meskheti-Dzhavakheti was under the sway of the Ottoman Empire (Khakhanov 1891: 2ff.; Vashapeli 1916). One of the arguments of the adherents of this view was that even in the nineteenth century many Muslim Meskhetians could still communicate well in the Georgian language. It is quite possible, however, that the adherents of this view oversimplified the ethnic history of the group, particularly if one compares it with another Muslim Georgian group, the Adzhar, who in spite of their conversion to Islam have retained, not only the Georgian language, but to some extent also the Georgian traditional culture and self-identification (Panesh and Ermolov 1990:20). Contrary to this, the traditional culture of Meskhetian Turks, though it contained some Georgian elements, was similar to the Turkish one (Panesh and Ermolov 1993:181). Apparently, the situation with Meskhetians was more complicated, and the possibility of direct participation of some Turkish elements in their formation, or ethnogenesis, to use the Soviet scientific parlance, should not be rejected out of hand. Some scholars assume that the Turkization of the area started as early as the Saljuk period (Shengelia 1968: 391–92; Panesh and Ermolov 1993: 178–79).

On the other hand, it is difficult to agree with those who insist that the Georgians did not play any role whatsoever in the formation of the Meskhetian Turks. Beginning in the Saljuk period, Meskheti was a frontier region between the Turkish and Georgian worlds, where Christians and Muslims, Georgians and Turks, lived side by side for many centuries while competing for the political power over this territory. (By the way, the most famous medieval Georgian poet, Shota Rustaveli, was a Christian Meskhetian.)

In 1886, 19.3 percent of the population of the Akhaltsikhskii Uezd (District) in Meskheti were Orthodox Georgians; 18.1 percent, Catholic Georgians; 19.4 percent, bilingual Muslims, who used both the Georgian and Turkish languages; and 43.2 percent, Turkish-speaking Muslims (Topchishvili 1989: 116). The process of Turkization in Meskheti continued even into the nineteenth century. Such family names as Tavdgiridze, Tsulakidze, Anakidze, Dvalishvili, Kipiani, as well as others, are of indisputable Georgian origin. Besides, there are documents from this period testifying that some people changed their Georgian names to Turkish ones (Topchishvili 1989: 115). In the beginning of this century, Nikolai Marr mentioned his meeting with a Muslim Georgian in the area, a man who claimed that his grandfather had been a Christian priest (Marr 1911:330).

Be that as it may, in the prewar period the Meskhetian Turks lived in 212 villages of southern and southwestern Georgia (Adigenskii, Akhaltsikhskii, Aspinskii, Akhalkalakhskii, and Bogdanovskii Districts) along the Turkish border, in some cases living for a long time side by side with Orthodox and Catholic Georgians, Armenians and Kurds (Panesh 1990: 17–18). Although the Muslims there maintained a degree of ethnic and cultural isolation from their neighbors, their separate ethnic self-identification at that time was rather vague and uncertain. Even their ethnic name was not yet fixed.

In the nineteenth and early twentieth centuries, the Meskhetian Turks were often called *ierli* (the locals, the natives), or Muslims, as well as Turks, Tatars (i.e., Azerbaidjanians), Adzar, and Muslim Georgians. In 1919–1921, the government of independent Georgia pursued an assimilation policy toward the Muslim groups in the republic. Regarding the Meskhetian Turks this policy continued in Soviet Georgia until 1926. Later, the majority of Meskhetian Turks began to be registered as "Turks." In the late 1930s a policy of Georgianization was resumed (Osipov 1993: 68–69). The Meskhetian Turks were ordered to change their Turkish surto Georgian ones; some of them were further told to take a Russified form of their names (Sarvanov et al. 1989).

Just at that time the Azerbaidjanians were ordered to change their ethnic name from the Azerbaidjanian Turks (Azerbaidjanskie Tiurki), or even simply Turks, as they had been called before, to Azerbaidjanians. Some Meskhetian Turks followed their example; some others registered as Georgians, but most, having been unable to anticipate the consequences, registered as Turks (Akiner 1986: 261; Panesh and Ermolov 1989: 119). Their neighbors continued to call them Turks in any case, just as Azerbaidjanians continue to be called Turks even now by many Georgians and particularly by Armenians. In fact, in the late 1930s, the Meskhetian Turks did not pay much attention to their official name and ethnic affiliation. Remarkably enough, they often continued to call themselves *ierli*, which did not have explicit ethnic connotations (Panesh and Ermolov 1989: 119).

In November 1944, the Meskhetian Turks along with some other smaller ethnic groups of southern Georgia, such as the Turkicized Armenians (Khemshils or Khemshins), Kurds, and Turkmen, were deported to Central Asia. The reasons for their deportation remained unclear for a long time. Since collaboration with Germans in the region of southern Georgia was impossible, and the imagination of the Soviet rulers was rather limited, the deportees were not provided with any explanation whatsoever, either written or oral, and their deportation was never mentioned in the official Soviet documents of that period.

Nothing remains but to hazard a guess. There are many evidences that at that time Stalin planned to invade Turkey and wished to clear the Transcaucasia of those ethnic elements who did not enjoy his confidence. It is no coincidence that the deportation of Meskhetian Turks was followed in 1949 by the deportation of Greeks, Lakhlukhs (Aramaic-speaking Jews), and some others. Apparently, Meskhetian Turks seemed to him particularly suspicious because of their linguistic, religious, and territorial proximity to the Turks in Turkey (Khazanov 1992a: 3).[2] It was also remembered that in 1918, during the Turkish offensive on Georgia through Meskheti, the Muslim population of this region had sided with the Turks (Bugai 1989: 136; Salykova and Ianovskii 1989).

Recently published documents provide more arguments in support of this conjecture. Apparently, a pretext for deportation was provided by Stalin's henchman Beria, who knew well the mood and intentions of the dictator.[3] In the report to Stalin, Molotov, and Malenkov on November

[2] A similar conclusion recently appeared in the Soviet press (see Bugai 1991b: 6).
[3] A Georgian dissident, Victor Rtskhiladze, claimed in 1977 that the deportation had been preceded by KGB provocation through the formation of an armed group from 20 deserters (see Fuller 1988: 2 n. 2).

28, 1944, Beria claimed that "a significant part of [Meskhetian] Turks, Kurds and Khemshils have been connected by ties of kinship with population of border areas of Turkey, involved in smuggling, revealed a desire to emigrate and served as the pool for recruiting espionage elements and implanting bandit groups" (Bugai 1991a: 110).

Official Soviet information on a number of the deported is still absent. The Western publications and some Georgian sources usually show the figures between 150,000 and 200,000 (Conquest 1970b: 11; Wimbush and Wixman 1975: 323; Fuller 1988: 1). The Meskhetian sources mention a smaller figure—115,500 (Arkhiv Samizdata, No. 6170: 9; Safarov 1989: 184; Salykova and Ianovskii 1989; Panesh and Ermolov 1990: 16); however, one should take into account that in 1944 about 40,000 men were serving in the Soviet army and were sent into exile a little later (Panesh 1989: 68). N. Bugai, a Soviet historian who studies the deportation of Soviet peoples, claims that about 100,000 persons were deported from Meskheti and that this figure includes not only Turks but also other ethnic groups (Bugai 1989: 142).[4] Another Soviet scholar, V. Zemskov (1990: 8), estimates that altogether the number of Meskhetian Turks, Kurds, Khemshils, and Azerbaidjanians (apparently, the same Meskhetian Turks) who were deported in 1944 from Georgia and arrived at their destinations in exile was 94,955.[5] According to the data presented in the Soviet Ministry for Internal Affairs' report of January 1, 1949, there were 81,575 deportees from Georgia (19,421 men, 25,107 women, and 37,047 children; about 3,000 of these children had already been born in exile [Zemskov 1990: 12, 13]). The figure of those who perished during deportation, or soon afterwards, also varies in different sources: from about 15,000 to 30,000 or 50,000 persons, mainly the elderly and children (Conquest 1970b: 109; Sarvarov et al. 1989; Salykova and Ianovskii 1989: 31; Pepinov 1989: 185; Zemskov 1990: 9, table 6; Tolz 1991: 19; Bugai 1991a: 111).

The deportees were resettled in small groups in the territories of Kazakhstan (29,497 persons), Kirgizia (8,911 persons), and above all Uzbekistan (42,618 persons), as the so-called special settlers, that is, people deprived of elementary civil rights. They were forbidden to change their residence; under the threat of imprisonment they had to appear once a month for registration in special commandants' offices; even marriages

---

[4] In November 1944 Beria reported to Stalin about the deportation of 91,095 persons from Georgia (Bugai 1991a: 100). Several years later, Colonel Shiian, the chief of the Ministry of Internal Affairs' Department of Special Settlements, claimed that the number of deported Turks, Kurds, and Khemshils amounted to 94,950 (Bugai 1991a: 111).

[5] This figure is based on the Soviet Ministry of Internal Affairs' archives data (see also Bugai 1991a: 111).

between dwellers of different settlements were forbidden (Khurshut 1988: 102ff.; Sarvanov et al. 1989; Pepinov 1989: 185–86; Zemskov 1990: 9, 10).

The discriminatory status of Meskhetian Turks was partly lifted, with one very important exception, after the 20th Congress of the Communist Party in 1956. While many other punished peoples were permitted to return home, the Meskhetian Turks were forbidden to return to southern Georgia. A decree of the presidium of the Supreme Soviet of the USSR dated October 31, 1957, stated the unwillingness of the Georgian government to permit the Meskhetian Turks (significantly enough, they were called the Azerbaidjanians in the decree) to return home, or even to settle in other regions of Georgia, allegedly because it lacked the capacity to resettle and to employ them. Instead, they were granted a right to migrate to Azerbaidjan (Bugai 1991c: 159).

After the war, at the insistence of the Georgian authorities the territory of Meskheti was declared an 85-kilometer-wide special frontier zone, which was practically closed to the Meskhetian Turks. They could not visit it even as guests and tourists. The territory itself was hurriedly settled by the Adzhar and Imeretians (West Georgians), who sometimes were moved there against their will. In West Georgia, troops destroyed homes of those who were ordered to move to Meskheti, and special measures were undertaken to prevent their return home (Salykova and Ianovskii 1989; Panesh and Ermolov 1993: 185).

During the last 30 years some of the Meskhetian Turks migrated to and settled in other parts of the Soviet Union: in Azerbaidjan, in the North Caucasus (particularly in North Ossetia, Kabardino-Balkaria, and Karachaevo-Cherkessia), in Stavropol'skii and Krasnodarskii Krai (Territories), and even in Moldavia. However, a majority of them continued to live in Central Asia, more than a half in Uzbekistan.

In the political sphere most of the Meskhetian activities were directed at obtaining permission to return to their homeland. Beginning in the late 1950s, they established some informal organizations whose only aim was repatriation to Georgia. The Constituent Congress of Meskhetian Turks, which secretly took place in Central Asia in 1962, founded the Provisional Organizing Committee for Repatriation to the Homeland. The committee coordinated the activities aimed at this goal and spread its influence to all the Meskhetian communities across the country. Ten Congresses of Meskhetian Turks took place during the 1962–1989 period (Panesh and Ermolov 1993: 186), and more than 200 delegations were sent to the authorities in Moscow and Tbilisi to advocate for Meskhetian rights (Panesh and Ermolov 1990: 19).

However, all these efforts were futile. The special decree of the presidium of the USSR Supreme Soviet issued on May 30, 1968, was ambiguous and hypocritical. While stating that the people deported from Georgia "enjoy the same right as do all citizens of the Soviet Union to live anywhere in the USSR in accordance with the legislation in force on labor and passport regulations," it immediately made an important exception by noting that "citizens of Turkish and Kurdish nationalities, Khemshils and Azerbaidjanians, who previously lived in the Georgian SSR, have settled permanently in the territory of the Uzbek SSR, the Kazakh SSR, and other union republics" (*Bulletin of the Supreme Soviet of the USSR* 23, [June 5, 1968]).

Beginning in the 1960s, the Soviet authorities more and more often began to resort to repression (including intimidation, interrogation, arrest, and imprisonment) of the activists of the Meskhetian Turks' movement for return to the homeland, in order to suppress it by force (Arkhiv Samizdata, No. 1532: 3ff.). At the same time, all the attempts to settle in Georgia undertaken by individual groups of Meskhetians were thwarted by the Georgian authorities.

On July 26, 1968, Mzhavanadze, the first secretary of the Georgian Communist Party, told representatives of the Meskhetian movement that there was no longer any room for them in Meskheti. He promised them only that 100 families a year might be permitted to settle in other regions of Georgia (Conquest 1970b: 189). However, even this promise was never fulfilled. Since the 1960s, only 186 families, 1,211 persons, managed to return to Georgia; even this insignificant minority was resettled in different parts of West Georgia, beyond the historical borders of Meskheti, and was soon ousted and forced to leave again (Arkhiv Samizdata, No. 1534: 1–2; Panesh and Ermolov 1990: 23). By 1989 only 35 families remained in Georgia; the only Meskhetian Turk who had resettled in Meskheti was forced to leave it (Salykova and Ianovskii 1989).

The main obstacle was the resistance of the Georgian authorities and of a significant part of the general public to the Meskhetians' return to Meskheti. When in June 1988, about 200 Meskhetian Turks demonstrated in the Borzhomi District of Georgia for their right to return to Georgia, clashes broke out with the local population (Fuller and Bohr 1989: 17).

The Georgians asserted that there was no vacant land in Meskheti anymore, a claim which the Meskhetian Turks still challenge. They point out that even now far from all the 212 villages that existed in the area before 1944 are settled, and that 70 percent of agricultural land there lies idle, partly because of the labor shortage, and partly because new settlers lack specific skills to practice the terrace agriculture, which had been characteristic in the region (Pain 1990b: 144; Panesh and Ermolov 1990: 23).

In fact, the Georgians do not wish to permit the Meskhetian Turks to return for quite different reasons. The ethnic composition of Georgia is complex enough, with various ethnic minorities often complaining about discrimination against them. The Georgian leadership has many troubles with autonomous formations already existing in the territory of Georgia, and has no wish whatsoever to create other ones. The Azerbaidjanians in Marneul'skii and Bolniskii Raions of Georgia have already demanded autonomy (*Novoe russkoe slovo*, July 5, 1989), and the Georgians are afraid that the return of Meskhetian Turks would eventually lead to the creation of a Meskhetian Turkish autonomous formation. Some leaders of the Meskhetian Turks gave the Georgians good reason for suspicion by insisting that their return should be accompanied by the creation of an autonomous republic or autonomous district of Meskhetian Turks, with the capital in Akhaltsikhe (Arkhiv Samizdata, No. 1532: 5).

Besides this, birthrates of some ethnic minorities in Georgia, particularly the Muslim ones, are higher than birthrates of the ethnic Georgians, and this situation greatly worries the Georgian officials and the general public. In 1988, the former Georgian minister of education, O. Kinkladze, claimed quite frankly in the Georgian semiofficial newspaper *Komunisti* that, "even if we take the mistakes of the past into consideration, for us to contribute to the future growth of the non-Georgian speaking population far exceeds all sensible bounds of hospitality" (Fuller 1989: 18).

It is true that, in the 1970s and even in the 1980s, Georgian opinion was not unanimous on the Meskhetian issue. Some intellectuals advocated repatriation of those who were ready to admit their Georgian origin, to change their family names, to learn the Georgian language, in other words to become Muslim Georgians and to renounce their Turkish affiliation. However, in the opinion of even these people, the so-called pro-Turkish-oriented Meskhetians should be barred from returning to their homes (Arkhiv Samizdata, No. 3001: 1-2; Fuller 1989: 18; Pain 1990b: 145).

Meanwhile, very interesting ethnic and political processes were developing in the midst of the deportees. Their educational level was very low. At the time of deportation only 63 of them had a higher education, and 957 had a secondary education; 27,489 Meskhetian Turks (62 percent of adults) were illiterate (Zemskov 1990: 14, table 17). They were resettled in small and dispersed groups, which numbered from several dozen to several thousand persons. Their traditional material culture was mainly destroyed, and new cultural traits in agriculture, animal husbandry, dress (except ritual and headdress), diet, housing, interior decoration, and so on, were borrowed from the Central Asian population. Under the circumstances, one might expect that the Meskhetian Turks would eventually have been assimilated by the Central Asians, who were related to them religiously and linguistically, particularly because, by all accounts, in the beginning the Uzbeks and other Central Asian peoples were rather sympathetic with their plight. In fact, the opposite happened.

Because of high birthrates their number is constantly increasing and, according to some sources, has already reached 400,000 (Panesh and Ermolov 1990: 1; A. Osipov, in personal communication with me, estimated their number at about 250,000). It is true that the last Soviet census of 1989 gives a lower figure—207,369; however, one should take into account that far from all Meskhetian Turks have been registered as such. For years many were even denied the right to register their nationality in legal documents. Thus, by 1988 in Kazakhstan, only a third of them were recorded as Turks on their passports. The rest had been arbitrarily declared members of other ethnic groups. In order to change this situation, they had to prove they were not of the nationality stated on their passports (*Izvestiia*, September 13, 1988).

In spite of the policy of enforced assimilation pursued by the Soviet authorities (suffice it to say that attempts to open schools with an education in the Turkish language failed), maybe even as a direct result of this policy, the Meskhetian Turks in exile, more than ever before and perhaps for the first time in their history, began to conceive of themselves as a separate people. Before 1956, the possibility of their assimilation was prevented by their inferior political and social status. Afterwards it was staved off by a specific goal of political mobilization, a return to the homeland, which their separate ethnic self-identification began to serve.

Correspondingly, some social and psychological mechanisms have emerged, effectively blocking the possibility of assimilation of the Meskhetian Turks by local populations. In spite of their dispersion, the Meskhetian Turks have managed to become organized in closed communities, in which they maintain contacts with each other but reduce to a minimum contacts with the locals. Before the deportation, communities of the Meskhetian Turks were based on kinship; however, contemporary communities are usually heterogeneous, and do not have direct genetic links with their predecessors. Their emergence was connected with a problem of ethnic survival in extreme conditions of exile. These communities have their own informal leaders and their own unofficial clergy (Osipov 1990: 142–43). In these communities traditional values have been revived and preserved, and the rule of ethnic endogamy that the Meskhetian Turks had practiced before their deportation has been reaffirmed.

At the same time the feeling of separateness, which was operating on the lines of a "we-they" opposition typical of all kinds of ethnic differentiation, was further intensified amongst Meskhetian Turks by the development of a kind of superiority complex. Considering themselves more advanced, they tended to look down upon the indigenous populations of

Central Asia, particularly because, denied avenues of social advancement, they had concentrated their efforts on the economic sphere and soon became more prosperous than their Uzbek or Kazakh neighbors. We-they opposition began to reveal itself in very specific sets of opposites with negative connotations: European-Asian (i.e., Meskhetian Turk–Central Asian), europeoid-mongoloid, sedentary-nomadic (the last two sets of opposites were revealed in a particularly clear way in Kirgizia and Kazakhstan) (Panesh 1989: 69–70).

The situation has been different only in Azerbaidjan, where by August 1988, about 40,000 Meskhetian Turks were living. They have found there a related cultural and ethnic environment; the Azerbaidjanian government and general public were favorably disposed toward them, and they did not feel themselves isolated and discriminated against. Some affirmative action measures were even introduced to facilitate their access to higher education. As a result, the Meskhetian Turks in Azerbaidjan tend to merge with the dominating nationality. However, their mass migration to Azerbaidjan was held up in the late 1950s (Panesh 1989: 70; Panesh and Ermolov 1990: 17) and resumed on a large scale only in 1989.

On the other hand, the Meskhetian Turks who migrated to the North Caucasus have considered their stay there only a temporary one, a stop on the way to Georgia. While being the most politically active amongst their compatriots, they have deliberately maintained isolation from the local population (Panesh 1989: 70–71).

The formation of a separate Meskhetian Turkish ethnicity was accompanied by political struggle and splits within the community. Some activists, not without reason, attributed these splits to the subversive activities of the KGB, which wished to divide them (Arkhiv Samizdata, No. 1532: 5–6). However, their search for self-identity was in no way initiated by the Soviet secret police. Already in 1964 some of them had founded the Turkish Society for the Defense of the National Rights of the Turkish People in Exile (Fuller 1988: 3). In April 1970 their leader, Enver Odabashev (Odabashogly), appealed to the Turkish Embassy at Moscow for protection and permission for the entire community to immigrate to Turkey if their demands were not met by the Soviet authorities (Arkhiv Samizdata, No. 1532: 5–6).[6]

Apparently, the Turkish government was far from happy with this appeal, and it was rejected. However, the group represented by Odabashev was in a minority. The majority, while insisting on their Turkish identity, did not reveal a desire to immigrate to Turkey. Sometimes they tended to

[6] In August 1971 Odabashev was imprisoned by the Soviet authorities for "slandering the Soviet Union."

stress that they were Soviet Turks. Others were ready to admit that they were Turkicized Georgians in order to achieve their main goal—the return to Meskheti, or even to any other place in Georgia (Tiutiunnik 1989; Panesh and Ermolov 1990: 19; Osipov 1993: 69–70). In 1976 their appeal was signed by about 7,500 persons (Arkhiv Samizdata, No. 2952: 2). Still other small groups claimed that they were Meskhetians (Meskhi) (Panesh 1989: 71).

This factional struggle came to a temporary end at the Ninth All-Union Congress of the Meskhetian Turks, which took place in Kabardino-Balkaria in July-August 1988 in an atmosphere of growing nationalism and self-awareness of many ethnic groups of the USSR. Remarkably enough, the Congress was opened with a religious ceremony and was blessed by a mullah.

In the subsequent discussion the partisans of Georgian identification were defeated and publicly admitted that their political line was erroneous. Two hundred seventy-six delegates declared this Congress to be the Congress of Unity. They elected the chief leader of their movement and decided to press for the return to their homeland and for the official recognition of the existence of separate Meskhetian Turkish ethnicity (Panesh and Ermolov 1990: 19; Panesh and Ermolov 1993: 188). The last declaration was a culmination of ethnosegregating processes intensified in their midst during the last decades. On the other hand, it virtually ended all the possibilities of reaching an agreement with the Georgians. Less than a year afterwards the tragic events in the Fergana valley followed (in addition to the previously cited literature, see also *Pravda Vostoka*, July 30, 1989; Mialo and Goncharov 1989; Ryzkov 1992: 217ff.), and later, the less-known conflict in the Syrdarya District of Uzbekistan (Brusina 1990: 25–26).

The reasons for these clashes still remain unclear, although it is obvious that to a large extent they should be considered the consequence of long-neglected internal problems of Uzbekistan, of its economic difficulties aggravated by the demographic explosion and growing unemployment. Thus, it is no wonder that a growing discontent with existing conditions aggravated ethnic competition for scarce resources. Many ordinary Uzbeks demonstrate hostility toward ethnic minorities, including Muslim ones. The relations between Uzbeks and Meskhetian Turks have been deteriorating for years, and one of the reasons for this might be their growing competition for lucrative positions in trade and services (Levin 1989: 119–20). However, some observers point out that the number of Meskhetian Turks occupied in these professions has actually been very small (Brusina and Osipov 1993: 20).

Nevertheless there is enough evidence to suspect that disturbances in the Fergana valley were not completely spontaneous, that they were thoroughly planned and organized in advance. The former Soviet prime minister Nikolai Ryzhkov, after his tour of the Fergana valley in June 1989, stated that the pogroms were a "well organized, large-scale, and skillfully implemented political action" (*Washington Post*, June 16, 1989). Somebody instigated and directed mob participation in pogroms. The question remains, who exactly?

The KGB and Interior Ministry claimed that "organized crime" and "corrupted elements" among the Uzbek officials were behind the disturbances (Tatur 1990: 20). In the late 1980s, this was the usual explanation of ethnic conflicts in the USSR. The problem was that the KGB always failed to catch these mysterious subversive elements.

During my 1990 summer visit to the Soviet Union, I had the opportunity to discuss this question with some of those Soviet experts on Central Asia, who tended to support the official Soviet explanation. They also pointed to some unspecified conservative groups in the Uzbek political elite and, at the same time, to their opponents, "extremists" in the Uzbek national movement inspired by the slogan "Uzbekistan for the Uzbeks." Other Soviet scholars insist that the Meskhetian Turks were chosen as a scapegoat almost accidentally, just because they were the least protected ethnic minority. They claim that in fact action had been planned against the Tadjiks. However, the Tadjiks are too numerous and can rely on the support of their compatriots in Tadjikistan, so it was decided that it would be too dangerous to initiate open hostilities against them. The Meskhetian Turks wished to remain neutral in interethnic animosities in Uzbekistan, particularly in the Uzbek-Tadjik tension; therefore, they had to face the music (Panesh and Ermolov 1993: 192-93). However, my informants among the Meskhetian Turks do not support this explanation. It does not seem plausible to me either, because it implies the existence of a strong and influential underground organization about which virtually nothing is known. The very existence of such an organization in the conditions of the late 1980s is unlikely. Nonexistent plots were too widespread in the Soviet propaganda lexicon and repressive practice (the most notorious was the so-called Doctors' Plot, which was used by Stalin in his preparations for deporting Jews to Siberia and the Far East [see Vaksberg 1994: 241ff.]) to borrow the plot theory without definite proof.

I should also mention another view circulating in the Soviet Union, a view that attributes the Fergana events to a provocation by the Moscow center and KGB and their allies in the Uzbek leadership. Thus, an Uzbek poet and a leader of the Erk Party, Muhammad Salikh, stated quite frankly: "The violence that occurred was instigated. Which organ instigated it— the KGB, the Central Committee [of the Uzbek Communist Party], or the center—we can not say with certainty, but it is very clear that all of the actions were planned in advance" (Bohr 1990: 22).

Another interesting but hardly convincing explanation was suggested by those Uzbeks who claimed that "the unrest was in fact instigated by Moscow operatives aiming to intimidate the Meskhetian Turk victims into fleeing to Russia, where their convenient presence would help to alleviate the acute rural labor shortage" (Critchlow 1991a: 19).

The Meskhetian Turks themselves claimed that they did not know who instigated the pogroms; however, they did not have any doubts that the pogroms were organized. For example, they mentioned that officers of the local traffic patrol provided marauders with information on their location, and that they noticed people in officers' uniforms amongst mobs participating in pogroms (Mitrofanov 1989).

It is clear, however, that at present neither the Moscow leadership nor the Uzbek authorities seek truth and justice. Only some immediate participants in the Fergana pogroms were prosecuted.

Most of the Meskhetian Turks who fled from Uzbekistan immediately after the pogroms or had to leave the country during the following year under pressure from the Uzbek authorities (Brusina and Osipov 1993:21) were not able to return, nor did they wish to. Some of them were resettled in depopulated regions of Central Russia (mainly in Smolenskaia, Orlovskaia, and Kurskaia Oblasts). Apparently, the Soviet leadership, which had failed to attract ethnic Russians back to these regions, decided to chance resettling the regions with the refugees. It was not the first such attempt. In the 1980s, the Soviet government tried in vain to lure the Uzbek peasants to Nechernozem'e (the non-black earth territories). However, the last attempt, involving the Meskhetian Turks, has failed as well.

The local Russians grumbled that they were denied privileges granted to the new Meskhetian settlers; the right-wing Russian chauvinists in Moscow made noise complaining that this resettlement would eventually result in the creation of "another Karabakh" (*Zemlia* 10 [August 1989]:218), and that "the indigenous population of Central Russia is diluted by an Asian conglomeration" (*Radio Liberty*, November 24, 1989; see also *Moscow News* [November 4-11, 1990]: 9; Panesh and Ermolov 1993: 194-95). As for Meskhetian Turks themselves, being unaccustomed to the natural and cultural environment there and to quite different agricultural systems and life-style, and confronted with a far from friendly attitude of the local population, they strove to leave these regions as soon as possible. By the beginning of 1990, fewer than 14,000 Meskhetian Turks were living in the four *oblasts* of Central Russia (*Izvestiia*, February 20, 1990).

11 constituent and autonomous republics of the Soviet Union. In some of these republics their presence is fraught with new ethnic conflicts. Thus, the Azerbaidjanian authorities encouraged those Meskhetian Turks who migrated to Azerbaidjan after the events in Fergana valley to settle in Nagornyi Karabakh and the neighboring areas, in addition to settling them in Sabirabadskii Raion and some other places where others of them had been living for a long time, and in the settlements left by the Russian sectarians (Molokans) (I am most grateful to Dr. R. Guseinov and Dr. A. Yamskov for this information). This measure is bitterly resented by Armenians. After the Armenian offensive on Khodzaly in February 1992, the Meskhetian Turks were deported a third time. Another territory in Azerbaidjan where the Meskhetian Turks have been resettled is the districts populated by the Lezgin, an ethnic minority which the Azerbaidjanian authorities tried to assimilate for a long time. No wonder the Lezgin also did not welcome the new migrants.

The Russian population in Stavropol'skii and Krasnodarskii Krais (Territories), other areas to which many Meskhetian refugees have recently moved, has begun to complain that they already have more than enough refugees, such as Armenians and Kurds, and that they do not wish to accommodate the new ones. Some people warn that the situation in these areas is becoming explosive. Thus, in the summer of 1990, 80 percent of participants in a referendum which took place in the Krymskii Raion of the Krasnodarskii Krai, where more than 10,000 Meskhetian Turks have tried to take refuge, supported the suggestion to expel them from the district (Dergachev 1990). Some desperate Meskhetian Turks announced that they were ready to commit suicide in protest against the outrage of local authorities (*Ekspress-khronika* 35, no. 108 [1989]). In November 1991, the Meskhetian Turks in the town of Kholmsky of Krasnodarskii Krai were beaten and their houses were damaged or destroyed by the local Slavic population. By the end of 1991, the Cossacks in the same *krai* threatened that they would expel the Meskhetian Turks to Central Russia if this were not done by the Russian government. In 1992, the authorities of the *krai* and the Georgian leadership came to the agreement that some Meskhetian Turks would be allowed to repatriate to Georgia, but so far this agreement remains only on paper. Only the Crimean Tatars in Krasnodarskii Krai sympathized with and helped the Meskhetian Turks (Panesh and Ermolov 1993: 195).

At the same time, the situation of the Meskhetian Turks in Central Asia continues to deteriorate. In the summer of 1991, those of them from the Enbekshikazakhskii Raion of Kazakhstan picketed the Turkish Embassy in Moscow with the slogan: "President Ozal, save your compatriots." They were afraid that the events in the Fergana valley could soon be repeated

in Kazakhstan, because the indigenous population had given them an ul-
timatum: leave the *raion* in three months. Remarkably enough, the president of Kazakhstan, N. Nazarbaev, provided them with only limited assurance. He promised that nobody would be compelled to leave Kazakhstan by force (Khovratovich 1991). Implicitly that meant that their "voluntary" departure would be rather welcome.

Meanwhile, the central Soviet leadership was paying at best only lip
service to the plight of Meskhetian Turks. In December 1989, the special
commission of the USSR Supreme Soviet decided that the Meskhetian Turks
should be allowed to return gradually to Georgia. It urged the central
and Georgian governments to work out a program to create a favorable
moral and psychological climate for their return (TASS, December 15,
1989). In July 1991, R. Nishanov, the chairman of the Soviet of Nationalities of the USSR Supreme Soviet, approached the Georgian president and
Parliament again with a request to consider the possibility of Meskhetian
Turks' return to Georgia (*Izvestiia*, July 19, 1991). Naturally, all these
belated appeals, as well as numerous efforts and appeals to the Soviet,
Russian, and Georgian authorities made by Meskhetian Turks themselves,
were in vain (*Izvestiia*, September 24, 1989: July 4, 1991). The solution
to their problem has hardly been helped by the awkward maneuvering of
some leaders of their Vatan (Homeland) organization, who have sometimes tried to ally with the right-wing Russian organizations in order to
win their support.

The chances of the Meskhetian Turks returning to Georgia look very
dim in the atmosphere prevailing now in Georgia. In 1989, G. Gumbaridze,
the former first secretary of the Georgian Communist Party, told one of
the Meskhetians' leaders that Uzbekistan was a "paradise" compared with
the current situation in Georgia (Fuller 1989). Sakharov had good cause
to call Georgia a "mini-empire" (interview in *Ogoniok* 31 [1989]). Some
Georgian nationalists have launched a campaign against ethnic minorities already living in Georgia and are hardly disposed to increasing non-
Georgian elements there.

A peaceful march on Georgia undertaken by Meskhetian Turks in August 1990 was stopped at her borders (*Ekspress-khronika* 31, no. 156
[1990]; Dergachev 1990). Their last hopes vanished when the coalition
Round Table–Free Georgia came to power after elections to the Georgian
Parliament in the autumn of 1990, and its leader, Zviad Gamsakhurdia,
became, first, the chairman of the Supreme Council of Georgia and, then,
her president. A former dissident, Gamsakhurdia considered ethnic minorities living in Georgia the major threat to the Georgian people. In one
of his speeches he called for removing all the non-Georgians who took

shelter in Georgia (*Molodezh' Gruzii*, September 7, 1990). In his interview to the Russian weekly he claimed:

> There was a time when the Turks were strangers in Georgia. Now they claim Georgian land as their own. We cannot grant their claims, because the Turks' native land is Turkey, not Georgia. Also, the lands in Meskheti are populated by Georgians and Armenians. What shall we do with these people? Some politicians think that by letting hundreds of thousands of Meskhetian Turks into Georgia we do service to democracy. In fact, there would be actual civil war and heavy bloodshed.

Gumsakhurdia also hurried to confirm his words with practical measures. He decided to populate Meskheti with the Georgians who were victims of the recent earthquake (*Kuranty*, August 1, 1991). The next Georgian leader, Shevardnadze, stated that Georgia's moral duty was to allow Meskhetian Turks to return; however, he hurriedly added that their return should be postponed again because of Georgia's economic difficulties. The assurance of Yu. Sarvarov, the chair of Vatan, that Meskhetian Turks are ready to defend with arms the territorial integrity of Georgia did not help (*Nezavisimaia gazeta*, November 11, 1992: 3).

No wonder the idea of immigration to Turkey as the only real solution to their plight reemerged among some Meskhetian Turks. Their representative, Tafur Abuzer, claimed in the summer of 1989: "There are no Meskhetian Turks, just as there are no Uzbek Turks. There are only Turks and Uzbeks, and if there is no land for us here, we should go to Turkey" (Mitrofanov 1989). At the Tenth Congress of Meskhetian Turks, which took place in Azerbaidjan on September 2, 1989, where about 180,000 of them are settled at present (or even 260,000, according to other data), 5,727 delegates stated that 70–80 percent of their people would like to immigrate to Turkey if they were not allowed to return to Georgia (Panesh and Ermolov 1993: 195–96). It looked as though the Soviet leadership was glad to solve the problem of Meskhetian Turks in such a way. The Turks' representatives were told by the Supreme Soviet and Foreign Ministry that there were no obstacles to their emigration (Khovratovich 1991). The Russian government does not consider the problem of Meskhetian Turks its own at all; for Russia it is just another minor nuisance.

The problem remains the same as it was 30 years ago: the Meskhetian Turks are not welcome in Turkey. In contrast with the situation of Germans, Jews, and Greeks, for Meskhetian Turks there is no country to go to. They have become everywhere the unwanted and persecuted ethnic minority. At the utmost, the Turkish government may now agree to accept, without any enthusiasm, a very limited number of them (Khovratovich 1991).

All in all, at present a just and prompt solution to the Meskhetian problem in the post–Soviet Union seems almost impossible. This is another crime of the Stalin era, aggravated by the policy of his successors, for which generations of innocent people still pay a high price.

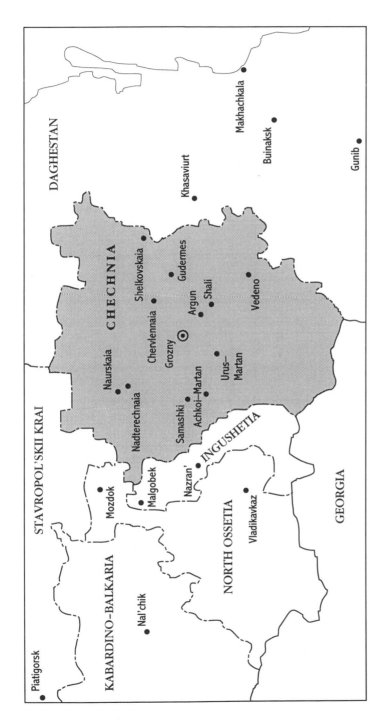

Map 5. Chechnia

211

8

A Last-Minute Postscript: The Chechen Crisis (as of May 21, 1995)

> In the Chechen language the word "freedom" is
> included even in the greeting formula.
> Russians say, "Be healthy";
> Americans, "Be well."
> Chechens say, "Be free."
> —Author

> No idea, including one that is very important to many
> Russians—the idea of the indivisibility of
> Russia—can be justified by war against a people.
> No democratic country can keep a people in its
> embrace by military force if they do not wish to be retained.
> —Elena Bonner, 1995

I am writing these last lines of the final draft of the manuscript at the moment when the war in Chechnia has already entered its sixth month, but is still far from being over. Russia has launched a war on those whom she considers her own citizens. This essentially colonial war, brutal and merciless, was unnecessary and avoidable; peaceful means to solve the problem had not been exhausted.

The confrontation between Chechnia and Moscow began not yesterday but more than three years ago, and the stages of this confrontation reflect the political transformation of the Russian leadership and its approach to the nationality problem in the country. By 1991, Checheno-Ingushetia remained one of the most impoverished and undeveloped regions not only of the Russian Federation but of the whole Soviet Union. Thus, it occupied last place in the quality of health care and first place in the mortality rate. One fifth of the able-bodied population of the republic, about 200,000 persons, could not find employment in Chechnia and Ingushetia and had to look for temporary or seasonal jobs in other parts

212

of the Soviet Union, mainly in Russia. Most of the employees in the oil industry, the only developed branch of the republican economy, were ethnic Russians (Vasilieva and Muzaev 1994: 58–59).

Growing dissatisfaction with the political and economic situation in the republic resulted in the creation of the nationalist Chechen National Congress in 1990, and culminated in the so-called Chechen revolution in the fall of 1991. In the aftermath of the August 1991 putsch, a charismatic leader of the radical nationalists, the former Soviet general Dzhokhar Dudaev, with the tacit support of Russian authorities in Moscow, ousted the republic's last communist leader, Doku Zavgaev, from power in Checheno-Ingushetia. Zavgaev lost Moscow's support because he was no longer able to control the situation in his republic. Besides, he practically took the side of the putschists, while Dudaev from the very first hours of the putsch opposed it and called for a nationwide resistance among his compatriots. (Three years afterwards the situation has changed again. The anti-communist Dudaev became an archenemy of Moscow, while the communist Zavgaev acts as an advisor of the Russian leadership on Chechen affairs.)

The romance between the Russian leadership and the Chechen nationalists was very brief. Dudaev's supporters resorted to force to dissolve the Supreme Soviet of the republic. Soon afterwards, on October 27, 1991, Dudaev was elected president of Chechnia, an event which the Moscow leadership had tried in vain to prevent and, then, refused to recognize. Immediately after his election, on November 1, 1991, Dudaev declared Chechnia a sovereign republic (Nakhchi-Cho), while the Ingush held a referendum during which a vast majority voted for the creation of a separate republic within the Russian Federation. That same month, Yeltsin made an unsuccessful attempt to declare a state of emergency in Chechnia and sent airborne troops to its capital, Grozny. This action immediately rallied the major political forces in Chechnia behind Dudaev. The Russian troops were surrounded at the airport by the armed Chechen volunteers. In the face of opposition from the Russian Parliament and from the general public, Yeltsin was forced to withdraw them. In the beginning of 1992, the Russian troops stationed in Chechnia also left the recalcitrant republic, leaving behind many weapons, and on July 4, 1992, Ingushetia was proclaimed by the Russian Parliament a separate republic within the Russian Federation. Thus, Chechnia's independence was recognized de facto, at least partly. Chechnia refused to sign the March 31, 1992, Federal Treaty and did not participate in the 1993 referendum on the constitution and in the parliamentary election in Russia.

Still, in 1992–1994, the possibility of compromise was feasible. In Moscow, some politicians and observers suggested that the solution could be

found by providing Chechnia the status of associated state. There are
many indications that Dudaev, despite his sometimes extremist rhetoric,
was actually trying to reach an accommodation with Moscow (*Moskovskii
komsomoletz*, March 14, 1995). Thus, during the October 1993 confrontation between Yeltsin and the Russian Parliament, Dudaev declared his
support for Yeltsin.

However, Yeltsin's leadership was trying to do everything to destabi-
lize the situation in Chechnia and to oust Dudaev from power. Some
people, who at one time or another were close to Yeltsin, told me that his
attitude toward Chechnia is to a large extent influenced by his personal
animosity toward Dudaev. Yeltsin considers his 1992 fiasco of sending
troops to Grozny as a personal humiliation, and this is something unfor-
given by the Russian president.

The only action against Chechnia that was excluded for the time being
was the direct military intervention because it was opposed by many influential politicians, some people in the military, and the general public.
In fact, not pro-Chechen, but rather anti-Chechen feeling prevails in Russia. "The cruel Chechen is crawling up the riverbank and sharpening his
dagger"—this famous line by the nineteenth-century Russian poet Mikhail
Lermontov, which goes back to the times of the Caucasian war, is known
by heart by generations of Russian school children. The Russian mass
media have certainly contributed to the spread of the negative attitudes
toward Chechens by depicting every Chechen as a criminal, mafiosi, and
potential terrorist. Still, the scars of Afghanistan are not yet forgotten in
Russia.

Nevertheless, when, in the fall of 1992, the Russian tanks moved into
Ingushetia, allegedly to prevent further bloodshed between the Ingush
and the Ossetians, they came to the Chechnia border. Some of my informants claim that the officers in command were told that they could cross
the border, if the Chechens would try to help the Ingush, and that, apparently, was just what Moscow hoped for. My informants further claim that
the Russian officers in the field did not welcome this idea; they entered
into direct negotiations with the Chechen commanders, and a possible
provocation was averted. What is known for sure is that Yegor Gaidar, at
that time the Russian acting prime-minister, personally came to the zone
of conflict, met with the Chechen vice-premier Mamodaev, and quickly
came to an agreement with him about the measures which defused the
tension. It was also decided at the meeting to have further negotiations
on the normalization of relations between Russia and Chechnia (*Izvestiia*,
January 12, 1995).

However, eventually the decision was made not to negotiate seriously
with Dudaev but to oust him from power by force and to bring Chechnia

back into the Russian Federation. Yeltsin's advisor, Emil Pain, admits that the president was demonstrating only an outward expression of the negotiation process. Thus, in April 1994, Sergei Shakhrai, a Russian politician who was one of the staunchest opponents of the legitimation of Dudaev's regime, and as early as January 1993 had tried to find in Grozny more complaisant partners (*Izvestiia*, January 17, 1995), was appointed to supervise the Russian delegations on the negotiations, which actually never took place (Pain and Popov 1995).

The authoritarian character of Dudaev's regime, which in May–June 1993 dispersed the Chechen Parliament and the Constitutional Court, was certainly only a minor factor, if it factored at all, in the decision not to negotiate. In some other countries of the ex–Soviet Union the governments are no less authoritarian; nevertheless, Russia maintains normal, sometimes even friendly, relations with them. Much more important was that Moscow considered Chechnia a part of Russia and a challenge to its dominance in the Caucasian region. Apparently, the growing dissatisfaction with Dudaev in Chechnia encouraged the Russian leadership to hope that the general could be ousted from power by the internal opposition, if this were assisted by Moscow. The economic situation in Chechnia was deteriorating; mismanagement, corruption, and incompetence of its government were evident. The republic became a haven of various kinds of criminal activities, including smuggling and the biggest trans-shipping center for arms trade in the North Caucasus. (In all fairness, it should be noted that these activities became possible, at any rate widespread, because they were conducted in close cooperation with some corrupt bureaucrats and businessmen in Moscow. Besides, Moscow's attempts at blockading Chechnia also contributed to the development of illegal business operations.) Many of Dudaev's initial supporters joined the opposition, and the country faced the danger of being torn by increasing factional strife.

Chechen society always belonged to an egalitarian and decentralized type. It lacked the nobility or any other hereditary privileged social stratum. As the Chechen saying goes, every Chechen is a king to himself, all Chechens are considered equal. At the same time they are divided along the clanal, territorial, and to some extent even confessional lines. The Chechen *teifs*, or clans, survived in the Soviet period and nowadays are becoming more and more salient in the political life of the country. Loyalty to one's clan remains a paramount valor in Chechen ethics, and blood feuds in Chechnia last for generations. In the recent past, the fear of them served as a restraining force. Chechen people do not easily shed the blood of their countrymen. In addition, the Chechens are divided into three major territorial groups: those who live in the Terek River valley (they underwent a stronger Russian influence than other groups); those who live in the piedmont area; and the mountaineers (economically the most impoverished and socially the most traditional group). In the Soviet period, political power in Chechnia was held by those who came from the plains; no wonder the mountaineers became the staunchest supporters of Dudaev. Last but not least, although all Chechens are Sunni Muslims, they are adherents of two different Sufi orders, or brotherhoods: the Naqshbandiya and the Qadyriah, which are competing with each other for influence in Chechen society. Significantly, while Dudaev and his most reliable supporters belong to the Qadyriah, his opponents, such as Umar Avturkhanov or Ruslan Khazbulatov, belong to the Naqshbandiya.

It is no wonder that in the past the Chechens refused even to elect, or to recognize, a national leader from their own midst, because they did not wish to give one clan or territorial group an advantage over others. Their only previous national leader was Sheikh Mansur, who lived in the eighteenth century and was the first to lead the Chechens in a war against the Russians (Bennigsen 1964). During the Caucasian war, in the nineteenth century, the Chechens recognized as their leader Imam Shamil', who was a Daghestani (Gammer 1994). Thus, Dudaev is the second Chechen in 200 years to have become a national leader, and it is not accidental that for 20 years he has lived outside Chechnia and belongs to a small and uninfluential clan.

By the summer of 1994, the leaders of the Nadterechnyi and the Urus-Martanskii Districts of Chechnia were in open opposition to Dudaev and wanted to reach an accommodation with Moscow. Many others, especially the intelligentsia in Grozny, also demonstrated anti-Dudaev sentiments, though simultaneously many of them remain supporters of Chechnia's independence. Only the mountain areas remain loyal to the Chechen president.

All these factors were apparently taken into account when the decision was made by Moscow to rely upon the internal opposition to Dudaev[1]—all, except one. The Chechens were always the most irreconcilable adversaries of the Russian rule in the North Caucasus. After the Caucasian war, they rose again in 1877–1878, and once more in 1920–1921 (Broxup 1992); in addition, small-scale guerrilla activity continued in the mountains till the revolution and even afterwards. In the Soviet period, the anti-religious campaign and collectivization provoked several more uprisings in Chechnia in 1926, 1929–1930, 1940, and 1942

---

[1] Even in the beginning of September 1994, when the opposition forces had already suffered some serious setbacks, Shakhrai stated that a mere 120 men were ready to defend Dzhokhar Dudaev (*Moscow News* 36 [September 2–8, 1994]: 1). It is hard to say whether this statement was based on ignorance, was a sheer lie, or both.

(Avtorkhanov 1992). The Soviet repressions were severe. In the brief period from the middle of 1936 to the end of 1938, 80,000 people were purged in Checheno-Ingushetia. Stalin exiled the Chechens to Central Asia in 1944; during the deportation a third of them perished. Still, they continued to resist, even in exile and in the hard-labor camps. Solzhenitsyn testifies that in the camps only one nation as a whole refused to accept the psychology of submission—the Chechens. After the 20th Congress of the Communist Party the Chechens and Ingush were allowed to return to their homeland; however, they were never trusted by the Soviet government. The ethnic Russians were put in charge of all local organs of power (Rywkin 1991). Thus, the Chechen reaction to any involvement by Moscow in their affairs could be quite predictable.

Moscow's scenario for the solution of the Chechen problem closely resembled the previous Soviet scenarios of the interventions in Hungary, Czechoslovakia, and Afghanistan. A few members of the Chechen opposition to Dudaev who were brought to Moscow and, in the summer of 1994, declared the creation of the Provisional Council issued decrees that did not deceive anybody. (Actually, these decrees were written by one of Yeltsin's advisors, who in a conversation with me confirmed his authorship.) One of these decrees, issued on September 2, 1995, called for Dudaev's ouster by military means as the only alternative to the civil war in Chechnia. In November 1994, the Russian government and the Chechen opposition announced the creation of the Cabinet of Ministers with 21 portfolios.

Although the Russian government at first denied any involvement in Chechen affairs, it immediately provided the opposition support, not only political but also material support, including money, arms supplies, and the dispatch of Russian military instructors. The opposition was trying to lure young men to join its forces by paying them high salaries, with the money generously provided by Moscow (*Moscow News* 38 [September 23–29, 1994]: 3). However, it soon became clear that hopes that the oppositionists would be capable of replacing Dudaev without direct intervention by the Russian army were but wishful thinking. In the beginning, some opposition leaders claimed that they opposed bringing Russian troops into Chechnia, but as early as September 1994 they admitted that they would not mind the assistance of several Russian battalions (*Moscow News* 39 [September 30–October 6, 1994]: 2). The very fact that the Provisional Council was founded in and backed by Moscow was enough for many Chechens not to support it. Several times Dudaev's forces inflicted heavy defeats on the opposition, and all its attempts to capture Grozny were properly rebuffed. Particularly embarrassing to Moscow was the last of these attempts, undertaken on November 26, 1994, during

which Dudaev's fighters captured a number of Russian soldiers and officers. In the beginning the Russian leadership denied its participation in
the fighting, then the captives were declared mercenaries, then volunteers, and only later was it admitted that the Russian military was involved
in the actions (*Novoe russkoe slovo,* November 29, 1994).

By November 1994, it became clear that, whatever one may think about
the situation in crime-ridden Chechnia and about the dubious legitimacy
of Dudaev's regime, it would be impossible to defeat Dudaev without a
direct and large-scale military intervention. However, everybody in Russia with an elementary knowledge of the history of the Caucasus and
Chechen-Russian relations understood that it would be difficult to win a
victory in such a war and even more difficult to subdue the Chechen
people. As early as September 1994 the liberal Russian weekly, *Moscow
News,* warned that "Dudaev may very well defeat the troops of the pro-
Russian Provisional Council, which could increase the danger of the Russian army's involvement in the conflict. This may compromise the pro-
Russian opposition, and the people will be forced to take up arms in order to rebuff aggression" (*Moscow News* 36 [September 9–15, 1994]: 3).
A month earlier, Yeltsin himself ruled out the use of force to retake Chechnia. Three months later he decided to resort to a military solution to the
Chechen crisis, against public opinion, against protests of liberals who at
that time still supported him, against the recommendation of Parliament,
and in spite of the reluctance of many disgruntled people in the army.
The famous saying claims that the only lesson that can be learned from
history is that nobody ever learned anything from it. The Russian leadership certainly belongs to this category of people. Even letting Chechnia
go would not lead to a breakup of the Russian Federation, first, because
so far most of the ethnic minorities in Russia did not demonstrate a strong
desire to secede; and, second, because in many of her autonomous formations the ethnic Russians are in the majority. On the contrary, keeping
Chechnia by force, at the risk of having another Afghanistan, will certainly
aggravate anti-Russian feelings in the North Caucasus and among other
non-Russian minorities in the country in general.

It is unclear at the moment and may remain unclear for a long time
why the decision to start a large-scale military campaign was made at all
and who is personally responsible for it.[2] The decision was made in great

---

[2] In accordance with some sources, including the president's advisor Pain (Pain and
Popov 1995), this decision had been advocated by the "force" ministers (defense, interior,
and security) and by some members of Yeltsin's "inner circle" including the chief of the
president's guard Korzhakov. It was made in closed meetings of the Russian Security Council
sometime in late November or early December. However, Shakhrai claims that, in fact, the
Security Council recommended only the blockade of Chechnia and a demonstration of

secrecy, at the moment when Dudaev made another attempt to reach an agreement with Moscow based on the Tatarstan model. He indicated that he would agree with providing Chechnia an associate state status within the Russian Federation, which in practical terms should mean that the status of his republic would be similar to that of Tatarstan. Dudaev stipulated two demands in regard to this solution. First, Russia should recognize him as the legitimate president of Chechnia. Second, he should be allowed to keep his guards, which would be incorporated into the Russian army as a special unit, just as this had been done with the North Ossetian regiments and with some Cossacks units. Dudaev's proposal was in no way rejected out of hand. On the contrary, Moscow sent a delegation to the Caucasus to negotiate with the representatives of the Chechen president. One member of this delegation told me that a few hours into the talks, on December 11, 1995, the participants received word about the beginning of the Russian military campaign in Chechnia. The Chechen operation was sanctioned only by Yeltsin's secret decree of November 30, 1994 (*Izvestiia*, May 12, 1995). In the opinion of many Russian legal experts, this alone makes the whole campaign illegal. On December 17, 1994, Dudaev offered talks again, that time without conditions. The Russian side replied with bombs and rockets.

Some people in Russia speculate that Defense Minister Pavel Grachev pursued the Chechen war in part to distract attention from a scandal connected with high-level corruption in the military (*Monitor* 6, no. 1 [January 9, 1995]: 2). This may be part of the truth, but only a small part. Grachev alone was hardly powerful enough to force the Russian leadership to make such a drastic decision. Likewise, a *post factum* economic explanation of the campaign, insisting that Russia needs Chechen oil (*Moskovskii komsomoletz*, January 12, 1995), does not seem convincing. In 1992, Chechnia produced only 3.6 million tons of crude oil of the Russian output of 354 million tons. In the following years its production continued to go down, and it was less than 1 percent of Russian oil production forecasted for 1995 (*Izvestiia*, January 12, 1995). It is true that an oil pipeline which connects Russian oil-producing areas with the refining center in Baku goes through Chechnia. However, before the war started there were already projects to build a new pipeline which would bypass Chechnia. Economically and politically its construction would cost Russia much less than military action. As for the oil refinery in Grozny, it was destroyed by Russian bombs soon after the war began.

---

force by concentrating troops on its borders, with a simultaneous continuation of negotiations with Dudaev (*Vecherniaia Moskva*, February 17, 1995).

According to an opinion which was circulating in the Russian liberal circles at the beginning of the war, the Chechen crisis was fanned deliberately, and its possible consequences, such as a guerrilla war or even terrorist acts, were anticipated and welcomed, since, in one way or another, they may allow the creation of an atmosphere favorable for authoritarian rule and/or for winning or even postponing the presidential elections. I am in no way sure that this opinion is correct, and especially complete, but nowadays many things are possible in the Russian political life. One thing is, however, clear. The Chechen war reflects Yeltsin's general shift to the right. Apparently, the president and his entourage wanted to comply with the offended vanity of the forces of Russian nationalism, imperialism, and militarism and attract the sympathies of those who back these forces, or are prone to their ideology. Thus, Shakhrai stated that a secession of Chechnia would encourage separatists in other North Caucasian republics and would weaken the Russian positions in Transcaucasia (*Vecherniaia Moskva,* February 17, 1995). A blitzkrieg in Chechnia, it was hoped, would once again enhance the president's fading image among the Russian voters and would bring other political dividends.

It soon became clear that the blitzkrieg had failed, although the Russian leadership continued to please itself with this illusion or simply preferred to stick to this lie. On November 1994, Pavel Grachev boasted to journalists that one regiment of his paratroopers could seize Grozny in two hours (*Novoe russkoe slovo,* November 29, 1994). On December 26, 1994, Yeltsin told the Russian Security Council that the military campaign was almost over; from that moment on only the police would introduce "order" in Chechnia. On January 18, 1995, after the Russian troops triumphantly hoisted a Russian flag over the collapsed hulk of the Presidential Palace in Grozny, as if it were the capital of a defeated enemy, Yeltsin assured the same council again that in a few days the military operation in Chechnia would be over and, then, the Ministry of Interior would maintain the law and order in Chechnia and would "protect the Chechen population" (*New York Times,* January 20, 1995; *Izvestiia,* March 10, 1995). On February 8, 1995, Yeltsin stated once more: "The situation is developing normally. Soldiers are not involved in combat activities but are engaged in creative work [*sic*!]. Only Interior Ministry units, in small groups, continue to disarm the militants" (*New York Times,* February 10, 1995).

Meanwhile, almost from the very beginning the military operation in Chechnia resulted in excessive violence. The Russian defense minister proclaimed the principle in accordance with which the Russian army should respond to every Chechen shot with a thousand of its own. Issuing the order to carry out huge artillery and air strikes at random (there are many reports that during the latter, pelter and needle bombs were used, though they are forbidden by international law), he consciously sacrificed the civilian population, including ethnic Russians in Grozny. When the "Grad" and "Uragan" volley-fire systems were put into operation it became clear that the casualties would be counted in the thousands. Many of the victims consisted of elderly people with no place to flee the onslaught (*Moscow News* 10 [March 17–23, 1995]: 2). As early as December 27, 1994, Yeltsin announced that the bombing of Grozny would stop. Actually, it did not, and for many weeks more bombs continued brutally to rain down on the city day and night, and all types of ammunition and ordnance were used in the city until it was reduced to rubble. (For comparison's sake, I would like to suggest to the reader that she or he imagine another situation: Quebec has seceded from Canada, and the government in Ottawa sends war planes to destroy Montreal or Quebec City).

The Russian aircraft also resorted to the method of "free hunting" on the roads when individual cars became their targets. The obvious goal of these and other similar actions was to demonstrate Russia's readiness to continue, if necessary, the war to the last Chechen, to force them into submission.

The result was the opposite. The invasion and the atrocities committed by the Russian army and particularly by the Interior Ministry forces did what Dudaev had previously failed to achieve. It united most Chechens. The recent supporters and opponents of Dudaev fought together against the Russian occupiers. In January 1995, I met in Moscow with Jebrail Gakaev, a former vice-president of the Chechen Academy of Sciences and one of the leaders of the opposition to Dudaev who had been forced by Dudaev to leave Grozny. He told me that all his relatives in Chechnia were fighting against the Russian troops and that two of his nephews had already died. The Russian maverick general Lebed', a veteran of the Afghan war and an outspoken critic of the Chechen war and the ways it was being conducted, from his own experience knew what he was saying when he stated:

> Bombardments have an unpleasant side effect: They engender wolves who for a very long time will not conceal their fangs. The most splendid soldiers are made of the people who are leaving their homes in the morning without even thinking about a war, but after returning home in the evening discover the place of their houses are now shell-holes in which their wives, children and parents had evaporated. . . . Only one thing remains to such people—revenge (*Segodnia*, May 17, 1995).

Only by the middle of March 1995, the Russian troops managed to capture the Naurskii, Nadterechnyi, and Shelkovskii Districts of Chechnia, and established relative control over the ruins of Grozny and some nearby settlements. By that time, at least 6 settlements in Chechnia were demolished completely, 80 more were partly ruined, and many atrocities against the civilian Chechen population, including looting, raping, and murdering, were already committed. According to different estimates, by then the Russian troops had lost about 5,000 men. In Chechnia, 20,000–25,000 civilians, among them 5,000 children, had been killed, and over 300,000 had become refugees (*Moscow News* 10 [March 17–23, 1995]: 2).

"Filtration camps" were already established in occupied parts of Chechnia and nearby North Ossetia to check whether the captured Chechens were fighters or civilians. This is not an easy task, since the Chechens owe their strength not to professionals but to rural inhabitants who voluntarily took up arms. Anyway, nobody is granted POW status; those who resist the Russian troops are considered bandits. People who have gone through these filtration camps testify that all the camps' prisoners are subjected to humiliation and torture (*Obshchaia gazeta*, February 16–22, February 23–March 1, 1995). Chechnia's economy suffered an estimated $45–52 billion in damages. "I like the situation in Russia"—this is how Yeltsin appraised the state of affairs in his country in the same month of March (*Moscow News* 12 [March 31–April 6, 1995]: 1). No remorse about those who were killed and were continuing to be killed. Apparently, the Russian president does not count the Chechens anymore.

The Russian deputy prime minister Shakhrai had predicted an end of the war by the end of April. By the end of that month, the Russian troops, resorting to scourged-earth tactics, seized the ruins of Argun, Gudermes, and Shali. The advancing forces have been delivering artillery and air strikes against all populated areas standing in their way and have demonstrated no interest in whether there were militants in these areas or just helpless civilians (*Moscow News* 13 [April 7–13, 1995]: 1). However, if the Russian politicians and generals had hoped that the Chechens would cease their resistance, their hopes turned out to be in vain. The war of extermination continued. Even those Chechen politicians who collaborate with the Russian government publicly accuse the Interior Ministery forces of looting, rape, and violence against civilians. They complain that such atrocities help Dudaev (*Obshchaia gazeta*, March 23–29, 1995: 2; *Moscow Times*, April 23, 1995: 15).

The grim reality of this war was revealed again in the massacre of Samashki, a settlement 18 miles west of Grozny, which was turned into a blood bath by the detachment consisting mainly of OMON (Special Purpose Police Detachments), riot police, and Interior Ministry forces. The clean-up operation lasted four days, at which time neither the press nor Red Cross representatives were let into the settlement. By that time the

Chechen fighters had already left Samashki, and the local residents had surrendered their weapons. Nevertheless, the carnage began immediately after the troops entered the settlement. Soldiers and special militia units backed by armored personnel carriers shot at every step. Suspicious houses were first pelted with grenades and then finished off with flame-throwers. An estimated 250 unarmed civilians, mainly women, children, and elders, were murdered. All male residents from the age of 14 to 90 who escaped the murder were detained in filtration camps (*Izvestiia*, April 12, 1995; *New York Times*, April 14, 1995; *Sunday Times*, April 16, 1995; *Literaturnaia gazeta*, April 19, 1995; *Moscow Times*, April 23, 1995: 15; *Moscow News* 15 [April 21-27, 1995]; *Obshchaia gazeta*, April 27–May 3, 1995). On the eve of V-E Day, the Russian liberal weekly bitterly re-marked: "The horrifying truth is that on the anniversary of its great vic-tory, Russia is treating the Chechen people in the same way as Nazi Ger-many treated the Russians" (*Moscow News* 16 [April 28–May 4, 1995]: 2). Still, during the victory celebrations in Moscow, in the presence of Presi-dent Clinton, Yeltsin assured the world that "there was no armed activity in Chechnia, the Ministry of Interior simply seized the weapons in the hands of some small criminal gangs" (*New York Times*, May 11, 1995).

At the moment, the war is not yet over. Only the plain districts of Chechnia have been captured, and at great cost. Still, by the middle of May 1995, the Russian authorities in Grozny, despite the imposed curfew and other punitive measures (e.g., young Chechens appearing in the streets were in danger of being shot without a trial or of being sent to the filtra-tion centers [*Komsomol'skaia pravda*, May 13, May 16, 1995]), were unable to cope with the guerrillas in the city. So far the Russian troops have not attempted to establish their control over the mountain areas of Chechnia, where the resistance may last for a long time. Pavel Grachev insisted several times that there would be no guerrilla warfare in Chech-nia (*Moscow News* 14 [April 14-20, 1995]: 2). Some Russian military experts are more cautious, but still claim that it is possible to eliminate the guerrillas there in less than two years by organizing a blockade of the mountains and starving their population to death or into submission (*Nezavisimaia gazeta*, January 14, 1995), but this remains to be seen. In addition, the danger of terrorist activities also cannot be excluded. Still, other questions remain: What kind of future relations with Russia does Yeltsin's leadership foresee for Chechnia? And does Russia intend to main-tain there a regime of military occupation? Those in this leadership who were responsible for the fatal decision to resort to force in Chechnia sabo-taged all attempts at its peaceful solution during half a year of the war. The warrant for Dudaev's arrest is as indicative in this respect as the appointment of an ethnic Russian and a former communist functionary, Nikolai Semenov, as Russia's vice-regent in Chechnia.

At the moment, the question is not only how much sovereignty is Moscow ready to yield to Chechnia but also with whom is the Kremlin going to negotiate its future relations with the recalcitrant republic? The government of *quislings* or *husáks* is not a solution for Chechnia. Even before the military actions began, people such as Umar Avturkhanov, Yaragi Mamodaev, and Doku Zavgaev had been referred to in Chechnia as the Moscow Chechens. Head of the puppet Chechen government, Salambek Khadzhiev, is characterized as a political kamikaze even by Yeltsin's advisor Pain (Pain and Popov 1995). Most Chechens consider these people a bunch of collaborators. They cannot even find a common language with each other. Their political survival depends solely on the presence and support of the Russian troops. In April 1995, one member of the local administration in Chechnia appointed by Moscow complained:"Essentially, we are all potentially dead men and will be destroyed at the first opportunity (*Moscow News* 13 [April 7–13, 1995]: 3). After the Russian military campaign in Chechnia had begun, the Provisional Council was subjected to mass-scale obstruction even by many of its former supporters. In April 1995, Yeltsin confirmed by his decree the creation of a new political body in Chechnia, the Committee of National Accord, which included some less-compromised members of the Chechen opposition to Dudaev. However, even Khadzhiev admits that electing a new legitimate power in Chechnia cannot be done at gunpoint.

It is too early to forecast an outcome of the Chechen crisis. It may well be that Russia will win an inglorious military victory in Chechnia. The question is whether this victory turns out to be a Pyrrhic one to the nascent Russian democracy. Detrimental effects of the Chechen war on the Russian political development are already quite evident.

The message that Russia is sending now to the near-abroad countries is fairly clear. In violation of the Treaty on the Conventional Armed Forces in Europe, Russia is deploying its new 51st army in the North Caucasus. On April 17, and again on April 19 and 20, 1995, Foreign Minister Kozyrev asserted the Kremlin's right to use direct military force to protect the ethnic Russians living in other ex–Soviet countries. Hitler made similar statements regarding the ethnic Germans. The consequences are well known.

The Chechen crisis proved to non-Russian citizens of the Russian Federation that the federative character of this state exists mainly on paper. Many of them are convinced now that the Russian Empire has never ceased to exist. At present, the Chechen example proves again how dangerous it is to suppress tensions in interethnic relations instead of looking for ways to alleviate them. Although the predictions that the invasion of Chechnia would result in the second Caucasian war turned out to be wrong, anti-Russian feelings in the North Caucasus are today stronger than ever during the last decades. In the beginning of the Chechen war, Russian forces that moved through Ingushetia and Daghestan met resistance from the local population in attempts to thwart the invasion of Chechnia. Ingush civilians, including women and children, barricaded roads and placed themselves in front of advancing columns. Some tanks and military vehicles were fired on, and others were captured and set ablaze. Similar events occurred in Daghestan. Ingushetia is already subject to "occasional" air strikes, and many people there are afraid that what has happened to Chechnia will soon be repeated in Ingushetia.

In less than half a year, from the beginning of the Chechen war, Russian society has moved from shock to stupor. The war is still extremely unpopular, but the prevailing feeling is that of impotence. Open protests in the military were suppressed after three deputy defense ministers, Generals Boris Gromov, Georgy Kondratiev, and Valery Mironov, as well as some other officers of lower rank, who raised objections against using the Russian army in Chechnia, were either fired, like Kondratiev, or removed from their positions. Most of the democrats moved to the opposition of Yeltsin, but their influence is decreasing. The liberal press continues to be very critical of the government's actions in Chechnia, but the government is increasing its control over the mass media including the press and is trying to muffle the most critical of them. The civil rights activists who openly oppose the Chechen war and tell the truth about it are vilified by the government and in the Parliament. While the Russian fascists promise to erect a monument to Grachev when they come to power (*Moscow News* 9 [March 3–9, 1995]: 5), he refers to the civil rights campaigners as "enemies of the people" and "skunks." In March 1995, the Russian Parliament overwhelmingly voted for dismissal of the human rights commissioner, Sergei Kovalev, for his criticism of the Chechen war. In April 1995, the head of the parliamentary commission on Chechnia, Stanislav Govorukhin, accused the strongest opponents of the war, liberal deputies Sergei Kovalev, Anatoly Shabad, and Lev Ponomarev, of "treason" and "Russophobia" and called for their prosecution for a "terrible crime against the Russian people and the Russian state at a time of war" (*Moscow Times,* April 23, 1995: 15).

The message that the Russian citizens are getting now is the same as they were used to during the 70 years of communist rule: they have no rights, while the authorities are accountable to no one. A small number of people within the ruling elite, who have exchanged *Das Kapital* for capital but do not wish to give up their political power, again decide in secrecy the destiny of the country while society passively sits by. In addition to the Chechen people, liberal democracy in Russia my prove to be the ultimate victim of the unwarranted and savage war. In fact, economic reforms and democracy already ceased to be one and the same in the country. A sad truth that not yet everybody wants to admit, especially in the West, is that, in a few post-Soviet years, Yeltsin the democrat has passed away, and the part of this man that was formerly first secretary of the regional Communist Party organization has taken the upper hand over the part of him that was a temporary ally of Sakharov. The authoritarian tendencies of Yeltsin's leadership are quite conspicuous and are growing stronger. The shallowness of Russia's newly acquired democratic attributes and institutions has been revealed to all her citizens by the president's ability to take shortcuts through the democratic political process, to ignore the legislature and public opinion, and to bypass the constitution.

In the beginning of 1995, when Yeltsin's popularity had been plummeting, when no less than 70 percent of those interviewed in opinion polls claimed that they did not trust the president (*Obshchaia gazeta*, March 16–22, 1995: 1) and only 3 percent of the interviewees wanted Yeltsin to be the next Russian president (*Obshchaia gazeta*, February 23–March 1, 1995: 1), many predicted that he did not have a chance to be reelected. At present this is far from clear, though at the moment no more than 4 percent of the Russian citizens want Yeltsin to be reelected (*Komsomol'skaia pravda*, May 17, 1995).

The more people become accustomed to the war, the less apt they are to remember who started it and who is to blame for it. Despite a common disapproval of the war, to a growing number of people prone to the official Russian propaganda, the main culprit is sought and found not in the Kremlin but in Chechnia. It is a "cruel Chechen" who kills innocent Russian soldiers. When one watches official programs on Russian TV, such as "Vremia" (Time), or reads the semiofficial newspapers spreading lies about the war in Chechnia, one may get the impression that time has turned back to the years of the Soviet invasion of Afghanistan. Unconfirmed or simply false information about castrated captive Russian soldiers, raped kindergarten children, or numerous mercenaries, including women from the Baltics, which some Russian politicians like Yegorov and Rybkin did not disdain repeating (*Moskovskii komsomoletz*, January 12, 1995; *Segodnia*, January 17, 1995; *Moskovskie novosti* 3 [January 15–22, 1995]: 10), became a constant subject in these media. According to one opinion poll, as early as February 1995, only 21 percent of Russians supported the opinion that Russian troops are opposed not by criminals but by the Chechen people, whereas 47 percent supported the government's version (*Moscow News* 8 [February 24–March 2, 1995]: 3). Under the circumstances, the ruling elite and the state bureaucracy have many possibilities for maneuvering and still have a good chance to remain in power after the parliamentary elections in 1995 and the presidential elections in 1996.

The bulk of the nomenklatura in Russia have managed to survive not only economically but also politically. Now they are on the counteroffensive on a wide front, not only in Chechnia but in Russia as well. Now they are smarter than they were a few years ago; they do not oppose privatization of state property anymore. This time their goal is to pursue the country's transition to a market economy but under the strict control of the ruling elite, that is, to follow a Russian variety of the essentially Chinese model. At the moment, the main obstacle to achieving this goal is not the liberal press (the Chechen crisis has demonstrated that this press can be ignored, at any rate for the time being, particularly because the most important mass media are under governmental control) or the democratic opposition (the Chechen crisis has proved again that at present this opposition has little influence), but rather the threat of the forthcoming elections with their unpredictable results.

The attempt to monopolize the Russian political scene by creating a system of two status-quo political blocs, in practical terms a "one-in-two" party headed by Prime Minister Chernomyrdin and Speaker of the State Duma Rybkin, was hailed by Yeltsin and seems aimed at propping him up. The very idea of these blocs was born amongst Yeltsin's close associates (*Izvestiia*, May 13, 1995). These blocs are designated to play correspondingly "right-of-center" and "left-of-center" roles. If Yeltsin's chances for reelection remain slim, Chernomyrdin may be considered as his possible successor. Thus, the idea of "centrism" should become part of the ruling elite's self-preservation.

So far this grand design faces difficulties in creating a left-of-center bloc. Rybkin's image of a fighter for social justice faded somewhat after it was learned that his plane, instead of carrying humanitarian cargo (medicine for orphanages), brought home the Speaker's furniture purchased during his official visit to the United States. However, Chernomyrdin's bloc has already been successfully created under the pretentious name Russia Is Our Home. At least half of this bloc's council consists of those who occupy leading positions in the federal executive power, and of barons of regional administrations (*Izvestiia*, May 13, 1995; *Nezavisimaia gazeta*, May 13, 1995).

The next goal is to make the party of power, as Chernomyrdin's bloc is already christened in Russia, the ruling party. This goal is not secured yet, but it is in no way unachievable, considering the enormous financial resources, the state-controlled propaganda machine, and the support of a significant number of regional nomenklatura who are at the disposal of the party of power. Besides, there is no guarantee that the forthcoming elections will be free and fair. Commenting on the creation of Chernomyrdin's party, Gorbachev noted that he was well conversant with the vast opportunities that similar structures had when they were supported by power (*Segodnia,* May 12, 1995). Oh yes, the former general secretary of the Communist Party of the USSR is acquainted with such opportunities very well; this time he was telling the truth.

The army that has tasted blood in an unjust war may also be dangerous to the country. At least every fifth Russian who served in the military in Chechnia needs psychiatric treatment (*Komsomol'skaia pravda,* May 16, 1995). This year the soldiers who have already learned their lesson of violence will start to return home, embittered against the democrats, who, to their mind, betrayed them by supporting the Chechens, as well as against the government, who sent them to the slaughterhouse in Chechnia. Who knows against whom these people may turn? And the generals? The generals are breathing down everyone's neck.

In 1991, Yeltsin offered the autonomous formations of the Russian Federation as much sovereignty as they could swallow. A few months afterwards, in August 1991, he climbed up a tank to stand against the forces of imperialism and totalitarianism. In October 1993, he did not find a better way to defend Russian democracy than by sending tanks to the Parliament. In December 1994, he apparently considered tanks the best way to foster interethnic peace in the Russian Federation. In 1991, Yeltsin was a hero of the Russian democrats and an archenemy of the Russian ultranationalists. Nowadays the gap between Yeltsin and the democrats is deepening while Barkashev, Zhirinovsky, Baburin, and people like them declare their unequivocal support of the president's action in Chechnia—a remarkable evolution of a politician in so short a time.

In 1990, when for the first time I was allowed to visit Moscow since living in the West for five years, I felt, like many other people there, that Big Brother had stopped watching us—at last. In any case people talked freely and did not care anymore whether they were overheard by the secret police or not. The situation remained the same over the next five years. I became used to it. In this respect there was no difference between Moscow, New York, or Jerusalem, or, maybe I had better say, no big difference. This spring, during my telephone conversations with my friends and informants in Russia, I was warned again, for the first time in many years, "This is not a matter for a telephone conversation. Let us discuss it when we meet." I do not know for certain whether Big Brother has resumed its old practice or not. What matters is that people have again become cautious. To those who were born and used to live in a totalitarian country, this is not a minor detail; this is a very indicative and alarming sign, indeed.

Conclusion

Every theory is bound
to meet its "no" sooner or later,
often very quickly after conception.
—Albert Einstein

The collapse of the communist regimes in the Eastern European countries and in the Soviet Union was met with a mixed reaction in Western academia and in intellectual circles in general. It was almost a personal tragedy to those who, while occupying comfortable positions in the capitalist society they hated, could not or did not wish to escape illusions about the nature of the communist regimes, to whom the magic of words like *communism*, *socialism*, or *revolution* gained an implicit moral approbation and clouded the totalitarian character of communist society. Raymond Aron once said that revolution is the opium for the intelligentsia. It was too difficult for those people to admit the demise of their revolutionary legacy. It is true that by the 1990s these people were already in the minority, at any rate in the United States. Still, to the very end they have tried to find good guys, good Bolsheviks in the history of the Russian Revolution, and to the very end they hoped that Soviet-style communism could be modified, reformed, and revived. This is why Gorbachev became their hero and their last hope. I suspect that these people cared for themselves, for their illusions and reputations, much more than for the people in communist countries, or even for the fate of socialism there and around the world.

There were also other scholars who admitted the desirability of a transition from totalitarian communism to liberal capitalism and welcomed this transition, but underestimated the difficulties connected with it. When the communist world began to open up politically, the concepts derived from the experiences of Spain, Portugal, Greece, and some Latin American countries were sometimes applied, particularly in the beginning, to the communist countries (see, for example, Bova 1991). It was too often

230

assumed that their transition to liberal democracy would be rapid and inevitable, almost automatic. Hence, Fukuyama's (1987) dictum on the end of history, predicting the close-at-hand victory of liberal democracy all over the world.

This conceptual extension was mistaken. The current development in many postcommunist countries proves that their communist past has left a very particular legacy which hinders their divorce from totalitarianism. What was certainly not sufficiently taken into account was that authoritarian capitalism is markedly different from totalitarian communism.

Authoritarian capitalism suppresses civil society but still has to tolerate, sometimes even to engender, some forms of societal self-organization, which in the proper conditions help to consolidate new democracies. In contrast, totalitarian communism resulted in the utter destruction of civil society. The state completely subjugated society, identified itself with society, and usurped the right to interpret public interests.

Authoritarian capitalism does not monopolize the economic sphere or abolish private property and the market system. Political elites have to coexist with economic ones. Therefore, during the transitional period the former can be bought by or incorporated into the latter. With the transition from authoritarian to liberal democratic capitalism, only the political order is changed while the economic one remains essentially the same. Under totalitarian communism, economic elites did not have an independent existence. With the transition from totalitarian communism, everything should be rebuilt or built anew from the bottom up: political order, social organization, the economic system, and ideology. This alone makes it rather difficult to expect that there will be any uniform transition to democracy. One cannot exclude the possibility that authoritarianism of various kinds—or even worse, neo-fascism—may in some cases become the alternative to the recent communist past.

Since much of this book is devoted to nationalism and related issues it is time to inquire what the Soviet experience and the experience of other communist countries can tell us about this phenomenon. However, first, I would like to clarify my own position on this issue. Doing so seems to me particularly appropriate at a time when, almost worldwide, people are ready to die and kill for various nationalistic ideologies. It should be stressed that I am using the term *nationalism* free of any value judgment, with no plus or minus sign attached. In itself nationalism is neither good nor bad. What is bad is when people begin to discriminate against others or to slaughter each other on the grounds of their nationality. Still, throughout history there has not been one idea, no matter how noble, in whose name people have not slaughtered each other.

The main conclusion, already trivial at the moment but still disputed by many Marxists only a few years ago, is that the appeal of communist ideology turned out to be weaker than that of nationalism. Not without reason, from its very beginning Marxism viewed nationalism as a rival and an enemy (Szporluk 1988: 14). But despite all efforts, it failed to defeat or to domesticate nationalism; on the contrary, nationalism was one of the main forces that buried communism. After all, the ideas of class solidarity, which were supposed to be stronger than any other ideas, became dominant amongst the working class only in a few countries and for relatively short periods. This should not be surprising, since the ideas of national solidarity are less exclusive and have an even stronger egalitarian appeal.

All those who belong to "us," rich and poor, people with university diplomas and those of little education alike, upper classes and lower classes, industrialists and workers, the party nomenklatura and political dissidents, constitute a nation. Nationalism claims that, in a way, all these people are kindred because they live in the same territory (or sometimes strive to acquire a territory they consider their own), they speak the same language, they share the same culture, they have a common historical memory and myths, and they have a common fate. Ironically, modern history often does its best to confirm these claims and feelings. All sorts of Jews—fervent Zionists and those who advocated a complete assimilation, religious and secular people, even converts, whether bankers or beggars—were condemned to Auschwitz; and all Chechens, Kalmyks, and Crimean Tatars—some of whom were communist party officials, others of whom had no kind feelings toward the Soviet rule—were deported from their homelands. Ethnic cleansings do not know the difference between economic classes, social strata, and political allegiances. They only strengthen loyalties among the persecuted, as well as among the persecutors, and the border between the former and the latter is sometimes only conditional and temporary.

Still, if not in its extreme, then in principle, nationalism in its "humanitarian" variety, so termed by Hayes (1950), does not imply that those who do not belong to "us" are necessarily our enemies. The nationalism of Mazzini and Masaryk held that a peaceful coexistence between different nations is possible. Marxism is much more merciless, not only to economic classes, but sometimes to peoples and nations as well. The common cause of the workers should be stronger than their loyalty to any nation. Those who are not "with us" are "against us." This alone denies a significant part of society, often its majority, the right of belonging to "us." Those who speak the same language, share the same culture, sometimes even live on the same streets should be considered class enemies. The country in which one was born and lives, and to which one usually has a strong emotional attachment, its rivers and lakes, forests and mountains, cities and monuments, history and traditions, is irrelevant. Working people have no country.

Already Marx and Engels felt that something was wrong with this concept. Hence, their division of nations into progressive and reactionary ones; hence, their anger at the Czechs and other Slavic peoples refusing to become Germans, and thereby challenging their supposedly iron laws of historical development. The founding fathers did not hesitate to hope that "the Slavic barbarians . . . these petty, bull-headed nations will be destroyed so that nothing is left of them but their names" (for more details see Connor 1984b: 5ff.; see also Cummins 1980).

Not Marxism but nationalistic ideologies which reflected the European powers' competition were at least partly responsible for World War I and not only forced but also lured the masses to follow loyally, or even to welcome its outbreak. It would be wrong to claim that mass nationalism had something to do with 1914. However, with its first gun volleys the Western social-democrats took the side of their respective nations, thus sacrificing the international solidarity of workers. And the workers themselves were affected by jingoistic fervor. Nationalism, when it was at its worse, won the second round of competition with Marxism.

World War I, the disintegration of the continental empires, and the Treaty of Versailles resulted in the emergence of new states in Central and Eastern Europe. However, history did not allow them much time to develop a secure national identity. Because of the region's great ethnic diversity and other factors, these states, squeezed between fascist Italy, nazi Germany, and the communist Soviet Union and confronted by secessionist and irredentist demands, can hardly be characterized as nation-states. In most of them the process of nation building took nonliberal, authoritarian, and exclusive forms. The ideologies of ethnic, not civic, nationalism prevailed. Loyalty to the state was supposed to be achieved through loyalty to a dominant nationality, and those who were not loyal enough or were suspected of being disloyal were not considered a part of the nation. Not only were numerous ethnic minorities oppressed, but also frequently they were denied the opportunity and the right to join the nation in the making. In nineteenth-century Europe, nationalism was often linked with a democratic impulse; in the period between the two world wars, this Janus revealed its other ugly face. In Moynihan's (1993) vivid comparison, it became Pandaemonium—the capital of hell in Milton's *Paradise Lost*, where Satan and demons rule.

Still, the very fact that the new states in Central and Eastern Europe strove for homogeneity, just as the Western European countries had striven

100 or 150 years earlier, was by no means accidental. Nor was it the result of a tragic historical mistake. Those who adhere to the functional theory of nationalism and hold that the industrial era demands the congruence of political, ethnic, and cultural-linguistic borders should not be surprised by the eagerness of new states to emulate and catch up hastily with their more advanced and successful Western counterparts. The fact that they were trying to do this in a way that did not conform to the Western liberal standards of the times, and that their nationalism was of an excluding ethnic order, did not make the underlying reasons for the process different. Theoretical concepts often look better on paper than in reality.

The dual monarchy of Austria-Hungary, with two politically and culturally dominant nationalities as its pillars (though the Hungarians, even after the 1867 compromise, played second fiddle to Austria and continued to regard Austria as an opponent) and numerous other subjugated nationalities, was unable to evolve into a nation-state. Although some of its former subjects or their descendants, even scholars, horrified by the consequences of the disintegration of the empire of the Hapsburgs, tend to idealize it, this empire was actually a relic of the premodern era. *Kaisertreuer* might be appealing to cosmopolitan and acculturated individuals, or, on the other hand, to uneducated peasants, or even to some nationalities that consider the empire a kind of protector against regionally stronger ones. But eventually it failed to curb the forces of frustrated nationalism, which turned ethnic groups into corporate bodies with political demands shifting from full autonomy to independent statehood. True, it was the war into which Austria-Hungary entered so thoughtlessly that turned out to be suicidal to the Hapsburg Empire (but after all, it was an empire, and empires have their own logic of behavior). It is also true that a strong link between unitary societies and economic and social modernization is not imperative. Still, I venture to claim that Austria-Hungary was doomed to eventual disintegration, if not by the war or by the modernization process per se, then by the forces that uneven and differential modernization in the plural societies calls into being (on different opinions about the Hapsburg Empire and its fate, see Seton-Watson 1977: 147ff.; Sked 1981, 1989; Klima 1993: 232ff.; Mann 1993b: 330–52; Niederhauser 1993: 254ff.). Those who insist that cultural homogeneity is really a condition of the smooth functioning of industrial society should be consistent (Gellner 1983: 69); this principle should be applicable not only to Western Europe but to Central and Eastern Europe as well.

In modern times, multiethnic empires can hinder the process of nation building and the emergence of nation-states, but they are unable to prevent it. Sooner or later the forces of nationalism destroy empires; and the later it happens, the more painful it is.

In the aftermath of World War II, the imposed communist regimes in Central and Eastern European countries promised a new start. Hitler, Stalin, and their followers in the region, with their policies of ethnocide, ethnic cleansing, and a change of political borders with a corresponding population exchange, made many of these countries much more homogeneous in the postwar period than they were in the period between the two world wars. Still, the old problems of nation-state building remained unsolved. The new rulers tried to substitute loyalty to a communist state for loyalty to a national state, but the very fact that they were brought to power and backed by Soviet troops has made them anti-national. Nationalism was more suppressed than defeated, but even its suppression was not complete. In countries such as Poland and Romania, the communists, in a vain attempt at legitimizing their power, tried not so much to overcome as to harness ethnic nationalism and to adopt it as a part of the official ideology (see, for example, Verdery 1991). Even the discrimination of ethnic minorities continued. Nothing did work or could work. By destroying or suppressing civil society, communism in these countries has only paved the way for the return of ethnic nationalism. When communism in East-Central Europe collapsed, the old national rivalries erupted again, and full-fledged ethnic nationalism, not infrequently in its extreme forms, reemerged and began to compete with the liberal scenario for the postcommunist future of the region. With respect to ethnic nationalism, one may notice only one innovation in comparison with the prewar period: nowadays anti-Semitism is adopted in a virtual absence of Jews.

In a way, Yugoslavia was an exception in the region. Marxism was put to a real test there. In the prewar period, from the 1920s, Yogoslavia was Serb dominated. After the war, there was a serious desire to find a remedy for the centrifugal forces. Marxism there tried to overcome nationalism through the ideological glue of communism, and an attempt at creating a common Yugoslav identity through federalism and consociational arrangements of power sharing. Eventually, nothing worked out. Ethnic tension was felt in the country long before its disintegration. Nationalism in Yugoslavia has won another victory, this time a bloody one.

Thus, the experience of communism in East-Central Europe has proved again that it is beyond the power of the Marxist alternative to withstand and overcome the forces of nationalism. After the communist intermezzo, the countries of the region resumed the process of nation building. Only the future will tell whether they will do it better than their prewar and, then, communist predecessors, and which of them will be capable of de-

veloping a nation on a civic basis defined not by exclusive ethnic criteria
but by inclusive citizenship.

World War I resulted in the disintegration of two other multiethnic continental empires: the Ottoman and the Russian. In both of them, empire
building preceded and impeded nation building. In the case of the Ottoman Empire, whatever one may think about nationhood in the Arab world,
the end of that empire at least gave birth to the modern Turkish nation.
In the former domain of Romanovs, the development took a different path.

In prerevolutionary Russia the very idea of nation was never expressed
explicitly, since it was denied an identity separate from the state. Even
the common definition of the Russian nation was virtually absent. The
state was conceived in political, legal, and territorial terms. By God's
grace, the tsars had a hereditary right to rule over the empire, that is,
over all countries, peoples, and subjects that came under their sway. Officially, the Russians were defined, not as an ancestorally related people
in primordialist terms, like those formulated by Fichte, Herder, or Novalis,
and certainly not in civic terms, but rather as a religious and linguistic
unity bound together by the ties of dynastic loyalty. Hence, the slogan of
official nationality declared during the reign of Nicholas I: "Orthodoxy,
Autocracy, Nationality" (Narodnost') (Riasanovsky 1967). Those who pro-
fessed Orthodox Christianity, spoke Russian, and were subjects of a tsar
could, if they wished, be considered Russians, at any rate from the legal
point of view. This could not solve the problems connected with the
multiethnic character of the Russian Empire and with the discrimination
of non-Russian ethnic groups. Besides, between 1881 and 1905, the government increasingly resorted to forced Russification.

In the nineteenth century, the concept of the Russian nation became a
problem also for the emerging Russian nationalism. This nationalism from
the very beginning was developing in opposition to the rationalist West
and such values as equality, liberty, and individualism. Two different per-
ceptions of the Russian nation—inclusive and exclusive—as well as the
criteria for inclusion, remained a matter of debate till 1917 even among
the liberals (Shelokhaev 1994). In all kinds of Russian nationalism, religion played a central role. Being Orthodox Christian became an important part of being Russian. Tuzenbach, a Russified German from Chekhov's
play *Three Sisters*, had to persuade his Russian friends: "On my word of
honor, I'm Russian. I cannot even speak German. My father is Orthodox." Among conservatives, the exclusive perception of the Russian nation predominated. In the opinion of Pobedonostsev, one of the most
influential politicians during the reign of Alexander III, non-Russians and
non-Orthodox Christians in principle could not be completely loyal subjects of the Russian Empire. This ambiguity is reflected even in the Rus-

sian language. It contains two different words describing the Russian nation which are very difficult to translate into other languages: *rossiiskii*, which is a political-territorial and only potentially a civic definition, and *russkii*, which is an ethnic definition. At present, just as in the past, Russian nationalists stress an ethnic character of the Russian nation by persistently using the term *russkii*, while liberals prefer to use the term *rossiiskii*, implying that it means a shared citizenship in a multiethnic nation-state.

Thus, the formation of the Russian nation by the time of the revolution was not yet accomplished. Suffice it to mention, it remained unclear who was a Russian even in ethnic terms; the government and many Russian nationalists considered the Ukrainians and Belorussians only ethnographic parts of the Russian people. Many Cossacks were not sure whether they should consider themselves a part of the Russian nation or not.

The same may be claimed, and with even more reason, about the majority of non-Russian ethnic groups in the empire. They certainly did not constitute homogeneous ethnic nations, even if one takes into account that nations are never completely homogeneous and that the process of their formation is never completely accomplished (Connor 1990). In most of the non-Russian regions of the empire the majority of the population consisted of illiterate or semiliterate peasants, with a great variety of dialects and local cultural characteristics, often even with uncertain ethnic consciousness and self-identification. Still, tsarist Russia was, in Lenin's words, a "prison house of people," and amongst many of them ethnic nationalism was gaining strength, fueled by discrimination and often articulated, advocated, and promoted by the emerging educated middle strata, and in a few cases by the nobility. As far as the empire remained invincible the nationalism of the non-Russian ethnic groups was usually more of a cultural than a political order; however, we know from the numerous historical examples that in the proper conditions the transition from a cultural nationalism to a political one can be accomplished in a very short time.

The February 1917 revolution suggested to non-Russian nationalities an equality of legal rights with Russians and even the possibility of autonomy in the future. Whether in the long run that would have been enough to prevent the non-Russian nationalities' desire to secede, which I doubt, remains a speculative question.

The October 1917 revolution was not only a political and social revolution; it was also accompanied by national liberation movements in many non-Russian parts of the former Russian Empire, although political and class loyalties often conflicted with ethnic ones. One of the reasons the Bolsheviks won the civil war is that, at the time, they made many concessions to the non-Russian nationalities, temporarily succeeding in neutralizing them or attracting the sympathy of some national movements or entering into coalitions with several others (Pipes 1974). After all, the Reds' promise of the right of nations to self-determination seemed more attractive than the Whites' armed insistence on the "Russia single and indivisible" principle. Self-determination promulgated by the Bolsheviks was a tactical maneuver. Still, Lenin understood the danger of Russian chauvinism for the future of the Soviet Union; his successors neglected his warning.

Communism has proved weaker than nationalism for more reasons than the inconsistency of the ethnic policy conducted in the Soviet Union and a number of Eastern European countries. Contrary to Hobsbawm's view, nationalism in the USSR was not created artificially. (It is surprising to hear what I would call an idealistic explanation from a dedicated Marxist like Hobsbawm, who only a few years ago [Hobsbawm 1990: 173] held the opposing view, praising communist regimes for their ability to curb nationalism.) Even some scholars of the non-Marxist school maintain similar opinions. They still tend to view, if not nationalism, then its implied political consequences as the outcome of a historical error, the creation of Woodrow Wilson and the principle of nations' right to self-determination, declared at the Treaty of Versailles and subsequently exported from Europe to other parts of the world (Kedourie 1993: 128; Moynihan 1993: 63ff.).

Meanwhile, there are those who believe that nationalism, especially nationalism in multiethnic states, constitutes, not a result of the good or bad will of individual agitators or of erroneous policies conducted by one government or another, but an unavoidable though secondary product of modernization and its unevenness. To them the explosion of nationalism in the Soviet Union was inevitable and predictable following the weakened repressive power of the state. Still, this explosion cannot be attributed to modernization alone; there were many other additional factors which also facilitated the growth of nationalism.

The Soviet nationality policy, in spite of its sophistication, eventually failed in many respects. Some of them deserve mentioning. Connected with the totalitarian specifics of the Soviet state, the policy prevented even the possibility of the emergence of a civic multiethnic nation in the form of the so-called single Soviet people (whose formation was many times officially declared to have already been achieved), because to non-Russian nationalities the propagandized form of nationalism disguised as Soviet patriotism meant, in practical terms, Russification and the compliance with a metropole hegemony.

At the same time, the Soviet nationality policy prevented a gradual transformation of the constituent republics of the USSR into nation-states. Suny (1993: 110ff.) claims that the Soviet Empire was instrumental in the territorialization of ethnicity and in the creation of territorial nations. One may agree with his first premise, but the second is more arguable. In all non-Russian union republics, as well as in many autonomous formations of a lower order, the loyalty to one's nationality prevailed over the loyalty to a given political-administrative unit. Only in the case of titular nationalities did these loyalties go more or less together. But the goal of titular nationalities was to maintain, and to preserve as much as possible, an ethnic character of their formations in order to secure their advantageous positions there. Ethnic minorities, such as the Abkhaz in Georgia, the Gagauz in Moldavia, and the Poles in Lithuania, as well as many dispersed nationalities in different non-Russian republics preferred to communicate not in the languages of the titular nationalities but in Russian, and to appeal to the Russian-dominated government when they had grievances against the government of the republic of their residence. From the point of view of the Soviet leadership, that was an almost ideal situation because it put this leadership in a position of supreme arbiter.

Besides, the Soviet model of ethnoterritorial pseudofederalism favored titular nationalities in the union republics only to the extent that was compatible with the dominant positions of ethnic Russians and of the Russian language in the country in general. All this left very little room for the development of multiethnic territorial nations in the non-Russian republics on the basis of languages and cultures of the titular nationalities. Thus, gaps between political, ethnic, and cultural realities were created, and were revealed in full in the post-Soviet period.

The Soviet nationality policy turned out to be detrimental even to the formation of the Russian nation. To a certain degree the Russians in the Soviet Empire remained at the Ottoman stage of national identity. They tended to identify Russia with the whole Soviet Union, just as Turks had tended to identify Turkey with the whole Ottoman Empire. Thus, their loyalty to the Soviet state and their loyalty to the Russian nation did not contradict each other. In the past this gave the Soviet rulers the opportunity to pass off imperial interests for Russian national interests. At present, the Russians are searching out a new base for their identity as a nationality and as a nation. A single unitary identity of the nation is still absent. Many Russians conceive the nation as an ontological category and/or confuse nation with nationality and ethnicity. It is remarkable that in the Russian language the word *nation* (*natsiia*) means "ethnic group," "a people," but not an aggregate of all citizens of a given state, hence, the ongoing debate about the character of the Russian Federation and about the status of ethnic minorities there. The problem of a civic versus an ethnic Russian nation is far from resolved. This is reflected in, among other things, the new terminology in the Russian public and official lexicon, which stresses the difference between the ethnic Russians and the Russophones (i.e., acculturated members of other nationalities who have Russian as their first or only language).

Empires must fall apart with time. In this regard, the Soviet Union was an anachronism, because its creation delayed the disintegration of the former Russian Empire for more than 70 years. The country has skipped the twentieth century and to some degree the nineteenth century also (Gellner 1991: 132). Although communism eventually turned out to be powerless against nationalism, the country now has to pay the price for this lapse.

So, it turns out that nationalism, which originally emerged at the outset of the modern period and gained strength during the nineteenth century, has not receded by the end of the twentieth century, but, contrary to many predictions, remains one of the main factors of the political development worldwide. It is not confined within the borders of the European continent anymore; it has demonstrated its compatibility with different political and economic systems.

So far only a few multiethnic states have managed to cope more or less successfully with the pressure of ethnic nationalism. The concept of a civic nation based on the equality of all citizens of a given state irrespective of their ethnic affiliation is not always sufficient for ethnic minorities, or for ethnic groups that consider themselves at a disadvantage. The equality of individual rights and opportunities cannot eliminate the problems of collective rights and of ethnic group status in a plural society. When ethnic demands are connected with claims on special rights in a certain territory and (or at least) on special political-autonomous status, the acknowledgment of cultural pluralism may not be enough.

Nationalities often act not at all the way theoreticians and politicians would have them act. How much of a success at merging separate peoples was the policy of linguistic and cultural Russification so actively imposed in the Soviet Union? When they had the chance, did these people listen to the numerous recommendations of the Western politicians and experts that it would be better for them to remain in the reformed Soviet Union? I would venture to predict that, if Soviet-like policies continue in post-totalitarian countries, the growth of nationalism among ethnic minorities in these countries is imminent. The moment people begin to believe that their ethnic affiliation is at a disadvantage and/or that their individual interests will be best protected only through the collective interests of their ethnic groups, we are looking at the birth of nationalism.

So far not only Marxist but also individual-oriented, classical, liberal theory and practice, which hold traditional notions of human rights and prefer to treat ethnic issues as purely personal questions to be solved by and through civil society and the equal application of law, have failed to address satisfactorily the rights of ethnic groups as corporate entities in plural societies, although they confirm the peoples' right to form political associations. The social contract envisioned by Hobbes, Locke, and their followers envisages the existence of only individual actors. As Young (1976: 525) noted, one of the foundations of threat avoidance in nation building is recognizing that the principle of equality must be envisaged in terms of collectivities as well as individuals. What ethnic minorities often strive for is not only protection against arbitrary discrimination but also a share in power and participation in decision making, as well as the ways and means to assert their separate ethnicity.

Whether we like it or not, it is just modern civilization that implies nationalism. This fact is recognized by most contemporary scholars, even though they differ in their explanations of the phenomenon of nationalism itself (cf., for example, Gellner 1983; Anderson 1983; Greenfeld 1992). It is true that nationalism can hardly be explained by industrialization only. Its first appearance was before industry, as early as the eighteenth century, and at that time the nascent nationalism was mainly connected with politics. But it also had to do with rationalization and modernization of states. Later, the advance of modernity and mass involvement in politics were often accompanied (and sometimes facilitated) by a growing importance of nationalism. Occasional attempts to prove the existence of nationalism in ancient and medieval societies (Armstrong 1982; Smith 1986) are not particularly successful. To be sure, instances of ethnic solidarity were in evidence in the past, but it is only in modern times that we are witnessing the wide rise of one of the main principles of nationalism: to each people a state of its own. The hopes that in the postmodern period ethnic and national identities are becoming vague and utterly meretricious are not yet substantiated enough.

About 150 years ago, the young Marx and Engels predicted in the *Communist Manifesto* that the global economy would reduce to naught all forms of nationalism and even the existence of separate nations. Surprisingly, similar predictions backed by very similar reasoning can still be found in our times (Hobsbawm 1990: 181-83). History has shown these predictions to err in wishful thinking. The global economy, the world market, and transnational corporations fall far from undermining national states or national cultures. Just as it was anticipated by Aron (1974), at present it is far from clear that Western Europe is moving toward a federation, let alone a unitary state (Mann 1993a: 115ff.). Coca-Cola, McDonald's, and Michael Jackson are no more a threat to national cultures than television and computers are. If they threaten anything, it is the pseudo–folk culture that purists would like to preserve by prohibitive measures. Some write that nationalism is a purely Western concept artificially transplanted to other parts of the world. In fact it is at present no more artificial than cars and airplanes, than the notion of economic growth based on technological advances—the key concept of modernization. It is quite possible that nationalism in Asia and perhaps in Africa will, instead of weakening, actually become a more decisive factor in their future development (A. D. Smith 1983). Actually, there was more room for assimilation in premodern societies than in modern or modernizing ones, particularly when ethnic groups develop into nationalities with literary languages, modern social structures, and political elites or counterelites.

Historical lessons not seriously taken into account avenge themselves not only in a one-sidedness of theoretical concepts but also in unpleasant political surprises. The idea that a strong and centralized power in multiethnic states can give prosperity to all its nationalities, though it may deny or reduce their right of self-determination, seems dubious, in the light of the Soviet experiment, when this right is denied by force. Human behavior is inspired by more than purses and stomachs. Besides, more often than not such power fails to deliver both prosperity and freedom. In principle, if ethnic and national identities are respected, then it may be possible to avoid a desire to secede, that is, a search for one's own state. However, whether and to what extent even the most thoughtful and considerate politics in plural societies, with good will, skill, and luck also, can satisfy all national claims remains to be seen. One thing, however, is obvious to me. The struggle against nationalism, whether under the banners of Marxism, classical liberalism, economic integrationism, or any other -ism, has so far proved to be futile. The only hope that remains for the foreseeable future is not to eradicate nationalism but to curb its excesses, in other words to make it civil.

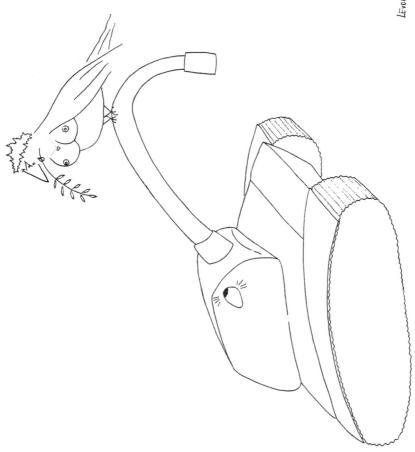

LEVON ABRAHAMIAN

243

Reference Materials

TABLES AND FIGURES

Table 1.1. Russian population distribution in the Soviet republics, by 1989 (in thousands of persons)

Republic	Total population	Russian population	Russian percentage of total population
Russian Federation	147,000	119,865	81.5
Ukraine	51,452	11,356	22.1
Kazakhstan	16,463	6,228	37.8
Uzbekistan	19,810	1,652	8.3
Belorussia	10,152	1,342	13.2
Kirgizia	4,258	917	21.5
Latvia	2,667	906	34.0
Moldavia	4,335	562	13.0
Estonia	1,565	475	30.3
Azerbaidjan	7,021	392	5.6
Tadjikistan	5,093	388	7.6
Lithuania	3,675	344	9.4
Georgia	5,401	341	6.3
Turkmenistan	3,523	334	9.5
Armenia	3,305	52	1.6

Source: 1989 population census.

Table 1.2. Percentage distribution of population in Latvia and Estonia, by ethnic group, 1959–1989

	1959	1970	1979	1989
Latvia				
Latvians	62.0	56.8	53.7	52.0
Russians	26.6	29.8	32.8	34.0
Belorussians	2.9	4.0	4.5	4.5
Ukrainians	1.4	2.3	2.7	3.5
Others	7.1	7.1	6.3	6.0
Estonia				
Estonians	74.6	68.2	64.7	61.5
Russians	20.1	24.7	27.9	30.3
Ukrainians	1.3	2.1	2.5	3.1
Belorussians	0.9	1.4	1.6	1.8
Others	3.1	3.6	3.3	3.3

Sources: Population censuses for the years shown.

Table 1.3. Number of students of special secondary schools and institutions of higher education receiving education in the languages of the Soviet nationalities, by September 1990

Republic	Special secondary schools		Institutions of Higher Education	
	Number (in thousands)	Percent of all students	Number (in thousands)	Percent of all students
Russian Federation				
in Russian	2,261.0	99.6	2,792.0	98.6
in Abazin	1.0	0.03	—	—
in Altay	0.1	0.01	—	—
in Ingush	—	—	0.03	0.0
in Komi-Permiak	0.1	0.01	—	—
in Tatar	2.0	0.1	2.0	0.1
in Chechen	—	—	0.1	0.0
in Chuvash	0.1	0.0	1.0	0.02
in Yakut	0.4	0.02	—	—
Ukraine				
in Ukrainian	160.0	21.2	134.0	15.2
in Russian	501.0	66.2	503.0	57.1
Belorussia				
in Belorussian	0.3	0.2	1.0	0.4
in Russian	142.0	99.1	186.0	98.6
in Lithuanian	—	—	0.4	0.2
Uzbekistan				
in Uzbek	186.0	71.1	222.0	65.1
in Russian	58.0	22.2	110.0	32.3
in Karakalpak	16.0	6.1	6.0	1.9
in Kazakh	1.0	0.4	1.0	0.3
in Tadjik	0.4	0.2	2.0	0.4
in Turkmen	0.1	0.02	—	—
Kazakhstan				
in Kazakh	21.0	8.7	39.0	13.6
in Russian	226.0	91.1	248.0	86.3
in Uzbek	0.1	0.5	—	—
in Uighur	0.1	0.4	0.2	0.1
in German	0.2	0.1	—	—
Georgia				
in Georgian	38.0	87.8	89.0	85.7
in Russian	5.0	12.0	14.0	13.1
in Azerbaidjanian	—	—	0.1	0.1
in Armenian	0.1	0.2	0.1	0.1
in Abkhaz	—	—	1.0	0.6
in Ossetian	—	—	0.4	0.4

(table continues on following page)

Table 1.3, continued

Republic	Special secondary schools		Institutions of Higher Education	
	Number (in thousands)	Percent of all students	Number (in thousands)	Percent of all students
Azerbaidjan				
in Azerbaidjanian	51.0	87.7	81.0	77.3
in Russian	7.0	12.3	24.0	22.5
Lithuania				
in Lithuanian	41.0	88.1	60.0	90.7
in Russian	5.0	10.9	6.0	8.9
in Polish	0.4	1.0	0.3	0.4
Moldova				
in Romanian	23.0	44.9	25.0	45.0
in Russian	26.0	51.3	30.0	54.6
Latvia				
in Latvian	18.0	49.9	26.0	56.0
in Russian	17.0	47.7	20.0	44.0
Kirgizia				
in Kyrgyz	8.0	18.0	14.0	23.4
in Russian	35.0	81.1	45.0	76.3
in Uzbek	0.3	0.8	.02	0.3
Tadjikistan				
in Tadjik	16.0	38.2	33.0	48.2
in Russian	23.0	56.8	30.0	44.1
in Uzbek	2.0	4.9	5.0	7.7
in Kyrgyz	0.03	0.1	—	—
Armenia				
in Armenian	45.0	98.1	56.0	81.7
in Russian	1.0	1.9	12.0	18.3
Turkmenistan				
in Turkmen	6.0	17.1	10.0	23.6
in Russian	28.0	82.9	32.0	76.4
Estonia				
in Estonian	12.0	65.4	21.0	79.8
in Russian	7.0	34.6	5.0	20.2

Source: Vestnik statistiki, 12 (1991): 53–54.

Table 1.4. Percentage distribution of students receiving education in the state languages of their republics, by type of educational institution, by September 1990

Republic	Secondary schools	Vocational schools	Institutions of higher education	Percentage of the titular nationality in the entire population of the republic (per 1989 census)
Russian Federation—in Russian	98.1	99.9	98.8	81.9
Ukraine—in Ukrainian	47.9	32.9	15.2	72.7
Belorussia—in Belorussian	20.8	—	0.4	77.9
Uzbekistan—in Uzbek	78.1	79.7	65.1	71.4
Kazakhstan—in Kazakh	32.3	16.4	13.6	39.7
Georgia—in Georgian	68.8	75.9	85.7	70.1
Azerbaidjan—in Azerbaidjanian	86.1	82.8	77.3	82.7
Lithuania—in Lithuanian	—	84.4	90.7	79.6
Moldova—in Romanian	60.2	61.7	45.0	64.5
Latvia—in Latvian	53.2	54.9	56.0	52.0
Kirgizia—in Kyrgyz	55.7	49.2	23.4	52.4
Tadjikistan—in Tadjik	67.2	66.1	48.2	62.3
Armenia—in Armenian	86.9	96.7	81.7	93.3
Turkmenistan—in Turkmen	76.6	58.0	23.6	72.0
Estonia—in Estonian	63.0	57.0	79.8	61.5

Source: *Vestnik statistiki,* 12 (1991): 47.

Table 2.1. Dynamics of in- and out-migrations of urban Russians in the territory of non-Russian Soviet republics, 1989–1991

Republics	In-migration			Out-migration			Balance		
	1989	1990	1991	1989	1990	1991	1989	1990	1991
Ukraine	174,968	160,490	—	130,060	112,225	—	+44,908	+45,265	—
Belorussia	35,968	28,393	26,466	22,507	24,530	17,088	+13,479	+3,863	+9,378
Uzbekistan	23,470	18,651	17,002	38,865	53,133	41,410	-15,395	-34,482	-24,408
Kazakhstan	65,588	61,391	57,119	75,620	71,406	59,784	-10,032	-10,015	-2,665
Georgia	5,434	3,871	—	8,974	10,095	—	-3,540	-6,224	—
Azerbaidjan	7,194	4,724	—	18,739	40,889	—	-11,545	-36,165	—
Lithuania	6,961	4,822	—	7,312	9,498	—	-351	-4,676	—
Moldavia	11,113	9,031	7,393	9,868	11,903	11,335	+1,247	-2,872	-3,942
Latvia	10,392	7,542	—	10,350	9,806	—	+42	-2,264	—
Kirgizia	12,171	10,271	8,958	13,551	19,739	18,972	-1,380	-9,468	-10,014
Tadjikistan	7,246	6,379	6,144	13,647	33,625	18,633	-6,401	-33,246	-12,489
Armenia	1,823	1,201	1,203	5,109	3,638	3,653	-3,286	-2,437	-2,450
Turkmenistan	6,942	5,338	5,217	9,672	10,110	9,640	-2,730	-4,772	-4,423
Estonia	6,958	4,350	3,133	6,124	6,029	6,640	+861	-1,679	-3,507

Source: Ostapenko and Subbotina 1993: 309, table 1.

Table 3.1. Major ethnic groups of the Russian Federation, 1989

Number[a]	Ethnic group	Total population	Population living in its autonomous formation in a territory within the Russian Federation
	Whole population	147,021,869	
1	Russians	119,865,946	0
2	Tatars	5,522,096	1,765,404
3	Ukrainians	4,362,872	0
4	Chuvash	1,773,645	906,922
5	Bashkirs	1,345,273	863,808
6	Belorussians	1,206,222	0
7	Mordovians	1,072,939	313,420
8	Chechens[b]	898,999	734,501
9	Germans[c]	842,295	0
10	Udmurt	714,833	496,522
11	Mari	643,698	324,349
12	Kazakhs	635,865	0
13	Jews[d]	551,047	8,887
	including:		
	Mountain Jews	11,282	0
	Bukharan Jews	1,407	0
	Georgian Jews	1,102	0
	Krymchaks	338	0
14	Avartsy[e]	544,016	496,077
15	Armenians	532,390	none
16	Buryat	417,425	341,185
17	Ossetians	402,275	334,876
18	Kabardinians[f]	386,055	363,492
19	Yakuts	380,242	365,236
20	Dargintsy[e]	353,348	280,431
21	Komi	336,309	291,542
22	Azerbaidjanians	335,889	0
23	Kumyks[e]	277,163	231,805
24	Lezgin[e]	257,270	204,370
25	Ingush	215,068	163,762
26	Tuvinians	206,160	198,448
27	Moldavians	172,671	0
28	Kalmyks	165,821	146,316
29	Gypsies	152,939	0
30	Karachay[g]	150,332	129.449
31	Komi-Permiaks	147,269	95,215
32	Georgians	130,688	0
33	Uzbeks	126,899	0
34	Karelians	124,921	78,928
35	Adyge	122,908	95,438
36	Koreans	107,051	0
37	Laktsy[e]	106,245	91,682

(table continues on following page)

253

Table 3.1, continued

Number[a]	Ethnic group	Total population	Population living in its autonomous formation in a territory within the Russian Federation
38	Poles	94,594	0
39	Tabasaran[e]	93,587	78,196
40	Balkars[f]	78,341	70,793
41	Khakas	78,500	62,859
42	Nogay[e]	73,703	28,294
43	Lithuanians	70,427	0
44	Altaitsy	69,409	59,130
45	Cherkes[g]	50,764	40,241
46	Finns	47,102	0
47	Latvians	46,829	0
48	Estonians	46,390	0
49	Kyrgyz	41,734	0
50	Turkmen	39,739	0
51	Tadjiks	38,208	0
52	Nentsy[h]	34,190	29,786
53	Abazins	32,983	0
54	Bulgarians	32,785	0
55	Evenks[h]	29,901	3,480
56	Khanty[h]	22,283	11,892
57	Crimean Tatars	21,275	0
58	Rutultsy[e]	19,503	14,955
59	Tats	19,420	0
60	Aguls[e]	17,728	13,791
61	Evens[h]	17,055	0
62	Shortsy	15,745	0
63	Chukchi[h]	15,107	11,914
64	Veps[h]	12,142	0
65	Nanaitsy[h]	11,883	0
66	Gagauz	10,051	0
67	Turks	9,890	0
68	Assyrians	9,622	0
69	Koriaks[h]	8,942	6,572
70	Mansi[h]	8,279	6,562
71	Abkhaz	7,239	0
72	Dolgans[h]	6,584	4,939
73	Tsakhurs[e]	6,492	5,194
74	Karakalpaks	6,155	0
75	Rumanians	5,996	0
76	Hungarians	5,742	0
77	Chinese	5,197	0
78	Kurds	4,724	0
79	Nivkhy[h]	4,631	0
80	Czechs	4,375	0
81	Selkups[h]	3,564	0

Table 3.1, continued

Number[a]	Ethnic group	Total population	Population living in its autonomous formation in a territory within the Russian Federation
82	Ul'chi[h]	3,173	0
83	Uighurs	2,577	0
84	Itelmens[h]	2,429	0
85	Udege[h]	1,902	0
86	Saami[h]	1,835	0
87	Eskimos[h]	1,704	0
88	Chuvantsy[h]	1,384	0
89	Nganasans[h]	1,262	0
90	Yukagirs[h]	1,112	0
91	Udins	1,102	0
92	Kets[h]	1,084	0
93	Orochi[h]	883	0
94	Tofalars[h]	722	0
95	Karaites	680	0
96	Aleuts[h]	644	0
97	Dungan	635	0
98	Negidaltsy[h]	587	0
99	Izortsy	449	0
100	Baluch	297	0
101	Talysh	202	0
102	Entsy[h]	198	0
103	Orochi[h]	179	0

Source: 1989 population census.

[a] In rank order of total population.

[b] The Chechen government declared a secession of their republic from Russia, which was not recognized by the Russian government.

[c] German autonomy in the Volga region was abolished in 1941, and so far all attempts to restore it have failed.

[d] The Jewish autonomous region in Siberia is a Soviet fiction and has never been considered by Russian Jews as their homeland.

[e] These groups share the Daghestan autonomous formation with many other ethnic groups; this situation causes ethnic frictions.

[f] Kabardinians and Balkars have a joint autonomous formation; this situation results in ethnic tension.

[g] Karachay and Cherkessians have a joint autonomous formation, which also results in ethnic tension.

[h] These peoples belong to the indigenous peoples of the North.

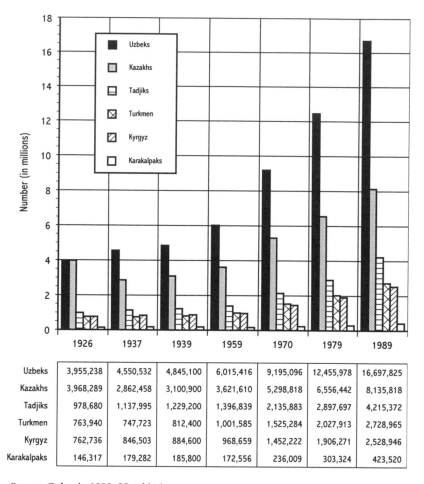

	1926	1937	1939	1959	1970	1979	1989
Uzbeks	3,955,238	4,550,532	4,845,100	6,015,416	9,195,096	12,455,978	16,697,825
Kazakhs	3,968,289	2,862,458	3,100,900	3,621,610	5,298,818	6,556,442	8,135,818
Tadjiks	978,680	1,137,995	1,229,200	1,396,839	2,135,883	2,897,697	4,215,372
Turkmen	763,940	747,723	812,400	1,001,585	1,525,284	2,027,913	2,728,965
Kyrgyz	762,736	846,503	884,600	968,659	1,452,222	1,906,271	2,528,946
Karakalpaks	146,317	179,282	185,800	172,556	236,009	303,324	423,520

Source: Guboglo 1993: 55, table 3.

Figure 4.1. Indigenous populations of Central Asia and Kazakhstan, 1926–1989

256

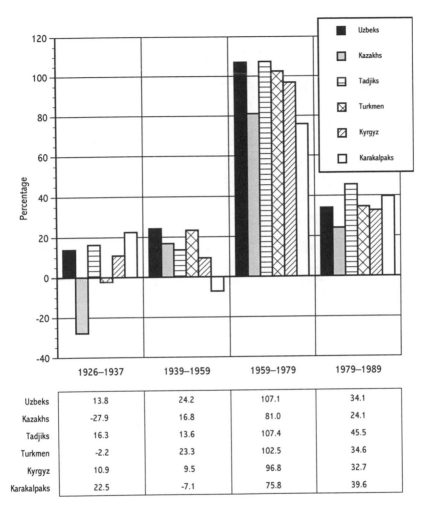

	1926–1937	1939–1959	1959–1979	1979–1989
Uzbeks	13.8	24.2	107.1	34.1
Kazakhs	-27.9	16.8	81.0	24.1
Tadjiks	16.3	13.6	107.4	45.5
Turkmen	-2.2	23.3	102.5	34.6
Kyrgyz	10.9	9.5	96.8	32.7
Karakalpaks	22.5	-7.1	75.8	39.6

Sources: Censuses of 1926, 1937, 1939, 1959, 1970, 1979, 1989; Sinnott 1992: 23.

Figure 4.2. Percentage growth/decline of indigenous populations of Central Asia and Kazakhstan, 1926–1989

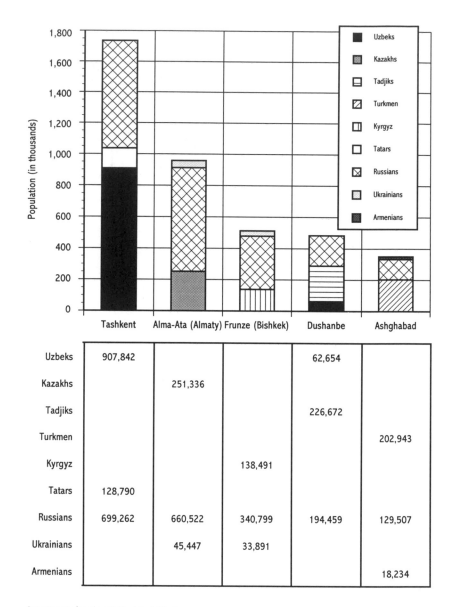

	Tashkent	Alma-Ata (Almaty)	Frunze (Bishkek)	Dushanbe	Ashghabad
Uzbeks	907,842			62,654	
Kazakhs		251,336			
Tadjiks				226,672	
Turkmen					202,943
Kyrgyz			138,491		
Tatars	128,790				
Russians	699,262	660,522	340,799	194,459	129,507
Ukrainians		45,447	33,891		
Armenians					18,234

Source: Guboglo 1993: 55, table3.

Figure 4.3. The populations of the most numerous ethnic groups in the capitals of Central Asia and Kazakhstan, 1989

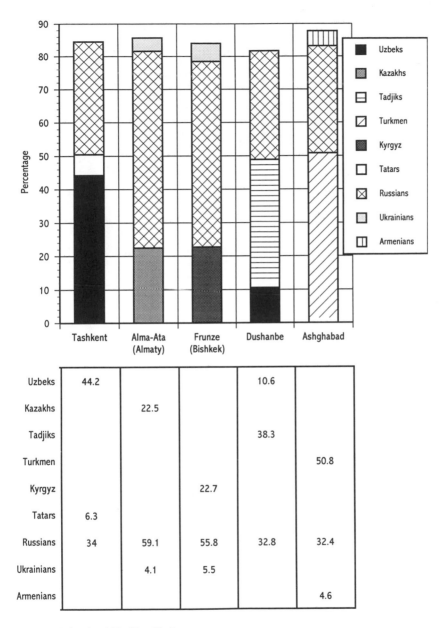

	Tashkent	Alma-Ata (Almaty)	Frunze (Bishkek)	Dushanbe	Ashghabad
Uzbeks	44.2			10.6	
Kazakhs		22.5			
Tadjiks				38.3	
Turkmen					50.8
Kyrgyz			22.7		
Tatars	6.3				
Russians	34	59.1	55.8	32.8	32.4
Ukrainians		4.1	5.5		
Armenians					4.6

Source: Guboglo 1993: 55, table 3.

Figure 4.4. Percentage distribution of the most numerous ethnic groups in the capitals of Central Asia and Kazakhstan, 1989

Table 4.1. Summarized coefficient of birthrates[a] among indigenous peoples of Central Asia, 1979 and 1989

People	1979	1989	1989 percentage of 1979 births
Tadjiks	7.511	5.949	79.2
Turkmen	7.685	4.904	63.8
Kyrgyz	7.757	4.834	62.3
Uzbeks	7.478	4.662	62.3
Kazakhs	5.787	3.584	61.9
Russians	1.819	1.955	107.5

Source: Vestnik statistiki 8 (1991): 68

[a] The summarized coefficient of birthrates is the average number of children born to a woman during her reproductive period of life.

Table 4.2. The percentage growth of urban population in Central Asia and Kazakhstan, 1926-1989

| Republic | Year | Percentage of urban vs. whole population | Indigenous urban population | | Russian urban population | |
			Its percentage to the whole indigenous population of the republic	Its percentage to the whole urban population of the republic	Its percentage to the whole Russian population of the republic	Its percentage to the whole urban population of the republic
Kazakhstan	1926	8.3	2.1	14.4	22.2	52.8
	1939	27.8	16.1	21.9	40.2	57.7
	1959	43.7	24.3	16.7	59.0	57.6
	1970	50.3	26.3	17.1	69.1	58.4
	1979	53.5	30.9	20.8	73.9	56.4
	1989	57.2	38.3	26.5	77.4	51.0
Uzbekistan	1926	23.8	18.3	57.2	85.0	19.3
	1939	23.1	14.3	40.3	80.8	35.5
	1959	33.1	20.2	37.2	83.7	33.4
	1970	36.7	23.0	41.1	89.1	30.4
	1979	40.8	28.6	48.1	93.4	24.8
	1989	40.7	30.5	53.3	94.9	19.3
Tadjikistan	1926	4.9	4.8	73.5	70.4	9.9
	1939	16.8	10.2	36.1	68.7	37.2
	1959	32.6	19.6	31.8	86.9	35.3
	1970	37.1	25.5	38.6	93.8	30.0
	1979	34.6	25.2	42.2	94.1	30.4
	1989	32.6	26.4	50.1	94.1	21.9
Kirgizia	1926	12.0	0.8	4.7	38.7	38.0
	1939	18.5	3.6	10.1	44.4	49.8
	1959	33.7	11.0	13.2	57.8	51.8
	1970	37.4	14.5	16.9	65.9	51.4
	1979	38.3	18.3	22.9	68.6	46.4
	1989	38.2	21.7	29.6	69.9	39.1
Turkmenistan	1926	12.3	1.4	8.2	84.9	53.3
	1939	33.3	10.5	18.6	89.1	49.8
	1959	46.2	26.3	34.7	94.5	35.4
	1970	47.9	31.7	43.4	95.7	29.0
	1979	47.4	33.0	47.6	96.5	25.7
	1989	45.4	33.7	53.4	96.7	20.1

Source: Fridman and Karazhas 1994: 8, table 2.

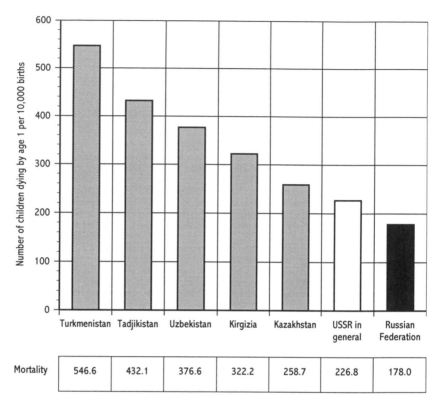

| Mortality | 546.6 | 432.1 | 376.6 | 322.2 | 258.7 | 226.8 | 178.0 |

Source: *Vestnik statistiki* 7 (1991): 78.

Figure 4.5. Infant mortality in Central Asia and Kazakhstan, the Russian Federation, and the USSR, 1989

Table 4.3. Professional distribution of the urban Russian population in Central Asia, by 1989

Republic	Blue-collar workers		Engineering staff		Employees in the administrative apparatus	
	Number	%	Number	%	Number	%
Kazakhstan	543,348	21.3	285,512	11.6	266,510	10.9
Uzbekistan	171,223	18.8	118,186	13.6	72,024	8.9
Kirgizia	66,466	20.8	41,034	12.9	22,524	7.1
Tadjikistan	38,145	10.1	26,968	14.2	18,104	9.6
Turkmenistan	31,474	18.3	22,843	13.3	17,615	10.3

	Higher, secondary, and elementary teachers and professors		Humanitarian intelligentsia		Party and government nomenklatura	
	Number	%	Number	%	Number	%
Kazakhstan	143,202	5.6	12,047	0.5	6,909	0.3
Uzbekistan	61,602	7.6	5,432	0.7	2,216	0.3
Kirgizia	21,975	6.9	1,898	0.6	877	0.3
Tadjikistan	15,405	8.1	1,445	0.8	1,401	0.7
Turkmenistan	13,116	7.6	1,008	0.6	774	0.5

Source: Tishkov 1993c: 18, table 4.

Table 4.4. The composition of titular nationalities and Russian university students in Central Asia, 1979 and 1989

	Titular nationalities				Russians			
	General number of students		Their no. per 10,000 people		General number of students		Their no. per 10,000 people	
Republic	1979	1989	1979	1989	1979	1989	1979	1989
Uzbekistan	171,876	234,142	437	443	37,607	35,149	419	413
Kazakhstan	115,400	154,836	584	563	89,028	89,130	285	287
Tadjikistan	31,259	41,315	395	397	8,297	8,129	379	402
Kirgizia	29,670	38,635	490	465	15,280	12,580	320	281
Turkmenistan	22,970	32,895	324	337	5,982	4,455	307	251

Source: Tishkov 1993c: 20, table 6.

Table 4.5. Number of Russians in the Soviet republics of Central Asia, 1979 and 1989

Republic	1979	1989	Total population in 1989
Kazakhstan	5,991,000	6,226,000	16,436,115
Uzbekistan	1,665,658	1,652,179	19,808,077
Kirgizia	912,000	916,000	4,257,700
Tadjikistan	395,000	387,000	5,089,000
Turkmenistan	349,000	334,000	3,512,190

Source: 1979 and 1989 population censuses.

Table 4.6. The balance of migrations to and from Central Asia (in thousands of people), 1961–1988

Republic	1961–1970	1979–1988
Kazakhstan	+431	-789
Uzbekistan	+257	-507
Kirgizia	+126	-157
Tadjikistan	+70	-102
Turkmenistan	+4	-84

Source: Perevedentsev 1993: 144, table 1.

Table 5.1. Numerical distribution of Kazakhstan's population, by ethnic group, 1926-1989

	1926	1939	1959	1970	1979	1989
Total population	6,193,000	6,139,000	9,295,000	13,009,000	14,685,000	16,463,000
Kazakhs	3,628,000	2,311,000	2,787,000	4,234,000	5,289,000	6,531,000
Russians	1,267,000	2,450,000	3,972,000	5,522,000	5,991,000	6,226,000
Ukrainians	859,000	658,000	761,000	933,000	898,000	896,000
Uzbeks	128,000	103,000	136,000	216,000	263,000	332,000
Tatars	79,000	104,000	192,000	288,000	313,000	328,000
Uighurs	62,000	37,000	60,000	121,000	148,000	186,000
Germans	42,000	50,000	648,000	858,000	900,000	956,000
Belorussians	26,000	30,000	107,000	198,000	181,000	183,000
Koreans	0	97,000	74,000	82,000	92,000	103,000
Others	102,000	299,000	558,000	557,000	610,000	722,000

Sources: Population censuses of 1926, 1939, 1959, 1970, 1979, and 1989.

Table 5.2. Percentage distribution of Kazakhstan's population, by ethnic group, 1926-1989

	1926	1939	1959	1970	1979	1989
Total population	100.0	100.0	100.0	100.0	100.0	100.0
Kazakhs	58.5	37.6	29.8	32.6	36.0	39.67
Russians	20.4	40.0	42.7	42.4	40.8	37.82
Ukrainians	13.9	10.7	8.2	7.2	6.1	5.44
Uzbeks	2.1	1.7	1.5	1.7	1.8	2.02
Tatars	1.3	1.7	2.1	2.2	2.1	1.99
Uighurs	1.0	0.6	0.6	0.9	1.0	1.13
Germans	0.7	0.8	7.0	6.6	6.1	5.82
Belorussians	0.4	0.5	1.1	1.5	1.2	1.11
Koreans	0.0	1.6	0.8	0.6	0.6	0.62
Others	1.7	4.8	6.2	4.3	4.3	4.38

Sources: Same as table 5.1.

Table 5.3. The Kazakh population in Kazakhstan, 1830–1991

Year	Population (in thousands)	Percentage of total population
1830	1,300	96.4
1850	1,502	91.1
1860	1,644	?
1870	2,417	?
1897	3,000	79.8
1926	3,628	58.5
1939	2,311	37.6
1959	2,787	29.8
1970	4,234	32.6
1979	5,289	36.0
1989	6,531	39.67
1992	7,297	43.2

Sources: Bekmakhanova 1980: table 28; *Aziatskaia Rossiia* 1914: 82; Population censuses of 1926, 1939, 1959, 1970, 1979, 1989; Suzhikov et al. 1993: 53.

Table 5.4. Ethnic composition of Kazakhstan's capital, Alma-Ata, 1959–1989 (in thousands)

Ethnic group	1959	1970	1979	1989	Percent
Total	456.5	729.6	899.7	1110.0	100.0
Russians	333.5	512.8	593.8	666.0	60.0
Kazakhs	39.4	88.2	147.9	250.0	22.5
Uighurs	8.0	19.1	26.4	42.0	3.9
Ukrainians	23.0	30.9	34.9	37.0	3.4
Tatars	12.5	19.8	24.0	30.0	2.8
Germans	10.0	13.3	18.1	23.0	2.1
Koreans	2.5	6.9	11.5	14.0	1.4
Jews	8.4	9.2	8.7	7.5	0.7
Belorussians	2.6	4.3	5.0	6.5	0.5
Uzbeks	1.5	3.1	3.7	5.6	0.5
Azerbaidjanians	1.1	2.3	3.3	4.5	0.4
Greeks	1.0	1.6	2.2	3.0	0.3
Dungans	0.5	1.3	1.6	2.5	0.2
Armenians	0.9	1.5	2.0	2.5	0.2
Mordovians	1.4	1.7	1.6	1.3	0.1
Others	11.6	12.5	14.9	15.0	1.4

Source: Suzhikov et al. 1993: 47, table 1.

Note: The reader should be warned that different publications of the same census often contain slightly different figures. The totals are shown here as they are shown in Suzhikov et al. 1993, even though the columns do not add exactly to these totals.

Table 6.1. Census counts of Yakuts in Yakutia and the entire Soviet Union, 1897–1989

Number in Yakutia	
1897	221,067
1917	224,960 (estimate)
1959	226,053
1970	285,749
1979	313,917
1989	365,236
Number in the entire Soviet Union	
1989	382,255

Source: Population censuses for the years shown.

Table 6.2. Percentage distribution of ethnic rural and urban population in Yakutia, by 1989

Ethnic group	Urban population		Rural population	
	Number	Percentage	Number	Percentage
Yakuts	94,017	25.7	271,219	74.3
Russians	496,305	90.2	53,958	9.8
Others	141,641	79.3	36,925	20.7

Source: Natsional'nyi sostav . . . 1990: 13, 17

APPENDIX

Ethnic composition of the Soviet Union, by 1989[a] (in rank order)

	Nationality	Number (in thousands)	Percentage who claim their nationality's language is their mother tongue	Percentage fluent in languages of the peoples of the USSR as their second language	
				In Russian	In other languages
	Total population	285,743	92.7	24.2	5.3
1	Russians	145,155	99.8	0.2	4.0
2	Ukrainians	44,186	81.1	56.2	8.5
3	Uzbeks	16,698	98.3	23.8	3.7
4	Belorussians	10,036	70.9	54.7	11.7
5	Kazakhs	8,136	97.0	60.4	2.9
6	Azerbaidjanians	6,770	97.7	34.3	2.2
7	Tatars	6,649	83.2	70.8	5.3
8	Armenians	4,623	91.7	47.1	5.0
9	Tadjiks	4,215	97.7	27.7	12.2
10	Georgians	3,981	98.2	33.1	1.0
11	Moldavians	3,352	91.6	53.8	4.4
12	Lithuanians	3,067	97.7	37.9	1.6
13	Turkmen	2,729	98.5	27.7	2.0
14	Kyrgyz	2,529	97.8	35.2	4.6
15	Germans	2,039	48.7	45.0	1.6
16	Chuvash	1,842	76.4	65.1	5.9
17	Latvians	1,459	94.8	64.4	2.5
18	Bashkirs	1,449	72.3	71.8	3.6
19	Jews	1,378	11.1	10.1	29.2
	Mountain Jews	19	75.8	54.8	16.7
	Georgian Jews	16	90.9	46.4	4.6
	Bukharan Jews	36	65.1	50.6	17.0
	Krymchaks	1.4	34.9	30.2	13.3
20	Mordvovians	1,154	67.1	62.5	8.9
21	Poles	1,126	30.5	43.9	17.3
22	Estonians	1,027	95.5	33.9	1.8
23	Chechens	957	98.1	74.0	0.8

Ethnic composition of the Soviet Union, by 1989[a] (in rank order), continued

	Nationality	Number (in thousands)	Percentage who claim their nationality's language is their mother tongue	Percentage fluent in languages of the peoples of the USSR as their second language	
				In Russian	In other languages
24	Udmurt	747	69.6	61.3	7.1
25	Mari	671	80.8	68.8	5.8
26	Avartsy	601	97.2	60.8	6.7
27	Ossetians	598	87.0	68.9	12.2
28	Lezgin	466	91.6	53.4	19.9
29	Koreans	439	49.4	43.3	3.7
30	Karakalpaks	424	94.1	20.6	11.4
31	Buryat	421	86.3	72.1	2.7
32	Kabardinians	391	97.2	77.7	0.7
33	Yakuts	382	93.8	64.9	1.5
34	Bulgarians	373	68.1	60.3	8.8
35	Dargintsy	365	97.5	68.0	1.8
36	Greeks	358	44.5	39.5	16.5
37	Komi	345	70.4	62.2	6.1
38	Kumyks	282	97.4	74.5	1.1
39	Crimean Tatars	272	92.6	76.1	8.0
40	Uighurs	263	86.6	58.3	10.8
41	Gypsies	262	77.4	63.3	13.8
42	Ingush	237	96.9	80.0	1.0
43	Turks	208	91.0	40.3	30.6
44	Tuvinians	207	98.5	59.2	0.4
45	Gagauz	196	87.5	71.1	6.9
46	Kalmyks	174	90.0	85.3	1.5
47	Hungarians	171	93.9	43.3	11.7
48	Karachay	156	96.8	79.2	1.0
49	Kurds	153	80.5	28.7	40.4
50	Komi-Permiaks	152	70.1	61.3	8.0
51	Romanians	146	60.9	50.8	11.6
52	Karelians	131	47.8	45.5	14.8
53	Adyge	125	94.7	81.7	1.5
54	Laktsy	118	93.6	76.5	2.9
55	Abkhaz	105	93.5	78.8	3.5
56	Tabasaran	98	95.9	62.5	5.3
57	Balkars	85	93.6	78.6	2.0
58	Khakhas	80	76.1	66.8	3.6
59	Nogay	75	89.9	79.3	1.4
60	Altaitsy	71	84.3	65.1	2.3
61	Dungan	69	94.8	70.8	2.9
62	Finns	67	34.6	35.4	10.8

(table continues on following page)

Ethnic composition of the Soviet Union, by 1989[a] (in rank order), continued

	Nationality	Number (in thousands)	Percentage who claim their nationality's language is their mother tongue	Percentage fluent in languages of the peoples of the USSR as their second language	
				In Russian	In other languages
63	Cherkes	52	90.4	76.3	2.2
64	Iranians	40	33.2	45.8	18.3
65	Nentsy	34.7	77.1	61.7	3.1
66	Abazins	34	93.4	78.1	4.4
67	Tats	31	71.9	64.1	13.3
68	Evenks	30.2	30.4	55.4	5.3
69	Baluch	29	96.9	4.6	56.3
70	Assyrians	26	59.6	43.7	19.9
71	Khanty	22.5	60.5	50.6	3.0
72	Talysh	22	90.4	5.5	73.5
73	Rutultsy	20	94.8	63.1	8.3
74	Tsakhurs	20	95.2	23.5	54.3
75	Aguls	19	94.9	68.4	6.5
76	Evens	17.2	43.9	52.5	9.6
77	Shortsy	17	56.7	52.7	7.1
78	Czechs	16	35.3	36.8	22.9
79	Chukchi	15.2	70.3	61.2	3.9
80	Veps	13	50.8	49.0	16.7
81	Nanaitsy	12	44.1	40.1	6.3
82	Chinese	11	32.9	30.5	5.1
83	Koriaks	9.2	52.4	46.6	6.4
84	Slovaks	9.1	37.9	51.9	25.8
85	Mansi	8.5	37.1	32.9	4.4
86	Udins	8	85.7	51.3	27.3
87	Arabs	7.7	61.5	51.3	17.7
88	Dolgans	6.9	81.8	66.4	2.4
89	Afghans	6.7	63.1	30.0	30.1
90	Nivkhy	4.7	23.3	19.9	3.9
91	Albanians	4	52.1	49.8	8.8
92	Selkups	3.6	47.6	42.6	4.1
93	Vietnamese	3.4	96.4	53.1	0.8
94	Spaniards	3.2	46.1	42.5	8.2
95	Ul'chi	3.2	30.8	24.0	8.0
96	Cubans	2.8	71.9	73.2	2.3
97	Serbs	2.7	40.8	51.1	8.6
98	Karaites	2.6	19.3	14.4	22.3
99	Itelmens	2.5	19.6	17.2	5.9
100	Udege	2	26.3	18.7	9.1
101	Saami	1.9	42.2	40.8	9.4

Ethnic composition of the Soviet Union, by 1989[a] (in rank order), continued

	Nationality	Number (in thousands)	Percentage who claim their nationality's language is their mother tongue	Percentage fluent in languages of the peoples of the USSR as their second language	
				In Russian	In other languages
102	Eskimos	1.7	51.6	48.4	4.5
103	Peoples of India and Pakistan	1.7	71.5	43.6	5.1
104	Chuvantsy	1.5	21.4	26.7	7.8
105	Italians	1.3	39.7	25.7	9.7
106	Nganasans	1.3	83.2	56.5	4.0
107	Kets	1.1	48.3	44.3	6.6
108	Yukagirs	1.1	32.8	37.5	16.6
109	Orochi	0.9	18.8	14.0	3.2
110	Croats	0.8	49.7	42.6	7.7
111	Dutch	0.8	31.5	30.7	6.0
112	Izortsy	0.8	36.8	37.8	24.1
113	Aleuts	0.7	26.6	24.5	4.8
114	Japanese	0.7	46.0	38.9	3.1
115	French	0.7	46.6	44.1	14.6
116	Tofalars	0.7	43.0	39.1	3.7
117	Austrians	0.5	29.6	28.8	11.5
118	Americans	0.3	63.2	45.8	12.3
119	English	0.3	57.8	48.6	7.2
120	Livs	0.2	43.8	34.1	35.0
121	Entsy	0.2	45.5	47.8	10.0
122	Oroki	0.2	44.7	40.0	3.2
	Others	32	31.0	23.0	14.5

[a] The figures vary slightly in different publications of the 1989 census materials.

REFERENCES

Abramian, L. A. 1990. Chaos and Cosmos in the Structure of Mass Popular Demonstrations (The Karabakh Movement in the Eyes of an Ethnographer). *Soviet Anthropology and Archeology* 29, no. 2: 70–86.

Abylgozhin, Zh. B., M. K. Kozybaev, and M. B. Tatimov. 1989. Kasakhstanskaia tragediia. *Voprosy istorii* 7.

Aitov, N. 1990. Kakaia statistika nuzhna sotsiologam? *Vestnik statistiki* 12: 52–54.

Aiubzod, S. 1993. Dal'niaia chuzhbina luchshe blizhnei. *Nezavisimaia gazeta,* May 27.

Akiner, S. 1986. *Islamic Peoples of the Soviet Union.* 2nd edition. London: KPI.

Aklaev, A. P. 1994. Zakonodatel'stvo o iazykakh i mezhetnicheskie konflikty v respublikakh Rossiiskoi Federatsii. In *Konfliktnaia etnichnost' i etnicheskie konflikty,* edited by L. M. Drobizheva, 15–40. Moscow: Institut etnologii i antropologii.

Alexandrov, Iurii. 1994. Ekonomicheskie izmeneniia, etnosotsial'naia stratifikatsiia i mezetnicheskie otnosheniia. In *Natsionalism i bezopasnost' v postsovetskom prostranstve,* edited by S. Panarin, 18–25. Moscow: Progress-Kompleks.

Alexeev, N. A. 1975. *Traditsionnye religioznye verovaniia yakutov v XIX-nachale XX v.* Novosibirsk: Nauka.

Alexeyeva, Ludmilla. 1985. *Soviet Dissent: Contemporary Movements for National, Religious, and Human Rights.* Middletown, Conn.: Wesleyan University Press.

Alieva, Svetlana (ed.). 1993. *Tak eto bylo. Natsional'nye repressii v SSSR,* Vols. 1–3. Moscow: Insan.

Alimdzanov, A. 1988. K estestvennomy ruslu. *Druzhba narodov* 5: 255–56.

Alimdzanov, A. 1989. Gor'kie uroki. *Druzhba narodov* 12.

Allworth, Edward A. 1989. The Changing Intellectual and Literary Community. In *Central Asia: 120 Years of Russian Rule,* edited by E. Allworth, 349–96. Durham and London: Duke University Press.

Allworth, Edward A. 1990. *The Modern Uzbeks.* Stanford: Hoover Institution Press.

Alma-Ata: 1986. 1991. Alma-Ata: Altyn Orda.

Amal'rik, Andrei. 1971. *Will the Soviet Union Survive until 1984?* New York: Harper and Row, Perennial Library.

Anderson, Benedict. 1983. *Imagined Communities: Reflections on the Origins and Spread of Nationalism.* London: Verso.

Andreev, Sergei. 1991. Traurnyi marsh. *Oktiabr'* 6: 161–85.

272

Andreyev, N. 1992. Central Asia Looks towards the East. *New Times* 39.

Ardaev, Vladimir. 1992a. Kazakhstan: Oppositsiia s tochki zreniia vlasti. *Izvestiia,* June 23: 3.

Ardaev, Vladimir. 1992b. Nursultan Nazarbaev: "nam pora oglianut'sia na sdelannoe." *Izvestiia,* November 16.

Ardaev, Vladimir. 1993. Budet li u Kazakhstana novaia stolitsa? *Izvestiia,* October 8: 4.

Arendt, Hannah. 1968. *The Origins of Totalitarianism.* Pt. 2. *Imperialism.* New York: Harcourt, Brace and World, Inc.; first published in 1951.

Argunov, I. A. 1985. *Sotsial'noe razvitie yakutskogo naroda. Istoriko-sotsiologicheskoe issledovanie obraza zhizni.* Novosibirsk Nauka.

Argunova, T. V. 1992. *Yakutsko-russkoe dvuiazychie.* Yakutsk.

Arifkhanova, Z. Kh. 1989. Ne prenebregat' etnicheskim faktorom. *Voprosy istorii* 5.

Armstrong, John A. 1982. *Nations before Nationalism.* Chapel Hill: University of North Carolina Press.

Aron, Raymond. 1968. *Democracy and Totalitarianism.* London: Weidenfeld and Nicolson.

Aron, Raymond. 1974. Is Multinational Citizenship Possible? *Social Research* (Winter): 638-56.

Aron, Raymond. 1977. *Plaidoyer pour l'Europe décadente.* Paris: R. Laffont.

Aron, Raymond. 1985. *History, Truth, Liberty.* Chicago and London: University of Chicago Press.

Asylbekov, M. Kh. 1991. O sotsial'noi, politicheskoi i etnicheskoi strukture Kazakhstana. *Izvestiia AN Kazakhskoi SSR,* seriia obshchestvennykh nauk 3: 43-47.

Atchabarov, B., and T. Sharmanov. 1990. Voda dlia regiona. *Zvezda vostoka* 4.

Atkin, Muriel. 1989. *The Subtlest Battle: Islam in Soviet Tadjikistan.* Philadelphia: Foreign Policy Research Institute.

Atkin, Muriel. 1992a. Islamic Assertiveness and the Waning of the Old Soviet Order. *Nationalities Papers* 20, no. 1: 55-74.

Atkin, Muriel. 1992b. Religious, National, and Other Identities in Central Asia. In *Muslims in Central Asia: Expressions of Identity and Change,* edited by Jo-Ann Gross, 46-72. Durham and London: Duke University Press.

Avtorkhanov, Abdurahman. 1992. The Chechens and Ingush during the Soviet Period and Its Antecedents. In *The North Caucasus Barrier: The Russian Advance towards the Muslim World,* edited by M. Bennigsen Broxup, 146-95. London: Hurst and Co.

Azamova, A. 1991. Kyrgyzstan. Third Way. *Moscow News* 49 (December 8-15).

Azamova, A. 1992a. Suspected of Defending Human Rights. *Moscow News* 50 (December 13-20).

Azamova, A. 1992b. The Prohibitive Cost of Dictatorship. *Moscow News* 40 (October 7-13).

Aziatskaia Rossiia. 1914. Vol. 1. St. Petersburg: Pereselencheskoe upravlenie.

Bahry, Romana M. (ed.). 1990. *Echoes of Glosnost in Soviet Ukraine.* Ontario, Canada: Captus University Publications.

Baialinov, K. 1990. "Shelkovaia revolutsiia," ili "zagovor demokratov?" *Komsomol'-skaia pravda,* November 21.

Baialinov, K. 1994. Kirgizy, ne Moskva l' za nami? *Komsomol'skaia pravda,* January 29.

Bakatin, Vadim. 1992. *Izbavlenie ot KGB.* Moscow: Novosti.

Bakvis, Herman. 1987. Alternative Models of Governance: Federalism, Consociatialism, and Corporatism. In *Federalism and the Role of the State,* edited by Herman Bakvis and William M. Chandler, 279-305. Toronto: University of Toronto Press.

Bakvis, Herman, and William M. Chandler. 1987. The Future of Federalism. In *Federalism and the Role of the State,* edited by Herman Bakvis and William M. Chandler, 306-17. Toronto: University of Toronto Press.

Balzer, Marjorie Mandelstam. 1992a. Dilemmas of the Spirit: Religion and Atheism in the Yakut-Sakha Republic. In *Religious Policy in the Soviet Union,* edited by Sabrina Ramet, 231-51. Cambridge: Cambridge University Press.

Balzer, Marjorie Mandelstam. 1992b. The Struggle against Chamans: A Comparison of Alaska and Yakutia. In *Shamanism kak religiia: Genezis, rekonstruktsiia, traditsii,* 18. Tezisy. Yakutsk: Izdatel'stvo YaGU.

Balzer, Marjorie Mandelstam. 1993. Two Urban Shamans: Unmasking Leadership in Fin-de-Soviet Siberia. In *Perilous States: Conversations on Culture, Politics and Nation,* edited by George E. Marcus, 131-64. Chicago and London: University of Chicago Press.

Balzer, Marjorie Mandelstam (ed.). 1990. *Shamanism: Soviet Studies of Traditional Religion in Siberia and Central Asia.* Armonk, New York: M. E. Sharpe, Inc.

Banac, Ivo (ed.). 1992. *Eastern Europe in Revolution.* Ithaca and London: Cornell University Press.

Barany, George. 1971. Hungary: From Aristocratic to Proletarian Nationalism. In *Nationalism in Eastern Europe,* edited by Peter F. Sugar and Ivo J. Lederer, 259-309. Seattle and London: University of Washington Press.

Barry, Brian. 1991. *Democracy and Power: Essays in Political Theory,* Vol. 1. Oxford: Clarendon Press.

Barth, Fredrik. 1969. Introduction. In *Ethnic Groups and Boundaries,* edited by F. Barth, 9-38. Boston: Little, Brown.

Bates, R. H. 1974. Ethnic Competition and Modernization in Contemporary Africa. *Comparative Political Studies* 6 (January): 457-84.

Batt, Judy. 1991. The End of Communist Rule in East-Central Europe: A Four-Country Comparison. *Government and Opposition* 26, no. 3: 368-90.

Beissinger, Mark B. 1992. Elites and Ethnic Identities in Soviet and Post-Soviet Politics. In *The Post-Soviet Nations: Perspectives on the Demise of the USSR,* edited by Alexander J. Motyl, 141-69. New York: Columbia University Press.

Beissinger, Mark B. 1993. Demise of an Empire-State: Identity, Legitimacy, and the Deconstruction of Soviet Politics. In *The Rising Tide of Cultural Pluralism: The Nation-State at Bay?* edited by Crawford Young, 93-115. Madison: University of Wisconsin Press.

Beissinger, Mark, and Lubomyr Hajda. 1990. Nationalism and Reform in Soviet Politics. In *The Nationalities Factor in Soviet Politics and Society,* edited by Lubomyr Hajda and Mark Beissinger, 305-22. Boulder: Westview Press.

Bek, A. 1994. Zhizn' pod avtomatom. *Nezavisimaia gazeta,* March 16.

Bekker, A. 1989. Chornyi rynok Chorsu. *Moskovskie novosti,* September 3.

Bekmakhanov, S. 1992. Kyrgyzy. *Nedelia* (February): 5.

Bekmakhanova, N. E. 1980. *Formirovanie mnogonatsional'nogo naseleniia Kazakhstana i Severnoi Kirgizii.* Moscow: Nauka.

Bennigsen, Alexandre. 1964. Un mouvement populaire au Caucase au XVIIIe siècle: La 'Guerre Sainte' du sheikh Mansur [1785-1791], page mal connue et controversée des relations russo-turques. *Cahiers du monde russe et soviétique* 5, no. 2: 159-205.

Bennigsen, A., and M. Broxup. 1983. *The Islamic Threat to the Soviet Union.* London: Croom Helm.

Bennigsen, A., and S. Enders Wimbush. 1985. *Muslims of the Soviet Empire: A Guide.* London: C. Hurst and Co.

Bentley, Arthur F. 1967. *The Process of Government.* Cambridge, Mass: Harvard University Press.

Bogdanov, I. 1988. Uchit'sia pravde. *Kommunist* 18.

Bogert, C. 1991. The Khan of Kazakhstan. *Newsweek,* July 8.

Bohr, A. 1989. Health Catastrophe in Karakalpakistan. *Radio Liberty Report on the USSR* (February 10).

Bohr, A. 1990. Inside the Uzbek Parliamentary Opposition: An Interview with Muhammad Salikh. *Radio Liberty Report on the USSR* 2, no. 46 (November 16): 18-22.

Bonner, Elena. 1995. An Open Letter to Boris Yeltsin. *Monitor* 6, no. 1 (January 9): 3.

Borisov, D., and N. Vladimirov. 1992. Zia ul-Haq: Will His Dream Come True? *Moscow News* 3 (January 19-26).

Bova, Russel. 1991. Political Dynamics of the Post-Communist Transition: A Comparative Perspective. *World Politics* 44: 113-38.

Bracewell, Wendy. 1993. National Histories and National Identities among the Serbs and Croats. In *National Histories and European History,* edited by Mary Fulbrook, 141-60. Boulder: Westview Press.

Brass, P. B. 1976. Ethnicity and Nationality Formation. *Ethnicity* 3: 225-41.

Brass, P. B. 1991. *Ethnicity and Nationalism: Theory and Comparison.* New Delhi: Sage Publications.

Bromley, Yu. 1990. Ethnic Problems and Perestroika. *Social Sciences,* Moscow, 21, no. 1.

Brown, B. 1990a. Kazakhs Now Largest National Group in Kazakhstan. *Radio Liberty Report on the USSR* 2, no. 19 (May 4): 19-20.

Brown, B. 1990b. Ethnic Unrest Claims More Lives in Fergana Valley. *Radio Liberty Report on the USSR* 2, no. 24 (June 15): 16-18.

Brown, B. 1990c. New Political Parties in Kazakhstan. *Radio Liberty Report on the USSR* 2, no. 35 (August 31): 10-11.

Brown, B. 1990d. Alma-Ata Commission of Inquiry Publishes Report. *Radio Liberty Report on the USSR* 2, no. 42 (October 19): 20–21.

Brown, B. 1991a. Interethnic Tensions, Unsolved Economic Problems. *Radio Liberty Report on the USSR* 3, no. 1 (January 4): 29–30.

Brown, B. 1991b. The Strength of Kazakhstan's Antinuclear Lobby. *Radio Liberty Report on the USSR* 3, no. 4 (January 25): 23–24.

Brown, B. 1991c. The All-Union Referendum in Central Asia. *Radio Liberty Report on the USSR* 3, no. 13 (March 29): 1–3.

Brown, B. 1991d. The Islamic Renaissance Party in Central Asia. *Radio Liberty Report on the USSR* 3, no. 19 (May 10): 12–14.

Brown, B. 1991e. Nursultan Nazarbaev of Kazakhstan: A Profile. *Radio Liberty Report on the USSR* 3, no. 22 (May 31): 10–13.

Brown, B. 1991f. Kazakhstan's Economic Reform Program. *Radio Liberty Report on the USSR* 3, no. 24 (June 14): 24–26.

Brown, B. 1991g. Central Asia: Mixed Reactions. *Radio Liberty Report on the USSR* 6, no. 36 (September 6): 43–47.

Brown, B. 1993. Central Asia: The First Year of Unexpected Statehood. *RFE/RL Research Report,* (January 1): 25–36.

Broxup, Marie Benningsen. 1992. The Last Ghazawat: The 1920–1921 Uprising. In *The North Caucasus Barrier: The Russian Advance towards the Muslim World,* edited by M. Bennigsen Broxup, 112–45. London: Hurst and Co.

Broxup, Marie Benningsen. 1994. The "Internal" Muslim Factor in the Politics of Russia: Tatarstan and the North Caucasus. In *Central Asia and the Caucasus after the Soviet Union: Domestic and International Dynamics,* edited by Mohiaddin Mesbani, 75–98. Gainesville: University Press of Florida.

Brusina, O. I. 1990. Mnogonatsional'nye sela Uzbekistana i Kazakhstana osen'iu 1989 g. (migratsii korennogo naseleniia). *Sovetskaia etnografiia* 3: 18–30.

Brusina, O. I., and A. G. Osipov. 1993. Mezhnatsional'nye otnosheniia: Vzgliad na problemy Uzbekistana. *Etnograficheskoe obozrenie* 3: 15–27.

Buchanan, Allen. 1991. *Secession: The Morality of Political Divorce from Fort Sumter to Lithuania and Quebec.* Boulder: Westview Press.

Bugai, N. F. 1989. K voprosu o deportatsii narodov SSSR v 30–40-kh godakh. *Istoriia* SSSR 6.

Bugai, N. F. 1991a. Deportatsiia: Beria dokladyvaet Stalinu. *Kommunist* 3.

Bugai, N. F. 1991b. Po resheniiu pravitel'stva SSSR. *Moscovskie novosti* 26 (July 30).

Bugai, N. F. 1991c. Pogruzheny v eshelony i otpravleny k mestam poselenii. . . L. Beria–I. Stalinu. *Istoriia SSSR* 1.

Bunich, A. 1992. Lakomnyi kusok. *Literaturnaia gazeta,* February 5.

Burke, J. 1992. Uzbek Leaders Pick Stability over Reform. *Christian Science Monitor,* December 11.

Burtin, Yu. G., and E. D. Molchanov (eds.). 1992. *God posle Avgusta: Gorech' i vybor.* Moscow: Literatura i politika.

Bushkov, B. I., and D. V. Mikul'sky. 1992. *Obshchestvenno-politicheskaia situatsiia v Tadjikistane: ianvar' 1992 g.* Institut etnologii i antropologii. Issledovaniia po prikladnoi i neotlozhnoi etnologii, dokument N 26, seriia A, Moscow.

Bushkov, B. I., and D. V. Mikul'sky. 1993. *Tadjikistan: Chto proiskhodit v respublike?* Institut etnologii i antropologii. Issledovaniia po prikladnoi i neotlozhnoi etnologii, dokument N 40, seriia A, Moscow.

Bychkova, Olga. 1990. A Border through the Republic? *Moscow News* 44 (October 7): 8.

Carlson, Charles. 1990. Kazakhs Refute Russian Territorial Claims. *Radio Liberty Report on the USSR* 2, no. 32 (August 10): 18–20.

Carlson, Charles. 1991. Turkmenistan: Inching towards Democratization. *Radio Liberty Report on the USSR* 3, no. 1 (January 4): 35–36.

Carrère d'Encausse, Hélène. 1981. *Decline of an Empire: The Soviet Socialist Republics in Revolt.* New York: Harper and Row.

Carrère d'Encausse, Hélène. 1985. The Islamic Minorities. *Soviet Jewish Affairs* 15, no. 1: 88–95.

Carrère d'Encausse, Hélène. 1992. *The End of the Soviet Empire: The Triumph of the Nations.* New York: Basic Books.

Cassesse, Antonio. 1986. *International Law in a Divided World.* Oxford: Clarendon Press.

Cavanaugh, C. 1992. Crackdown on the Opposition in Uzbekistan. *RFE/RL Research Report* 1, no. 31 (July 31): 20–24.

Chazan, N. 1986. Ethnicity in Economic Crisis: Development Strategies and Patterns of Ethnicity in Africa. In *Ethnicity, Politics and Development,* edited by D. Thompson and D. Ronen, 137–78. Boulder: Lynne Reimer Publishers.

Chervonnaia, S. M. 1993. *Abkhazia—1992: Postkommunisticheskaia Vandeia.* Moscow: Mosgorpechat'.

Chesko, S. V. 1988. Vremia stirat' "belye piatna." *Sovetskaia etnografiia* 6: 3–15.

Chesko, S. V. 1990. Sredniaia Aziia i Kazakhstan: Sovremennoe sostoianie i perspektivy natsional'nogo razvitiia. *Rasy i narody* 20: 106–27.

Chesko, S. V. 1993. *Ideologiia raspada.* Moscow: Institut etnologii i antropologii.

Chicherina, N. G. (ed.). 1990a. *Grazhdanskie dvizheniia v Latvii 1989.* Moscow: TsIMO.

Chicherina, N. G. (ed.). 1990b. *Grazhdanskie dvizheniia v Tadjikistane.* Moscow: TsIMO.

Chichlo, B. 1987. Histoire de la formation des territoires autonomes chez les peuples turco-mongoles de Sibérie. *Cahiers du monde russe et soviétique* 28, nos. 3–4: 361–402.

Chornovil, Vyacheslav. 1968. *The Chornovil Papers.* New York: McGraw-Hill.

Cohen, Stephen F. 1991. Gorbachev the Great. *The New York Times,* March 11.

Cohen, Stephen F. 1992. What's Really Happening in Russia. *The Nation* (March 2): 262–63.

Colton, Timothy J. 1986. *The Dilemma of Reform in the Soviet Union.* New York: Council of Foreign Relations.

Connor, Walker. 1973. The Politics of Ethnonationalism. *Journal of International Affairs* 27, no. 1: 1–21.

Connor, Walker. 1984a. Eco- or Ethno-nationalism. *Ethnic and Race Studies* 7, no. : 342–59.

Connor, Walker. 1984b. *The National Question in Marxist-Leninist Theory and Strategy.* Princeton, N.J.: Princeton University Press.

Connor, Walker. 1990. When Is a Nation? *Ethnic and Racial Studies* 13, no. 1: 92–102.

Connor, Walker. 1992. Soviet Policies toward the Non-Russian Peoples in Theoretic and Historic Perspective: What Gorbachev Inherited. In *The Post-Soviet Nations: Perspectives on the Demise of the USSR,* edited by Alexander J. Motyl, 30–49. New York: Columbia University Press.

Connor, Walker. 1994. *Ethnonationalism: The Quest for Understanding.* Princeton, N.J.: Princeton University Press.

Conquest, R. 1970a. Russia's Meskhetians—A Lost Peoples. *The Times,* August 5.

Conquest, R. 1970b. *The Nation Killers: The Soviet Deportation of Nationalities.* New York: Macmillan Company.

Conquest, Robert (ed.). 1986. *The Last Empire: Nationality and the Soviet Future.* Stanford: Hoover Institution Press.

Critchlow, J. 1990. Further Repercussions of "The Uzbek Affair." *Radio Liberty Report on the USSR* 2, no. 18 (May 4): 20–22.

Critchlow, J. 1991a. *Nationalism in Uzbekistan: A Soviet Republic's Road to Sovereignty.* Boulder: Westview Press.

Critchlow, J. 1991b. Uzbekistan: What Ever Happened to Marxism-Leninism? *Radio Liberty Report on the USSR* 3, no. 12 (March 22): 17–20.

Cummins, I. 1980. *Marx, Engels and National Movements.* London: Croom Helm.

Dakhshleger, G. F. 1965. *Sotsialno-ekonomicheskie preobrazovaniia v aule i derevne Kazakhstana (1921–29 god).* Alma-Ata: Nauka.

Davlet-uulu, N. 1992. Independent Kyrgyzstan: Current Political and Economic Situation. *Umid/Hope* (Spring).

Dement'eva, Irina. 1994. Voina i mir Prigorodnogo raiona. *Izvestiia,* January 25–29.

Demko, G. J. 1969. *The Russian colonization of Kazakhstan, 1896–1916.* Bloomington: University of Indiana Press.

Denisenko, E. 1993a. Respublika vyshla iz rublevoi zony. *Nezavisimaia gazeta,* May 12.

Denisenko, E. 1993b. Piat' dnei, kotorye potriasli respubliku. *Nezavisimaia gazeta,* May 15.

Denisenko, E. 1993c. Mesiats s somom. *Nezavisimaia gazeta,* June 8.

Dergachev, A. 1990. Bezhentsy v svoei strane. *Izvestiia,* October 12.

Desiatov, V. 1991a. President Nazarbaev: "Novyiu volny' budem delat' svoimi rukami." *Nezavisimaia gazeta,* October 16: 3.

Desiatov, V. 1991b. Kazak v Kazakhstane tozhe chelovek. *Nezavisimaia gazeta,* November 19: 3.

Deutsch, Karl W. 1961. Social Mobilization and Political Development. *American Political Science Review* 55: 493–514.

Diakonov, N. 1992. Sovremennye aspekty demograficheskogo vozrozhdeniia i razvitiia yakutskogo naroda. Manuscript.

Diakonova, E. N. 1990. Simvolika v yakutskom obriade "yasyakh": 1990. In *Problemy izucheniia traditsii v kulture narodov mira,* vyp. 1, 48–57. Moscow: Institut etnografii.

Dienes, L. 1987. *Soviet Asia: Economic Development and National Policy Choices.* Boulder: Westview Press.

Doyle, Michael W. 1986. *Empires.* Ithaca, N.Y.: Cornell University Press.

Drobizheva, L. M. 1991. Etnicheskoe i istoricheskoe samosoznanie narodov SSSR na rubezhe poslednego desiatiletiia XX veka (v kontse 80-kh—nachale 90-kh gg.). In *Dukhovnaia kul'tura i etnicheskoe samosoznanie,* vyp. 2, 65–82. Moscow.

Drobizheva, L. M. 1994. *Natsional'noe samosoznanie i natsionalism v Rossiiskoi Federatsii.* Moscow: Institut etnologii i antropologii RAN.

Dubnov, A. 1993a. Asiatic Faces of Russia's Adversity. *New Times* 49: 16–18.

Dubnov, A. 1993b. The Tadjikistan Catastrophe. *New Times* 6 (February): 10–13.

Dubnov, A. 1993c. Habits and Ways of the CIS Central Asian Republics Do Not Encourage Further Discussions of Human Rights. *New Times* 23 (April): 3.

Dubnov, A. 1993d. What Currency Circulates in Bishkek? *New Times* 18 (June): 15–17.

Dzanguzhin, Rustem. 1993. Kakim ia vizhu novyi Kazakhstan. *Prostor* 9: 173–84.

Dzhamgerchinov, B. 1959. *Prisoedinenie Kirgizii k Possii.* Moscow: Izdatel'stvo sotsial'no-ekonomicheskoi literatury.

Dzyuba, Ivan. 1974. *Internationalism or Russification? A Study in the Soviet Nationalities Problem.* Philadelphia: Ukrainian Political Science Association in the United States.

Eickelman, D. F., and K. Pasha. 1991. Muslim Societies and Politics: Soviet and US Approaches—A Conference Report. *Middle East Journal* 45, no. 4: 630–44.

Elebaeva, A. B. 1991. *Grazhdanskie dvizheniia v Kyrgyzstane.* Moscow: TsIMO.

Eliade, Mircea. 1951. *Le chamanisme et les techniques archaïques de l'extase.* Paris: Librairie Payot.

Emerson, Rupert. 1960. *From Empire to Nation: The Rise to Self-Assertion of Asian and African Peoples.* Cambridge, Mass.: Harvard University Press.

Enloe, C. H. 1973. *Ethnic Conflict and Political Development.* Boston: Little, Brown and Co.

Eremeev, S. 1991. Prezhdevremennye pokhorony. *Nedelia* 49, (December 2–9): 6–7.

Ericson, Richard E. 1992. Soviet Economic Structure and the National Question. In *The Post-Soviet Nations: Perspectives on the Demise of the USSR,* edited by Alexander J. Motyl, 240–71. New York: Columbia University Press.

Esman, Milton J. 1989a. Economic Performance and Ethnic Conflict. In *Conflict and Peacemaking in Multiethnic Societies,* edited by Joseph V. Montville, 477–90. Lexington, Mass.: Lexington Books.

Esman, Milton J. 1989b. Political and Psychological Factors in Ethnic Conflicts. In *Conflict and Peacemaking in Multiethnic Societies,* edited by Joseph V. Montville, 53–64. Lexington, Mass.: Lexington Books.

Eyal, J. 1989. Soviet Moldavia: History Catches Up and a Separate Language Disappears. *Radio Liberty Report on the USSR* 1, no. 8 (February 24): 25–29.

Fedorova, E. N. 1993. *Narodonaselenie Yakutii.* Novosibirsk: Nauka.

Fierman, W. (ed.). 1991. *Soviet Central Asia: The Failed Transformation.* Boulder: Westview Press.

Filonyk, A. O. 1994. Kyrgyzstan. In *Central Asia and the Caucasus after the Soviet Union,* edited by Mohiaddin Mesbahi, 149–63. Gainesville: University Press of Florida.

Focus on Kazakhstan. 1990. *Central Asia and Caucasus Chronicle* 9, no. 1: 3–6.

Forsyth, James. 1992. *A History of the Peoples of Siberia: Russia's North Asian Colony 1581–1990.* Cambridge: Cambridge University Press.

Fragner, Bert G. 1994. The Nationalization of the Uzbeks and Tajiks. In *Muslim Communities Reemerge: Historical Perspectives on Nationality, Politics, and Opposition in the Former Soviet Union and Yugoslavia,* edited by Andreas Kappeler et al., 14–32. Durham and London: Duke University Press.

Fridman, L. A., and O. V. Karazhas. 1994. *Strukturnye sdvigi v narodnom khoziaistve Tsentral'noi Azii i Zakavkaziia (po materialam perepisei naseleniia 1926–1989 gg.).* Vestnik Moskovskogo Universiteta, Seriia 13, Vostokovedenie, 2, pp. 3–23.

Fukuyama, Francis. 1987. The End of History. *National Interest* (Summer): 3–18.

Fuller, E. 1988. Deportation of Meskhetians Discussed in Georgian Press. *Radio Liberty Research* 168, no. 88 (April 12).

Fuller, E. 1989. What Are the Meskhetians' Chances of Returning to Georgia? *Radio Liberty Report on the USSR* 1, no. 26 (June 30): 17–18.

Fuller, E., and A. Bohr. 1989. Chronology of Ethnic Disturbances in Transcaucasia and Central Asia. *Radio Liberty Report on the USSR* 1, no. 27 (July 7): 16–18.

Furtado, Charles F., and Andrea Chandler (eds.). 1992. *Perestroika in the Soviet Republics: Documents on the National Question.* Boulder: Westview Press.

Fyodorov, A. 1992. What Do Students Want: Bread or Freedom? *Moscow News* 6 (February 29).

Gafarly, M. 1994. V respublike vykhodiat tol'ko pravitel'stvennye gazety. *Segodnia,* January 11.

Galiev, A. V. 1990. Bezrabotitsa v Srednei Azii i Kazakhstane na sovremennom etape. In *Vsesoiuznaia nauchnaia sessiia po itogam polevykh etnograficheskikh i antropologicheskikh issledovanii 1988–1989 gg.,* chap. 1, 127–28. Alma-Ata. Tezisy dokladov.

Gammer, Moshe. 1994. *Muslim Resistance to the Tsar: Shamil and the Russian Conquest of Chechnia and Daghestan.* London: Frank Cass.

Gdlian, T. 1989. Piramida. *Strana i mir* 4, no. 58.

Gdlian, T., and Nikolai Ivanov. 1994. *Kremliovskoe delo.* Rostov-na-Dony: AO Kniga.

Geertz, Clifford. 1963. The Integrative Revolution: Primordial Sentiments and Civil Politics in the New States. In *Old Societies and New States,* edited by C. Geertz, 105–57. New York: Free Press.

Gellner, Ernest. 1964. *Thought and Change.* London: Weidenfeld and Nicolson.

Gellner, Ernest. 1979. *Spectacles and Predicaments.* Cambridge: Cambridge University Press.

Gellner, Ernest. 1983. *Nations and Nationalism.* Ithaca, N.Y.: Cornell University Press.

Gellner, Ernest. 1991. Nationalism and Politics in Eastern Europe. *New Left Review* 189: 127-34.

Gellner, Ernest. 1992. Nationalism in the Vacuum. In *Thinking Theoretically about Soviet Nationalities: History and Comparison in the Study of the USSR,* edited by Alexander J. Motyl, 243-54. New York: Columbia University Press.

Gellner, Ernest. 1994. *Encounters with Nationalism.* Oxford: Blackwell Publishers.

Gerasimov, I. P. (ed.). 1969. *Kazakhstan.* Moscow: Nauka.

Ghai, Yash. 1993. *Ethnicity and Governance in Asia: A Report to the Ford Foundation.* N.p.

Glazer, Nathan, and Daniel P. Moynihan. 1975. Introduction. In *Ethnicity: Theory and Experience,* edited by Nathan Glazer and Daniel P. Moynihan, 1-26. Cambridge, Mass.: Harvard University Press.

Goble, P. 1990. Islamic "Explosion" Possible in Central Asia. *Radio Liberty Report on the USSR* 2, no. 7 (February 16): 22-23.

Gorbachev, Mikhail. 1992. *Dekabr'-91: Moia positsiia.* Moscow: Novosti.

Gordon, Milton M. 1975. Toward a General Theory of Racial and Ethnic Group Relations. In *Ethnicity: Theory and Experience,* edited by Nathan Glazer and Daniel P. Moynihan, 84-110. Cambridge, Mass.: Harvard University Press.

Gorokhov, S. N. 1992. Bor'ba s shamanizmom v Yakutii. In *Shamanism kak religiia: Genezis, rekonstruktsiia, traditsii.* Tezisy. Yakutsk: Izdatel'stvo YaGU.

Govorukhin, S. 1990. Repetitsiia? *Moskovskie novosti* 7 (February).

Gray, J. 1986. *Liberalism.* Milton Keynes, England: Open University Press.

Greenfeld, Liah. 1992. *Nationalism: Five Roads to Modernity.* Cambridge, Mass.: Harvard University Press.

Grigorieva, A. M. 1991. *O narodnoi meditsine yakutov.* Yakutsk.

Guboglo, M. N. 1984. *Sovremennye etnoiazykovye protsessy v SSSR.* Moscow: Nauka.

Guboglo, M. N. 1993. Etnodemograficheskaia i iazykovaia situatsiia v stolitsakh soiuznykh respublik SSSR v kontse 80-kh-nachale 90kh godov. *Otechestvennaia istoriia* 1.

Guboglo, M. N. (ed.). 1992. *Etnopoliticheskaia mozaika Bashkortostana,* t. 1-2. Moscow: TsIMO.

Guboglo, M. N., and S. M. Chervonnaia (eds.). 1992. *Krymskotatarskoe natsional'noe dvizhenie,* t. 1-2. Moscow: TsIMO.

Guboglo, M. N. and S. M. Chervonnaia. 1994. Krymskotatarskii vopros i sovremennaia situatsiia v Krymu. In *Mezhnatsional'nye otnosheniia v Rossii i SNG,* edited by Paul Goble and Gennady Bordiugov, 88-120. Moscow: ITs AIRO-XX.

Hajda, Lubomyr, and Mark Beissinger (eds.). 1990. *The Nationalities Factor in Soviet Politics and Society.* Boulder: Westview Press.

Hall, John A. 1988. *Liberalism: Politics, Ideology and the Market.* London: Paladin Grafton Books.

Hall, John A. 1993. Nationalisms: Classified and Explained. *Daedalus* 122, no. 3: 1-28.

Hall, John A. 1994. *Coercion and Consent.* Cambridge: Polity Press.

Hayes, Carlton J. H. 1950. *The Historical Evolution of Modern Nationalism.* New York: Macmillan Company.

Hechter, M. 1976. Ethnicity and Industrialization: On the Proliferation of the Cultural Division of Labor. *Ethnicity* 3: 214-24.

Heiberg, Marianne. 1989. *The Making of the Basque Nation.* Cambridge: Cambridge University Press.

Helgesen, Malvin M. 1994. Central Asia: Prospects for Ethnic and Nationalist Conflict. In *Ethnic Nationalism and Regional Conflict: The Former Soviet Union and Yugoslavia,* edited by W. Raymond Duncan and G. Paul Holman, Jr., 137-53. Boulder: Westview Press.

Hill, Ronald J. 1993. Managing Ethnic Conflict. *Journal of Communist Studies* 9, no. 1: 57-74.

Hill, Ronald J., and John Löwenhardt. 1991. Nomenklatura and Perestroika. *Government and Opposition* 26, no. 2: 229-43.

Hobsbawm, Eric J. 1962. *The Age of Revolution 1789-1848.* New York: New American Library.

Hobsbawm, Eric J. 1990. *Nations and Nationalism since 1780.* Cambridge: Cambridge University Press.

Hobsbawm, Eric J. 1993. The New Threat to History. *The New York Review of Books* 40, no. 21 (December 16): 62-64.

Hobsbawm, Eric, and Terence Ranger (eds.). 1992. *The Invention of Tradition.* Cambridge: Cambridge University Press.

Hoppál, Mihály. 1992. Urban Shamans: A Cultural Revival in the Postmodern World. In *Studies in Shamanism,* edited by Mihály Hoppál and Anna-Leena Siikala, 197-209. (Ethnologica Uralica, 2.) Budapest: Akademiai Kiado.

Horowitz, Donald L. 1985. *Ethnic Groups in Conflict.* Berkeley: University of California Press.

Hough, Jerry. 1991. Understanding Gorbachev: The Importance of Politics. *Soviet Economy* 7, no. 2: 89-109.

Hroch, Miroslav. 1985. *Social Preconditions of National Revival in Europe.* Cambridge: Cambridge University Press.

Hyman, A. 1994. Central Asia and the Middle East: The Emerging Links. In *Central Asia and the Caucasus after the Soviet Union: Domestic and International Dynamics,* edited by Mohiaddin Mesbani, 248-67. Gainesville: University Press of Florida.

Iablokov, A. 1988. Pestitsidy, ekologiia, sel'skoe khoziaistvo. *Kommunist* 15.

Ionescu, D. 1989. Soviet Moldavia: The State Language Issue. *Radio Liberty Report on the USSR* 1, no. 22 (June 2): 19-22.

Ionin, L. 1991. A Coup Tomorrow? *New Times* 51 (December 24-30): 4-6.

Iranian Religious Propaganda in Turkmenistan. 1987. *Radio Liberty* 375, no. 87 (September 22).

Isakov, Konstantin. 1991. Next Stop the Moon? *New Times* 51: 36-38.

Ivanov, A. 1992a. Ulybka prezidenta. *Literaturnaia gazeta,* May 20.

Ivanov, A. 1992b. I zdes' chuzhye, i tam ne nuzhny. *Literaturnaia gazeta,* August 26.

Ivanov, A. 1993. Verkhovaia ezda na zabore. *Literaturnaia gazeta,* April 14.

Ivanov, A. 1994. Etnopoliticheskaia situatsiia v Respublike Sakha (Yakutiia). In *Narody Severa i Sibiri v usloviiakh ekonomicheskikh reform i demokraticheskikh preobrazovanii,* edited by Z. P. Sokolova, 89–112. Moscow: Institut etnologii i antropologii.

Kabilov, T. 1989. Kooperativnoe dvizhenie v respublikakh Srednei Azii—magistral'noe napravlenie radikal'noi ekonomicheskoi reformy. *Voprosy ekonomiki* 5.

Kalinkin, N. 1993. Peace and calm in Tashkent. *New Times* 20 (May): 13–15.

Kalyshev, A. B. 1991. Ob etnicheskom aspekte mezhnatsional'nykh semei v Kazakhstane. *Izvestiia AN Kazakhskoi SSR,* seriia obshchestvennykh nauk 3: 48–53.

Kamal, Jamal. 1992. Do You Care? *Umid/Hope* (Spring).

Karklins, R. 1986. *Ethnic Relations in the USSR: The Perspective from Below.* Boston: Allen and Unwin.

Kasenov, U. 1994. Vneshniaia politika Rossii v Tsentral'noi Azii. *Nezavisimaia gazeta,* March 16.

Kask, Peet. 1994. National Radicalization in Estonia: Legislation on Citizenship and Related Issues. *Nationalities Papers* 22, no. 1: 379–91.

Keane, John. 1988. *Democracy and Civil Society.* London and New York: Verso.

Kedourie, Elie. 1993. *Nationalism.* 4th edition, expanded. Oxford: Blackwell Publishers.

Khakhanov, A. 1891. Meskhi (Etnograficheskii ocherk). *Etnograficheskoe obozrenie* 3–4.

Khalim, A. 1988. Yazyk moi—drug moi. *Druzhba narodov* 6.

Khazanov, Anatoly M. 1988. The Current Ethnic Situation in the USSR: Perennial Problems in the Period of "Restructuring." *Nationalities Papers* 16, no. 2: 147–70.

Khazanov, Anatoly M. 1989. *The Krymchaks: A Vanishing Group in the Soviet Union.* Jerusalem: Hebrew University, Marjorie Mayrock Center for Soviet and East European Research.

Khazanov, Anatoly M. 1990a. The Ecological Situation and the National Issue in Uzbekistan. *Environmental Policy Review* 4, no. 1: 20–28.

Khazanov, Anatoly M. 1990b. The Ethnic Situation in the Soviet Union as Reflected in Soviet Anthropology. *Cahiers du monde russe et soviétique* 31, nos. 2–3: 213–22.

Khazanov, Anatoly M. 1991. *Soviet Nationality Policy during Perestroika.* Falls Church, Va.: Delphic.

Khazanov, Anatoly M. 1992a. Meskhetian Turks in Search of Self-Identity. *Central Asian Survey* 11, no. 4: 1–16.

Khazanov, Anatoly M. 1992b. Nomads and Oases in Central Asia. In *Transition to Modernity,* edited by John A. Hall and I. C. Jarvie, 69–89. Cambridge: Cambridge University Press.

Khazanov, Anatoly M. 1994a. The Collapse of the Soviet Union: Nationalism during Perestroika and Afterwards. *Nationalities Papers* 22, no. 1: 157–74.

Khazanov, Anatoly M. 1994b. Nationalism and Neo-Shamanism in Yakutia. *MDIA* 12.

Khazanov, Anatoly M. 1994c. Underdevelopment and Ethnic Relations in Central Asia. In *Central Asia in Historical Perspective,* edited by B. Manz, 144-63. Boulder: Westview Press.

Khazanov, Anatoly M. 1995. The Ethnic Problems of Contemporary Kazakhstan. *Central Asian Survey* 14, no. 1: 243-64.

Khodzhamuradov, A. 1984. Uspekhi melioratsii zemel' v Turkmenskoi SSR. *Problemy osvoeniia pustyn'* 5.

Khovratovich, V. 1991. Sovetskie turki v poiskakh krova. *Izvestiia,* July 22: 3.

Khurshut, A. 1988. Turki. *Literaturnyi Kirgizstan* 12.

Kirch, M., and A. Kirch. 1988. The National Process in Estonia Today. *Nationalities Papers* 16, no. 2: 171-76.

Kiselev, V. 1991. Bol'shoi krug. *Moskovskie novosti* 21 (May 26): 11.

Kiyanitsa, Victor. 1991. Why Did Nazarbaev Get All the Russian Votes? *Moscow News* 50 (December 15-22): 3.

Kiyanitsa, Victor. 1992. Nursultan Nazarbaev. *Moscow News* 3 (January 19-26): 4.

Klima, Arnost. 1993. The Czechs. In *The National Question in Europe in Historical Context,* edited by Mikulás Teich and Roy Porter, 228-47. Cambridge: Cambridge University Press.

Kohn, Hans. 1967. *The Idea of Nationalism.* 2nd edition. New York: Collier-Macmillan.

Kolarz, Walter. 1969. *The Peoples of the Soviet Far East.* Archon Books.

Komarov, B. 1978. *The Destruction of Nature in the Soviet Union.* London: Pluto Press.

Kommunisticheskaia partiia Kazakhstana. 1990. *Organizatsionno-politicheskoe razvitie.* Alma-Ata: Spravochnik.

Konovalov, V. 1993. Nursultan Nazarbaev: Novaia kontseptsiia i novaia initsiativa. *Izvestiia,* June 5.

Konsratov, E. 1989. Postav' sebia na ego mesto. *Izvestiia,* October 5.

Konstantinova, N. 1993. Girls Read the Koran. *Moscow News* 14 (April).

Korostelev, A. D. 1994. Dinamika etnicheskago sostava sel'skikh poselenii Bashkortostana (K probleme tataro—bashkirskoi mezhetnicheskoi napriazhennosti). In *Konfliktnaia etnichnost' i etnicheskie konflikty,* edited by L. A. Drobizheva, 67-92. Moscow: Institut etnologii i antropologii.

Koroteeva, V. V., and M. N. Mosesova. 1988. Problemy natsional'nykh iazykov i ikh otrazhenie v obshchestvennom soznanii. *Sovetskaia etnografiia* 5: 4-14.

Kostiukova, Irina. 1994. Sel'sko-gorodskie migranty v Bishkeke: Sotsial'nye problemy i uchastie v natsional'no-politicheskom dvizhenii. In *Etnosotsial'nye Protsessy v Kyrgyzstane,* edited by N. P. Kosmarskaia and S. A. Panarin, 75-93. Moscow: Institut Vostokovedeniia PAN.

Kotliakov, V., S. Zonn, and E. Chernyshev. 1988. Sovremennoe sostoianie, ratsional'noe osvoenie i okhrana prirodnykh resursov Iugo-Vostoka. *Vestnik AN SSR* 5.

Kovalev, A. 1989. Kto i pochemu za chertoi bednosti. *Ekonomicheskaia gazeta* 25 (June).

Kozlov, S. 1993a. Chevron Impatient to Drill in Kazakhstan. *Independent Newspaper* 3, no. 24—4, no. 1.

Kozlov, S. 1993b. Kongress antiiadernogo dvizheniia pod ugrozoi sryva. *Nezavisimaia gazeta,* April 7.

Kozlov, S. 1993c. Nazarbaev—lider SNG? *Nezavisimaia gazeta,* June 2.

Kozlov, S. 1993d. Nezavisimye zhurnalisty boriutsia za svoi prava. *Nezavisimaia gazeta,* May 18.

Kozlov, S. 1993e. Nursultan Nazarbaev: "Nyneshnii kurs dollara—eto chepukha, pridumannaia rossiiskim bankom." *Nezavisimaia gazeta,* June 4.

Kozlov, S. 1993f. Pravo pervoi nefti. *Nezavisimaia gazeta,* April 10.

Kozlov, S. 1993g. Ugrozy bonapartizma v Kazakhstane bol'she net. *Nezavisimaia gazeta,* May 6.

Kozlov, S. 1993h. V Alma-Ata poiavilis' dissidenty. *Nezavisimaia gazeta,* May 28.

Kozlov, S. 1994. Nabliudateli SBSE byli sub'ektivny. *Nezavisimaia gazeta,* March 15: 3.

Kozlov, V. I. 1988. Osobennosti etnodemograficheskikh problem v Srednei Azii i puti ikh resheniia. *Istoriia SSSR* 1.

Kozlov, V. I. 1990. Natsional'nyi vopros: Paradigmy, teoriia i politika. *Istoriia SSSR* 1.

Kozlov, V. I. 1993. Natsionalism, natsional-separatizm i russkii vopros. *Otechestvennaia istoriia* 2: 44-64.

Kozybaev, I. M., and M. K. Kozybaev. 1994. *Istoriia Kazakhstana: Khrestomatiia.* Almaty: Atamyra.

Kozyrbaev, I. I. 1990. *Istoriografiia Kazakhstana: Uroki istorii.* Alma-Ata: Rauan.

Kreindler, Isabelle T. (ed.). 1985. *Sociolinguistic Perspectives on Soviet National Languages: Their Past, Present and Future.* Berlin: Mouton de Gruyter.

Krivochapkine, V. G. 1992. L'écologie médicale du bassin du fleuve Vilioui dans les conditions de la mise en exploitation industrielle intensive de son territoire. *Questions Sibériennes* 2: 35-40.

Krupnik, Igor. 1991. The Nationalities Question in the USSR: Looking for Explanations. In *National Processes in the USSR: Problems and Trends,* edited by V. Tishkov, 79-101. Moscow: Nauka Publishers.

Ksenofontov, G. V. 1992. *Shamanism: Izbrannye trudy.* Yakutsk: Sever-Iug.

Kuandykov, A. 1994. Kazakhi v Kazakhstane: Integratsiia i sovremennost'. In *Obshchestvenno-politicheskaia stabil'nost',* edited by B. B. Baimagambetova et al., 21-23. Kustanai: Kustanaiskaia oblastnaia administratsiia.

Kuanyshev, Zh. I. 1991. Natsional'naia politika i politicheskaia zhizn' Kazakhstana v seredine 50kh-80e gody: Novye podkhody. In *Mezhnatsional'nye problemy i konflikty: Poiski putei ikh reshenii,* chap. 1, 40. Bishkek.

Kubekov, M. 1990. Gorbachev, kak vsegda, ni pri chiom. *Russkaia mysl',* October 26: 3.

Kuderina, L. D. 1994. *Genotsid v Kazakhstane.* Moscow: Skorpion.

Kudriavtsev, A. V., and A. Sh. Niyazi. 1994. "Politicheskii islam": Nachalo 90-kh. In *Sovremennyi islam: Kul'tura i politika,* edited by V. V. Naumkin, 95-128. Moscow: Rossiiskii Tsentr strategicheskikh i mezhdunarodnykh issledovanii.

Kukushkin, Yu. S. (ed.). 1993. *Russkii narod—istoricheskaia sud'ba v XX veke.* Moscow: Anko.

Kulakovsky, Alexei. 1990. *Snovidenie shamana.* Moscow: Khudozhestvennaia literatura.

Kunaev, Dinmukhamed. 1992. *O moem vremeni.* Alma-Ata: Dauir.

Kuznetsov, A. I., and L. I. Missonova. 1993. *Etnosotsial'noe polozhenie evenov v Eveno-Bytantaiskom raione Yakutii.* Institut etnologii i antropologii. Issledovaniia po prikladnoi i neotlozhnoi etnologii, dokument N 35. Moscow.

Laqueur, Walter. 1994. *The Dream That Failed: Reflections on the Soviet Union.* New York: Oxford University Press.

Landa, R. L. 1993. Islamskii fundamentalism. *Voprosy istorii* 1.

Latifi, O. Platina. 1988. *Pravda*, November 21.

Lebedev, A. V. 1991. *Grazhdanskie dvizheniia v Belorussii.* Moscow: TsIMO.

Lebedeva, M., and O. Panfilov. 1994. Bozor Sobir otpushchen na svobody s ispytatel'nym srokom. *Izvestiia,* January 19.

Lempert, David. 1993. Changing Russian Political Culture in the 1990s: Parasites, Paradigms, and Perestroika. *Comparative Studies in Society and History* 35, no. 3: 628–46.

Levin, L. 1989. Pylaiushchee leto Fergany. *Zvezda vostoka* 10.

Levin, M. G., and A. P. Potapov (eds.). 1956. *Narody Sibiri.* Moscow-Leningrad: Izdatel'stvo AN SSSR.

Lewis, I. M. 1984. What Is a Shaman? In *Shamanism in Eurasia,* pt. 1, edited by M. Hoppál, 3–12. Göttingen.

Lijphart, Arend. 1977. *Democracy in Plural Societies: A Comparative Exploration.* New Haven: Yale University Press.

Lindblom, Charles E. 1977. *Politics and Markets: The World's Political-Economic Systems.* New York: Basic Books.

Lubin, Nancy. 1984. *Labor and Nationality in Soviet Central Asia: An Uneasy Compromise.* Princeton: Princeton University Press.

Lushin, Yu. 1992. Bol'shoi sekret "v mirnykh tseliakh." *Ogonek* 2 (January 11–18): 14–15.

McCauley, M. 1970. Kazakhstan and the Virgin and Idle Lands Programme, 1953–64. *Mizan* 12: 100–111.

McRae, Kenneth. 1988. *Conflict and Compromise in Multilingual Societies: Switzerland.* Waterloo, Ontario: Wilford Laurier University Press.

Maksimov, P. S. 1990. Natsional'nye otnosheniia i tendentsii ikh razvitiia v respublike. In *Mezhnatsional'nye otnosheniia v regione (po materialam Yakuskoi ASSR),* edited by P. S. Maksimov, 5–24. Yakutsk: Yakutskii nauchnyi tsentr.

Malashenko, A. 1992. Muftii, mully, imamy i politika. *Nezavisimaia gazeta,* October 23.

Malashenko, A., and V. Moskalenko. 1992. Proigralo li religioznoe dvizhenie v Tadjikistane? *Nezavisimaia gazeta,* January 31.

Malia, Martin. 1994. *The Soviet Tragedy: A History of Socialism in Russia, 1917–1991.* New York: Free Press.

Mann, Michael. 1993a. Nation-States in Europe and Other Continents: Diversifying, Developing, Not Dying. *Daedalus* 122, no. 3: 115–40.

Mann, Michael. 1993b. *The Sources of Social Power.* Vol. 2. *The Rise of Classes and Nation-States, 1760-1914.* Cambridge: Cambridge University Press.

Manz, Beatrice Forbes. 1987. Central Asian Uprisings in the Nineteenth Century: Ferghana under the Russians. *Russian Review* 46: 267-81.

Manz, Beatrice Forbes (ed.). 1994. *Central Asia in Historical Perspective.* Boulder: Westview Press.

Marchintsev, Victor K., Vadim G. Krivochapkine, and Rouslan N. Kopylov. 1992. Les problèmes d'écologie biogéochimique liés à l'industrialization intensive de la Iakoutie. *Questions Sibériennes* 2: 25-28.

Marcy, Sam. 1990. *Perestroika: A Marxist Critique.* New York: WW Publishers.

Marr, N. Ya. 1911. *Dnevnik poezdki v Shavshetiiu i Klardzhetiiu.* Sankt-Petersburg.

Marx, Karl. 1973. *The Revolutions of 1848,* edited by D. Fernbach, Harmondsworth: Penguin Books.

Mayall, James. 1990. *Nationalism and International Society.* Cambridge: Cambridge University Press.

Meeting Report. 1991. *Kennan Institute for Advanced Russian Studies* 9, no. 4.

Meillassoux, Claude. 1993. Toward a Theory of the "Social Corps." In *The Curtain Rises: Rethinking Culture, Ideology, and the State in Eastern Europe,* edited by Hermine G. De Soto and David G. Anderson, 2-42. Atlantic Highlands, N.J.: Humanities Press.

Merquior, J. G. 1992. Thoughts on Liberalisation. In *Transition to Modernity: Essays on Power, Wealth and Belief,* edited by John A. Hall and I. C. Jarvie, 317-42. Cambridge: Cambridge University Press.

Mialo, K., and P. Goncharov. 1989. Zarevo Fergany. *Novoe vremia* 36: 37.

Micklin, P. P. 1987. The Fate of Sibaral: Soviet Water Polities in the Gorbachev Era. *Central Asian Survey* 6, no. 2.

Micklin, P. P. 1991. The Water Management Crisis in Soviet Central Asia. *The Carl Beck Papers in Russian and East European Studies,* N. 905. University of Pittsburgh Center for Russian and East European Studies.

Mill, John Stuart. 1975. *Three Essays: On Liberty. Representative Government. The Subjection of Women.* London: Oxford University Press; first published in 1861.

Milosz, Czeslaw. 1991. Some Call It Freedom. *The New York Times,* August 8.

Miminoshvili, Roman, and Guram Pandzikidze. 1990. *Pravda ob Abkhazii.* Tbilisi: Merani.

Minkin, A. 1988. Zaraza ubiistvennaia. *Ogonek* 13.

Mirrakhimov, M. 1990. Glavnye prichiny ne lezhat sverkhy. *Moskovskie novosti* 30 (June 29).

Mitrofanov, S. 1989. Natsional' nyi vopros—bezvyigryshnyi variant dlia Gorbacheva. *Novoe russkoe slovo,* July 3.

Motyl, Alexander J. 1987. *Will the Non-Russians Rebel? State, Ethnicity, and Stability in the USSR.* Ithaca and London: Cornell University Press.

Motyl, Alexander J. 1989. The Sobering of Gorbachev: Nationality, Restructuring, and the West. In *Politics, Society, and Nationality Inside Gobachev's Russia,* edited by Seweryn Bialer, 149-73. Boulder and London: Westview Press.

Motyl, Alexander J. 1992. The End of Sovietology: From Soviet Studies to Post-Soviet Studies. In *The Post-Soviet Nations. Perspectives on the Demise of the USSR,* edited by Alexander J. Motyl, 302–16. New York: Columbia University Press.

Moynihan, Daniel Patrick. 1993. *Pandaemonium: Ethnicity in International Politics.* Oxford: Oxford University Press.

Muiznieks, N. 1990. The Pro-Soviet Movement in Latvia. *Radio Liberty Report on the USSR* 2, no. 34 (August 24): 19–24.

Mukomel', V. I. 1989. Vremia otvetstvennykh reshenii. *Sotsiologicheskie issledovaniia* 1.

Mursaliev, A. 1992. O chem streliali v Tashkente. *Komsomol'skaia pravda,* January 25.

Mutiso, G. C. 1975. *Kenya: Politics, Policy and Society.* Nairobi: East African Literature Bureau.

Nagel, Joane. 1986. The Political Construction of Ethnicity. In *Competitive Ethnic Relations,* edited by S. Olzak and J. Nagel, 93–112. Orlando: Academic Press.

Nahaylo, Bohdan, and Victor Swoboda. 1990. *Soviet Disunion: A History of the Nationalities Problem in the USSR.* New York: Free Press.

Narzikulov, R. 1992. Vostok—delo slishkom tsvetistoe. *Nezavisimaia gazeta,* February 5.

Naselenie SSSR: Po dannym vsesoiuznoi perepisi naseleniia 1979 goda. 1980. Moscow: Statistika.

Naselenie SSSR: Spravochnik. 1983. Moscow: Izdatel'stvo politicheskoi literatury.

Nash, Manning. 1989. *The Cauldron of Ethnicity in the Modern World.* Chicago and London: University of Chicago Press.

Natsional'nyi sostav naseleniia Yakutskoi ASSR. 1990. *Statisticheskii sbornik,* N 3. Yakutsk: Goskomstat.

Naumova, O. B. 1991. Evolution of Nomadic Culture under Modern Conditions: Traditions and Innovations in Kazakh Culture. In *Rulers from the Steppe: State Formation on the Eurasian Periphery,* edited by Gary Seamen and Daniel Marks, 291–307. Los Angeles: Ethnographic Press.

Naumova, O. B. 1992. Nekotorye aspekty formirovaniia sovremennoi bytovoi kul'tury kazakhov v mnogonatsional'nykh raionakh Kazakhstana. In *Sovremennoe razvitie etnicheskikh grupp Srednei Azii i Kazakhstana,* edited by A. N. Zhilina and S. V. Cheshko, chap. 1, 5–50. Moscow: Institute etnologii i antropologii.

Nazarbaev, Nursultan. 1990. An Interview. *Ogonek* 51 (December 15–22): 3–6.

Nazarbaev, Nursultan. 1991a. *Bez pravykh i levykh.* Moscow: Molodaia gvardiia.

Nazarbaev, Nursultan. 1991b. Priznaiu tol'ko nravstvennuiu politiku. *Izvestiia,* July 1: 3.

Nazrulloev, Kh. 1993. Strasti po Tadjikistanu. *Nezavisimaia gazeta,* April 10.

Nekrich, A. M. 1978. *The Punished Peoples.* New York: W. W. Norton and Company.

Niederhauser, Emil. 1993. The National Question in Hungary. In *The National Question in Europe in Historical Context,* edited by Mikulás Teich and Roy Porter, 248–69. Cambridge: Cambridge University Press.

Niiazov, F., and K. Baialinov. 1991a. Akaevu tozhe. *Komsomol'skaia pravda,* October 15.

Niiazov, F., and K. Baialinov. 1991b. Chuzhoi sredi svoikh. *Komsomol'skaia pravda,* September 5.

Nikolaev, Vladimir. 1990. V peredi trudnaia raborta. 1990. *Molodezh' Yakutii* (August 9): 3.

Nikolaev, Vladimir, and I. P. Ushnitskii. 1990. *Tsentral'noe Delo: Khronika Stalinskikh repressii v Yakutii.* Yakutsk: Yakutsk Press.

Niyazi, A. 1994. Tadjikistan. In *Central Asia and the Caucasus after the Soviet Union: Domestic and International Dynamics,* edited by Mohiaddin Mesbahi, 164–90. Gainesville: University Press of Florida.

Novikov, A. G. 1992. Vozmozhno li segodnia oboitis' bez shamanstva? In *Shamanism kak religiia: Genezis, rekonstruktsiia, traditsii,* 38–39. Tezisy. Yakutsk: Isdatel'stvo YaGU.

Novikov, Iu. 1990. Uroki istorii. *Zvezda vostoka* 6.

Novoprudsky, S. 1993. Integratsii ne predviditsia. *Nezavisimaia gazeta,* May 28.

Nurmukhamedov, S. B., V. K. Savosko, and P. B. Suleimenov. 1966. *Ocherki istorii sotsialisticheskogo stroitel'stva v Kazakhstane (1933–1940).* Alma-Ata: Nauka.

Nurullayev, A. 1992. Need to Shape Up Religious and Civic Accord. *Moscow News* 15 (April 12–19).

Okey, Robin. 1982. *Eastern Europe 1740–1980.* London: Hutchinson and Co. Publishers.

Okladnikov, A. P. 1949. *Istoriia Yakutii,* Vol. 1. Yakutsk: Yakutgosizdat.

Okoneshnikov, V. I. 1992. K voprosu o metafisike yakutskogo shamanstva. In *Shamanism kak religiia: Genezis, rekonstruktsiia, traditsii,* 112–13. Tezisy. Yakutsk: Izdatel'stvo YaGU.

Olcott, Martha Brill. 1987. *The Kazakhs.* Stanford: Hoover Institution Press.

Olcott, Martha Brill. 1990. Central Asia: The Reformers Challenge a Traditional Society. In *The Nationalities Factor in Soviet Politics and Society,* edited by L. Hajda and M. Beissinger, 253–80. Boulder: Westview Press.

Olcott, Martha Brill. 1994. Ceremony and Substance: The Illusion of Unity in Central Asia. In *Central Asia and the World,* edited by Michael Mandelbaum, 17–46. New York: Council on Foreign Relations Press.

Olgun, M. 1992. Central Asian Profiles: Muhammed Salikh. *Umid/Hope* (Fall).

Orazbekov, E. 1991. Razvitie etnokul'turnykh vzaimosviazei kak factor stabilizatsii mezhetnicheskikh otnoshenii (na primere Kazakhstana). In *Mezhnatsional'nye problemy i konflikty: Poiski putei ikh resheniia,* 51. Bishkek.

Orlik, Iu. 1992. Tsenzura v Uzbekistane suverenna. *Izvestiia,* November 13.

Osipov, A. G. 1990. Nekotorye osobennosti obshchinnykh otnoshennii v srede sovremennogo turetskogo naseleniia Srednei Azii i Kazakhstana. In *Vsesoiuznaia nauchnaia sessiia po itogam polevykh etnograficheskikh i antropologicheskikh issledovanii 1988–1989 gg.* Alma-Ata.

Osipov,A. G. 1993. Ideologicheskii faktor v protsesse formirovaniia samosoznaniia malykh etnicheskikh grupp (na primere meskhetinskikh turok). In *Prava i status natsional'nykh men'shinstv v byvshem SSSR,* edited by I. L. Babich and S. V. Sokolovskii, 63–77. Moscow: Institut etnologii i antropologii.

Ostapenko, L. V., and I. A. Subbotina. 1993. Nekotorye problemy russkikh v blizhnem zarubezh'e: Migratsiia, zaniatost', konflikty. *Rossiiskii etnograf* 2: 283–312.

Pain, E. 1990a.A People without Land, a Government without State. *Moscow News* 35 (September 9–16): 9.

Pain, E. 1990b. O probleme turok-meskhetintsev. In *Vsesoiuznaia nauchnaia sessiia po itogam polevykh etnograficheskikh i antropologicheskikh issledovanii 1988-1989 gg,* pt. 1, 144–45. Alma-Ata.

Pain, Emil, and Arkadii Popov. 1995. Ot popustitel'stva k bezumiiu. (Chechenskii krizis i politika Rossii s 1991 po 1994 gg.) Unpublished manuscript.

Panarin, Sergei. 1993.A Long Good-Bye? *Moscow News* 15 (April 9).

Panarin, Sergei. 1994a. Bezopasnost' russkoiazychnogo menshinstva v Tsentral'noi Azii i politika Rossii. In *Natsionalism i bezopasnost' v postsovetskom prostranstve,* edited by S. Panarin, 26–35. Moscow: Progress-Kompleks.

Panarin, Sergei. 1994b.The Ethnohistorical Dynamics of Muslim Societies within Russia and the CIS. In *Central Asia and the Caucasus after the Soviet Union: Domestic and International Dynamics,* edited by Mohiaddin Mesbahi, 17–33. Gainesville: University Press of Florida.

Panesh,E. Kh. 1989. Sovremennye etnokul'turnye kontakty meskhetinskikh turok. In *Etnicheskie i etnograficheskie gruppy v SSSR i ikh rol' v sovremennykh protsessakh.* Tezisy dokladov. Ufa.

Panesh, E. Kh. 1990. Etnokul'turnye kontakty meskhetinskikh turok v kontse XIX-pervoi polovine XX v. In *Kratkoe soderzhanie dokladov sredneaziatsko-kavkazskikh chtenii.* Moscow.

Panesh, E. Kh., and L. B. Ermolov. 1989. Turki-Meskhetintsy. (Evolutsiia kultury pri smene etnicheskikh kontaktov.) In *Etnokontaktnye zony v Evropeiskoi chasti SSSR.* Moscow: Moskovskii filial Geograficheskogo obshchestva SSSR.

Panesh, E. Kh., and L. B. Ermolov. 1990.Turki-Meskhetintsy (istoriko-etnograficheskii analiz problemy). *Sovetskaia etnografiia* 1.

Panesh, E. Kh., and L. B. Ermolov. 1993. Meskhetinskie Turki: Dinamika etnokul'-turnykh i sotsial'no-politicheskikh izmenenii. In *Etnosy i etnicheskie protsesy,* edited by V. A. Popov. Moscow: Vostochnaia literatura.

Panfilov, O. 1992. Strana ozabochennogo presidenta. *Nezavisimaia gazeta,* May 20.

Panfilov, O. 1993a. Chei Su-25 byl sbit nad Tadjikistanom. *Nezavisimaia gazeta,* May 5.

Panfilov, O. 1993b. Rossiia posylaet v Tadjikistan eshche odin batalion. *Nezavisimaia gazeta,* April 29.

Panfilov, O. 1993c. Skrytyi terror. *Nezavisimaia gazeta,* May 14.

Pechenev, V. A. 1991. Kremlevskie tainy—Vverkh po lestnitse vedushchei vniz. *Literaturnaia gazeta,* January 30.

Pepinov, F. 1989. Slezy v sobstvennom dome. *Druzhba narodov* 11.

Perevedentsev, V. I. 1993. Raspad SSSR i problema repatriatsii v Rossiiu. In *Bezhentsy,* edited by A. G. Zdravomyslov, 142-59. Moscow: Rossiiskii Nezavisimyi Institut Sotsial'nykh i Natsional'nykh Problem.

Peters, Ya. 1989. Slushat' i uslyshat'. *Druzhba narodov* 1.

Peterson, D. J. 1987. Unemployment in the USSR. *Radio Liberty Report on the USSR* (August 25).

Petrov, A. 1993. Naidet li moskovskaia militsiia uchastnikov napadeniia na uzbekskikh politemigrantov? *Nezavisimaia gazeta,* December 11.

Pipes, Daniel. 1994.The Event of Our Era: Former Soviet Muslim Republics Change the Middle East. In *Central Asia and the World,* edited by Michael Mandelbaum, 47-93. New York: Council on Foreign Relations Press.

Pipes, Richard. 1974. *The Formation of the Soviet Union: Communism and Nationalism 1917-1923.* Revised edition. New York: Atheneum.

Pipes, Richard. 1975. Reflections on the Nationality Problems in the Soviet Union. In *Ethnicity: Theory and Experience,* edited by Nathan Glazer and Daniel P. Moynihan, 453-65. Cambridge, Mass.: Harvard University Press.

Pi-Sunyer, Oriol. 1993. The Spanish Route to Democracy: A Model for Eastern Europe in Transition? In *The Curtain Rises: Rethinking Culture, Ideology, and the State in Eastern Europe,* edited by Hermine G. De Soto and David G. Anderson, 305-33. Atlantic Heights, N.J.: Humanities Press.

Poliakov, S. P. 1989. *Traditsionalism v sovremennom sredneaziatskom obshchestve.* Moscow: Znanie.

Poliakov, S. P. 1992. *Everyday Islam: Religion and Tradition in Soviet Central Asia.* Armonk, New York: M. E. Sharpe, Inc.

Polonskaia, L. R. 1994. Islamskaia legitimizatsiia sovremennykh gosudarstvennykh struktur musul'manskogo mira (na primere SNG). In *Sovremennyi islam: Kul'tura i politika,* edited by V. V. Naumkin, 26-70. Moscow: Rossiiskii Tsentr strategicheskikh i mezhdunarodnykh issledovanii.

Pomerants, G. 1989. Po tu storonu zdravogo smysla. *Iskusstvo kino* 10.

Ponomarev, V. 1989. Kirgiziia. *Spetsial'nyi vypusk informatsionnogo tsentra Moskovskogo Narodnogo Fronta.* Moscow.

Ponomarev, V. 1991. *Samodeiatel'nye obshchestvennye organizatsii Kazakhstana i Kirgizii 1987-1991 (opyt spravochnika).* Moscow: Institut issledovaniia ekstremal'nykh protsessov.

Popper, Karl. 1988.The Open Society and Its Enemies Revisited. *The Economist* (April 23): 19-22.

Portnikov, V. 1992a. Ia ne khotel chtoby respublika raskololas' nadvoe. *Nezavisimaia gazeta,* May 28.

Portnikov, V. 1992b. Niiazov, Karimov, Akaev—protiv novogo Soiuza. *Nezavisimaia gazeta,* October 1.

Portnikov, V. 1992c. Strana ozabochennogo presidenta. *Nezavisimaia gazeta,* May 20.

Powell, G. Bingham, Jr. 1982. *Contemporary Democracy: Participation, Stability, and Violence.* Cambridge: Harvard University Press.

Programma Kommunisticheskoi Partii Sovetskogo Soiuza, novaia redaktsiia. 1986. Moscow: Politizdat.

Przeworski, A. 1991. *Democracy and the Market: Political and Economic Reforms in Eastern Europe and Latin America.* Cambridge: Cambridge University Press.

Pulatov, T. 1990a. Mass Exodus Hits Central Asia. *Moscow News* 41 (October 21–28): 7.

Pulatov, T. 1990b. Osh: Classical Central Asian Conflict. *Moscow News* 26 (July 8–15): 15.

Rabushka, Alvin, and Kenneth A. Shepsle. 1972. *Politics in Plural Societies: A Theory of Democratic Instability.* Columbus, Ohio: Charles E. Merril Publishing Co.

Ramet, Sabrina Petra. 1994. Primordial Ethnicity or Modern Nationalism: The Case of Yugoslavia's Muslims Reconsidered. In *Muslim Communities Reemerge: Historical Perspectives on Nationality, Politics, and Opposition in the Former Soviet Union and Yugoslavia,* edited by Andreas Kappeler et al., 111–38. Durham and London: Duke University Press.

Razakov, Talant. 1993. *Oshskie sobytiia na materialakh KGB.* Bishkek: Renessans.

Rebane, Ya. 1989. Stroit' vmeste razumnye otnosheniia. *Kommunist* 4.

Reznichenko, G. 1992. Aral: Simply Choked. *Umid/Hope* (Spring).

Riasanovsky, Nicholas V. 1967. *Nicholas I and Official Nationality in Russia, 1825–1855.* Berkeley and Los Angeles: University of California Press.

Rizaev, S. 1990. Za kompleksnuiu sistemu v rabote s kadrami. *Voprosy istorii KPSS* 10.

Rogowski, Ronald. 1974. *Rational Legitimacy: A Theory of Political Support.* Princeton: Princeton University Press.

Ro'i, Y. 1991. The Soviet and Russian Context of the Development of Nationalism in Soviet Central Asia. *Cahiers du monde russe et soviétique* 32, no. 1: 123–41.

Roiz, Maks. 1993. *Chuzhak v Kremle.* Moscow: Biznes-Press.

Rorlich, A.-A. 1989. Novyi Uzen': A Small City with Major Problems. *Radio Liberty Report on the USSR* 1, no. 42 (October 20): 22–24.

Rotar', I. 1991. Kinorezhisser protiv byvshego pervogo sekretaria. *Nezavisimaia gazeta,* November 9.

Rotar', I. 1992a. Gossekretar' ushel v otstavky. *Nezavisimaia gazeta,* January 16.

Rotar', I. 1992b. Voina bez pobeditelei. *Nezavisimaia gazeta,* September 9.

Rotar', I. 1992c. Volneniia v Dzhelal-Abade. *Nezavisimaia gazeta,* October 28.

Rotar', I. 1993a. Drugie russkie. *Nezavisimaia gazeta,* June 2.

Rotar', I. 1993b. Kak mozhno dogovorit'sia po-khoroshemy? *Nezavisimaia gazeta,* May 18.

Rotar', I. 1993c. Rossiia vtiagivaetsia v novuiu nenuzhnuiu voinu? *Nezavisimaia gazeta,* May 27.

Rotar', I. 1993d. Slaviane v Srednei Azii. *Nezavisimaia gazeta,* May 5.

Rotar', I. 1993e. Tadjikskie bezhentsy v Rossii i na Ukraine. *Nezavisimaia gazeta,* April 7.

Rotar', I. 1993f. Ugroza parlamentskogo-prezidentskogo krizisa. *Nezavisimaia gazeta,* April 17.

Rotar', I. 1993g. Zatoptan dvukhmesiachnyi rebenok-repatriant. *Nezavisimaia gazeta,* May 14.

Rotar', I. 1994. Sredniaia Aziia: Nekorennye v novom mire. *Nezavisimaia gazeta,* January 20.

Rothschild, Joseph. 1981. *Ethnopolitics: A Conceptual Framework.* New York: Columbia University Press.

Royce, A. P. 1982. *Ethnic Identity.* Bloomington: Indiana University Press.

Rubin, Barnett R. 1994. Tadjikistan: From Soviet Republic to Russian—Uzbek Protectorate. In *Central Asia and the World,* edited by Michael Mandelbaum, 207–24. New York: Council on Foreign Relations Press.

Rudenko, B. 1989. Solenye peski Aralkum. *Nauka i zhizn'* 10.

Rumer, Boris. 1987. Central Asia's Cotton: The Picture Now. *Central Asian Survey* 6, no. 4.

Rumer, Boris. 1989. *Soviet Central Asia: "A Tragic Experiment."* Boston: Unwin Hyman.

Rumshiskaya, M., and A. Cherkasov. 1991. A Poet and the Czar? *New Times* 32 (August 13–19): 34–35.

Rybakovskii, L. L. 1987. *Migratsiia naseleniia: Prognozy, factory, politika.* Moscow: Nauka.

Rywkin, Michael. 1982. *Moscow's Muslim Challenge: Soviet Central Asia.* London: C. Hurst and Co.

Rywkin, Michael. 1991. The Communist Party and the Sufi Tariqat in the Checheno-Ingush Republic. *Central Asian Survey* 10, nos. 1/2: 133–45.

Rywkin, Michael. 1994. *Moscow's Lost Empire.* Armonk, N.Y.: M. E. Sharpe, Inc.

Ryzhkov, Nikolai. 1992. *Perestroika: Istoriia predatel'stv.* Moscow: Novosti.

Sacks, Michael Paul. 1990. Ethnicity and Class in the USSR. *Nationalities Papers* 18, no. 1: 57–59, 90–93.

Safarov, J. 1989. Tragediia moego naroda. *Druzhba narodov* 11.

Saidbaev, T. S. 1984. *Islam i obshchestvo.* 2nd edition. Moscow: Nauka.

Saidbaev, T. S. 1991. Rossii ne grozit islamskaia revolutsiia. *Izvestiia,* November 28.

Sakharov, Andrei. 1989. Interview. *Ogoniok* (June 31): 25–27.

Sakhatov, M. N. 1993. Opposition Arrested before Baker's Visit. *Moscow News* 8 (February 23–March 1).

Salamatov, M. 1990. Why Infant Mortality Is So High in Turkmenia. *Moscow News* 26 (July 8–15): 13.

Salykova, M., and S. Ianovskii. 1989. Gde syn tvoi, zemlia? *Ogonek* 50 (December): 31.

Samoilenko, A. 1989. I opiat' komendantskii chas. *Literaturnaia gazeta,* June 28: 3.

Samoilenko, A. 1993. Im nel'zia doveriat' gosudarstvo. *Literaturnaia gazeta,* June 16.

Sarvanov, Yu., et al. 1989. Liudi ne prostiat. *Glastnost'* 29 (May).

Satvaldyev, A. N. 1991. *K kharakteristike religioznoi situatsii v Shakhimardane (Uzkekistan).* Institut etnologii i antropologii. Issledovaniia po prikladnoi i neotlozhnoi etnologii dokument N 31, seriia A, Moscow.

Savvinov, D. D. 1992. Les problèmes écologiques du fleuve Vilioui. *Questions Sibériennes* 2: 29-34.

Seligman, Adam B. 1992. *The Idea of Civil Society.* New York: Free Press.

Seligman, Adam B. 1995. Animadversions upon Civil Society and Civic Virtue in the Last Decade of the 20th Century. In *Civil Society: Theory, History, Comparison,* edited by John A. Hall, 200-23. Cambridge: Polity Press.

Seroshevsky, V. L. 1993. *Yakuty: Opyt etnograficheskogo issledovaniia.* Moscow.

Seton-Watson, Hugh. 1977. *Nations and States: An Enquiry into the Origins of Nations and the Politics of Nationalism.* Boulder: Westview Press.

Sheehy, A. 1973. The Crimean Tatars, Volga Germans and Meskhetians: Soviet Treatment of Some National Minorities. *Minority Rights Group Report* 6.

Sheehy, A. 1988a. Kazakh Lecturer Disseminates Unorthodox Views on Nationality Question. *Radio Liberty Research* 81, no. 88 (February 18): 1-3.

Sheehy, A. 1988b. Opposition to Family Planning in Uzbekistan and Tadjikistan. *Radio Liberty Report on the USSR* (April 5).

Sheehy, A. 1989a. Interethnic disturbances in Western Kazakhstan. *Radio Liberty Report on the USSR* 1, no. 27 (July 7): 11-14.

Sheehy, A. 1989b. Russian Share of Soviet Population Down to 50.8 Percent. *Radio Liberty Report on the USSR* 1, no. 42 (October 20): 1-5.

Sheehy, A. 1989c. Uzbeks Requesting Further Reduction of Cotton Target. *Radio Liberty Report on the USSR* 1, no. 8 (February 24): 19-21.

Sheehy, A. 1990. Fact Sheet on Declarations of Sovereignity. *Radio Liberty Report on the USSR* 2, no. 45 (November 9): 23-25.

Shelokhaev, V. V. 1994. Problema "zoologicheskogo" i kulturnogo natsionalisma v liberal'noi kontseptsii natsional'nogo voprosa. In *Vsaimodeistvie politicheskikh i natsional'no—etnicheskikh konflictov,* pt. 1, edited by A. G. Zdravosmyslov, 135-48. Moscow: Tsentr sotsiologicheskogo analiza mezhnatsional'nykh konfliktov.

Shengelia, N. N. 1968. *Seljuki i Gruziia v XI v.* Tbilisi: Metsniereba.

Shermukhamedov, P. 1990. Trudno zhit' bez Arala. *Zvezda vostoka* 2.

Shibutani, Tamatsu, and Kian M. Kwan. 1965. *Ethnic Stratification.* New York: Macmillan.

Shils, Edward. 1957. Primordial, Personal, Sacred and Civil Ties. *British Journal of Sociology* 7: 113-45.

Shishigin, E. S. 1991. *Rasprostranenie christianstva v Yakutii.* Yakutsk: Yakutskii Gosudarstvennyi Ob'edinennyi Musei Istorii i Kul'tury Narodov Severa.

Shoismatulloev, Sh. 1994. Tadjikistan v fevrale 1990 goda: Nachalo vsekh nachal. In *Analiz i prognoz mezhnatsional'nykh konfliktov v Rossii i SNG. Ezhegodnik,* 171-70. Moscow: Tsentr sotsiologicheskogo analiza mezhnatsional'-nykh konfliktov.

Simchenko, Yuri. 1993. Obychnaia shamanskaia zhizn': Etnograficheskie ocherki. *Rossiiskii etnograf* 7.

Sinnot, P. 1992. The Changing Structure of Central Asia's Population. *Umid/Hope* (Spring).

Sitnianskii, G. Yu. 1994. Slavianskoe naselenie Talasskoi doliny: Nastroeniia i politicheskie simpatii. In *Chelovek v mnogomernom obshchestve: Etnichnost' i pravo,* edited by I. L. Babich and S. V. Sokolovskii, 92-106. Moscow: Institut etnologii i antropologii.

Sked, Alan. 1981. Historians, the Nationality Question, and the Downfall of the Habsburg Empire. *Transactions of the Royal Historical Society,* fifth series, 31: 175-83.

Sked, Alan. 1989. *The Decline and Fall of the Habsburg Empire, 1815-1918.* London: Arnold.

Smith, Anthony D. 1979. *Nationalism in the Twentieth Century.* New York: New York University Press.

Smith, Anthony D. 1983. *State and Nation in the Third World.* Brighton: Harvester Press.

Smith, Anthony D. 1986. *The Ethnic Origins of Nations.* Oxford: Basil Blackwell.

Smith, Graham (ed.). 1990. *The Nationalities Question in the Soviet Union.* London and New York: Longman.

Sokolovsky, V. G. 1926. *Kazakhskii aul.* Tashkent.

Solchanyk, Roman. 1991. The Changing Political Landscape in Ukraine. *Radio Liberty Report on the USSR* 3, no. 24: 20-23.

Solntsev, V. M., and V. Yu. Mikhal'chenko (eds.). 1992. *Iazykovaia situatsiia v Rossiiskoi Federatsii.* Moscow.

Soper, J. 1988. Nationality Issues under Review in Kirgizia. *Radio Liberty Research* 49, no. 48 (January 29).

Spillover Effects of Religious Broadcasts in Iran on Soviet Muslims. 1980. *Radio Liberty* 142, no. 80 (April 14).

Sredniaia Aziia i Kazakhstan: prioritety i al'ternativy razvitiia. Editorial paper. 1989. *Kommunist* 15.

SSSR v tsifrakh v 1989 gody: Kratkii statisticheskii sbornik. 1990. Moscow: Finansy i Statistika.

Staniszkis, J. 1991. *The Dynamics of the Breakthrough in Eastern Europe.* Berkeley: University of California Press.

Statisticheskie materialy ob ekonomicheskom i sotsial'nom razvitii soiuznykh i avtonomnykh respublik, avtonomnykh oblastei i okrugov. 1989. Pt. 1. Moscow.

Stepovoi, A., and G. Shipit'ko. 1990. Predskazannyi vzryv. *Izvestiia,* June 25.

Stubbs, Richard. 1989. Malaysia: Avoiding Ethnic Strife in Deeply Divided Society. In *Conflict and Peacemaking in Multiethnic Societies,* edited by Joseph V. Montville, 287-99. Lexington, Mass.: Lexington Books.

Subtelny, Orest. 1994. American Sovietology's Greatest Blunder: The Marginalization of the Nationality Issue. *Nationalities Papers* 22, no. 1: 141-55.

Sultangalieva, A. K. 1994. Islam v Kazakhstane. *Vostok* 3: 72-80.

Suny, Ronald. 1991. Incomplete Revolution: National Movements and the Collapse of the Soviet Empire. *New Left Review* 189: 111-25.

Suny, Ronald. 1993. *The Revenge of the Past: Nationalism, Revolution, and the Collapse of the Soviet Union.* Stanford: Stanford University Press.

Suzhikov, M., et al. 1993. *Mezhnatsional'nye otnosheniia v Kazakhstane.* Almaty: Gylym.

Svoik, P., and E. Lan'ko. 1994. *Sud'ba Kazakhstana kak gosudarstva.* Almaty: Evraziia.

Szporluk, Roman. 1988. *Communism and Nationalism: Karl Marx versus Friedrich List.* New York: Oxford University Press.

Tamir, Yael. 1993. *Liberal Nationalism.* Princeton: Princeton University Press.

Tatimov, Makash. 1990. *Auyldafy demografiialyk ahual.* (In Kazakh.) Almaty: Kainar.

Tatur, S. 1990. Nashe vremia. *Zvezda vostoka* 1.

Taylor, Alan J. P. 1948. *The Habsburg Monarchy 1809-1918.* London: H. Hamilton.

Tillett, Lionel. 1969. *The Great Friendship: Soviet Historians on the Non-Russian Nationalities.* Chapel Hill: University of North Carolina Press.

Tilly, Charles. 1975. Reflections on the History of European State-making. In *The Formation of National States in Western Europe,* edited by C. Tilly, 3-83. Princeton: Princeton University Press.

Tishkov, V. A. 1991. Etnichnost' i vlast' v SSSR. (Etnopoliticheskii analiz respublikanskikh organov vlasti.) *Sovetskaia etnografiia* 3: 3-18.

Tishkov, V. A. 1993a. Materialy po problemam mezhnatsional'nykh otnoshenii v Rossiiskoi Federatsii. *Rossiiskii etnograf* 1: 5-36.

Tishkov, V. A. 1993b. *Mezhnatsional'nye otnosheniia v Rossiiskoi Federatsii.* Moscow: Rossiiskaia Akademiia Nauk.

Tishkov, V. A. 1993c. Russkie ukhodiat. (Migratsii i bezhentsy v SSSR: Russkie.) *Rossiiskii etnograf* 3: 5-20.

Tiutiunnik, V. I. 1989. Kto oni, meskhetinskie turki? *Sovetskaia kul'tura,* June 17.

Tolz, V. 1991. New Information about the Deportation of Ethnic Groups under Stalin. *Radio Liberty Report on the USSR* 3, no. 17 (April 26): 16-20.

Topchishvili, R. A. 1989. Posemeinye spiski Tifliskoi gubernii 1886 g. kak etnograficheskii istochnik. *Sovetskaia etnografiia* 6: 109-17.

Ukhlin, D. 1993. Flashbacks. *Moscow News* 15 (April 9).

Usmanov, L. 1992. Guns Fired at Hungry Crowds. *Moscow News* 4 (January 26–February 2).

Usmanov, L. 1993a. Politika v eksportnom ispolnenii. *Literaturnaia gazeta,* May 12.

Usmanov, L. 1993b. Vostochnye edinoborstva. *Literaturnaia gazeta,* June 9.

Usmanov, L. 1994. Opredelit li "islamskii faktor" budushchee strany? *Nezavisimaia gazeta,* January 6.

Uteshev, A. S., and S. E. Semenov. 1967. *Klimat i vetrovaia eroziia pochv.* Alma-Ata: Kainar.

Utkin, K. D. 1991. "Tuskul" (Vozrozhdenie). Yakutsk.

Vakhtin, Nikolai. 1992. *Native Peoples of the Russian Far North.* London: The Minority Rights Group International Report.

Vaksberg, Arkady. 1994. *Stalin against the Jews.* New York: Alfred A. Knopf.

van den Berghe, Pierre L. 1981. *The Ethnic Phenomenon.* New York: Elsevier.

Vashapeli, G. 1916. *Turetskaia Gruziia, Lazistan, Trapezund i Chorokhskii krai.* Moscow.

Vasilieva, N. D. 1992. Shamanstvo v Yakutii v 1920-1930 gg. In *Shamanstvo kak religiia: Genezis, rekonstruktsiia, traditsii.* Tezisy. Yakutsk: Izdatel'stvo YaGU.

Vasilieva, Ol'ga, and Timur Muzaev. 1994. *Severnyi Kavkaz v poiskakh regional'noi ideologii.* Moscow: Progress.

Velsanar, Ak-Mukhammed. 1990. Tam, gde ne vyrastaet posokh. *Moskovskie novosti* (April).

Velychenko, Stephen. 1994. Restructuring and the Non-Russian Past. *Nationalities Papers* 22, no. 2: 325-35.

Verdery, Katherine. 1991. *National Ideology under Socialism: Identity and Cultural Politics in Ceausescu's Romania.* Berkeley: University of California Press.

Verkhovsky, A. 1991. Kirgizia: Kak i v Rossii? *Russkaia mysl',* December 6.

Vitebsky, Piers. 1990. Yakut. In *The Nationalities Question in the Soviet Union,* edited by Graham Smith, 304-19. London and New York: Longman.

Vitkovskaya, G. 1992. Forced Migrants. *Moscow News* 11 (March 15-22): 11.

Vormsbekher, G. 1989. Kak my predstavliaem sebe vosstanovlenie Nemetskoi ASSR. *Sovetskaia etnografiia* 6: 29-33.

Vorob'ev, A. I. 1990. Vremia lozungov ukhodit. *Ogniok* 14.

Vozgrin, V. E. 1994. *Imperiia i Krym—Dolgii Pyt' k Genotzidy.* Bakhchisarai.

Vyzhutovich, V. 1991. Nabiev-Khodonazarov, 57: 31. *Izvestiia,* November 26.

Wallerstein, Immanuel. 1974. *The Modern World System: Capitalist Agriculture and the Origins of the European World Economy in the Sixteenth Century.* New York and London: Academic Press.

Weiner, Myron. 1971. Political Participation: Crisis of the Political Process. In *Crisis and Sequences in Political Development,* edited by Leonard Binder et al., 159-204. Princeton: Princeton University Press.

White, Clovis L. 1988. Comparative Ethnic Stratification: A Critical Review of Theory and Research. *Research in Race and Ethnic Relations* 5: 1-23.

Wimbush, S. Enders. 1986. The Soviet Muslim Borderlands. In *The Last Empire: Nationality and the Soviet Future,* edited by R. Conquest. Stanford: Hoover Institution Press.

Wimbush, S. E., and R. Wixman. 1975. The Meskhetian Turks: A New Voice in Soviet Central Asia. *Canadian Slavonic Papers* 17, nos. 2/3: 320-40.

Winrow, G. 1992. Turkey and Former Soviet Central Asia: National and Ethnic Identity. *Central Asian Survey* 11, no. 3: 101-11.

Wixman, R. 1988. *The Peoples of the USSR: An Ethnographic Handbook.* Armonk, N.Y.: M. E. Sharpe, Inc.

Wolfson, Z. 1990. Central Asian Environment: A Dead End. *Environmental Policy Review* 4, no. 1: 29-46.

Yakovlev, Alexandr. 1992. *Predislovie. Obval. Posleslovie.* Moscow: Novosti.

Yamskov, A. N. 1992. *Sovremennye problemy i veroiatnye napravleniia razvitiia natsional'no-gosudarstvennogo ustroistva Rossiiskoi Federatsii.* Moscow: Polinaks.

Yamskov, A. N. 1994. Etnichnost' v mezhnatsional'nykh konfliktakh posle raspada SSSR. In *Analiz i prognoz mezhnatsional'nykh konfliktov v Rossii i SNG,* 54-77. Moscow: Rossiiskii Nezavisimyi Institut Sotsial'nykh i Natsional'nykh Problem.

Yeltsin, Boris. 1994. *Zapiski prezidenta.* Moscow: Izdatel'stvo Ogonek.

Yemelyanenko, V. 1993. Sangak Safarov, Also Known as the Tajik Robin Hood. *Moscow News* 15 (April 9).

Young, Crawford. 1976. *The Politics of Cultural Pluralism.* Madison: University of Wisconsin Press.

Young, Crawford. 1992. The National and Colonial Question and Marxism: A View from the South. In *Thinking Theoretically about Soviet Nationalities: History and Comparison in the Study of the USSR,* edited by Alexander J. Motyl, 67–97. New York: Columbia University Press.

Zainutdinov, Sh. 1994a. Bespretsedentnaia otkrytost' Uzbekistana. *Izvestiia,* February 3.

Zainutdinov, Sh. 1994b. Uzbekistan i Kazakhstan obrazuiut edinoe ekonomicheskoe prostranstvo. *Izvestiia,* January 12.

Zaionchkovskaia, Zh. 1994. Etnicheskie konflikty. *Segodnia,* January 5.

Zaslavsky, Victor. 1992. Nationalism and Democratic Transition in Postcommunist Societies. *Daedalus* 121, no. 2 (Spring): 97–121.

Zeimal', E. 1988. Narodnosti i ikh iazyki pri sotsializme. *Kommunist* 15.

Zemskov, V. N. 1990. Spetsposelentsy (po dokumentam NKVD-MVD SSSR). *Sotsiologicheskie issledovaniia* 11.

Zhambulov, D. A. 1991. Problemy sotsial'nogo razvitiia v Kazakhstane. In *Mezhnatsional'nye problemy i konflikty: poiski putei ikh resheniia,* chap. 1, 98–99. Bishkek.

Zhirinovsky, Vladimir. 1993. *Poslednii brosok na Iug.* Moscow.

Zhukov, I. 1991. My teper' budem zhit' po novomy. *Nezavisimaia gazeta,* October 29.

Zhukov, I. 1992a. Praviashchei partii do vsego est' delo. *Nezavisimaia gazeta,* February 13.

Zhukov, I. 1992b. Pravitel'stvo znaet, chto delaet. *Nezavisimaia gazeta,* May 22.

Ziiadullaev, S. 1989. Razvitie proizvoditel'nykh sil' Uzbekistana. *Voprosy ekonomiki* 5.

Zinin, Yu. N., and A. V. Malashenko. 1994. Azerbaijan. In *Central Asia and the Caucasus after the Soviet Union: Domestic and International Dynamics,* edited by Mohiaddin Mesbahi, 99–115. Gainesville: University Press of Florida.

Zisserman-Brodsky, Diana. 1994. Sources of Ethnic Politics in the Soviet Polity: The Pre-Perestroika Dimension. *Nationalities Papers* 22, no. 2: 337–45.

Zubov, A. 1993. Posleslovie k epokhe etnicheskikh revoliutsii. *Znamia* 5.

Zuev, V. 1991. *Aral'skii tupik.* Moscow: Prometei.

Zykov, F. M. 1994. *Etnopoliticheskaia situatsiia v Respublike Sakha go i posle vyborov 12 dekabria 1993g.* Institut etnologii i antropologii. Issledovaniia po prikladnoi i neotlozhoi etnologii, dokument N 71, Seriia A. Moscow.

INDEX